ADOLESCENCE

ADOLESCENCE

Margaret A. Lloyd

Suffolk University

1817

HARPER & ROW, PUBLISHERS, New York
Cambridge, Philadelphia, San Francisco,
London, Mexico City, São Paulo, Singapore, Sydney

Sponsoring Editor: *Susan Mackey*
Project Editor: *Bob Greiner*
Cover Painting: *Harry Borgman, represented by The Yellow Brick Road*
Text Art: *Fineline Illustrations, Inc.*
Photo Research: *Mira Schachne*
Production: *Willie Lane*
Compositor: *ComCom Division of Haddon Craftsmen, Inc.*
Printer and Binder: *R. R. Donnelley & Sons Company*

ADOLESCENCE

Library of Congress Cataloging in Publication Data
Lloyd, Margaret A., 1942–
    Adolescence.

    Includes indexes.
    1. Adolescent psychology.   2. Socialization.
I. Title.
BF724.L63   1985   155.5   84-25309
ISBN 0-06-044067-8
85 86 87 88 9 8 7 6 5 4 3 2 1

Contents in Brief

Contents in Detail

Preface

RATIONALE

My intent in writing this book has been to facilitate both the learning and teaching of adolescent psychology. That is, the content, organization, and presentation of the material as well as the style of writing have been designed to encourage the use of an experience-based approach to teaching course content. I have found that such an approach increases student interest and understanding of the material without detracting from the presentation of substantive information. This text has been written for use in one-semester undergraduate courses in the psychology of adolescence and is aimed at sophomores, juniors, and seniors who have had an introductory course in psychology.

CONTENT AND ORGANIZATION

The book is organized into two sections. *Part I: The Foundations of Adolescent Development* introduces the study of adolescence and provides an overview of the fundamentals of the subject matter. The material on theoretical approaches, current issues, and research methods has been combined into a single chapter to coincide with the amount of time most instructors can give to such material in a one-semester, introductory level course. Chapters 2, 3, and 4 survey the fundamental changes that take place in the physical, cognitive, and personality domains during adolescence.

Part II: Developmental Issues in Adolescence focuses specifically on nine important aspects of adolescent development. All nine chapters in Part II include a closing section ("Getting Involved"), which presents a series of exercises and/or case studies and questions that may be used by students on an individual basis or for either general classroom or small group discussion.

An appendix on small group communication processes is included for use by those students whose instructors opt to use a small group discussion format in their courses.

Chapter 6: Sex Roles and Identity is included because of its current relevance and because the nature and process of identity development appear to be different for males and females. In addition, I have attempted to point out other sex differences in the adolescent experience and to draw attention to the relevance of social class, racial, ethnic, and cross-cultural variations among adolescents.

INSTRUCTIONAL AIDS

Each chapter is introduced with an outline and concludes with a chapter summary and glossary. Important terms are printed in italic type and are defined in the text (and in the glossaries at the end of each chapter and in the master glossary at the end of the book).

Photographs, graphic illustrations, and tables have been included to emphasize important points, but not, I hope, in such numbers that would interrupt the continuity of the written material.

The final sections of the chapters in Part II include material for involving students with the subject matter.

PEDAGOGICAL OPTIONS

One of the major features of this book is its flexibility for use in a variety of course formats. For example, instructors who are not interested in a discussion format can easily use the book to interest and involve students on an exclusively individual basis and/or to prompt unstructured discussion in the regular classroom setting.

Instructors who prefer large class discussion or small group discussion formats will find helpful, specific information in the *Instructor's Manual* by which to structure such discussions. The appendix on small group processes has been included to facilitate effective small group discussions and to free instructors from having to present material that is tangential to adolescent psychology.

Before deciding how to use the book, instructors will find it helpful to skim the appendix and the chapters in Part II, paying special attention to the exercises, case studies, and questions at the ends of each of these nine chapters. The *Instructor's Manual* spells out the details of the small group discussion approach and should be useful in giving specific information with which to make this decision.

INSTRUCTOR'S MANUAL

I have prepared an *Instructor's Manual,* which includes multiple-choice and essay questions for all chapters, explicit and detailed instructions for using the text in several group discussion formats, as well as suggestions for using the book in nondiscussion courses. In addition, it contains a list of films organized by chapter and descriptions of several course projects.

ACKNOWLEDGMENTS

This book could never have been written without the assistance and support of numerous individuals. Cathy Axon, Betsy Brooks, Cori Christou, Jim Coleman, and Mary Florio, Suffolk University reference librarians, all provided invaluable reference assistance.

In particular, I want to thank my undergraduate student assistants over several years without whose perseverance in locating and xeroxing hundreds of articles this book would never have been written: Verleen Fletcher, Mari Garnache, Gary Krause, Lisa Stephenson, and Paul Martin, especially.

I am also much indebted to several editors who helped with this book: George Middendorf, Kathleen Robinson, Susan Mackey, and Robert Greiner, as well as the staff of Harper & Row, for their guidance and support. For their valuable comments and suggestions about the original manuscript, I want to thank the following reviewers: John Armstrong, Edinboro State College; Janis Bohan, Metropolitan State College; Richard Booth, Black Hawk College; David Elkind, Tufts University; Lillian M. Grayson, Simmons College; Harold D. Grotevant, University of Texas at Austin; Duane Harmon, Southern Connecticut State College; Stan Henson, Arkansas Tech University; George W. Herrick, State University of New York Agricultural and Technical College; Anthony B. Olejnik, Northern Illinois University; Tirzah Schutzengel, Bergen Community College; W. E. Scoville, University of Wisconsin; Steve Truhon, Michigan State University; Kathleen M. White, Boston University.

Also, in this context, I want to mention my colleague and friend, Susan Schenkel, who willingly listened and helped me clarify a number of ideas. Of course, it goes without saying that the responsibility for the assertions in this text rests with me.

I am deeply grateful for the long-term support and encouragement of many colleagues, students, and friends—especially Elizabeth Barrett Balis and Judith Holleman Elmusa. Finally, thanks go to Evelyn Torrey Tracey, who faithfully typed the manuscript for this book and patiently made numerous revisions.

Margaret A. Lloyd

ADOLESCENCE

one

THE FOUNDATIONS OF ADOLESCENT DEVELOPMENT

Chapter 1 Outline

Perspectives on Adolescence and Youth

ADOLESCENTS: WHO ARE THEY?

Overview

*Adolescence** (from a Latin word meaning "to grow up") is a transitional stage between childhood and adulthood. In some ways adolescents resemble the children they were, yet the many changes they undergo during this stage ensure that they will be different from children in many respects. Similarly, we see glimpses of the adults the adolescents will become, but more often we observe that they don't behave like adults. As adolescents mature, we see fewer resemblances to children and more similarities to adults.

Adolescent psychology is the study of physical, cognitive, personality, and social development in individuals beginning at puberty (the attainment of the capacity to reproduce) and continuing until the assumption of adult responsibilities in society. Typically, these changes occur between the ages of 13 and 22.

Chronological age by itself, however, isn't necessarily a valid index of the onset or termination of adolescence. For example, some 14-year-olds may not have reached puberty, while others may have done so several years earlier. Similarly, some 18-year-olds may be supporting themselves and living in their own homes (and therefore are considered adults), while others may still be in school and financially and emotionally dependent on their parents (and therefore are adolescents).

Because this period spans a number of years, it is often divided into substages. For our purposes we will use the term *early adolescence* to describe individuals of junior high school age or 12 to 14 years, *middle adolescence* to describe those of high school age or 14 to 17, and *late adolescence* to describe those of college age or 17 to 22 (Muuss, 1982). While this division into substages has useful, practical applications, it is impor-

*Most italicized words can be found at the end of each chapter and in the Glossary section at the end of the text.

Adolescents of the same age can vary widely in physical maturation and other aspects of development.

tant to remember that it is an oversimplification. It is based on educational level (chronology) rather than on developmental criteria (puberty or identity, for example), and educational level and developmental status aren't necessarily synonymous.

Developmental Tasks of Adolescence

Adolescents can also be identified by the level of development they have reached in the capabilities and skills needed to function effectively as adults. These developmental tasks include achieving a sense of identity, attaining emotional and financial independence from parents, relating effectively with peers, becoming a sexual person, and choosing and preparing for an occupation (see Figure 1.1).

Compared to children, adolescents are physically more mature, are more skilled and sophisticated in cognitive abilities, have more complex and integrated personalities, and have more effective social skills. These developmental changes mean that adolescents are capable of taking a more active role in their own development than are children.

CURRENT ISSUES IN ADOLESCENT PSYCHOLOGY

Defining the Boundaries of Adolescence

In Western cultures adolescence has traditionally been viewed as synonymous with the teenage years. Recently, however, it has been acknowledged that adolescence spans a wider age range, and it is now often described as beginning earlier, and lasting longer than the teens.

During the past 150 years the average age of onset of puberty has dropped.

Figure 1.1 Many significant changes take place during adolescence. © 1982, The Washington Post Company, reprinted with permission.

Moreover, pressures on preteens from parents, the media, and peers to grow up sooner and faster have increased (Elkind, 1981). For example, note the recent television advertisements which depict boys and girls (especially) in designer clothing and sexy poses. Even though most 11- and 12-year-olds haven't reached puberty, some are pushed toward and, in fact, do imitate adolescent behavior.

Adolescence has been extended at the other end as increasing numbers of youth continue their education beyond high school and postpone the assumption of adult responsibilities. Kenneth Keniston (1970) has suggested that the fact that postindustrial society demands higher levels of educational attainment of its citizens has produced a new stage of development, which he calls *youth*. While not all individuals pass through this stage, there is a growing number of young people who have developed beyond adolescence, but who haven't yet assumed adult responsibilities.

Hence, in today's Western cultures adolescence lasts longer than it has in the past. Moreover, there aren't agreed upon criteria marking the transition from adolescence to adulthood. In contrast, in non-Western, nonindustrialized cultures, the adolescent period is shorter (several weeks to several years in length). Also, formal rituals *(puberty rites)* are often used to signify to the adolescent and the larger society that a young person has attained adult status.

Recognizing Gender, Social Class, Ethnic, and Racial Differences

Because middle-class adolescents are more numerous and easier to study, they are overrepresented in research findings. This means that the experiences of lower- and

Societal pressures in American society "push" young people into adolescent experiences at earlier ages.

upper-socioeconomic status (SES) youth are less likely to be discussed. Also, literature dealing with troubled adolescents and delinquents has been unduly weighted by data drawn from youth in the lower socioeconomic statuses. Clearly, psychologists need to know more about lower-middle-SES (blue collar) youth and those in the highest socio-economic status.

In addition, much theorizing about the adolescent experience has been based on a male model of psychological development. When females have been studied and their experiences have been found to be different from males' experiences, females have often been ignored or portrayed as deviant or deficient (Gilligan, 1982).

It is becoming increasingly clear that it's misleading to portray the adolescent experience in this culture as a homogeneous one. Moreover, using one sex, one race or one social class as a standard by which to judge the others can lead to serious miscon-ceptions. Therefore, we'll attempt to make distinctions among adolescents with regard to gender, class, ethnic, and racial differences, where such distinctions are relevant and important and when research findings are available.

Need for Cross-Cultural Perspectives

Western psychologists (and American ones, in particular) have rarely studied adoles-cents in other cultures. This makes it difficult to know to what extent adolescent experiences in other cultures are similar to those of youth with whom we are famil-iar.

The particular experience of adolescence in American society (and in others, as well) is influenced by gender, race, age, and socioeconomic status.

In recent years the number of cross-cultural studies by developmental psychologists has increased. These studies have compared adolescents in different cultures in areas such as parenting styles and outcomes, cognitive development, self-esteem, identity and moral development. Such cross-cultural research enables us to revise and refine generalizations which have accumulated from years of research with American adolescents. The findings also give us useful perspectives on our own culture. When we can, we'll discuss cross-cultural findings relating to adolescent development.

The "Generalization Gap"

It has been asserted that adolescence was invented by Western industrialized societies at the beginning of the twentieth century (Kett, 1977). Also much of what was said about adolescence and many policies and programs affecting adolescents were based more on philosophical and moral assumptions about how adolescents *should* act than on observations of how they really behaved (Kett, 1977). Thus, our initial understandings of adolescence were often stereotypes and myths.

Today, although the adolescent period has been studied extensively, there are still serious problems in separating reality from myth. Joseph Adelson, a well-known adolescent psychologist, refers to this problem as the "generalization gap" or the tendency to make generalizations based on research using adolescent subjects who are atypical of most youth (Adelson, 1979).

Typically, researchers have limited their investigations to certain groups of

The experience of adolescence varies across cultures.

adolescents: those who are similar to the researchers (white, upper-middle-SES, often male) and those who capture researchers' attention because they are visible (delin-quents, rebellious youth, disturbed youth). This has led to misconceptions about adolescents and to a lack of information about the coping experiences of more "typi-cal" and less visible adolescents. For example, it may be surprising to learn that "Taken as a whole, adolescents are *not* in turmoil, *not* deeply disturbed, *not* at the mercy of their impulses, *not* resistant to parental values, *not* politically active, and *not* rebellious" (Adelson, 1979, p. 37). Happily, there are signs that the problem of the "generalization gap" is beginning to diminish. Still, it remains a concern for the present.

HISTORICAL ROOTS OF THE STUDY OF ADOLESCENCE

Early Views of Childhood and Adolescence

Before the twentieth century adolescence was not distinguished from childhood. Also, it was not until the end of the nineteenth century that there was a widespread effort to apply methods of scientific inquiry to the study of behavior. Prior to the late nineteenth century, people's views of human nature and related issues were based on theological and philosophical beliefs. These attitudes also influenced ideas about development in children and adolescents. Consider, for example, some of Aristotle's ideas about youth.

> Of the bodily desires, it is the sexual by which they are most swayed and in which they show absence of self-control. . . . They have exalted notions, because they have not yet been humbled by life or learned its necessary limitations. All their mistakes are in the direction of doing things excessively and vehemently. . . . They think they know everything, and are always quite sure about it. (Roberts, 1966, pp. 1389a–1389b)

Some of these early writers viewed children as inherently "evil," while others saw them as naturally "good." Based on these assumptions, educators, philosophers, clergy, and physicians put forth their ideas about the best ways to rear and educate children. (Psychology, as a professional entity, didn't exist.)

Charles Darwin's Influence

In 1859 an event occurred which was to transform the entire basis of study of children. With the publication of Charles Darwin's *The Origin of Species,* there was a shift to the idea that adult human behavior originated in childhood and developed over time through life experience (and was not totally governed by heredity as was thought to be true of nonhuman animals). Hence, it was seen as important actually to observe children and to evolve hypotheses about human development from these *empirical* observations rather than solely from rational assumptions about the nature of humankind. Here we see, then, the emergence of the study of human development as a scientific endeavor (Mussen, Conger, & Kagan, 1979).

Later Views

Adolescence gained its identity as a distinct stage in the lifespan because of a number of simultaneous demographic, social, economic, and academic developments in the early twentieth century (Bakan, 1971; Kett, 1977). During this period children and adolescents became more of an economic liability and less of an asset. On the farm children helped with the livestock and harvesting, but in the city, they often didn't work. Also, jobs became increasingly complex, and this reduced the usefulness of children and adolescents in the workplace.

The enactment of compulsory education laws which kept children in school until age 16 (and out of the workplace) was also a factor. Too, laws were passed giving special status to juveniles and setting them apart from adults, based on the belief that youth needed protection and special attention from society.

Next, we'll review a number of major theories of adolescence and trace the evolution of adolescent psychology from the early 1900s to the present.

THEORETICAL VIEWS OF ADOLESCENCE

At the present time there isn't a single unified and comprehensive theory which explains adolescent development. Instead, there are a number of theories which view adolescents from different perspectives and which focus on particular aspects of their development (physiology, cognition, personality, social behavior). Many of these theories haven't been extensively tested, so we don't yet know how valid they are. As we discuss the theories, we'll attempt, when possible, to indicate which ideas have been verified through research and which have failed to stand up to testing.

Biological Theories

G. Stanley Hall (1844–1924)   G. Stanley Hall is credited with inaugurating the modern scientific study of adolescence. He was also the first American to earn a Ph.D. in psychology in the United States and the founder of the American Psychological Association. His two-volume book entitled *Adolescence,* published in 1904, set forth his *theory of recapitulation* and was a major influence until the 1930s.

Essentially, Hall's theory was a restatement of Darwin's concepts and related biological ideas in psychological terms. His theory held that (1) the historical experiences of the human species were built into the genetic structure of each individual and (2) the development of each individual reflected (recapitulated) the stages through which humankind had passed during its evolution from lower forms. For example, since at one time human beings were considered to be barbarians, there was a corresponding period early in each individual's development characterized by playing robbers, pirates, soldiers, etc. (Grinder & Strickland, 1963). Interestingly, it was not until the age of 25 or so that Hall saw individuals as reaching the "civilized" stage.

Hall's stage of development which corresponded to adolescence was labeled "puberty" and spanned the years from about 12 to 24, not far from contemporary views (Muuss, 1982). Many contemporary psychologists have criticized Hall's theory for overemphasizing the biological determinants of development and ignoring the role of cultural factors. In fact, he believed that cultural influences were the more dominant force in adolescent development, but not in childhood (Grinder & Strickland, 1963).

An idea of Hall's which has found little support in research is his view of adolescence as being a time of "storm and stress" (referred to as *Sturm und Drang* by Hall). He suggested that adolescence was necessarily a period of emotional

G. Stanley Hall, 1844–1924

upheaval and turmoil because of the conflicts between the biologically determined physical changes of puberty and society's demand on the adolescent for social and emotional maturity. (The investigation of this assertion was the focus of Margaret Mead's doctoral research which we'll discuss shortly.)

Hall, also, has been critized for characterizing development in adolescence as occurring in abrupt spurts rather than as gradual and continuous in nature (Grinder & Strickland, 1963).

Arnold Gesell (1880–1961)   Arnold Gesell is probably best known for his studies describing the process of human growth and development from birth through the age of 16. As director of the Yale University Clinic of Child Development, he and his staff worked with thousands of children from New Haven, Connecticut, over many years. Through the use of observations, interviews, and tests, they codified children's behavior patterns into longitudinal "growth gradients" to show the sequences of development through which children passed as they matured. In addition, they described the outstanding characteristics of each age. Consider some of his comments about the 16-year-old: "He is more tolerant of the world in general. . . . Company of friends is usually preferred to company of family. . . . Relationships with the family have actually improved; arguments are fewer. . . . He has grown into a self-possessed sense of independence" (Gesell, Ilg, & Ames, 1956, pp. 250–254).

As you can see, the descriptions are rather vague, but at the same time suggest clear-cut distinctions between ages which don't really exist. (This is a common criticism of stage theories, particularly those which use age to divide the developmental sequence, since developmental changes are not controlled by chronology.) Nonetheless, Gesell's books established norms of development for the different ages of childhood and adolescence and were widely read by parents and teachers. During the 1940s and 1950s his ideas were very influential.

Gesell's studies of development were based on a biologically oriented theory which viewed both physical and psychological growth as genetically determined and basically unmodifiable by the environment. He accounted for individual differences in development through the notion that each person is born with a particular constitution and inborn maturational sequence. He did acknowledge that environmental factors (primarily home and school) were important in determining individual differences; he termed this aspect of development *acculturation*. However, he believed that acculturation could never outweigh maturation with regard to influencing development (Gesell et al., 1956).

Gesell's ideas were influenced by Hall, but he did not agree with all of Hall's ideas about adolescence. For example, both men viewed the period of adolescence as extending from the ages of about 12 to 24, but Gesell didn't view adolescence as a time of storm and stress. Gesell believed that the adolescent's most important task was that of finding himself or herself, and saw the adolescent period as critical in moving from childhood to adulthood (Gesell et al., 1956).

Gesell has been criticized for making artificial distinctions between age groups; he didn't portray development as the continuous process we now believe it to be. Also, his subjects were drawn primarily from the upper-middle to upper socioeconomic statuses and were of above-average to superior intelligence. Gesell didn't think that these factors would invalidate his norms since he was describing aspects of development which were supposedly biologically based and, therefore, common to all children. Today, psychologists wouldn't agree with his assumptions.

Psychoanalytic Theories

Sigmund Freud (1856–1939)   Sigmund Freud was the first person to put forth a comprehensive theory of personality. He believed that human behavior was motivated by unconscious and irrational forces rather than by conscious, rational ones, as was commonly held at that time. Moreover, Freud believed that the two strongest and most important human motives were sex and aggression. Needless to say, his ideas were seen as shocking and unacceptable by most of the Victorian community. Although not all of Freud's ideas are accepted today, historically they have strongly influenced our views of adolescent development. Freud didn't rule out the importance of environmental factors in personality development, but, like Hall, he placed greater emphasis on the role of biological and instinctive forces. In line with this reasoning, he also asserted that the nature and sequence of personality development was universal.

Freud's *theory of psychosexual development* held that each person passes through a series of invariant stages in which instinctual energies (libido) are vested in particular *erogenous zones* of the body (mouth, anus, genitals). Each stage is characterized by heightened sensitivity of the associated erogenous zone which becomes a vehicle for obtaining gratification for a period of time (see Table 1.1).

Thus, psychological development begins in the first year with the *oral stage* in which the mouth is particularly sensitive to stimulation, and activities such as sucking and chewing are experienced as especially pleasurable. The *id,* one of the three structures of personality, is present at birth. The id is governed by irrational and biological forces and seeks to gratify basic instinctive needs.

During the second year the individual enters the *anal stage;* the anus is sensitized

Sigmund Freud, 1856–1939, and Anna Freud, 1895–1982

Table 1.1   FREUD'S STAGES OF PSYCHOSEXUAL DEVELOPMENT

Approximate age	Stage	Characteristics
Birth–2	Oral	Gratification sought through the mouth (sucking, eating, chewing)
2–3	Anal	Gratification sought through activities of elimination
3–6	Phallic	Gratification sought through genital self-stimulation (autoerotic orientation); Oedipal or Electra complex in operation
6–puberty	Latency	Sexual impulses in a dormant state
puberty on	Genital	Gratification sought through genital stimulation (altruistic orientation); reawakening of Oedipal or Electra complex

and the sensations of excretion become pleasurable. It is during this stage that the second structure of personality, the *ego,* begins to develop. The ego is the rational, evaluating aspect of personality and aids the individual in adapting to the external world.

The *phallic stage* spans the years from 3 to 6 and is a particularly significant period. It is during this stage (in which the genitals are sensitized) that sex-role identification and moral development take place and that *Oedipal* or *Electra* conflicts arise. The latter refer to Freud's idea that 3- to 6-year-old children experience an unconscious attraction to the opposite-sex parent, along with negative feelings toward the same-sex parent (the Oedipus complex refers to boys' attractions to their mothers and the Electra complex, to girls' attractions to their fathers).

During the phallic stage, the *superego,* the third structure of the personality, begins to develop. The superego is the moral aspect of personality and is composed of internalized representations of parental and societal standards, expectations, and values.

According to Freud, the next six years or so constitute a *latency period* during which sexual and aggressive energies are repressed into the unconscious. These are relatively quiet years.

Last comes the stage that is associated with adolescent development—the *genital stage.* Interestingly, Freud didn't place great emphasis on adolescence as a period of development, no doubt because he believed that the first five to six years were the most critical ones in personality growth. As was true in the phallic stage, the libido is invested in the genitals during the adolescent period. However, whereas the younger child's search for gratification is primarily autoerotic (self-stimulation), the adolescent supposedly has an "altruistic" orientation, that is, sexual gratification in the service of reproducing the species (Freud, 1925). Here, we see the beginnings of the striving for a mature sexual relationship.

Another event which Freud suggested occurred during adolescence was the reawakening of the Oedipal (Electra) conflict. The conflict concerns the usually unconscious sexual attraction of the child to the opposite-sex parent (the Oedipal attraction of a boy to his mother and the Electra attraction of a girl to her father). The successful resolution of this conflict results in identification of the child with the parent of the same sex, thus ensuring "appropriate" sex-role identification and the onset of the latency period. With the onset of puberty these sexual feelings are again awakened. Now, however, there is an internalized incest taboo so that the adolescent is usually uncon-scious of these feelings and doesn't act on them. For example, Freud suggested that one outcome of this event is that the first serious love of adolescents is often an older person of the opposite sex who reminds them of the mother or father.

Another phenomenon related to the reappearance of the Oedipal conflict is adolescent rebellion against parents and other authority figures. Freud's explanation for this phenomenon was that the rebellion was related to adolescents' needs to free themselves from emotional dependency on both their parents. This emotional de-attachment permits, among other things, the selection of an appropriate love object. At the same time the adolescent also feels the unconscious pull toward his or her parents. Therefore, to establish autonomy the adolescent is often, for a time, hostile and rejecting of his or her parents and other authority figures, although Freud asserted that some individuals (mainly females) never make this "break" with their parents (even if they do marry). Eventually, ties to the parents are usually reestablished once the adolescent feels he or she has safely negotiated the emotional de-attachment process.

Anna Freud (1895–1982)   The major contribution of Anna Freud was to extend the practice of psychoanalysis to children and education. In addition, she developed more thoroughly psychoanalytic theory as it related to the adolescent years (A. Freud, 1937/1966). She held that the hormonal and physiological changes that bring about pubescence and puberty also add to the strength of libidinal energy. This increase in libidinal energy awakens already existing oral, anal, and phallic conflicts that have been dormant since the end of the phallic stage. These conflicts are the causes of the erratic behavior (storm and stress) described as typical of adolescents by psychoanalytic writ-ers. Once puberty begins, sexual impulses become dominant. This change of focus motivates adolescents to begin to integrate adult sexuality into their personalities.

Anna Freud suggested that there are several important differences between chil-dren and adolescents with regard to personality development. For one thing, the *superego* displaces disapproving parents as the primary control over unacceptable impulses. This means that there are many internal struggles (especially between sexual impulses and guilt) as the ego attempts to accommodate the id and the superego. This fact is viewed as a major cause of adolescent turmoil.

Another characteristic distinguishing adolescents from children is the use of *ego defense mechanisms* by adolescents. (Ego defense mechanisms are unconscious reac-tions by the ego to protect itself from threatening impulses and information.) Anna Freud believed that two defense mechanisms particularly characteristic of the adoles-cent period are asceticism and intellectualization. *Asceticism* is characterized by self-denial, that is, the young person refuses to engage in any kind of activity that is unconsciously associated with instinctual wishes, especially sexual ones. Thus, some adolescents may renounce alcoholic beverages, dancing, sleep, or sexual activities. The unconscious dynamic operating is the fear that even the slightest indulgence in a particular behavior will necessarily lead one to become a slave to this impulse. *In-tellectualization* refers to the intense intellectual debating of philosophical, moral, and political issues. In fact, what appears to be an intellectual discussion often turns out also to have ego defensive motives, that is, adolescents usually debate so intensely only those issues that are experienced as personal conflicts. The intellectual discussion of such issues allows young people to get some distance from and control of the intense feelings usually associated with such impulses.

Anna Freud was more concerned with pathological than with "normal" development and she dicussed two possible negative consequences of the increase in libido in adolescence. If the ego is not strong enough to withstand this additional "pressure" from libidinal energies, the adolescent may become an adult who is impulsive and unable to tolerate frustration or the adolescent may develop too rigid and defensive a superego which will limit his or her interest in and enjoyment of sexuality and other instinctive desires.

Like Hall, Anna Freud believed that adolescent storm and stress was normal. Moreover, she felt that a lack of turmoil was indicative of developmental difficulties and a cause for concern.

Social Psychological Theories

Both the theorists dicussed in this section were schooled in the psychoanalytic tradition, but went on to develop personality theories that focused less on sexuality and placed heavy emphasis on the role of the social environment in development.

Harry Stack Sullivan (1892–1949)   According to Sullivan's interpersonal theory of psychiatry, the basic motivating force in human personality development is the avoidance of the anxiety that grows out of troublesome interpersonal interactions. Hence, individuals strive for positive, intimate contacts with others and acceptance by them. As people grow, their interactions with others become increasingly complex and more

Harry Stack Sullivan, 1892–1949

selective. Moreover, it is through social interactions that the "self-system" matures, that is, others play a significant role in the way we come to perceive ourselves.

Sullivan's theory (1953) is based on six stages of development beginning with infancy and continuing through late adolescence (see Table 1.2). During *preadolescence* (10 to 12 years) a need for intimacy develops such that a child is motivated to seek an intensely close relationship with a peer of the same sex (an *isophilic relationship* or a *chum,* in Sullivan's words). This relationship is characterized by both individuals sharing practically everything about themselves with each other—hopes, fantasies, fears, etc. A chum relationship is significant for several reasons. For one thing, it's the first time that a child comes to see another human being as like himself or herself in essential ways. This means that the child can identify with another and know that others also experience pain, loneliness, and joy. Thus begins the movement away from the self-centeredness of childhood toward the more mature feelings of love and altruistic concern for other human beings.

Having a chum is also important because a child can know that he or she is important and worthwhile to another. Such a realization can be a powerful therapeutic force for children who may have developed negative opinions of themselves (usually because of painful interactions with parents). Here we see that Sullivan's view of development assumes that important personality changes can and do occur after the first five or six years of life—an important difference from orthodox Freudian theory. According to Sullivan, the preadolescent phase is the most peaceful one in the human life cycle.

Some children are unable to establish an isophilic relationship because of the anxiety associated with the risk of reaching out for close relationship with a peer. While not taking the risk enables them to maintain a feeling of personal security, it also means that they will experience loneliness and will miss the important developmental experiences of "chumship."

The tranquility of preadolescence is replaced by turmoil in *early adolescence* (12 to 16 years). Here we see similarities with the views of Hall and the Freuds (although the causes of stress differ according to the three theorists). For Sullivan, the turmoil of adolescence is due to the conflicting needs for personal security, interpersonal intimacy, and "lustful satisfaction." Sexual feelings are triggered by the hormonal and physiological changes of puberty. In addition, the young person who previously developed a strong

Table 1.2   SULLIVAN'S STAGES OF PERSONALITY DEVELOPMENT

Approximate age	Stage	Characteristics
Birth–2	Infancy	Need to be free from anxiety and to feel secure
2–6	Childhood	Need for adult attention and validation of experiences
6–10	Juvenile	Need to form peer relationships
10–12	Preadolescence	Need for interpersonal intimacy in an isophilic relationship (chum)
12–16	Early adolescence	Need for interpersonal intimacy, sexual satisfaction, and personal security in a heterophilic relationship
16–20	Late adolescence	Need for a "special" heterophilic relationship and to find one's place in society

attachment to a member of the same sex must now transfer these feelings to a member of the opposite sex (a *heterophilic relationship*). The newness and difficulty of these challenges is made even harder by most cultures because of sexual taboos and negative sanctions placed on sexual behavior, particularly for youth of this age. The positive outcome of early adolescence is the establishment of a "pattern of preferred genital activity." According to Sullivan, this usually, but not always, means the ability to establish and maintain an emotionally and sexually intimate relationship with someone of the opposite sex. As can be seen, then, the storm and stress of early adolescence, according to Sullivan, is a result of interpersonal conflicts rather than intrapersonal ones.

Once an adolescent is clear about his or her sexual preference, Sullivan suggested that the work of *late adolescence* (16 to 20 years) is devoted to developing more sophistication and variety in interpersonal relationships and establishing an emotionally and sexually intimate relationship with a special person. In addition, individuals continue to develop intellectually and to look for a satisfying role in the larger society. Ideally, the development of a socially competent and satisfied individual continues past late adolescence, but Sullivan noted that in many cases beliefs have already become so rigid as to foreclose opportunities for later growth.

Sullivan had little to say about female personality development. He acknowledged that there were important developmental differences between the sexes, but felt that he couldn't confidently describe female development because most of his psychotherapy patients were male.

Erik Erikson (1902–   )   As you will see, cultural anthropological research contradicted the assertions of Hall and the Freuds that particular personality characteris-

Erik Erikson, 1902–

tics develop in human beings regardless of cultural differences. By the time that Erik Erikson began writing *Childhood and Society* (1950), he had the benefit of such anthropological findings and constructed a theory that modified in several ways the Freudian theory of psychosexual development. Hence, Erikson is classified as a "neo-Freudian" theorist.

First, Erikson's "eight stages of man" extended psychoanalytic theory to encompass the total life span from birth through later adulthood (see Table 1.3). Second, he focused more on the ego than on the id and superego. Third, his theory adds a social element to Freud's psychosexual emphasis.

Erikson, like Freud, asserts that personality development proceeds according to a genetically determined sequence. Unlike Freud, however, Erikson claims that the nature of one's culture also determines the particular manner in which various developmental crises are resolved. In this way Erikson attempts to integrate Freud's theory of psychosexual development and known facts of physical and social development.

Each of Erikson's eight stages brings with it new expectations for the individual, who is faced with trying to maintain his or her own "sense of self" while trying to adapt to the cultural demands specific to that stage. The conflict at each stage brings to the individual the potential of both positive and negative experiences related to a central theme. These themes are described in terms of two possible outcomes (one positive, one negative). For example, the conflict in adolescence can result in either the achievement of *ego identity* (having a sense of oneself) or in *identity diffusion* (being confused about who one is and what is meaningful in life).

As each new stage of development is encountered, a new conflict arises with its two possible resolutions. If the conflict is resolved successfully, then the positive quality (for example, identity achievement for adolescents) is incorporated into the ego structure, which facilitates further ego development. On the other hand, if the conflict isn't satisfactorily resolved, then the negative quality (identity diffusion) is incorporated into the ego, and this results in damage to the developing ego.

According to Erikson, adolescence provides a *psychosocial moratorium,* that is, time out from adult responsibilities to be used for "identity experiments" in order to answer such questions as "Who am I?" and "What do I want to do with my life?"

From Table 1.2 you can see that the developmental conflict of young adulthood is that of intimacy versus isolation. Young adults need to learn to relate to others on an emotionally intimate basis. In order to do this successfully, Erikson insists that a

Table 1.3   ERIKSON'S "EIGHT STAGES OF MAN" AND FREUD'S CORRESPONDING PSYCHOSEXUAL STAGES

Erikson's stages	Age	Freud's stages
Basic trust vs. mistrust	Birth–2	Oral
Autonomy vs. shame and doubt	1–3	Anal
Initiative vs. guilt	3–6	Phallic
Industry vs. inferiority	6–puberty	Latency
Identity vs. identity diffusion	Adolescence	Genital
Intimacy vs. isolation	Young adulthood	No corresponding stage
Generativity vs. stagnation	Middle adulthood	No corresponding stage
Ego integrity vs. despair	Later adulthood	No corresponding stage

young person must have resolved the conflict of adolescence successfully and developed a sense of identity. Feelings of isolation, which may occur because of fears of closeness with others, cause individuals to withdraw from others. (Erikson's ideas will be discussed in greater detail in Chapters 5 and 6.)

Cultural Anthropological Theories

Early field studies of cultures other than our own conducted by anthropologists clearly demonstrated that the characteristics found in youth in Western cultures were *not* always found in adolescents in other cultures.

Ruth Benedict (1887–1948)   Ruth Benedict (1938) theorized that the degree of continuity between the roles of children and those of adults is the central factor in the impact of a given culture on an individual's personality. The nature of the transition from childhood to adulthood also has important implications for the adolescent's experience: smooth or continuous transitions cause little adolescent conflict and turmoil, whereas sudden or discontinuous transitions cause emotional strain and conflicts.

Benedict described the Samoan society as a *continuous* culture and ours as a *discontinuous* culture. In continuous cultures, such as Samoa or some Indian tribes, there are either no changes in expected behaviors as a child matures or the changes occur so gradually that they are not difficult. In most Western, technological cultures the shifts in expectations are relatively sudden. In addition, some changes must occur in major aspects of personality, ones not easily transformed in a relatively short period of time. For example, sexual attitudes can be particularly difficult to change, and during adolescence we are asked to *un*learn beliefs about sexuality we were taught earlier, for instance, that sex is dirty or evil.

Margaret Mead (1901–1979)   Margaret Mead's doctoral dissertation was conducted to test Hall's assertion that adolescence was a universally stormy and stressful period. (These findings were published in her classic work, *Coming of Age in Samoa,* in 1928.)

While Mead didn't deny the role of biological factors in development, particularly at adolescence, she also didn't, at least in her earlier writings, attempt to explain specifically the relationship between biological and cultural determinants of personality. Hence, this approach was termed *cultural determinism,* which implied that culture was the dominant force in personality development. We should note that later cultural anthropological writings take a less "extreme" position and incorporate biogenetic factors into theory, just as contemporary psychoanalytic theorists have accepted the role of social factors in personality development (Muuss, 1982).

Recently, Mead's Samoan work has been criticized on several counts (Freeman, 1983). She spent only nine months in Samoa. She didn't speak the language and so had to rely on interpreters, who may not have given her accurate information. As a woman, she was excluded from the meetings of the chiefs where important information was exchanged. Also, Mead had a cultural deterministic bias which may have influenced her observations and interpretations. These things make it likely that Mead may have been in error in describing Samoan society as peaceful and the adolescent period as nonstressful.

Margaret Mead, 1901–1979

Still, this refutation of Mead's early work in Samoa doesn't mean that cultural variations don't have an impact on human experience and behavior. For example, other anthropological studies have described many societies in which adolescence isn't turbulent (Vogt, 1983). (Also, we should note that Mead made many more contributions to cultural anthropology than this single study.)

The early cultural anthropologists made some important contributions to the study of adolescent development. First, their research provided clear-cut evidence against Hall's theoretical assertion of the universality of storm and stress. Second, they attempted to explain some of the causes of this stress or absence of it. Third, their work helped shift the balance from a biogenetic view of adolescent development to one that acknowledged the role of cultural factors as well.

Behavioristic Views

Behaviorists assert that whatever behaviors, values, and ideas a particular culture endorses will be adopted by its members and that psychological development is dependent on learning these expectations and behaviors. Behaviorism focuses on elucidating the principles which govern learning. Emotional behavior and feelings are learned primarily through a process of *classical* or *respondent conditioning,* which Ivan Pavlov first described and John Watson extended. Motor skills (walking, driving a car, playing a musical instrument), social interaction skills, and verbal behaviors (language) are learned according to the principle of *operant conditioning* or *instrumental learning* which B. F. Skinner and his colleagues elaborated.

"Radical behaviorism" (so-called to distinguish it from a more recent development of "cognitive behaviorism") is concerned only with observable behaviors. Of course, this orientation rules out from legitimate psychological study a great deal of significant human experience which is "private" in nature and therefore not open to observation (thoughts and subjective feelings are two examples). Albert Bandura, whose ideas we will discuss in this section, is better described as a cognitive behaviorist than a radical behaviorist, such as Watson or Skinner. Bandura views cognitive events as relevant to psychological study and attempts to study them within a controlled, socially relevant experimental context.

Albert Bandura (1925–   )   Social learning theory uses and extends principles of classical and operant conditioning and adds principles to explain human social behavior. For example, this approach places a great deal of emphasis on the role of social models in the process of socialization. Parents, peers, teachers, and television characters are probably the most significant models which influence adolescents. Bandura has labeled this type of learning—in which we learn by observing the actions of others and the consequences of their actions—*observational learning* (or modeling or imitation).

Observational learning is a process whereby an *observer* (a child, an adolescent, or an adult) watches a *model* (another person who performs certain behaviors) and learns to perform the actions which were observed. As children grow up, parents serve as models, as do siblings, teachers, relatives, and other persons who are important to

Albert Bandura, 1925–

them. Moreover, models are not limited to real people. There are *symbolic models* as well, for example, the characters, human or cartoon, on television and in motion pictures. The current discussions about the relationship between violence in the media and aggressive behavior are a direct outgrowth of social learning research which has demonstrated the considerable part models play in "teaching" aggression to children and adolescents (and adults).

The processes of modeling and operant and classical conditioning operate continuously. Current behavior is always a product of *past* social learning experiences and *present* social environmental conditions. For adolescents, past experiences include parenting practices, childhood educational experiences, and childhood peer interactions. Present conditions include parent-adolescent interactions, peer interactions, and current educational experiences.

When there are significant changes in social role expectations, we expect behaviors to change accordingly and within the context of earlier learning. At adolescence we see role changes between adolescents and their parents, adolescents and peers, adolescents and educational institutions. Changes in social expectations don't necessarily produce dramatic behavioral changes. In those instances where dramatic changes do occur (as in delinquent or emotionally disturbed youth), Bandura suggests that inadequate socialization (past experiences) or stresses in the current social environment are the causes. He feels, however, that the number of youth in whom this occurs is small —approximately 10 percent of the population—and doesn't view the adolescent period as one characterized by storm and stress (1964).

Unlike many of the theories we have already discussed, social learning theory is a *non*developmental theory, that is, the life span is not marked off into stages with particular characteristics and explanatory concepts. Rather, behavioristic theories assume that the same principles of development, namely, those of classical and operant conditioning and observational learning, obtain at all levels of development in human beings; therefore, the idea of stages is irrelevant and misleading (Bandura, 1964). While Bandura doesn't deny the importance of constitutional variables in personality development, he hasn't chosen to study them because he believes that the study of social learning influences is a more productive avenue of research at this time (Bandura & Walters, 1963).

Cognitive-Developmental Views

In contrast to theories which deal primarily with personality development and social behavior, this viewpoint focuses on another aspect of human functioning—cognitive development (thinking and reasoning). Significant changes in the nature of thinking occur during adolescence, and many aspects of personality, such as identity and moral beliefs, appear to be affected by cognitive processes as well.

Jean Piaget (1896–1980)   Piaget's formal education was in biology, not in psychology. Not long after he earned his doctorate in Switzerland, however, he became fascinated with the development of logical thought and worked for a time with Alfred Binet, the originator of the first intelligence test. He spent countless hours observing and interviewing children and adolescents (including his own) in order to try to understand the

Jean Piaget, 1896–1980

nature of their thinking and the structure of intelligence. (Piaget also formulated a theory of the development of moral judgment, but since it deals primarily with children, we won't consider it.)

Based on his observations, he put forth a four-stage theory in which he attempted to describe and explain cognitive development. He asserted that the *sequence* of the stages is the same in all human beings, regardless of cultural factors; however, the *rate* of movement from one stage to another may vary from one individual to another. In this sense cognitive development is dependent on biogenetic and maturational factors. It would be inaccurate, however, to label Piaget's theory a maturational one because he does stress the importance of interactions between people and their physical environments in the development of thinking. Also, the nature of a particular culture will determine, to some extent, the *content* of thought.

Because we'll discuss Piaget's theory in detail in Chapter 3, we'll describe only its major aspects at this point. According to Piaget, thinking becomes more and more complex as individuals mature. Cognitive development moves from physically based sensations and perceptions and corresponding motor activity to highly abstract reasoning. At about age 11 there is a critical shift in children's thinking from the use of elementary logic with reference to concrete objects and events to the use of more sophisticated logical thinking about abstract ideas. In Piaget's model this shift in thinking marks the emergence of the last stage of cognitive development, that of *formal operational thought.*

Formal operational thinking is important not only in its own right (because it gives the adolescent greater flexibility and sophistication of thought), but also because it affects the adolescent's emotional and social development. It figures importantly in identity achievement, future aspirations, parental and peer relationships, religious and ethical beliefs, political concerns, and sexual behavior, among other adolescent issues.

Lawrence Kohlberg (1927–   )   Lawrence Kohlberg has extended Piaget's ideas in the area of moral reasoning and development. Kohlberg believes that an individual's level of moral reasoning is based on his or her level of cognitive development. Like Piaget, Kohlberg has constructed a stage theory and maintains that the order in which individuals pass through the various stages is invariant and universal because moral development has a biogenetic basis. Unlike Piaget, however, who assumes that chronological age is a critical factor in movement from stage to stage, Kohlberg asserts that the age at which a given stage of moral development begins is largely dependent on cultural and societal factors. At adolescence the individual is theoretically capable of achieving the adult level of moral reasoning; however, the actual level of development is also related to the level of moral reasoning dominant within a society, which is not necessarily the highest possible level of reasoning (Kohlberg, 1969). We'll discuss Kohlberg's ideas in detail in Chapter 10.

Developmental Task Orientation

Robert Havighurst (1900–   )   The concept of *developmental task* was contributed by Robert Havighurst, who defines the term as follows:

> a task which arises at or about a certain period in the life of an individual, successful achievement of which leads to his happiness and to success with later tasks, while failure leads to unhappiness in the individual, disapproval by the society and difficulty with later tasks. (1979, p. 2)

In some respects Havighurst's tasks resemble Erikson's developmental crises in that the individual must learn new skills appropriate to particular stages of development. In addition, mastery of each task is a prerequisite for moving to the next task. Havighurst's tasks for each period of development, however, are more specific than those of Erikson.

Havighurst considered the adolescent period to span the years from 12 to 18. His

Robert Havighurst, 1900–

developmental tasks for this period and for early adulthood are listed in Table 1.4. Havighurst places most emphasis on emotional and social development during adolescence, with some mention of physical competence. Since he is writing for readers in the United States, he lists some developmental tasks that are relevant only to industrialized societies (particularly the United States) and not other cultures, for example, preparing for an economic career.

Review of Theoretical Approaches

Each of the theories we have discussed adds some useful ideas or emphases to our understanding of adolescence. Let's summarize these contributions from a contemporary perspective. While psychologists today don't embrace the particulars of either Hall's or Gesell's theories, neither do they deny the importance of hereditary and physiological factors in adolescent development. Sigmund and Anna Freud point out the importance of psychological motives, particularly the sexual drive, at adolescence and offer an explanation for the particular conflicts and resulting fluctuations in emotionality observed in adolescence. Sullivan stresses the importance of interpersonal relationships in personality development. Erikson integrates cultural anthropological findings into Freud's psychosexual theory of personality development and views adolescence as the crucial period for identity achievement.

The work of Benedict and Mead provides a valuable cross-cultural perspective on adolescent development so that we can more easily discern the operations of biology and culture in adolescence and see more clearly the unique character of our own and other cultures.

Bandura disputes the validity and usefulness of a stage theoretical approach to development, asserting instead that human social behavior is governed by principles of learning which don't change over the life span. Piaget elucidates the nature of intellec-

Table 1.4 HAVIGHURST'S DEVELOPMENTAL TASKS OF ADOLESCENCE AND EARLY ADULTHOOD

Adolescence (12–18)	Early adulthood (18–30)
1. Achieving new and more mature relations with age mates of both sexes	1. Selecting a mate
2. Achieving a masculine or feminine social role	2. Learning to live with a marriage partner
3. Accepting one's physique and using the body effectively	3. Starting a family
4. Achieving emotional independence of parents and other adults	4. Rearing children
5. Preparing for marriage and family life	5. Managing a home
6. Preparing for an economic career	6. Getting started in an occupation
7. Acquiring a set of values and an ethical system as a guide to behavior—developing an ideology	7. Taking on civic responsibility
8. Desiring and achieving socially responsible behavior	8. Finding a congenial social group

Source: From *Developmental Tasks and Education,* Third Edition by Robert J. Havighurst. Copyright © 1972 by Longman Inc. Reprinted by permission of Longman Inc., New York.

tual development and suggests that important changes in flexibility and sophistication of thinking come about in adolescence. These changes in thinking, moreover, influence some aspects of personality functioning in young persons. Kohlberg extends Piaget's ideas by constructing a theory of moral development which has implications for adolescent development. Havighurst puts forth an eclectic theory of stage-specific developmental tasks that individuals need to master as they mature. His developmental tasks for adolescents focus on emotional and social development.

Our subject matter can be viewed from many perspectives. While it's tempting, from the point of view of wanting clear-cut answers, to choose one theory as best, we encourage you to take an *eclectic* view of adolescence, that is, take what's useful from each viewpint. This is the orientation we've adopted in this book because we feel that this approach provides the best understanding of adolescent development in all of its complexity.

RESEARCH IN ADOLESCENT PSYCHOLOGY

As behavioral scientists, psychologists construct hypotheses and theories about adolescent development and attempt to verify them. As research verifies and refutes hypotheses, psychologists slowly build models and theories to describe and explain aspects of adolescent development. It is to the "hows" of this verification process that we now turn.

Research Approaches

Research in adolescent psychology is governed by two types of questions. Some researchers are interested in studying change and stability in particular aspects of psychological functioning as related to chronological age; for example, does occupational choice crystallize as youth grow older? Such questions are *developmental* in nature. Other researchers may not be interested in uncovering trends in development, but rather in studying particular facets of adolescent development, for example, where do adolescents get their initial information about sex? Such questions would be considered *nondevelopmental*.

Developmental Questions   Psychologists use three different approaches to study developmental questions. These approaches, or research designs, may be viewed as "plans for gathering information" about the question of interest (Hetherington & Parke, 1975, p. 12). They are summarized in Table 1.5 and described below.

Longitudinal approach   The longitudinal approach involves repeated testing of the same group of individuals over an extended period of time. The length of the time span varies, depending on the questions being investigated and the time and resources available to the researcher. A study may extend over many years. For example, the California Growth Studies on the effect of early and late physical maturation in adolescence on later development spanned some 20 years. Adolescent research of this duration is rare (and extremely valuable). More typical longitudinal studies extend over a four- to eight-year period.

Longitudinal research can demonstrate long-term developmental trends which can clarify understanding of stability and change in the physical, cognitive, emotional, or social spheres of functioning during adolescence. One of its major drawbacks is obviously the length of time it takes to complete. Other drawbacks include subject attrition and the high cost of conducting an extended study. By subject attrition we mean loss of subjects, usually due to problems in keeping track of them in a highly mobile society over many years in order to do the necessary follow-up testing. For these reasons, longitudinal studies are not the most common type of developmental research.

Cross-sectional approach In a cross-sectional design different age groups are tested at the same time. Like the longitudinal approach it is a method of exploring developmental questions, but it is a more efficient method of gathering information, it takes less time, and it costs less to conduct.

The main drawback to this approach is that it is difficult to ensure that the functioning in the different age groups is comparable. This problem is avoided in longitudinal studies.

A study by Anne Constantinople (1969) on the development of identity during the college years is an example of a cross-sectional study. Constantinople tested groups of freshmen, sophomore, junior, and senior males and females and compared their scores on a test of identity achievement. In this way she was able to ascertain the developmental level of each class as well as the trend (it was positive) toward identity achievement from freshmen through senior years.

Combined longitudinal and cross-sectional approach A design that combines features of the longitudinal and cross-sectional approaches has several important ad-

Table 1.5 COMPARISON OF THREE DEVELOPMENTAL RESEARCH DESIGNS

	Longitudinal		Cross-sectional		Combined longitudinal and cross-sectional	
Main feature	Same age group of individuals (Group A) tested at several age points		Different age groups of individuals (Groups A, B, C) tested once		Different age groups of individuals (Groups A, B) tested at two or more age points	
	Age	*Group*	*Age*	*Group*	*Age*	*Group*
	12	A	12	A	12	A
	15	A	15	B	15	A B
	18	A	18	C	18	B
Approximate time for data collection	8 years		Time required to test each person once (typically less than 1 year)		4 years	

Source: Adapted from E. Mavis Hetherington and Ross D. Parke (1975). *Child Psychology: A Contemporary Viewpoint.* New York: McGraw-Hill, p. 11. Copyright © 1975 by the McGraw-Hill Book Company. Adapted by permission.

vantages. Not only is it possible to discern the particular developmental status for each of several age groups (as in the cross-sectional study); we are also able to measure the effects of repeated testing (for example, the 15-year-old group in Table 1.5). The time required for the combined approach is shorter than that needed for the longitudinal study (although it is longer than that required for the cross-sectional study).

Another feature of this type of design is that it makes it possible to separate age effects from time-of-birth (historical-cultural) effects. For example, consider a hypothetical cross-sectional study that investigates the attitudes of 20-, 30-, and 40-year-olds and finds that they are different. The researcher has no way of knowing whether the attitude differences are due to the difference in chronological age of the three groups or to the fact that the groups grew up in dissimilar cultural environments (growing up in the 1940s was a considerably different experience from growing up in the 1960s). Longitudinal studies cannot isolate the effects of these two variables either.

With the combined longitudinal–cross-sectional design, it is possible to separate these effects. As an example of this approach, we will use a study by Warner Schaie and Charles Strother (1968) which measured changes in cognitive functioning in subjects ages 20 to 70. Subjects were divided into groups of equal numbers of males and females within a five-year age interval (20–24, 25–29, and so forth). The subjects were all tested and then were re-tested seven years later. This design is longitudinal because each subject was tested at two different ages. It is cross-sectional because groups of different ages were tested at about the same time. (Actually, it is *two* separate cross-sectional studies because these groups were tested twice.)

Figure 1.2 shows the subjects' scores on the reasoning subtest of an intelligence test (in this study, 50 was considered an average score). The data from the two cross-sectional studies were averaged, and these scores were then plotted to form a single cross-sectional curve. As you can see from Figure 1.2, the cross-sectional curve shows a peak in reasoning ability around the age of 25, a sharp drop after age 35, and a decline after age 50. On the other hand, the longitudinal curve shows a more constant level of ability, with a peak at about age 40 and no significant decrease until age 60.

Studying these two curves together illustrates the usefulness of the combined design in isolating age and historical-cultural factors. The cross-sectional curve indicates that different-aged subjects show differences in reasoning ability. Without the accompanying longitudinal data, we might draw erroneous conclusions, such as 45-year-olds have lower reasoning ability than 25-year-olds. But the longitudinal data show that reasoning abilities remain relatively constant over these years. The explanation of the differences in results between the cross-sectional and longitudinal portions of the study lies in the fact that the educational experiences of the younger subjects were superior to those of the older subjects. Schaie and Strother (1968) also suggest that "genetic improvement in the species" might also be a cause of the differences. With this design, then, it's possible to separate the cultural-historical factor from the age variable.

All of these approaches can be useful in the study of adolescent development. Which design a researcher chooses is determined mainly by the strengths and limitations of the approach in relation to the particular question under investigation.

Nondevelopmental Questions   Let us now turn to the nondevelopmental research questions in which there is no particular concern for uncovering developmental trends,

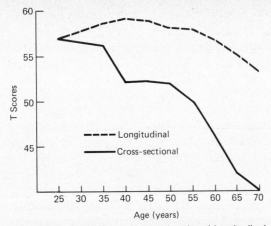

Figure 1.2   Estimated cross-sectional and longitudinal age gradients for reasoning. *Source:* Redrawn from K. Warner Schaie and Charles R. Strother (1968). A cross-sequential study of age changes in cognitive behavior. *Psychological Bulletin, 70,* 675. Copyright 1968 by the American Psychological Association. Reprinted by permission of the author.

but interest in some aspect of psychological functioning at a particular point in development. For example, one study used college freshman males to look at the relationship between the resolution of the identity crisis and two other factors, degree of autonomy and trust in other people. This wasn't a cross-sectional study because there was only one group of subjects, and it wasn't longitudinal because the subjects were tested only once. It's true that each subject took several tests, but each test was taken only once and all were taken within a short span of time.

Research Methods in Adolescent Psychology

Now we will review four types of systematic procedures psychologists use to gather data. Any of these methods may be part of any of the three previously mentioned designs. Each procedure has strengths and weaknesses. A good researcher adopts the method or combination of methods that will provide the most accurate and useful answers to the questions he or she is asking.

Observational Methods   Observation is one of the oldest methods used in developmental psychology. The researcher observes the subjects and records all the observations. It's important to note that the researcher doesn't interfere in any way with what is going on, but just observes and records what "naturally" unfolds. For example, a psychologist interested in sex differences in aggressive behavior in high school classrooms would go to the classrooms and as unobtrusively as possible record students' acts of aggression. When possible, the recording of responses is carefully controlled, and mechanical and electronic devices are often used for increased accuracy (with the subjects' consent, of course).

The observational method is usually used to study behaviors and interactions of groups of individuals, rather than of single individuals. The actions of each individual in a group are recorded and then all the data are considered together to enable the psychologist to make a general statement. In our example the researcher would analyze data to make a general statement about aggressive behavior in adolescent girls and boys.

This method is often, but not always, used as a precursor to more sophisticated types of research. It serves as a means of "getting the lay of the land" before investing more time and money in a more controlled and intensive research effort.

Observation has several drawbacks. (1) The observer may find it difficult to observe and record what is going on in an unbiased way. (2) It is often difficult to make an accurate record of all that is taking place. (3) Since the method requires noninterference, the investigator cannot cause the behavior of interest to occur, but must wait until it happens spontaneously. (4) There is no way of establishing conclusively the causes of events which are observed. The main advantage of observational methods is that it is often useful to have information about behavior as it occurs in natural settings rather than in the laboratory (and most observational studies occur in natural settings).

Clinical Methods Clinical methods combine observation with more systematic inquiry such as asking probing questions and psychological testing. These methods typically focus on one person at a time and are used in a clinical rather than a natural setting. (Anywhere the researcher administers the tests or asks the questions, such as a psychologist's office, is considered a clinical setting.)

One clinical method for obtaining data is the interview. Although the investigator may be interested in a particular issue, a particular sequence of questions is less important than understanding the subject's ideas and feelings as clearly as possible. The series of questions asked continually probes to elicit as fully as possible the subject's frame of reference and ideas about the issue under discussion. For example, Kohlberg makes extensive use of clinical interview data in his work on moral development. Clearly, there are drawbacks to the use of open-ended questions and to a flexible questioning style. The most obvious of these is the lack of the investigator's objectivity. There are numerous opportunities for the questioner to make subjective interpretations and inferences and to suggest "desirable" answers.

A more objective clinical data-gathering device is the individually administered standardized psychological test, such as the Stanford-Binet Intelligence Test or the Wechsler Intelligence Scales. Each individual is asked the same set of questions and given the same amount of time in which to respond. Because of these standardized procedures, individual scores can be compared.

Because every device is limited in the type and amount of data it can elicit and by problems of subjectivity, no single piece of clinical evidence is used by itself. The accepted practice is to administer a number of such tests and to combine these with clinical observations in order to obtain the most accurate representation of the individual being tested.

Survey Methods Survey methods rely on asking subjects questions, usually in a standardized format. Surveys may be done by written questionnaires or face-to-face interviews. In adolescent psychology subjects are usually questioned about their attitudes and values (toward religion or premarital sex, for example) or typical behaviors ("How often do you date during the week?").

The questionnaire format usually takes less time to complete than interviewing, thereby permitting the use of a greater number of subjects. It's also less expensive. One drawback to the questionnaire is that it doesn't allow for a flexible exchange often needed to clarify questions for the subject and to clarify the subject's answers to be sure the investigator has interpreted them correctly. Obviously, the interview format offers this option.

Both the questionnaire and the interview, however, suffer from a serious limitation. There is no way to determine the accuracy of the subjects' answers. Psychologists know that people (understandably) want to appear in the best possible light and so may deceive the researcher, they may simply forget, or they may not know information and offer "best guesses" as facts.

A well-known survey by Elizabeth Douvan and Joseph Adelson (*The Adolescent Experience,* 1966) is an example of a study that utilized this method. Some 3,500 adolescents (boys from 14 to 16 years of age and girls from 11 to 17) were interviewed on an individual basis. Each interview took from one to four hours and included questions about interpersonal development, femininity, leisure activities, and personality development.

With survey research a central concern is the *sample,* or who is included in the survey. It is most important that the sample, those who are surveyed, are representative of the *population,* or the larger group about whom generalizations will be made (recall our earlier comments about the "generalization gap"). For example, in the Douvan and Adelson survey interviews were arranged through schools in the United States. Their study, therefore, characterizes American adolescents of the ages interviewed who were in school at that time. Obviously, it wouldn't be accurate to say that their results were representative of all adolescents since the sample didn't include young people in other cultures or American adolescents who were not enrolled in school because they were in penal institutions or hospitals or had dropped out. It's important to know the characteristics of the individuals in the sample so that it can be ascertained whether the sample, is, in fact, representative of the larger population, as it is intended to be. This helps ensure the accuracy of conclusions.

Experimental Methods   The essence of experimental methods is the aspect of *control* which the experimenter has in designing and conducting the research. With observational methods the investigator is limited to waiting and watching for the behavior of interest to appear; he or she may not interfere in the situation to make the behavior more likely to occur. In survey and clinical methods the investigator is more active in the data-gathering process, and thereby assumes more control and influence over the subject's responses. In experimental methods the experimenter's control is even greater.

In an experiment the experimenter manipulates one or more variables *(independent variables)* while holding all other variables constant. Then, the experimenter looks for an effect of the independent variable on the subject's behavior (the *dependent variable*).

In an experiment some subjects are assigned to the *experimental group,* a group of subjects who are exposed to the independent variable. Others are assigned to a *control group,* a group of subjects similar in all respects to the experimental group but not exposed to the independent variable. One of the critical features of the experiment is the *random assignment* of subjects to these groups. By randomly assigning each subject to either the experimental or control group, the experimenter can assume that the two groups are comparable and that any differences which are found between the two groups must, therefore, be caused by the variation which has been intentionally introduced in the experimental group. This allows us to determine the causes of problems we're interested in. Other methods don't provide this information, as a rule.

One of the tests of the reliability of an experimental procedure and the validity of its results is *repeatability.* Another experimenter (or the original experimenter) should be able to repeat the experiment and get the same results.

Experimental methods have their weaknesses. For one thing, they can't always be used in psychology because the nature of the subject matter isn't always amenable to experimental control. For instance, if we are interested in studying the "plasticity" of development at adolescence, we couldn't take 75 children from delivery rooms, keep 25 of them in dark closets for 12 years, place 25 in "moderate care" facilities, and 25 in enriched environmental settings in order to measure the differences among groups during the adolescent years! Moreover, experiments typically take place in laboratories or in "artificial environments" and conclusions drawn from these studies may not be accurate when applied to "real world" situations.

One attempt to deal with the problem of the artificial environment is the use of *experimental field studies* instead of or in addition to experimental laboratory studies. (Note that the word *experimental* is critical in the label experimental field studies, as there are field studies that are not experimental.) Experimental field studies are performed in the field, that is, in the "real world," in which the experimenter attempts to maintain as much control as possible over the conditions being studied. Obviously, we have a "trade-off" here, for to the extent that the experiment takes place in the "real world," there is less control over extraneous factors which could affect the outcome of the study.

Let's look at an experimental field study. The purpose of the research was to investigate whether college women's participation in consciousness-raising groups would have any effect on the subjects' self-esteem, feminist attitudes and behaviors, or need for social approval (Follingstad, Robinson, & Pugh, 1977). Twenty-two female undergraduate volunteers were randomly assigned to one of two types of consciousness-raising experiences: a marathon group, which met only once for a 16-hour period, or an 8-week group, which met for 2 hours a week for 8 weeks. (This experiment used two experimental groups.) The control group consisted of 12 other undergraduate women who were tested on the same measures as the experimental groups, but who did not participate in either experimental group. All subjects were tested before the group experience (pretest), one day after (posttest), and one month after (follow-up).

Among other things, it was found that the profeminist attitudes and behaviors of the subjects in the two experimental groups were significantly stronger at the time of posttesting and follow-up than those of the control subjects. Secondly, no significant differences were found between the two experimental groups on any of the variables. When compared with control subjects, marathon participants showed slightly higher pro-feminist attitudes, but no other differences. Eight-week subjects showed significantly more profeminist behavioral changes and increases in self-esteem than controls. No significant differences between groups were obtained with regard to the need for social approval.

The experimental design of this study enabled the researchers to determine what kind of group experience was responsible for producing particular personality and behavioral changes (cause and effect could be determined). This permits the objective evaluation of the effectiveness of such groups. In addition, the findings suggest certain changes in format for consciousness-raising groups to increase their effectiveness in producing changes in group members.

Special Problems in Studying Adolescents

Before concluding this section on research, we want to mention a research-related issue: that of the special problems which arise in the study of adolescents. The first problem is the disparity between chronological age and physical and psychological development during adolescence. This problem is complicated by the fact that, especially during early adolescence, females are typically $1\frac{1}{2}$ to 2 years more advanced in physical development than boys. Consequently, research groups comprised of subjects of the same chronological age often produce widespread differences among subjects. These results are not only confusing in themselves, they can also mask more subtle effects a researcher is attempting to study.

A second problem concerns the validity of adolescent subjects' responses obtained in research. This is a problem with subjects at any age, but several factors combine to make it more serious in adolescent research. For one thing, adolescents are at a "self-conscious" age. When questions of a "personal" nature are asked (about sex or sex roles, for example), individuals may adjust their answers, often unwittingly, in the direction they feel will make them look best. Obviously, this presents a problem for the psychologist who must assume that subjects' responses are true, unless there are ways of detecting untruthful answers, and detection is not always possible. We can hope that reassurances of anonymity and confidentiality promote honesty among subjects, but we can't guarantee it.

A third problem concerns the developmental fact that adolescent attitudes and beliefs are undergoing self-examination and may change relatively rapidly. An adolescent may not really know how he or she feels about religion at the time such a question appears on a survey. Or, what is true at one time may not be so six months later. This rapid change makes it difficult to get a clear idea of adolescents' attitudes and values.

We alluded to a fourth problem earlier when we discussed the composition of Douvan and Adelson's (1966) national survey which didn't include high school dropouts or adolescents in hospitals or penal institutions (from about the age of 15, school dropouts become a "sizable group"). As psychologists interested in adolescents, we need to know about *all* of them, not just those in educational institutions.

This concern takes a slightly different twist when we shift our focus to late adolescence and youth. Typically, most research with these groups is done with college students, even though half of high school graduates don't attend college. Moreover, there is considerable diversity among late adolescent college students in terms of competencies, the types of institutions they attend, and the different effects of different environments (Astin, 1977). As researchers, it's important that psychologists be able to identify accurately the causes of differences observed among adolescents.

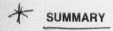

SUMMARY

The psychology of adolescence is the study of the physical, cognitive, personality, and social changes which take place in individuals beginning at puberty and continuing until the assumption of adult responsibilities in society. The major developmental tasks of adolescence include achieving a sense of identity, attaining emotional and financial independence from parents, relating effectively with peers, becoming a sexual person, and choosing and preparing for an occupation.

Current issues in adolescent psychology include the definition of the boundaries of adolescence, the recognition of important gender, class, ethnic, and racial differences in the adolescent experience, the need for cross-cultural perspectives on the adolescent experience, and the need to increase the validity of generalizations about adolescents.

Adolescence began to be identified as a separate stage in the life span in the early twentieth century. Early theories of adolescence stressed the biological determinants of behavior (Hall, Gesell, Sigmund and Anna Freud). Later theories emphasized socio-cultural determinants (Sullivan, Erikson, Benedict, and Mead). More recently, we have seen an awareness of the interaction of biological and social forces, with the emergence of other viewpoints such as the cognitive, social learning, and developmental task orientations. No single theory can adequately explain the complexities of adolescent development.

Typically, three approaches are used to research developmental questions related to adolescence and youth. These include the longitudinal, the cross-sectional, and the combined longitudinal/cross-sectional designs. Researchers are also interested in non-developmental questions about adolescents. Some major research methods utilized in the study of adolescents and youth include the following: observational, clinical, survey, and experimental.

GLOSSARY

adolescence   a transitional stage of development between childhood and adulthood, generally beginning around age 13 and ending about age 22.

adolescent psychology   the study of the physical, cognitive, personality, and social changes which take place in individuals beginning at puberty and continuing until the assumption of adult responsibilities in society.

classical conditioning (Pavlov)   the process of repeatedly pairing two stimuli (an unconditioned and a neutral stimulus) with the result that the initially neutral stimulus acquires the capacity to elicit the response originally elicited by the unconditioned stimulus.

combined longitudinal/cross-sectional approach   a research approach which combines the features of the longitudinal and cross-sectional designs, with the primary advantage of making it possible to separate age from time-of-birth effects.

cross-sectional approach   a research design in which different age groups (14, 16, 18, for example) are tested at the same time on the same questions to ascertain changes and stability in development with age.

developmental tasks (Havighurst)   Attitudes and skills which are best learned at particular stages of development.

eclectic   Choosing what appears to be the best from a variety of sources.

ego (Freud)   The rational aspect of personality which aids the individual in adapting to the external world.

empirical   based on systematic observation or experiment rather than solely on reasoning.

formal operations (Piaget)   The fourth and last stage of cognitive development which begins about age 11 and is characterized by the ability to think logically about abstract ideas.

genital stage (Freud)   The last stage of psychosexual development, beginning about age 11, when an individual is motivated toward sexual gratification with another person and when the Oedipal or Electra complex is reawakened.

heterophilic relationship (Sullivan)   A relationship which is sought because another person is significantly different from oneself, namely, the opposite gender.

id (Freud)   The structure of personality present at birth, governed by irrational and biological forces, which seeks to gratify basic instinctive needs.

identity (Erikson)   A stable sense of oneself, the developmental task of adolescence.

interpersonal theory of psychiatry (Sullivan)   A theory which considers social interactions to be the major factor in personality development.

isophilic relationship (Sullivan)   A relationship which is sought because another person is very similar to oneself, namely, the same gender.

longitudinal approach   A research design in which the same subjects are tested repeatedly over a period of time.

observational learning (Bandura)   Learning how to do something by watching someone else do it (imitation, modeling).

operant conditioning (Skinner)   Strengthening a response by reinforcing it.

puberty   Attainment of sexual maturity; usually about age 13 females, with onset of menstruation; about age $14\frac{1}{2}$ in males, with ejaculation of sperm.

puberty rites   Formal initiation ceremonies which mark the passage from childhood to adult status; characteristic of tribal societies.

recapitulation theory (Hall)   The view that all individuals repeat the major stages of human evolution as they mature.

superego (Freud)   The moral agent of the personality consisting of internalized parental and societal standards, expectations, and values.

youth (Keniston)   A relatively new stage of development composed of older adolescents who haven't yet assumed adult responsibilities; characteristic of industrial societies which require postsecondary education of their citizens.

Chapter 2 Outline

chapter 2

Physical and Sexual Development

In this chapter we will focus on the physical, physiological, and sexual changes that occur during adolescence and on the psychological and social implications of these changes for young people. During adolescence two major physical transformations occur: the body of the child changes into that of an adult and the physical differences between the sexes are established.

Let's begin with some definitions. *Pubescence* is a two-year span which precedes puberty, during which physical and physiological changes leading to physical and sexual maturity take place. It is during pubescence that the *adolescent growth spurt* begins—at about $10\frac{1}{2}$ years of age in girls and about two years later in boys at $12\frac{1}{2}$ years. It is called a "spurt" because of the relatively sudden increases in body height and weight. This spurt might more accurately be termed the *pre*adolescent growth spurt because it actually occurs *prior* to puberty, which is the criterion usually used to indicate the beginning of adolescence (Hurlock, 1973).

We take the view that *puberty* is an extension of pubescence and marks the stage during which the more critical sexual functions reach maturity. Although some psychologists do not distinguish between pubescence and puberty, we want to maintain the distinction because pubescence technically occurs during childhood and puberty marks the beginning of adolescence.

We also make a conceptual distinction between physical and sexual development. Nonetheless, it is important to remember that the processes of attaining adult physical size and the capacity to reproduce are closely interwoven at the biological level, especially through the action of hormones.

PHYSICAL CHANGES DURING ADOLESCENCE

Physical growth is like other aspects of development in that it is a gradual and continuous process and is often asynchronous in nature. That is, different parts of the body develop at different rates of speed. For example, hands and feet grow before arms and legs. In addition, increases in height and weight occur before the onset of sexual maturity, and these as well as other physical changes continue after the ability to reproduce is attained.

Throughout this chapter we will refer to *normative* ages for physical development, but it is important to remember that these norms represent statistical averages and that there is a great deal of variability around any given average age. For example, the average age at which menstruation begins is 13 years, but the range of onset varies from 9 to 18 years. While extreme deviations from developmental norms may indicate problems which require medical attention, these cases are relatively rare.

By looking at the children in a seventh grade classroom, it would be easy to see that adolescents of the same age vary considerably in size. In fact, adolescents of the same chronological age can vary as much as six years in actual maturational age. Figure 2.1 shows the degree of variation for three 12¾-year-old girls and three 14¾-year-old boys. Obviously, chronological age is not an accurate index for measuring maturational age. A more reliable criterion for determining maturational level for clinical purposes is *skeletal age*. As a person matures, the soft cartilage in the skeleton changes to bone, so it is possible to measure skeletal maturity by monitoring this process. To measure skeletal age, X-rays of the bones of the hand and wrist are taken and the proportion of bone to cartilage in this area is measured and compared to a standard scale.

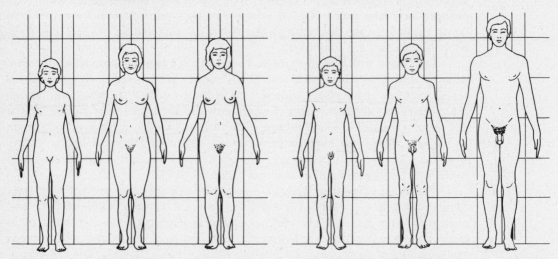

Figure 2.1   Variability in pubertal development. All three girls are 12¾ years and all three boys are 14¾ years of age but in different stages of puberty. *Source:* Redrawn from "Growing Up," by J. M. Tanner. Copyright © 1973 by Scientific American, Inc. All rights reserved. Reprinted by permission.

Adolescent Growth Spurt

The adolescent growth spurt refers to the sudden increases in height and weight which occur before puberty. It is triggered by an increase in hormones secreted by the endocrine glands. Endocrine glands include the pituitary, adrenals, thyroid, parathyroids, pancreas, and gonads or sex glands (ovaries in females; testes in males). Figure 2.2 shows the location and functions of the major endocrine glands. *Hormones* are biochemical substances secreted directly into the bloodstream by the endocrine glands. They act as an internal communication network for body cells by telling the various cells what to do and when to act. Each hormone has specific body organs which it affects. Some hormones are secreted constantly; others follow rhythmic cycles. The hypothalamus, a structure in the brain, plays a key role in the regulation of the endocrine glands and thus in the onset and regulation of the adolescent growth spurt.

The *pituitary gland* is a pea-sized structure situated at the base of the brain. It is often called the "master gland" because it not only produces bodily changes directly,

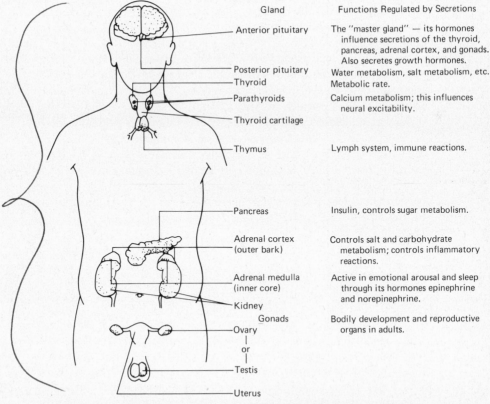

Gland	Functions Regulated by Secretions
Anterior pituitary	The "master gland" — its hormones influence secretions of the thyroid, pancreas, adrenal cortex, and gonads. Also secretes growth hormones.
Posterior pituitary	Water metabolism, salt metabolism, etc.
Thyroid	Metabolic rate.
Parathyroids	Calcium metabolism; this influences neural excitability.
Thyroid cartilage	
Thymus	Lymph system, immune reactions.
Pancreas	Insulin, controls sugar metabolism.
Adrenal cortex (outer bark)	Controls salt and carbohydrate metabolism; controls inflammatory reactions.
Adrenal medulla (inner core)	Active in emotional arousal and sleep through its hormones epinephrine and norepinephrine.
Kidney	
Gonads	Bodily development and reproductive organs in adults.
Ovary or Testis	
Uterus	

Figure 2.2 Location and functions of the major endocrine glands. *Source:* Redrawn from *Psychology: An Introduction,* by Paul Mussen, Mark R. Rosenzweig, et al. Copyright © 1977 by D. C. Heath and Company. Reprinted by permission of the publisher.

but also affects the functioning of other endocrine glands. It influences body metabolism, body growth, muscular strength, and motor coordination, as well as perspiration levels. The pituitary gland secretes a number of hormones, but the one which is most important in physical development is called *human growth hormone (HGH)*. HGH plays an important role in the growth and shaping of the skeleton. It is this hormone that regulates the height of a person and the length of limbs. Too much causes *giantism* and too little causes *dwarfism*. Normal growth also depends on a balance between growth hormone and the sex hormones, as well as nutrition.

Increases in height and weight are usually closely correlated during the adolescent growth spurt. Height change is generally the more significant of the two, as failure to increase in height within the average range of development may signify a hormonal deficiency or imbalance. Over- or underweight problems, on the other hand, usually are related to nonphysiological factors such as diet and exercise.

Increases in Height   A child's height prior to the onset of the adolescent growth spurt is highly correlated with adult height ($r = .80$). This means, for example, that a child in the twenty-fifth percentile in height before the growth spurt is very likely to be in the same percentile after puberty (Tanner, 1970). The magnitude of actual height increase during the adolescent growth spurt is another factor with regard to a person's ultimate height.

As can be seen from Figure 2.3, there are sex differences in the onset of the adolescent growth spurt and in the actual height gains. In girls the growth spurt begins approximately two years earlier than in boys. It may begin as early as $9\frac{1}{2}$ years of age or as late as 15. Typically, in American girls it starts at about age $10\frac{1}{2}$, reaches peak velocity at 12, and decelerates markedly by 14. Growth gradually ceases at about age 17 (Roche, 1979). This two-year lead in development is not solely an adolescent characteristic. Girls are born with slightly more mature skeletons and nervous systems, and this developmental lead gradually increases throughout childhood.

In boys, although the growth spurt may begin as early as $10\frac{1}{2}$ years or as late as 16, typically height increases start about the age of $12\frac{1}{2}$, reach peak acceleration around 14, and drop off sharply by 16. Height increases in boys cease for the most part by age 21 (Roche, 1979).

Increases in Weight   Increases in weight which accompany the height changes of the adolescent growth spurt reflect increases in the size of bones, muscles, and body organs, as well as increases in subcutaneous fat (a layer of fatty tissue under the skin).

Here, also, we see sex differences. On the average girls weigh somewhat less than boys from birth to age 7, become heavier than boys from age 9 or 10 until about age $14\frac{1}{2}$, and weigh less than boys after age $14\frac{1}{2}$. Also, muscles contribute more to body weight in boys than in girls, and subcutaneous fat comprises more of girls' body weight than boys'.

The onset of menstruation *(menarche)* seems to be related to body weight. One study of adolescent females showed that menstruation began at the same average weight (106 pounds or 47.8 kilograms) in girls who reached menarche at both earlier and later

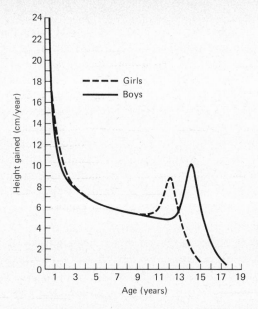

Figure 2.3 Typical individual curves showing velocity of growth in height for girls and boys. *Source:* Redrawn from J. M. Tanner, R. H. Whitehouse, and M. Takaishi (1966). "Standards from birth to maturity for height, weight, height velocity and weight velocity: British Children, 1965. *Archives of Diseases in Childhood, 41,* 455–471. Reprinted by permission of the New England Journal of Medicine.

chronological ages (Frisch & Revelle, 1970). The authors suggest that the point at which fatty tissue constitutes about 17 percent of body weight is the critical factor in the onset of menstruation. Related to this hypothesis, it has been found that obese children reach puberty about one year earlier than children of average weight. Moreover, menstruation usually stops in females who suffer from a psychological disorder termed *anorexia nervosa,* which results in severe loss of weight, among other symptoms.

Other Bodily Changes

As a rule, skeletal and muscle development follows a regular pattern of somewhat asynchronous growth such that the head, hands, and feet attain mature size before the legs and arms. This sometimes causes adolescents to feel temporarily clumsy and awkward. Also, the body fills out before the shoulders reach their maximum width. With changes in muscle and fat tissues, the spindly arms and legs of children take on more adult-shaped proportions.

Boys experience greater growth in muscles and, as we mentioned before, muscle tissue makes up a larger proportion of total weight than in females. Girls have a greater ratio of fatty tissue to total body weight.

Along with height and weight changes, the adolescent's *face* begins to look more adultlike. The forehead becomes wider and higher, the nose gets larger, the mouth widens, the lips grow fuller, and the jaw becomes more pronounced.

The *eyes* reach almost adult size before adolescence, but there is some increase in size (from cornea to retina) which, some speculate, may be responsible for an observed sudden increase in nearsightedness during adolescence.

Skin problems are often associated with puberty. These occur because of the increased activity of the *sebaceous* (oil) *glands* in the skin. *Apocrine* (sweat) *glands,* located in the armpit, mammary, genital, and anal regions, enlarge during puberty. The increased perspiration produced by these glands may be acted on by skin bacteria to cause body odors.

Body hair in both sexes changes from its preadolescent downy texture to the longer, thicker, coarser, and more kinky hair seen at maturation. Body hair grows first in the pubic region; this occurs relatively early in development (10 to 11 in girls, 12 to 13 in boys). Axillary (underarm) hair and body hair usually appear at about the time that pubic hair growth is completed, some two years after the onset of pubic hair growth. How much hair a person develops seems to be regulated largely by heredity. Facial hair in boys begins to grow at about the same time as axillary hair.

In the trunk, sex differences in the overall shape and proportion of the body become noticeable. The most obvious are the male's greater height and breadth of shoulders and the female's wider hips.

In addition to the more obvious changes in the body exterior at adolescence, equally impressive changes take place inside the body, such as an increase in the size of digestive organs, the heart, and the lungs. Obviously, these changes have important effects on circulation, respiration, digestion, and metabolism. For instance, blood volume increases at puberty (more rapidly in males), and blood pressure rises steadily from infancy on (the average male having higher blood pressure than the average female). Changes in lung size and respiratory function begin at about $11\frac{1}{2}$ years of age. Boys show a greater increase in size than girls because lungs develop according to demands made on them, and girls tend to be less active than boys. Changes also occur in digestive organs, such as an increase in the size of the stomach. Nutritional requirements obviously become greater in order to sustain physical growth on so many fronts.

We should add that not all parts of the body undergo dramatic changes at adolescence. For example, most of the development of the brain occurs before adolescence. By age $2\frac{1}{2}$ the brain has grown to approximately 75 percent of its adult weight, and by age 10 it has attained 95 percent (Tanner, 1970).

Increases in Physical Strength and Motor Coordination

The increases in physical strength at adolescence are directly related to the increases in muscular size, skeletal growth, body weight, and neural organization. This area is one in which sex differences are particularly apparent. For instance, boys on the average have somewhat larger muscles than girls, except during the age span from $12\frac{1}{2}$ to $13\frac{1}{2}$ years when the earlier onset of the growth spurt causes girls to move ahead temporarily (Tanner, 1970).

Various devices are used to measure physical strength. The abilities most often measured are the hand grip, the arm pull (the ability to pull one's hands apart as they each hold a dynamometer handle at chest level), and the arm thrust. Longitudinal data indicate that girls show a small increase in arm strength compared to boys, as measured by right grip and arm pull. It also appears that American boys are much stronger than girls after adolescence. It has been suggested that this reflects not only the larger size of the boys' muscles, but also a greater capacity to "develop more force per gram of muscle tissue" (Tanner, 1970, p. 95).

With regard to motor coordination, there do not seem to be sex differences until about age 14, at which time boys show average increases in coordination over girls on a variety of tasks. Whereas American boys continue to develop coordination after age 14, American girls do not show much change in coordination after that age (Malina, 1974).

Studies comparing the physical fitness of American adolescents with young people from other countries (England, Japan, Sweden, for example) have shown that American adolescents are often inferior (Cureton, 1964). Moreover, it is clear that youth who participate in physical education programs which include sustained exercises show superior physical fitness compared to youth whose physical education consists mainly of play and games. Some have criticized American physical education as being weak in this regard.

The impact of training on physical fitness has important implications for the sex differences in physical strength we noted in American youth. In our culture adolescent boys are encouraged to play sports and engage in vigorous physical activity to a much greater extent than girls are. No doubt there are many reasons for this state of affairs, but sexist beliefs and practices are important factors.

Compared to male sports, female athletic activities have been given less adequate funding, inferior facilities and equipment, lower paid coaching, less public attention, and fewer rewards (Gilbert & Williamson, 1973). These conditions have begun to change with the advent of Title IX of the Education Amendments of 1972 and of Title IX Guidelines of 1975 which require all educational institutions which receive federal funding to maintain equal athletic facilities and opportunities for boys and girls.

Females must also contend with sexist beliefs which discourage their interest and participation in sports. Several studies have found that females' participation in sports has limited social acceptance among the general public (Snyder & Kivlin, 1977). Moreover, 65 percent of college female high-level athletes agreed that "there is a stigma attached to women's participation in sports" (Snyder & Kivlin, 1977). Interestingly, the authors of this study also found that the female athletes reported more traditional sex-role attitudes than a comparison group of nonathletes.

Some discriminatory beliefs and practices are "protective" in intent. For example, it has been argued that female reproductive organs are more susceptible to injury than male organs, that heavy exertion interferes with menstruation, and that females are more likely to be injured or have accidents than males. However, there is no evidence to support these assertions (Gilbert & Williamson, 1973).

Also, it is commonly suggested that girls who engage in vigorous sports will develop large muscles (obviously, a prior assumption here is that it is acceptable for only males to be muscular). Whereas physical activity does develop muscle tone, which fitness experts advise is good, muscle size seems to be more related to hormonal activity than to athletic participation.

These various factors have resulted in less physical activity among girls. While sex differences in physical strength and coordination are not due solely to differences in training and practice, these factors can play an important role in the level of development reached. For example, some early studies showed that English and Japanese girls demonstrated some improvement in physical skills during adolescence, whereas American girls showed almost none (Cureton, 1964). The major difference between the American girls and the other girls was the amount of physical training they received in their physical education classes. Cross-cultural studies are beginning to indicate that adolescent girls are showing slight but continual improvement in skill performance through age 17 (Malina, 1974). It will be interesting to see if the changes brought about by Title IX will produce corresponding changes in attitudes toward sport participation and increased strength and coordination in American adolescent girls. One recent study indicated that attitudes toward women in sport are becoming more positive (although college women's attitudes were more positive than college men's) (Nixon, Maresca, & Silverman, 1979).

Trends Toward Larger Size and Earlier Onset of Puberty

There has been a clear-cut trend over the past 150 years for children to become larger (at all ages) and to reach puberty earlier, as Figure 2.4 indicates. Such a gradual trend over a period of decades or a century is known as a *secular trend.* While there are many causes of this secular trend, cross-cultural and longitudinal data suggest that a lessening of disease and higher nutritional levels are especially important (Tanner, 1971). Recently, a "stimulation/stress factor" hypothesis has been proposed which suggests that such factors as the presence of noise, crowding, and artificial light may also bring about these changes (Adams, 1981).

Current assessments indicate that these trends are slowing down or have ceased for many middle- and upper-socioeconomic groups in industrialized countries (Roche, 1979).

Participation in sports has become more acceptable and popular for girls.

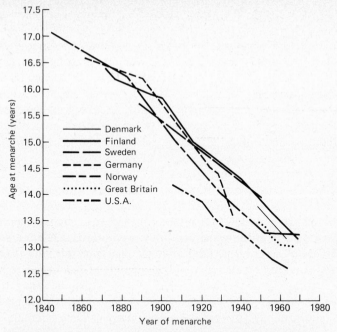

Figure 2.4   Secular trend in age at menarche: 1840–1960. *Source:*
Redrawn from "Growing Up" by J. M. Tanner. Copyright © 1973 by
Scientific American, Inc. All rights reserved. Reprinted by permission.

SEXUAL DEVELOPMENT

In this section we will elaborate on the changes which occur during pubescence and
puberty in order to describe more clearly the process of sexual maturation.

Pubescence

The average age range of this period is between $10\frac{1}{2}$ and 13 years in girls and between
$12\frac{1}{2}$ and $14\frac{1}{2}$ years in boys. This stage is seen as an immature phase of development
during which the (pre-)adolescent growth spurt begins and during which *secondary sex
characteristics* begin to appear. Secondary sex characteristics are those features which
distinguish one sex from another, but which are not essential for reproduction. They
include such things as voice changes, body hair distribution, breast development, and
body shape. During the pubescent stage children begin to take on the physical features
which characterize adults of their respective sexes. However, the capacity to reproduce
is not yet developed. Recall that since puberty is taken as the criterion for the onset
of adolescence, boys and girls in the pubescent stage are technically not yet adolescents.

Puberty

We can view this stage as a maturing period during which the *primary sex characteristics* begin to develop and function. Primary sex characteristics are the structures
necessary for reproduction to take place. Note that nonsexual body changes, such as

those in height and weight, are not completed at the beginning of this stage. American girls reach menarche at the average age of 13 with further sexual maturation continuing until approximately age 16. American boys begin to produce sperm and ejaculate at the average age of $14\frac{1}{2}$ with complete sexual maturation occurring by about 18 (Tanner, 1970). It is with menarche in girls and ejaculation of sperm in boys that adolescence technically begins.

After the attainment of sexual maturation, adolescents continue to mature physically until secondary sex characteristics are fully developed and the body has reached adult height and proportions. In girls such growth continues until about 17 years of age and in boys until about age 21 (Roche, 1979).

Table 2.1 portrays the actual sequence of the body changes which take place in males and females in the process of sexual maturation. Although there is variation among individuals as to the timing of these changes, the sequence of the changes is constant. Observe the position of the onset of menarche or mature sperm production within the total context of the sexual maturation process in Table 2.1. Note that the ages given for these events in the table are later than those given in the text because the table is based on older data (recall our discussion of the secular trend).

Criteria Marking the Advent of Puberty   Because sexual maturation takes place over time and involves a number of bodily changes (many of them internal), it is difficult

Table 2.1   AVERAGE AGE AND SEQUENCE OF APPEARANCE OF SEXUAL CHARACTERISTICS IN BOTH SEXES

Age	Boys	Girls
9–10		Growth of bony pelvis Budding of nipples
10–11	First growth of testes and penis	Budding of breasts Pubic hair
11–12	Prostatic activity	Changes in vaginal epithelium and the smear Growth of external and internal genitalia
12–13	Pubic hair	Pigmentation of nipples Breast development
13–14	Rapid growth of testes and penis Subareolar node of nipples	Axillary hair Menarche (average: 13½ years; range: 9–17 years). Menstruation may be anovulatory for first few years.
14–15	Axillary hair Down on upper lip Voice change	Earliest normal pregnancies
15–16	Mature spermatozoa (average: 15 years; range: 11¼–17 years)	Acne Deepening of voice
16–17	Facial and body hair Acne	Arrest of skeletal growth
21	Arrest of skeletal growth	

Note: The age of menarche and the age of production of mature sperm given here are later than those given in the text because the table is based on older data.

Source: From Lawson Wilkins, Robert M. Blizzard, and Claude J. Migeon (Eds.) (1965). *The Diagnosis and Treatment of Endocrine Disorders in Childhood and Adolescence* (3rd ed.). Courtesy of Charles C Thomas, Publisher, Springfield, Illinois.

to pinpoint specific events which can serve as useful criteria for the onset of sexual maturity. Because menstruation in girls is taken as a visible sign of sexual maturation, the first menstrual period or *menarche* is popularly used as the criterion for sexual maturity in girls. In fact, however, menarche is not always a valid index of a female's capacity to reproduce because most girls are sterile for 12 to 18 months following the menarche (but adolescents should not count on this as being true!). Breast development and the presence of pubic hair in girls serve as important social criteria of adolescence in the absence of visible external genitals.

In boys no comparable clear-cut sign of sexual maturity exists. The capacity to ejaculate sperm is used as a popular index of puberty in males (the onset of sperm production not being a visible event). The first ejaculation usually occurs through masturbation, rather than *nocturnal emission* (or "wet dream," in which ejaculation occurs during sleep and is sometimes accompanied by erotic dreams). Nocturnal emissions do not usually occur until almost a year after ejaculatory capacity has been attained (Katchadourian, 1977). As with girls, this sign of puberty in boys may not be a valid index of actual maturity because early ejaculations may contain seminal fluid but no active sperm.

For research purposes a variety of criteria are usually employed to determine the onset of puberty because of the variability in maturation rates of the primary and secondary sex characteristics.

Hormonal Changes

The hypothalamus, a structure in the brain, signals the pituitary gland when the process of sexual maturation is to begin. In addition to HGH (human growth hormone), the pituitary produces other hormones. Three of these, together called *gonadotropic hormones* or gonad-stimulating hormones, are especially important in the sexual maturation process.

Just before puberty, there is a gradual increase in the gonadotropic hormones secreted by the pituitary gland. This additional secretion causes the immature gonads (ovaries or testes) to grow in size and begin to mature. At the same time the gonads become more sensitive to the gonadotropic hormones. The combination of these two conditions appears to trigger the onset of puberty—although it is not yet clear how all of this happens.

As the ovaries and testes develop, they produce ova and sperm, respectively, as well as their own hormones. The gonadal hormones (estrogens and progesterone in females and androgens in males) cause the various sex-related changes in the primary genital organs and the development of the secondary sex characteristics. We will discuss hormonal development and maturation in greater detail below, as we review male and female development separately.

PROCESS OF SEXUAL MATURATION IN MALES

Hormonal Changes

At the onset of sexual maturation, male gonadotropic hormones stimulate growth and development of the testes and cause them to produce androgens. Of the androgenic hormones, testosterone is the most important. It is responsible for controlling the development of the primary sex characteristics: the testicles, a number of ducts and glands that store and transport sperm and secrete portions of the semen (such as the prostate gland and the seminal vesicles), and the penis. Testosterone is also important in the development of secondary sex characteristics such as deepening of the voice, broadening of shoulders, and the development and patterning of facial, body, and pubic hair.

Prior to pubescence males and females carry approximately equal amounts of both male and female hormones. At pubescence, however, the gonads begin producing greater amounts of androgens in males and estrogens and progesterone in females. For example, the testosterone level in women's blood is about one-sixth of that in men's. Likewise, estrogens increase only slightly in males at pubescence, but show a considerable increase in females.

Male Primary Sex Characteristics

In regard to sex characteristics the terms *primary* and *secondary* refer to the relative importance of the characteristics in sexual function and not to their sequence of development. Secondary sex characteristics begin developing before primary characteristics and continue developing after primary characteristics have matured. As you read this section, you may find it helpful to refer to Figure 2.5.

Testes (Testicles)   The *testes* (sing. testis) are two oval glands contained in the *scrotum*, a protective baglike structure which is suspended from the body, just behind the penis. (The testes are external structures because sperm production cannot take place at normal body temperatures.) The testes have two important functions: (1) to produce sperm, one of the two necessary components for sexual reproduction, and (2)

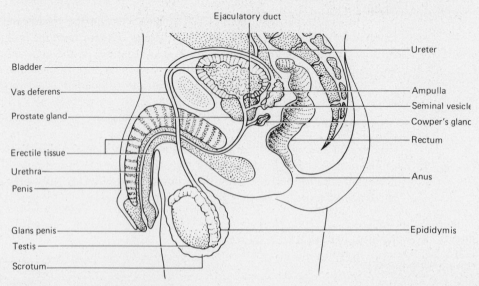

Figure 2.5 Male reproductive system.

to produce testosterone, an androgenic hormone. At puberty the testes increase in size due to growth of the glands which produce sperm.

In the early stages of puberty sperm production is slow and somewhat irregular because the hormonal feedback mechanisms are not yet functioning smoothly. Once the male reproductive system is mature, 10 to 30 billion sperm cells are produced regularly each month throughout a male's life. Nocturnal emissions usually occur when the reproductive apparatus is relatively mature.

Penis The *penis* is the male sex organ, and it and the testes are the first sexual structures to show growth at puberty. Normally, the penis is in a flaccid state, but with sexual excitement or stimulation it becomes engorged with blood and becomes erect. In the flaccid state penis size varies considerably among males (from $2\frac{1}{2}$ to 4 inches in length), but these size differences tend to disappear in the state of erection (average length is slightly more than 6 inches). Contrary to popular belief, the size and shape of the penis aren't related to "body build, race, virility, or ability to give and receive sexual satisfaction" (Katchadourian & Lunde, 1975, p. 26).

The penis contains the *urethra,* a long tube which transports both urine and semen. During ejaculation a sphincter at the base of the bladder is closed by the expansion of tissue in the penis so that urine does not pass through the urethra and semen does not enter the bladder.

Other Structures The *prostate gland* and the *seminal vesicles* produce the liquid portion of the semen, that is, the fluid in which sperm are transported.

The *epididymis* is a coiled tube which runs along the back and top of each testis. It is here that sperm cells mature and are stored after they are produced in the testes. The mature sperm are either released through the vas deferens and ejaculatory duct during ejaculation or they disintegrate and are reabsorbed.

The *vas deferens* is a long tube which transports the sperm from the epididymis to the *ejaculatory duct.* During ejaculation the vas deferens contracts and propels the sperm cells into the ejaculatory duct where sperm mix with fluids secreted by the prostate gland and seminal vesicles to form semen (or seminal fluid).

Male Secondary Sex Characteristics

Secondary sex characteristics in males are caused largely by the male hormones (androgens) (see Table 2.1). They include the following hair changes: recession of the hair from the temples (which, alas, for some men does not stop!) and growth of facial, axillary, pubic, and chest hair. Secondary sex characteristics also include the distribution of body fat and muscle which produce the more angular, broad-shouldered and narrow-hipped male body shape. Because of increased levels of both female hormones and androgens at puberty, approximately 80 percent of males experience breast enlargement for a brief time. In addition, deepening of the voice, which also occurs by age 14 or 15, is a result of the growth of the larynx (voice box) and the lengthening of the vocal cords.

PROCESS OF SEXUAL MATURATION IN FEMALES

Hormonal Changes

A group of hormones called *estrogens* are the most important female hormones. They are secreted by the ovaries in varying amounts throughout a monthly cycle. They are important in the maintenance of the normal size and functioning of the uterus, uterine (fallopian) tubes, and vagina. They stimulate the preparation of the uterine lining for possible pregnancy. They are also responsible for the development of secondary sex characteristics.

A second important hormone, *progesterone,* is also produced by the ovaries for about 13 days after ovulation (the expulsion of the egg from the ovary). Progesterone might be thought of as the "pregnancy hormone" because it causes the uterine glands to begin secreting nourishing substances and increases the uterine blood supply. It also stimulates the mammary glands of pregnant women, causing breasts to enlarge. Progesterone is responsible for the length of the menstrual cycle from ovulation to the next menstruation. Furthermore, it keeps breast tissue firm and healthy and reduces the possibility of painful menstruation and other gynecological problems.

Another hormone important in female sexual maturation is *testosterone,* an androgenic hormone. In females this hormone is produced by the adrenal glands (not the ovaries) and increases only very slightly at puberty. It appears to play an important role in female sexual arousability.

Female Primary Sex Characteristics

The secretion of the gonadotropic hormones, the estrogens and progesterone, at puberty stimulates the growth of the female sex organs (see Figure 2.6).

Ovaries   The ovaries produce mature ova (eggs), discharge the ova (ovulation), and secrete estrogens and progesterone. The two ovaries are about the size of walnuts and

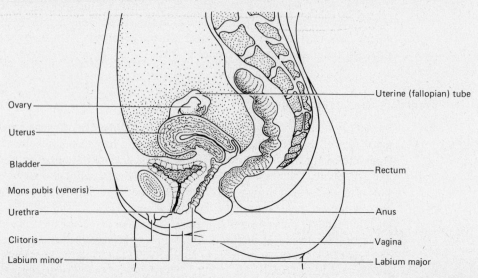

Figure 2.6   Female reproductive system.

are located in the pelvic region on either side of the uterus. The ovaries typically alternate in the once-a-month production of a mature ovum.

There are two important differences between the production of sperm and eggs. First, whereas a man produces sperm on a regular basis, a woman is born with a given number of immature eggs (about 400,000). Second, a woman ceases to discharge an egg each month around the age of 45 or 50 (menopause), whereas a man continues to produce sperm until he dies. (Thus, after menopause women are no longer capable of producing children, whereas a man's reproductive capacity may continue throughout his life.)

Uterine (Fallopian) Tubes The two 4-inch-long uterine (or fallopian) tubes branch off the uterus on either side. The end of each tube lies close to an ovary. Fingerlike structures at that end move and produce currents which wave the ripe egg into the tube as it is expelled from the ovary. It is in the uterine tube that fertilization may take place if sperm are present. Whether fertilized or not, the egg moves down the tube to the uterus.

Uterus The uterus (or womb) is a hollow, pear-shaped structure located above and behind the bladder. It is the repository for the fertilized egg. During pregnancy the developing fetus is nourished and supported in the uterus. At the end of the uterus is the *cervix,* the narrow passageway into the vagina. It is through this opening that the fetus is expelled during childbirth. If an egg has not been fertilized, it will be expelled along with part of the uterine lining through the cervix during menstruation.

Vagina The vagina is a flexible, tubular structure approximately 4 to 6 inches in length. It is the passageway for the entry of sperm during intercourse, the passageway for the discharge of menstrual fluids, and the birth canal.

Other Structures The structures we have described above are internal female genitalia. External female genitals are collectively called the *vulva* ("the covering"). They include the mons pubis (veneris), the labia majora and minora, the clitoris, and the introitus.

The *mons pubis* or *mons veneris* (Mount of Venus) is the soft mound of fatty tissue that covers the pubic bone. During puberty it becomes covered with coarse, curly hair. The *labia majora* (greater lips) are the two folds of skin which run back from the mons veneris. During puberty hair grows along the major lips. The *labia minora* (lesser lips) are two hairless folds of skin between the major lips. Between the minor lips lie the urethral and vaginal openings. The *introitus* (vaginal opening) is the entrance to the vagina. The *clitoris,* a small erectile structure, lies at the forward end of the major lips. The clitoris is highly sensitive to stimulation and during sexual excitement becomes engorged with blood and increases somewhat in size.

Female Secondary Sex Characteristics

The secondary sex characteristics in females include a wider pelvic measurement (girth) and shorter height (on the average) than males. Also included are fatty tissue deposits on the hips and buttocks, breasts, and pubic and axillary hair (see Table 2.1). As in boys, the amount and density of body hair are determined by heredity. In girls the voice deepens due to the increase in the size of the larynx, but the change is not as great as it is in boys.

Menstrual Cycle

The average age among American girls for the beginning of menstruation is about 13 years, with a range of from 9 to 18 years (Zacharias et al., 1976).

The ovaries contain structures called *follicles.* Each follicle consists of a cell capable of developing into an ovum surrounded by a spherical layer of cells. At birth a woman has approximately 200,000 of these follicles in each ovary. Of this original number, only 300 to 400 actually develop into mature eggs; the rest degenerate.

Each month usually only one follicle matures. Several days after the onset of menstruation (the 1st day of menstruation is taken as the 1st day of the menstrual cycle and days are counted from that time), one follicle moves toward the surface of an ovary. As it matures, the follicle secretes estrogens. On about the 14th day of the cycle, the follicle ruptures and releases an egg from the ovary (ovulation). The released egg, then, travels down the uterine (fallopian) tube, where it may be fertilized if sperm are present, to the uterus.

There are hormonal changes which correspond with the various phases of the menstrual cycle. Estrogens, made by the maturing follicle during the first 14 days of the cycle, begin at a relatively low level on the 1st day and rise to a peak at about the 14th day (ovulation). This increased production of estrogens causes the uterine lining to build up in preparation for sustaining possible pregnancy.

After ovulation the follicle that produced the egg begins producing progesterone, which causes the uterine lining to begin secreting both estrogens and progesterone (in differing amounts) for about 12 days after ovulation.

If pregnancy does not occur, the estrogen and progesterone levels rapidly drop off toward the end of the cycle. This hormonal decrease brings on menstruation. In menstruation the part of the uterine lining which had been built up in case of pregnancy is sloughed off and discharged, along with the unfertilized egg, through the vagina. During this time a new ovarian follicle starts growing thus initiating a new cycle.

Menstruation usually lasts about 5 days. The average cycle is about 28 days with a range of from 20 to 36 days. Usually a woman "settles down" to a cycle of days within this range which becomes typical for her.

At least 150 different physical and psychological symptoms have been associated with the menstrual cycle such as irritability, tension, depression, headache, weight gain, and feeling fat due to water retention (Parlee, 1973). Women do not necessarily experience the same or any symptoms from month to month. Depending on how premenstrual symptoms are defined, their incidence among women can vary from 25 to 100 percent (J. H. Williams, 1977). Approximately 50 percent of women experience menstrual cramps at some time in their lives (J. H. Williams, 1977).

For many years the belief persisted that cramps were wholly psychogenic ("all in one's mind"). While this may be so in some cases, research indicates that there are physical causes of menstrual discomfort (J. H. Williams, 1977). Typically, severe cramps disappear after childbirth, but pregnancy is not necessarily recommended as a cure!

Another issue is the relationship between female hormonal fluctuations and mood states and behavior. This is often termed the *premenstrual syndrome (PMS)* or *premenstrual tension.* Because of inadequate research methodology and the considerable variability in research findings, Mary Brown Parlee (1973) has concluded that there is no evidence to support the notion of a premenstrual sydrome defined as a *class* of behaviors which fluctuates with monthly hormonal changes. Moreover, it is not clear at this time to what extent symptoms some women associate with menstruation are physical or psychological in origin.

PROBLEMS RELATED TO HEALTH AMONG ADOLESCENTS

General Health Status and Mortality Rates

In general, the health of American adolescents is rated as "good" (Kovar, 1979). Still, a national survey of 12- to 17-year-old American adolescents and their parents indicated that both the adolescents and their parents hold inaccurate perceptions of the status of young persons' health (U.S. National Center for Health Statistics, 1975). The survey revealed that almost 60 percent of adolescents and 67 percent of their parents rated their health as either "excellent" or "very good." Approximately 36 percent of adolescents rated their health as "average," while only about 5 percent judged it as "fair" or "poor." On the other hand, a related study based on actual physical examinations of these young people revealed that approximately 21 percent (4.9 million) suffered from illnesses or physical handicaps which interfered with normal growth and development.

The survey also reported that family income and health were negatively correlated, that is, greater numbers of health problems were associated with lower family incomes.

While most adolescents are in good health, it is important to note that some youth engage in behaviors which can have negative consequences for their short- and long-term physical and emotional health—poor eating habits, drug abuse (including cigarettes and alcohol), and sexual intercourse without contraception. Moreover, risk-taking behavior in automobiles is a serious problem among young white males, that being the single most important cause of death among adolescents (Kovar, 1979).

There is a sizable increase in mortality rates for males beginning at about 14 years of age. One study found that the mortality rate for 15- to 19-year-old males more than doubled compared to that for 10- to 14-year-old males (Heald, 1976). Among adolescent white females, the rate decreased somewhat as age increased. It appears, therefore, that adolescence is a particularly hazardous time for males. It is noteworthy that diseases and physical conditions account for 30 percent of adolescent deaths, compared to the 70 percent death rate due to accidents, homicides, and suicides (Kovar, 1979).

Nutrition and Weight

Because of the tremendous physical growth that occurs, nutritional requirements are increased during adolescence. Emotional needs and social pressures also figure in an adolescent's eating habits. For example, feeling accepted by one's peers is especially

Car accidents account for a large number of deaths among male adolescents.

important to young people, and it is quite common for adolescents to "hang out" together in favorite eating places.

Adolescents can have enormous appetites. Moreover, the foods they often seem to prefer—soft drinks, ice cream, french fries, pastries—are not particularly nutritious and are high in calories. If adolescents eat large quantities of such foods in addition to their regular meals, they are likely to gain weight. If they eat these foods in place of more balanced meals, they are likely to develop vitamin or protein deficiencies.

Obesity   Clinically defined, obesity is a weight 20 percent over the average for a person's age, height, and build; overweight refers to a weight 10 percent over the average. Estimates of the incidence of obesity among adolescents vary from 10 to 30 percent; approximately 80 percent of children who are overweight remain so as adults (Paulsen, 1972). Not only is obesity a health hazard in itself (being related to cardiovascular disease, high blood pressure, and gynecological problems, among others), being overweight can also cause problems in the adolescent's personal and social adjustment.

The causes of obesity are complex and are both physiological and psychological in nature. It should be noted that obese adolescents (girls, at least) are not always "big eaters," but they are not good exercisers either. It is the fact of underactivity which seems to be a particular problem in obesity. Psychologically, obese adolescents may suffer from feelings of low body esteem (Hendry & Gillies, 1978). These feelings are likely to perpetuate overeating in that the adolescent may eat as a means of attempting to "solve" or compensate for psychological or social adjustment problems. Clearly, a vicious circle can get set in motion here such that the adolescent eats when he or she feels bad, feels bad about eating too much, and then eats because he or she feels bad about overeating and being overweight, and so forth. At least one study has shown that obese adolescents, especially girls, seem to have a strong drive toward sociability and peer acceptance, compared to underweight adolescents (Hendry & Gillies, 1978).

Underweight   The problem of being underweight occurs less frequently among adolescents. There are numerous causes of low body weight. Aside from medical problems (which are relatively infrequent), these causes include poverty, drug use, "fad" diets which do not provide enough nutrients for growth, and avoidance of a wide variety of foods due to "picky" food preferences.

Underweight adolescents consider their bodies to be less "deviant" than obese adolescents. However, they are more likely to avoid heterosexual contacts, to be somewhat withdrawn, and to show greater involvement with television compared to obese and average-weight adolescents (Hendry & Gillies, 1978).

In addition, there is an "underweight disorder" which is particularly common among adolescent girls: *anorexia nervosa* (literally, "nervous loss of appetite"). Anorexia is usually viewed as having psychological origins. It is a serious problem which has a 10 to 15 percent mortality rate. We will discuss this problem further in Chapter 13.

Acne

Acne or "pimples" is the most common medical problem of adolescence. This disorder of the skin is characterized by pimples on the face, but they may also appear on the

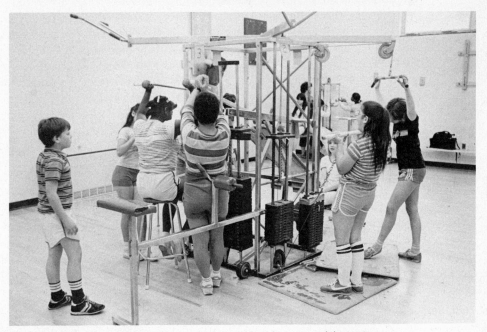

Maintaining an optimum body weight can be a problem for some adolescents.

upper chest, shoulders, and back. Although the exact cause of acne is not known, it appears that androgens (male hormones) cause excess activity of the oil-producing glands of the skin. Because of the increase in androgens at adolescence (particularly among boys), acne is more common among boys than girls. Acne also occurs more frequently in girls with very irregular menstrual cycles. When acne occurs early in adolescence, it is more likely to be severe. Since acne problems seem to end with adolescence, there is some speculation that it is the change in hormone production or a hormonal imbalance (not just the level of androgens) that causes the disorder.

Skin problems are caused by the increase in size and activity of oil-producing glands, along with slower development of the skin ducts through which the oil is discharged onto the surface of the skin. Skin ducts become clogged, and when oil comes to the surface and is exposed to the air, it dries and turns dark, causing a "blackhead" to form. When blackheads become infected because of bacteria present on the skin, pimples (acne) develop.

Because acne is painful (physically and psychologically) and can cause permanent scarring in severe cases, it is important that medical treatment be sought. Although there has been little evidence that over-the-counter remedies are particularly effective, a 1982 report submitted to the Food and Drug Administration by a panel of scientists reported that nonprescription drug products containing benzoyl peroxide alone or sulphur alone reduced skin lesions ("Study seeks," 1982). The best home treatment appears to be keeping the skin clean with soap and water, avoiding squeezing the pimples, and avoiding covering the blemishes with cosmetics.

Diet can also be a factor in skin problems. For a long time it was held that high-fat foods such as chocolate, nuts, and fried foods aggravated skin problems. While this may be true for some individuals, medical authorities now suggest that high-fat foods are not generally a problem in this regard. Rather, they advise that high-iodide foods (lettuce, saltwater fish, for example) exacerbate skin problems (Arundel, 1971).

Considering the importance of physical appearance to most adolescents and their concern with popularity, it is not surprising that acne can cause feelings of inferiority. One survey of high school students indicated that most of the students who had acne reported that they felt that they did not get as many invitations to parties as their peers, that they felt uncomfortable with people, and that they felt that others sometimes stared at them (Schachter, Pantel, Glassman, & Zweibelson, 1971).

SOCIAL AND PSYCHOLOGICAL EFFECTS OF PHYSICAL DEVELOPMENT

The fact that adolescents' bodies are increasing in size and maturing both physically and sexually has important social and psychological consequences for young people. For one thing, as children begin to look more like adults, social standards for acceptable conduct change. In addition, adolescents begin to alter their expectations of themselves as well as their feelings about how others should relate to them. In this section we will discuss a number of issues related to physical and sexual maturation.

Body Image

Because our bodies are the most tangible manifestation of ourselves, it is reasonable that we place considerable importance on our physical characteristics. In addition, our culture places a great deal of emphasis on physical attractiveness, especially in the context of social relationships. It is not surprising, then, that studies have shown that our feelings about ourselves are related to our feelings about our bodies, and vice versa.

In part because of the many important changes occurring during this period, early adolescents tend to be quite self-conscious, especially about their bodies and physical features (Hamburg, 1974). (Cognitive changes which also take place at this time are another critical component of this self-consciousness.) Adolescents worry about whether they are keeping pace developmentally with their peers because physical characteristics are particularly important at this time with regard to social acceptance and self-esteem. Real or perceived irregularities in facial features—a too large or too small nose, crooked teeth, or acne—are of special concern to adolescents. Great significance is also attached to being too fat or too thin or having too small or too large breasts, too much or too little pubic and other body hair. The cultural notion that the male should be the taller member of a couple poses particular problems for early adolescents because girls are often taller than most of their male age-mates, the adolescent growth spurt having started earlier in girls. The physical exposure in gym classes and locker rooms can be a source of embarrassment to junior high school students, especially those who are early or late maturers.

A study of male and female high school juniors from the upper-lower class looked at the relationship between adolescent appearance and self-concept (Musa & Roach, 1973). It found that girls who rated themselves at least equal to their peers on personal appearance also scored higher on a measure of personal adjustment than did those girls who rated their personal appearance as less desirable than their peers. No such relation-

Adolescents can be quite self-conscious about their bodies and physical features.

ship was found for boys. This study also found that 44 percent of the girls would have liked to have changed something about their appearance compared to only 12 percent of the boys. Girls most often wanted to change their hair, weight, clothes, or figure, in that order; boys preferred to change their clothes, facial characteristics, hair, or weight, in that order. This study illustrates the fact that appearance is likely to be more of a concern for females than males.

These rapid changes in physical development also mean that adolescents feel clumsy and awkward until they become comfortable with their bodies and familiar with their physical capabilities and limitations. Because of differing societal expectations for girls and boys, concern with physical coordination is more likely to be a worry for boys. Parents, teachers, and peers who are understanding and supportive of youth at this stage can be especially helpful to adolescents in helping them cope with these insecurities.

Effects of Early and Late Maturation

A number of studies have compared adolescents who mature early with those who mature later to see whether there are any measurable social or psychological effects of the timing of the onset of puberty. It is important to keep in mind, however, that the subjects of these studies have usually been white and middle-class.

One of the findings of such studies is that early or late maturation is less of a problem for girls than for boys, both during adolescence and later in life. Also, the findings on this issue with regard to boys are relatively consistent; with regard to girls, however, the results have often been contradictory, making clear-cut conclusions difficult. We will discuss these effects as they concern girls first.

Girls　Early-maturing girls seem to have less prestige and be less popular among their peers through the sixth grade (Faust, 1977). The early maturer, being unlike most of her female peers, seems to suffer a temporary loss of prestige until the developmentally average girls catch up with her. Once this happens (usually in the seventh grade), the early-maturing girl gains status among her peers (Faust, 1977).

Early maturation can be a problem for girls in other respects. For instance, because she appears physically mature, she is likely to begin dating earlier than her peers and to date older boys because boys her own age are less developed than she. While she gains status from this attention, she may experience anxiety because she may not be emotionally mature or socially sophisticated enough to handle the difficulties which can arise in these situations (Clausen, 1975; Simmons, Blyth, Van Cleave, & Bush, 1979). Moreover, her parents may fear that her early sexual maturation and interest in the opposite sex may lead to sexual involvement and unwanted pregnancy. Such concerns may lead parents to attempt to exert unreasonable control over their daughter's social activities, thereby straining their relationship and placing additional stress on the girl.

On the other hand, some experts suggest that there may be some long-term advantages for girls who are early maturers, precisely because they have to cope quickly with (not overwhelming) developmental and social stress. Recently, it has been shown that in adulthood, early-maturing girls show much better problem-solving and coping skills than late-maturing girls who may not have had to deal with the challenges of physical changes and social demands in so short a time (Livson & Peskin, 1980).

Those girls who have not attained menarche by the developmental average of about 13 years fall into the category of late maturers. Because they do not look as mature as their mature age-mates, they may not be asked out on dates as frequently as their age-mates and often worry about when they will start to look "older." Still, late maturers have been found to be outgoing and socially poised. As mentioned above, however, there is some evidence that late-maturing girls may not develop as much skill in problem-solving and coping as early maturers.

It is important to remember that these characterizations of early and late maturers should not be taken as descriptive of all such girls because of the variability in the findings. We can note, however, that the negative effects of early and late maturation are much less marked in girls than in boys.

Boys Early maturing boys are taller, stronger, and better coordinated than their peers. Consequently, they have athletic, social, and leadership advantages over age-mates who mature later. However, early attainment of adult physical stature may bring on adult responsibilities too soon. When this happens, these boys may have less time as well as fewer opportunities and rewards for intellectual and social "exploration"— an important aspect of the adolescent period. As a result, it has been found that in adulthood early-maturing boys have less well-developed and more conventional cognitive and coping skills than late-maturing boys (Livson & Peskin, 1980). Note that this is the opposite pattern as found for girls.

The timing of physical maturation varies among adolescents of the same age.

Compared to early or average maturers, late-maturing boys may feel less confident than their age-mates because of the emphasis placed on body build, strength, and coordination for males. Lack of development in these areas can interfere with both athletic and social success. It is not surprising, then, that late-maturing boys are more likely to suffer from negative self-concepts and feelings of inadequacy, dependency, rejection, and rebelliousness (Clausen, 1975). In the long run, however, later-maturing males appear to have some advantages. As adults, they tend to have greater intellectual curiosity, more social initiative, and more creative solutions to problems (Livson & Peskin, 1980).

Negative Effects of Inadequate Sex Education

Although we'll discuss sexuality and sex education in detail in Chapter 11, we do want to make brief reference to these issues at this point. Adolescents are particularly alert to the sexual developments in their own bodies, as well as those of their peers. While they may not be as aware of the hormonal changes taking place inside, these hormones play an important role in sensitizing youth to their own sexual feelings and in making them sexually responsive to others. These bodily changes, together with our culture's emphasis on sex, naturally cause adolescents to have considerable curiosity about sexual development, sexuality, and sexual relationships. Good sex education can go a long way in clarifying misperceptions and in alleviating unnecessary anxiety.

Unfortunately, inadequate sex education appears to be the rule rather than the exception. Consequently, most adolescents must find other outlets for their curiosity —"dirty" jokes and pictures, erotic literature, and the exchange of sexual gossip, often full of inaccuracies! Kissing, petting, masturbation, and sexual intercourse are also outlets for adolescents' sexual tension and curiosity about sex. Lack of adequate information about sexual development can cause some youth to develop negative feelings associated with masturbation, menstruation, and the first ejaculation.

Masturbation   Masturbation (self-stimulation of genitals, often resulting in orgasm) occurs earlier and is more common among males than females, no doubt due to the greater accessibility of their sex organs. There are many myths about the "evils" of "self-abuse" (as it was once called!). It is popularly believed to cause pimples, poor eyesight and even blindness, mental illness, and impotence. Nonetheless, almost all experts agree that masturbation is a "normal" activity which does not cause any harmful effects itself. The only problem associated with masturbation comes from the guilt or anxiety experienced by those who engage in it. Such feelings are learned from adults and peers who have negative attitudes about masturbation because of misconceptions about it. The more important issue here concerns the frequency of masturbation and the role it serves for adolescents. If it becomes a compulsive activity over which the adolescent feels he or she has no control or if it is used as a substitute for social relationships, this would indicate that attention might be given to developing more self-assurance and social competence.

First Ejaculation   Boys are capable of erections and orgasms from birth on, but it is not until adolescence that ejaculation occurs. The first ejaculation more often occurs as a result of masturbation than through a nocturnal emission or wet dream. One study found that 20 percent of boys were frightened after their first ejaculation and that only 6 percent felt that they had been adequately prepared for the event by their parents (Shipman, 1968).

Menstruation   For many reasons, menstruation is more of a concern to girls than the first ejaculation is to boys. Menstruation is associated with mainly negative attitudes and expectations in the larger society and also among adolescent girls and boys (Clarke & Ruble, 1978). Attitudes toward ejaculation are more likely to be positive.

Negative attitudes about menstruation are often passed on from mother to daughter; for example, the menstrual period has often been referred to as "the curse." In addition, there is often physical discomfort and sometimes real pain associated with menstruation. Also, the menstrual period involves bleeding which is usually associated with injury or sickness. On the other hand, because the menarche is taken as a sign that a girl has become a woman, there is some pride in the event or at least relief that she is "normal." It is not uncommon, then, for the adolescent girl to develop ambivalent or negative feelings about menstruation as expressed by the following girl in her journal: "I want . . . my period. Right now I see Sara [an older girl who was having her period for the first time] practically dying. But I want it. I know as soon as I get it, I'll hate it. . . . I just want to prove that I am growing" (Stubbs, 1982).

Recently, researchers have begun to investigate the psychological significance of menarche. The findings of these studies strongly suggest that this event is a pivotal one. For example, it has been found that, compared to premenarcheal girls, postmenarcheal girls have more sexually differentiated body images and show greater acceptance of themselves as females (Koff, Rierdan, & Silverstone, 1978). Research suggests that the menarche is an event through which girls begin to integrate a sense of themselves as sexually mature persons into a broader self-concept and identity (Rierdan & Koff, 1980).

Unfortunately, for most girls (those in the United States and in many other countries as well), menarche is rarely presented or discussed as an emotionally significant event, but rather as a hygiene problem to be coped with; that is, attention is focused on how to use sanitary napkins or tampons in order to avoid embarrassment (Logan, 1980; Whisnant, Brett, & Zegans, 1979).

Females also have to cope with unfounded taboos such as refraining from bathing, swimming, and physical exercise during the menstrual period. Bathing is certainly desirable, and moderate exercise and swimming have been found to relieve menstrual cramps (T. W. Anderson, 1965).

SUMMARY

Physical growth and development in adolescence begins with the (pre-)adolescent growth spurt. Numerous other physical and physiological changes take place during this time which have the effect of giving children the beginnings of adultlike body shapes, features, strength, and functioning. Differences between the sexes in body shape and other physical characteristics become more apparent at this time. Some sex differences, such as those in physical strength and coordination, appear to be caused in part by differing social expectations for the sexes.

Puberty marks the beginning of adolescence. Girls reach puberty approximately two years earlier than boys. During puberty primary sex characteristics begin to develop and function. The criterion for the onset of puberty is the menarche for girls and the first ejaculation of sperm for boys. Puberty appears to be occurring earlier over the past 150 years, mainly due to higher nutritional levels and lessening of disease.

As with nonsexual physical growth, sexual development is triggered and controlled by hormonal activity. The primary male hormones are the androgens. Primary sex organs in males include the testes, penis, prostate gland, epididymis, and vas deferens. The female sex hormones are the estrogens and progesterone. The primary sex characteristics in females include the ovaries, uterine (fallopian) tubes, uterus, and vagina.

Health-related problems which pose particular difficulties for adolescents include inadequate nutrition, over- and underweight, and acne.

The physical and sexual changes which occur during pubescence and puberty have social and psychological effects on adolescent development. Important issues in this respect include body image and self-esteem, early and late maturation, and the negative effects of inadequate sex education with regard to masturbation, first ejaculation, and menstruation.

GLOSSARY

adolescent growth spurt   A sudden increase in height and weight that occurs during pubescence at about age $10\frac{1}{2}$ in girls and about $12\frac{1}{2}$ in boys.

anorexia nervosa   An eating disorder characterized by self-starvation and severe loss of weight.

endocrine glands   Ductless glands which secrete hormones directly into the bloodstream (pituitary, adrenals, thyroid, parathyroids, pancreas, and gonads).

hormones   Substances secreted by endocrine glands into the bloodstream which regulate physiological and sexual development and functioning.

menarche   The first menstrual period.

menstruation   The monthly discharge of blood and uterine material which occurs in sexually mature females.

ovaries   Female sex glands which produce ova and sex hormones (estrogens and progesterone).

penis   The male sex organ.

primary sex characteristics   Structures essential for reproduction (testes, prostate gland, seminal vesicles, and penis in the male; ovaries, uterine tubes, uterus, and vagina, in females).

puberty   Attainment of sexual maturation, marked by the onset of menstruation in females (at about age 13) and by the ejaculation of sperm in males (at about age $14\frac{1}{2}$).

pubescence   A period of about two years preceding puberty during which rapid physical and physiological changes take place leading to physical and sexual maturity; starts about age $10\frac{1}{2}$ in girls and about $12\frac{1}{2}$ in boys.

scrotum   The sac of skin containing the testes.

secondary sex characteristics   Bodily features that distinguish between the sexes, but are not essential for reproduction (voice pitch, body hair distribution, breast development, body shape).

skeletal age   The most reliable criterion for determining the level of maturation, measured by the proportion of bone to cartilage in the hand and wrist.

testes   Male sex glands which produce sperm and sex hormones (androgens).

Chapter 3 Outline

chapter *3*

Intellectual and Cognitive Development

The dramatic changes in the adolescent's body and physical capacities often draw our attention away from the equally important transformations which take place in intellectual and cognitive functioning. In this chapter we will discuss characteristics and development of adolescent thought and how intellectual and cognitive development affects aspects of personality and social development.

There are many definitions of *intelligence* and many ways of measuring this capacity. We have chosen to use Wechsler's definition: "the aggregate or global capacity of the individual to act purposefully, to think rationally and to deal effectively with his environment" (1958, p. 7). *Cognition* is a related term which refers to the underlying processes which govern our abilities to think and act; these include perception, reasoning, learning, and memory.

Both heredity and environment (opportunities for learning) are important determinants of intellectual ability. Heredity is usually viewed as setting the outside limits of intellectual capacity, while experiences (or lack of them) are believed to determine the extent to which these limits can be realized.

GROWTH AND STABILITY OF INTELLIGENCE

Growth Rate in Intellectual Functioning

The rate of intellectual growth is much greater during childhood and adolescence than at any other time (see Figure 3.1). If we take 17 as the criterion age with regard to the level of intellectual functioning as measured by IQ, individuals develop 50

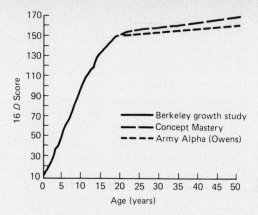

Figure 3.1　A composite growth curve of intelligence from birth to age 50. *Source:* Nancy Bayley (1955). On the growth of intelligence. *American Psychologist, 10,* 816.

percent of their mature intelligence from conception to age 4, another 30 percent between the ages of 4 and 8, and the remaining 20 percent between the ages of 8 and 17 (Bloom, 1964).

Stability of Intelligence

For many years it was assumed that a person's level of intelligence remained constant throughout life. It was believed that if an individual was given an IQ test at age 10 and was retested at ages 20, 30, and 40, the score would be approximately the same on all testings. Any differences could be attributed to the motivational state of the individual at the time of testing or to errors in measurement.

Now we know that scores on IQ tests given during childhood are not reliable indications of intellectual functioning at adolescence or adulthood. Using adolescent IQ scores to predict adult intellectual ability, however, results in more reliable estimates. Still, it is clear that the degree of stability once believed to be characteristic of IQs can no longer be assumed. For example, repeated testings of children and adolescents between 6 and 18 years showed variations of 15 or more IQ points in over half of the subjects and another third showed variations of as much as 20 points (Honzik, 1973).

Personality factors also have been found to influence the direction and degree of intellectual development. For example, gains in IQ (from the early teens to adulthood) occurred in individuals who were able to cope with life's frustrations and difficulties in constructive and realistic ways (Haan, 1963). Subjects whose IQ scores decreased during this time were more likely to resort to defense mechanisms such as denial of reality and rationalization.

Important implications stem from the question of IQ stability. If an IQ score is constant throughout life, then decisions can be made early about a person's intellectual ability and potential for success in school, since this is what IQ tests are designed to measure. If, however, IQs vary over time, such early judgments may be in error and can result in inappropriate and unfair treatment of adolescents. The fear of parents that a child might be unable to escape from a "negative label" based on a single test score is not entirely groundless. For example, Jerome Dusek (1975) found that teachers' judgments of students' abilities can "follow" students from one classroom and grade level to others. He also found evidence that teachers' expectations are related to students' academic performance in some cases. Regardless of ability level, all students benefit from being encouraged to learn, so it is obviously important for those who work with adolescents to be mindful of such possible negative outcomes and to try to avoid unfair judgments and treatment.

TWO VIEWS OF INTELLIGENCE: PSYCHOMETRIC AND DEVELOPMENTAL

Intelligence has been studied by psychologists in two rather different ways. The *psychometric* or *mental test* approach views intelligence as one of many traits which human beings possess in varying amounts. The distinguishing feature of intelligence for those of this orientation is the capacity for rational or logical thought.

Within the psychometric view there are many theories about the nature of intelligence. For example, Charles Spearman advanced the notion that intelligence is a single, general trait, whereas J. P. Guilford believes that intelligence is comprised of 120 different subcomponents. Obviously, our assumptions about the nature of intelligence will determine how we will assess the extent to which this capacity is present in a person.

Intelligence tests were designed to measure the differences in intellectual capacity

Teachers' attitudes and expectations can be important factors in students' academic performance.

between one person and another. Such tests yield an *intelligence quotient* (IQ) which enables us to compare a person's level of intellectual functioning with that of others. The use of such tests also permits the plotting of curves of the rate of intellectual growth over the life span.

As useful as this information is in predicting school success, it doesn't tell us anything about the *nature* of the individual's thought processes. In other words, we know *if* a person can solve a particular problem on an IQ test, but we don't know *how* he or she arrived at the answer.

A second approach to the study of intelligence attempts to answer the question of how. It is termed the *developmental* approach, and is best exemplified by the work of Jean Piaget. This orientation focuses on the particular way in which a person goes about solving a problem and on the qualitative changes in thought processes as individuals mature.

Are these two views incompatible? Some experts say that although they appear discrepant, the two approaches are really looking at the same phenomena from two different perspectives. On the other hand, some research findings suggest that psychometric and Piagetian tests are measuring different phenomena (Stephens, McLaughlin, Miller, & Glass, 1972). Not enough research has been completed to date for us to be able to resolve this question. Let us agree that both views are useful, depending on the purpose for which we might need information. We will discuss these two views in more detail below.

PSYCHOMETRIC VIEW OF INTELLIGENCE

Intelligence Tests

Measures of intelligence are often grouped into two categories: *group* and *individual* tests. As the first term suggests, group tests can be given to large numbers of individuals at one time. Since they are written tests, they are more easily administered and scored, but they are not as sensitive measures of intelligence as individual tests. The California Test of Mental Maturity and the Armed Forces Qualification Test are examples of group tests. Individual tests are given to one person at a time by a specially trained professional. These tests take more time to give, score, and interpret, but they are more sensitive measuring devices than group tests. The Stanford-Binet Intelligence Test, the Wechsler Intelligence Scale for Children, and the Wechsler Adult Intelligence Scale are examples of individual intelligence tests.

The Stanford-Binet and the Wechsler scales are the intelligence tests most commonly used by psychologists for purposes of clinical and educational assessment. The Stanford-Binet is an adaptation of the first test designed to measure intelligence. In 1904 the French government established a commission to study the problem of how to ensure educational benefits for retarded children. A critical question was how to determine which children could profit from instruction in regular schools and which would need special schools. Alfred Binet and Theodore Simon designed and constructed a psychological test for this purpose. The test, administered on an individual basis, was based on the evaluation of a selected number of abilities which they believed were related to school achievement (logical reasoning and memory, for example).

In all of these IQ tests the individual's test performance is compared with the average performance level for individuals in his or her own age group. This yields a percentile rank for each person, and from this rank the IQ is calculated. For example, a person who falls at the 76th percentile performs as well or better than 76 percent of the population, or we could say that only 24 percent of the population scores higher than this individual. Table 3.1 lists the IQs on the WAIS, their classification, and the percentage of adults in each category.

It is important to distinguish between intelligence tests and achievement and aptitude tests. *Intelligence tests* are designed for the purpose of predicting a person's future academic success. *Achievement tests* are designed to measure what an individual actually knows in specific content areas such as English or social studies. *Aptitude tests* are constructed to determine how well one might learn new information or skills of a particular nature. The Scholastic Aptitude Test (SAT) and the Graduate Record Examination (GRE) are aptitude tests.

Some psychologists have suggested that intelligence tests need to be broadened in scope. David McClelland (1973) has suggested that psychologists should change the predicting function of IQ tests away from "grades in school" to "grades in life." According to him, such a test would include at least the following components: communication skills, moderate goal-setting, patience, and ego development. While such a test would certainly be valuable, it is questionable whether it could serve as a substitute for current intelligence tests which do seem to provide important information. Whether IQ tests move in this proposed direction or remain as they are presently constructed, it is essential to know what a test is designed to do and how effectively it does this.

Use of Intelligence Tests with Adolescents

Intelligence tests are given to adolescents for a number of purposes. They may be used to assess intellectual capacity when there is a question about this. For example, if a student is not doing well in courses, it is important to determine whether or not the

Table 3.1 CLASSIFICATION OF IQ SCORES ON THE WECHSLER ADULT INTELLIGENCE SCALE (AGES 16–75)

IQ	Classification	Percentage
Above 130	Very superior	2.2
120–129	Superior	6.7
110–119	Bright-normal	16.1
90–109	Average	50.0
80–89	Dull-normal	16.1
70–79	Borderline	6.7
Below 70	Retarded	2.2

Source: Adapted from David Wechsler (1958). *The Measurement and Appraisal of Adult Intelligence.* Baltimore: Williams & Wilkins, p. 42. Copyright 1958 by The Williams & Wilkins Co, Baltimore. Adapted by permission.

student is actually performing as well as he or she could. If the student has course grades of D's and F's and an IQ of 130 (see Table 3.1), we would suspect that there might be personal or home problems which were interfering with academic achievement.

Intelligence tests may be included in a battery of psychological tests to obtain a profile of an individual's overall psychological functioning. Similarly, IQ tests (as well as others) can be used in vocational counseling to assess an adolescent's capacities for particular jobs or professions when IQ is relevant.

A Note about Scholastic Aptitude Tests   Intelligence tests can be used as screening devices for college or graduate school admission, but it is much more common to use aptitude tests such as the Scholastic Aptitude Test (SAT), the American College Testing Program's test (ACT), or the Graduate Record Examination (GRE). (These tests are expressly designed to predict academic performance in college or graduate school, and scholastic aptitude and IQ test scores are highly correlated.)

Educators have been concerned about the decline in both verbal and math SAT scores since 1963 (see Figure 3.2). (We should note that math scores rose by one point both in 1982 and 1983—apparently due to the improved performance by females— while verbal scores rose two points in 1982, but dropped one point in 1983. Whether the recent concern about the quality of education will bring about an upward trend in test scores remains to be seen.)

The possible causes of this decline were investigated by the College Entrance Examination Board, the administrators of the SAT program (Advisory Panel, 1977). The investigators suggested that the major cause of the decline between 1963–1970 (18 points on verbal, 14 points on math) appeared to be the significant changes in the composition of the student group that took the SATs. During this time educational

An adolescent's IQ can be measured by intelligence tests.

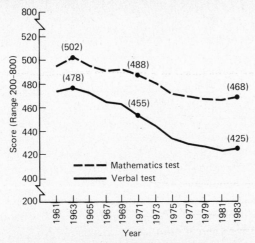

Figure 3.2 Scholastic Aptitude Test scaled score averages of college-bound high school seniors, 1960 to 1983. *Source:* Data compiled from College Entrance Examination Board, *On further examination: Report of the advisory panel on the Scholastic Aptitude Test decline, 1977* and *National Report on College-Bound Seniors, 1982.* Copyright 1977 and 1983 by Educational Testing Service. Reprinted by permission.
        Note: Scores from 1961 to 1965 are averages for all candidates taking the test. Scores from 1967 to 1983 are averages for high school seniors taking the test.

opportunities were opened to large numbers of students who had not taken the test before and whose scores lowered the average scores for those years. As we shall discuss later, lower-socioeconomic status students typically score lower on tests like the SAT, which has the effect of pulling the average scores down. Also, during this time more women began taking the test, and this pulled the math scores down. In addition, the investigators found that more students who were applying to community colleges and technical schools were taking the test. Taken together, these three factors accounted for two-thirds to three-quarters of the decline in scores between 1963 and 1970.

        The investigators found that other factors had to be involved in post-1970 decline in scores (31 points on verbal, 18 points on math) because the composition of the group taking the SATs changed little after 1970, but the decline in scores (particularly verbal) was considerably greater than the 1963–1970 decline. And, as the panel noted, other standardized test score averages showed similar decline patterns. How did the investigators explain this phenomenon? Several factors are worth mentioning. The panel noted that in many high schools there had been a shift away from the mastery of skills and knowledge and "a tendency to avoid precise thinking and the demand it makes on both students and teachers. . . . We attach central importance to the restoring of the traditions of critical reading and careful writing" (p. 46). (Students from high schools which did not make these shifts did not show the typical SAT score declines.) Similarly, the investigators suggested that there appeared to be increasing trends in education toward automatic promotions, lowering the reading levels of textbooks, inflating grades, and reducing homework.

Another problem, the investigators believed, was the amount of time students spent watching television (and the types of programs they watched), at the expense of homework, reading, and writing. While it is true that some educational television programs (such as "Sesame Street") seem to be improving academic performance in young children, there is no evidence of such positive effects on older children (Liebert, Sprafkin, & Davidson, 1982). Among other things, television appears to foster attitudes toward learning of expecting to be entertained. Changes in curricula, teaching methods, and students' television-watching habits would no doubt prove effective in reversing the post-1970 declining trend in SAT scores.

Criticisms of Intelligence Tests

When IQ tests were originally designed, they were thought to measure innate intelligence, that is, general intellectual ability free from environmental influences. Now, however, there is abundant evidence that IQ tests are not culture-free or even *culture-fair* for many groups. Most IQ tests in current use are biased in ways which benefit white, middle-class individuals. One obvious consequence of the use of culturally biased intelligence tests is that individuals from lower socioeconomic statuses and certain ethnic minority groups do not score as well as middle-class whites. (As we will see later, some would interpret such score differences as reflecting innate differences between groups, but this explanation is unlikely.) Obviously, a child who has never been exposed to ideas about which the test asks will score lower than a child who has had such exposure. This is the basic problem facing lower-class and nonwhite children and adolescents.

Another problem in this area lies not so much in the tests themselves, but in how the tests are used and by whom. As we have mentioned, IQ test scores and teacher evaluations can "follow" children from grade to grade, often with damaging results.

A related controversy has arisen with regard to college and graduate school entrance tests such as the SAT and GRE. Because so much weight is placed on these exam scores, some states (New York, California) have required the national testing services to provide test-takers with information indicating which answers they missed and the correct answers to the questions. Aside from the obvious upheavals in test administration such a policy change brings about, other questions are also raised. For instance, how valid are test scores when some individuals have had access to previous tests and some have not, since it appears that studying can raise test scores in some cases (Slack & Porter, 1980). We cannot predict the outcome of this controversy, but we can say that the discussion of these and related issues should prove to be beneficial in that it opens important social concerns to public scrutiny.

DEVELOPMENTAL VIEW OF INTELLIGENCE

Piaget's Theory: Stages of Cognitive Development

Piaget held that intelligence is a peculiarly human capacity which operates in place of instinct in animals. It is thus seen as an evolutionary development which permits greater freedom for human beings. In his view both internal and external factors are important in the development of thinking, as well as active interplay between the individual and the environment. Four factors are essential to the process of cognitive development: maturation of the nervous system, experience interacting with objects in the physical environment, social interactions, and equilibration, or the self-regulating process of continual cognitive reorganization (Inhelder & Piaget, 1958). In the course of cognitive maturation, simple reflex actions of the infant are eventually integrated and internalized into logical thought processes due, in part, to the development of mental imagery (symbols) and language.

Piaget's research led him to conclude that all human beings progress through the same stages of cognitive development in the same sequence, but that cultural and social experiences can accelerate or retard the rate of this progression. Accordingly, while he listed age ranges for the onset and termination of the different stages in cognitive development (see Table 3.2), he remained cautious as to the general applicability of ages. He noted, for example, that the stage of formal operations appears to begin at about 11 or 12 years, but that these types of thought processes are not present in the thinking of so-called primitive societies (Inhelder & Piaget, 1958).

Sensorimotor   According to Piaget, the infant lacks the abilities to engage in symbolic thought and to use language. Consequently, children under 2 years of age must rely on immediate physical sensations, perceptions, and motor activity to make sense out of and to control their environments. Accordingly, Piaget labeled this stage *sensorimotor* intelligence. While the characteristics of cognitive functioning at this age are crude compared with later stages, Piaget believed that these represent the beginnings of intellectual development.

Preoperational   The use of elementary symbols (images and words) to represent sensations, perceptions, and actions heralds the child's movement to the second stage, *preoperational* thought. Typically this stage begins about the age of 18 months or 2 years, when children first begin to talk. During the preoperational period children are unable to distinguish between symbols and their referents. Consequently, it is often cognitively impossible for them to see much beyond the present moment or literal appearance of things, although increased language skills and continuous interactions

Table 3.2 PIAGET'S STAGES OF COGNITIVE DEVELOPMENT

Stage	Estimated age	Distinguishing features
Sensorimotor	Birth–18 months	Reliance on immediate physical sensations, perceptions, and motor activity to interact with environment
Preoperational	18 months–7 years	Language; rudimentary use of symbols; prelogical thinking and problem solving
Concrete operations	7–11 years	Logical thinking about concrete events
Formal operations	11–15 years (and through adulthood)	Logical thinking about abstract ideas

with their social and physical environments help bring their perceptions more in line with "objective reality."

Concrete Operations   At about the age 6 or 7, the child advances to the third stage, that of *concrete operations.* During this period we see the emergence of *logic* in the child's thinking. Piaget termed these logical thought processes (logical) *operations.*

With the advent of logical thinking, children become more flexible in their thinking, begin to understand relationships between events, and can group objects on the basis of properties held in common. For example, a preoperational child has difficulty arranging a handful of sticks of various lengths in order of length; a child in the concrete operations stage has no such difficulty. Or, take the interesting problem of conservation of quantities. A child is shown two glasses of the same size with equal amounts of liquid in them. The child watches while the experimenter pours the liquid from one of the glasses into a shorter, fatter glass. When asked which glass has more liquid (the taller, thinner one or the shorter, fatter one), the preoperational child will usually say the taller one, even though he or she watched the experimenter pour the liquid from one glass into the other. The child capable of concrete operational thought can solve the conservation problem; he or she is able to comprehend the idea that a change in external reality (the appearance or shape of the different glasses) does not alter underlying reality (actual amount of liquid present).

Formal Operations   It is not until the child is able to think logically about *hypothetical events and objects* that the period of *formal operations* has been attained. This stage is estimated to begin between the ages of 11 and 15. With the onset of formal operational thought, Piaget believed that all of the necessary structural "thinking equipment" had developed. Nonetheless, he felt that these structures needed a great deal of refinement in order to be considered fully developed.

Recall that concrete operational thinking is logical thought, but it is limited to problems about observable events and objects which exist in the present. Formal operational thought widens the scope of cognitive activity so that adolescents are able not only to think about the present (what currently exists or is empirically given), but also to conceive of past and future events. Also, rather than being limited to the tangible or concrete, the formal operational person can grasp problems in which verbal statements are substituted for objects. For instance, children in the concrete operational period have difficulty solving verbal problems like this one: "Edith is lighter than Suzanne and Edith is darker than Lily. Which is the darkest of all three?" (Inhelder & Piaget, 1958, p. 252).

The hallmark of formal thought is that reality becomes secondary to possibility. (This is a reversal in the direction of thinking from the concrete operational period, in which possibilities exist only as extensions of what is given or what has already occurred.) One of the significant implications of this change is that it permits the adolescent to deal with hypothetical problems which require the acceptance of an assumption and the use of logical analysis. For example, children under 12 often have difficulty accepting contrary-to-fact assumptions ("Assume that cats fly") in order to solve hypothetical problems. They are likely to declare that cats can't fly and that therefore the problem is unsolvable. Older children are able to accept the hypothetical assumption and continue with the problem-solving.

Another characteristic of formal thinking is that adolescents can engage in combinatorial thought, that is, they are able to consider the effects of more than two variables operating at the same time. Combinatorial thinking is important in systematic hypothesis testing (versus trial and error) with regard to complex problems. This more sophisticated approach to problem-solving requires that the individual be able to consider all possible combinations of all factors in a problem and to test these in such a way as to permit only one factor to vary at a time; in other words, to observe the effects of one variable while holding all other factors constant. For example, in one of Piaget's problems children are shown a jar containing a yellow-colored liquid and five other jars containing colorless liquids and are asked to produce the yellow liquid from some combination of the remaining five jars. A combination of three of the colorless liquids produces the yellow color; the other two jars contain either water or a bleaching agent. When 7- to 11-year-olds are presented with this problem, they usually start by combining two liquids at a time, and after this procedure fails to work, they stop trying to solve the problem in a systematic manner. Instead, they start trying to solve it on a "hit-or-miss" basis; for example, they might try mixing liquids from all the jars together. In contrast, children over 12 usually stick with a systematic problem-solving approach by testing all possible combinations of one, two, or three liquids until the yellow solution is produced (Piaget & Inhelder, 1958).

Still another aspect of formal operations is the ability to think about thoughts. As a result of this development, adolescents become aware of and can evaluate the content and logic of their own thoughts as well as those of others.

One of the significant outcomes of these changes in thinking is that adolescents are freed from the cognitive limitations of the present; they are now able to conceive of possibilities which could not be imagined before. The ability to conceive of future events is one of the reasons they spend so much time fantasizing, planning, and worrying about their lives to be. As we will discuss shortly, the idealism of adolescence is related to this new mode of thought. Another outcome is that adolescents are able to understand metaphor. Witness their fascination with the use of symbolism and satire in cartoons (Elkind, 1970). The adolescent's delight with double entendre in jokes (especially sexual) is also a manifestation of this new development in cognition.

A particularly important and interesting aspect of cognitive development is *egocentrism,* or the tendency to view reality in line with our own idiosyncratic perceptions. This tendency becomes less pronounced as we grow older because we are able to test our perceptions against those of other people and against physical reality, according to Piaget. Egocentrism in adolescence is a particularly interesting phenomenon because it appears to account for much of the experience and behavior typical of young people of this age. We will discuss egocentrism in more detail in the last section of this chapter.

Evaluation of Piagetian Theory

Piaget's ideas about the number and sequence of cognitive developmental stages appear to be supported by research (Weisz & Zigler, 1979), but his theories have been criticized on a number of fronts.

Cognitive changes are one of the reasons adolescents spend a lot of time fantasizing, planning, and worrying.

One issue that has been questioned is his assumption that all cognitive processes are essentially the same in nature and function. Even though most of his research utilized physical and mathematical problems, he assumed that social thought operated in the same manner. Piaget later proposed expanding the content of problems to test in social as well as physical domains.

Some research indicates that distinctions can be made between physical or mathematical thinking and interpersonal or social thinking (Damon, 1979; Keating & Clark, 1980). For example, one study of 12-, 14-, and 16-year-olds found more subjects to be competent in formal reasoning on physical tasks than on interpersonal tasks. No clear-cut conclusions can be drawn yet, but we can say that thinking appears to differ in different content areas.

Another Piagetian idea which critics have questioned is whether formal thought is attainable by all people and, if so, at what age. Based on earlier work with European children, Piaget proposed that formal operations developed between the ages of 11 and 15. One study of American subjects compared one group of 14-year-olds, two groups of 16- and 17-year-olds, and one group of adults on formal operational thinking (Dulit, 1972). The 14-year-olds and one of the groups of 16- and 17-year-olds were average school achievers; the second group of 16- and 17-year-olds were gifted students; and the adults (aged 20 to 55) were of average intelligence. It was found that only 25 to 33 percent of the average older adolescents and adults and only 60 percent of the gifted adolescents were able to function at the fully formal level. (Boys performed at this level significantly more often than girls.) Hence, there is evidence that formal operational thinking does not appear to be completely developed by the end of high school and that many American college students don't engage, entirely, in formal thought (Elkind, 1962; Moshman, 1979). Moreover, some adults never achieve formal operational thinking (Graves, 1972). Hence, it seems reasonable to conclude that the age of onset of formal operations has been overestimated in the past.

Research indicates that mildly retarded American children and adolescents develop cognitively at a slower rate than adolescents of average intelligence and that retarded individuals do not appear to engage in formal operational thinking (S. Jackson, 1965). Recall also that gifted adolescents were found to be more successful in formal thinking than their average peers. It does not appear, then, that chronological age is the critical factor determining the onset of the period of formal operations. The more relevant variable in this regard seems to be *mental age.*

Cross-cultural research indicates that formal thinking is not widespread in other cultures, particularly those less technologically based (Dasen, 1972; Neimark, 1970). It is suggested that this may be so because Piaget's conceptualization of the development of thought is strongly rooted in the ideal of Western scientific thought (Greenfield, cited in Gallagher & Noppe, 1976). In many cultures such hypothetical-deductive reasoning may be quite alien. Moreover, it is essentially impossible to determine the presence of formal operational thought without developing tests which are relevant to a particular culture or society.

It has been suggested that formal operations may not be achieved unless one's environment demands it (Dulit, 1972). For instance, American high school and college curricula exert such pressures, and European secondary schools and universities proba-

Formal operational thinking may not be relevant in all cultures.

bly make even greater demands of this nature. This is not necessarily so in all cultures. Here, too, we should keep in mind that much of the everyday thinking and behavior in our own culture, especially for some, operates at a concrete level and does not require formal thought.

In conclusion, we can say that Piaget's theory has had and continues to have a major impact on psychology, even though we may see modifications in some of his ideas and methods of investigation.

GENDER, CLASS, AND RACIAL DIFFERENCES IN INTELLECTUAL AND COGNITIVE FUNCTIONING

Discussions of differences in intellectual and cognitive functioning related to gender, class, and race are always controversial because of the possible implications and interpretations of research findings. Many people have understandable (and no doubt justifiable) fears that gender, race, or class differences will be seen as innate and unchangeable and may be used to justify existing social conditions which may, in fact, be the causes of these differences. This is of particular concern to those who are relatively powerless in society as they attempt to move a resistant social system in order to gain equal access to social, economic, and political opportunities.

Gender Differences

Sex differences in overall intelligence have not usually been found because IQ tests have been intentionally designed to minimize such differences. More productive questions are whether there are sex differences in specific intellectual abilities and whether we can determine if heredity or environment is more influential in causing any observed differences? While biological factors (hormonal changes at puberty, for example) cannot be ruled out, today the more common explanations for sex differences are related to experiences. For example, a recent study found that second-grade teachers spent more of their instructional time with girls in reading and with boys in math (Leinhardt, Seewald, & Engel, 1979). In addition, the amount of time spent with students was significantly related to the children's achievement. Such findings provide evidence of differential treatment of girls and boys leading to later sex differences in specific performance areas.

We might also note that at least one longitudinal study has yielded some sobering findings with regard to sex differences in intelligence (Kangas & Bradway, 1971). As can be seen in Figure 3.3, this study showed that the higher the level of men's preadult IQ, the greater the IQ gain into adulthood, whereas the higher the level of women's preadult IQ, the less the IQ gain into adulthood. Since intellectual performance appears dependent, at least in part, on ongoing stimulation, it seems likely that the life experiences of most women in this study after high school were not as intellectually stimulating as those of men.

We will consider three aspects of intellectual functioning in which sex differences have been consistently found: verbal, quantitative, and spatial. Then, we will briefly survey some other findings.

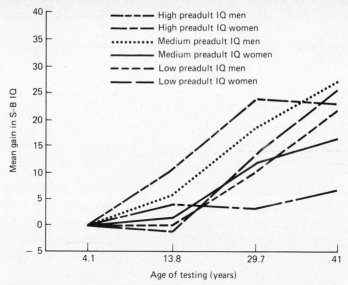

Figure 3.3   Average gains in Stanford-Binet IQ at successive ages for men and women of differing preadult IQ levels. *Source:* Jon Kangas and Katherine Bradway (1971). Intelligence at middle age: A thirty-eight year follow-up. *Developmental Psychology, 5* (2), 336. Copyright 1971 by the American Psychological Association. Reprinted by permission of the author.

Verbal Abilities   Verbal abilities include such competencies as vocabulary size, word fluency, spelling, sentence complexity, reading comprehension, and logical reasoning with language. Early studies showed that girls performed at a higher level of verbal ability than did boys. However, a comprehensive review of the research in this area by Eleanor Maccoby and Carol Jacklin (1974) indicates that the early studies did not find particularly large differences in verbal functioning and some later studies show no consistent sex differences in children younger than 10 or 11. Maccoby and Jacklin note one major exception. A number of studies of "disadvantaged" children from preschool through the second grade have found that "girls clearly test higher in a variety of language skills, including reading, vocabulary, and the understanding of relational terms" (p. 84). They also report that several studies of British children found that boys scored higher on vocabulary tests and had fewer reading problems than girls did. Hence, as one of the British researchers proposed, there may be "sex-specific cross-cultural differences in reading." (Recall the finding that second-grade American teachers spent more classroom time with girls in reading.)

Studies of children about 10 or 11 which have found sex differences (many, but not all have) indicate that girls do better than boys on both simple verbal tasks (spelling, punctuation) and complex ones (understanding of complex logical relations). In addition, girls maintain their superiority in high school and college. In a longitudinal study, however, it was found that boys' verbal skills caught up with girls' and sometimes surpassed them (Bradway & Thompson, 1962). They also found that such gains were related to the amount of formal education the subjects had had during adolescence and early adulthood, as well as the quality of the experiences to which they had been exposed after high school and college.

Quantitative Abilities   With regard to sex differences in mathematical abilities, the findings present an interesting picture. Maccoby and Jacklin (1974) reported that no sex differences in these functions are found in young children, although, again, gender appears to interact with class in that "culturally disadvantaged" girls do better than their male peers. At about the time of onset of puberty, however, there is a change. Boys usually perform better than girls on quantitative tasks (but at least one study has found the opposite in Hispanic youth [Schratz, 1978]). Males also score higher on the mathematical aptitude section of the SAT and this superiority seems to persist in adulthood.

What might cause this change at this time? For one thing, mathematics is still considered a "masculine" area and this no doubt discourages many girls from taking math courses in high school. Obviously, we would predict that these girls would not perform as well as boys who have taken math courses. However, at least one study using seventh-grade subjects found that males still outperformed females even when the girls and boys had taken the same number of math courses (Benbow & Stanley, 1980).

Attempts to explain such differences are currently focusing on the issue of "math anxiety" or "mathophobia" (Tobias, 1978). While both sexes can suffer from the fear of numbers and related concepts, Sheila Tobias believes that the sex-role expectations for girls that math is "masculine" and that excelling in it may lead to loss of popularity make "math anxiety" more prevelant among women and more difficult to overcome. Although we can say that sex differences in math abilities appear about the time of puberty and persist, we are not yet clear about the specific reasons why this is so. While most psychologists would probably agree that environmental influences are responsible for most of the sex differences, the possibility of genetic or hormonal causes cannot be ruled out at this time (Burstein, Bank, & Jarvik, 1980).

Spatial Ability   This aptitude has been measured in many different ways, and it is not clear that the abilities being measured are all similar in nature. For example, some spatial ability tests measure an individual's ability to recognize objects that have been rotated in space on paper or the ability to follow the message from one voice when two voices are speaking. These tests are thought to measure analytical ability (separating one element from another). Like mathematical abilities, no differences in spatial ability appear until the beginning of adolescence. And, like mathematical functioning, the differences appear to favor males.

Many of the studies in this area use visual spatial tasks, and the results are usually interpreted to mean that males are better at tasks involving analytical ability. At least one psychologist has suggested that these observed differences might more accurately be interpreted to mean that males excel at spatial visualization (because of their more extensive experience with it), but this does not mean that they surpass females in the more general ability of analytic reasoning (Sherman, 1971). At least one finding reported by Maccoby and Jacklin supports this contention. For example, males do not appear to excel on the analysis of nonvisual spatial problems. As with other special abilities, the basis for sex differences is not completely understood yet.

Other Findings   Whether or not there are sex differences related to the achievement of formal operations is not clear at this time. Results of studies are conflicting. Some indicate that boys are superior to girls on tasks involving formal operational reasoning (Dulit, 1972; Protinsky & Hughston, 1979); others show no differences (White & Friedman, 1977; Williams & Brekke, 1979). As with the other areas of cognitive functioning we have mentioned, when differences are found to exist, explanations of the differences are most often rooted in environmental influences.

Cross-cultural research in the area of gender differences and intellectual abilities provides additional evidence for the idea that the sex differences we have mentioned are related to different sex-role expectations in American society. For instance, a study comparing Central Eskimos and Nsenga Africans found almost no sex differences among subjects aged 9 to 40 in these groups on a variety of cognitive tasks (MacArthur, 1973).

A great deal of research indicates that females consistently achieve higher grades than males do from elementary school through college (Cross, 1971; Tavris & Wade, 1984). Also, Maccoby and Jacklin report that girls have fewer problems in school as well as fewer reading and speech problems. Females at the high school and college levels continue to achieve higher grades than males, in spite of the fact that studies either show no cognitive differences between the sexes or favor males. Some attribute the girls' higher grades to their being more willing to obey teachers' requests (Maccoby & Jacklin, 1974), but it seems unlikely that this explanation alone is sufficient to account for the paradox.

Social Class Differences

The factor of socioeconomic status (SES) usually is defined in terms of one or more of the following criteria: parents' income, educational attainment, and occupational level. Because SES encompasses a number of significant variables, social class by itself does not enable us to determine more specific causes of some of the effects associated with it. (This is an important point because although psychologists are not able to change a person's socioeconomic standing—would that we could!—we can ameliorate and even sometimes prevent problems which are class-related, if we know what specific features of the environment are critical to the problem.) Think for a moment about the ways in which the experiences of an adolescent from a lower-SES environment differ from those of an adolescent from a middle- or upper-SES environment. Such things as the following come to mind: less money, larger family (and therefore less attention), little or no access to good health care, inadequate nutrition, lower educational levels of parents, less intellectual stimulation in the home, less value placed on education, more rigid sex-role stereotypes, poorer educational resources, fewer opportunities for activities outside the home and school, lower vocational aspirations of parents for themselves and their children, and social stigmas associated with lower-class status (Thoday & Gibson, 1970). Note, too, that some of these factors operate before birth as well as afterward and can have effects on prenatal development. These conditions characterize environments which have been shown to have pervasive detrimental effects on various aspects of human development; for this reason we use terms such as "deprived" or "culturally disadvantaged" to refer to individuals who live in these settings.

With regard to intellectual functioning, the findings related to social class are relatively clear-cut: the higher the SES of the parents, the higher children and adolescents will score on IQ tests. (You can see that the "rich get richer and the poor get poorer" in more respects than one.) On the average the differences in IQ scores between children in the highest and lowest classes is about 20 points (Backman, 1972). Also, the longer children and adolescents are exposed to a deprived environment, the greater the impact of the setting. Hence, we see the emergence of a "cumulative deficit"; that is, individuals fall further behind as they progress in school. Robert Hess and Virginia Shipman (1965) state that "in scholastic achievement they are retarded an average of 2 years by grade 6 and almost 3 years by grade 8; they are more likely to drop out of school before completing a secondary education; and even when they have adequate ability are less likely to go to college" (p. 870).

Such findings indicate that class status in this country has major impacts on intellectual development. In the next section, we will see that SES factors are usually also related to race and ethnic group membership.

Racial and Ethnic Group Differences

Most of the studies in this area show that American whites score 10 to 20 points higher on intelligence tests than do blacks and those from certain ethnic minorities (Backman, 1972). These findings have led some psychologists to raise the question of whether whites are genetically superior to blacks with regard to intelligence (Jensen, 1969). As we mentioned earlier, this notion was not favorably received by blacks or by many psychologists.

For one thing, there is a problem of cultural bias in IQ tests. Standardized IQ tests often work against those from disadvantaged or ethnic minority backgrounds, especially when there is lack of familiarity with standard English. Another problem with conclusions of genetic inferiority is that most research fails to equalize differences in environmental conditions between whites and other groups. In particular, proportionately more blacks and minority group members fall into the lower socioeconomic statuses, and we have already seen that prolonged exposure to deprived environments has significant impacts on intellectual functioning. The importance of deprived versus advantaged environments for achievement by black children is demonstrated by a study that found that black children who had been adopted by advantaged white parents scored above the national average for white students on intelligence and academic achievement (Scarr & Weinberg, 1976).

Such information helps us understand the role of the environment related to intellectual functioning, but much more research into this question is needed before we will be able to understand the role of genetics. Indeed, given the complexity of the factors and their interrelationships, there is good reason to speculate that we may never be able to resolve this issue definitively.

It is important to be aware of the negative effects of prejudice and discrimination based on gender, racial, ethnic, and class stereotypes. While it is impossible to predict a given individual's IQ on the basis of one of these external characteristics, many of us still persist in believing that we can. Such false beliefs can then create *self-fulfilling prophecies* in which our biased and unfair treatment of children and adolescents serves to convince them that they are, in fact, just as we perceive them to be—in this case, not very smart. In adolescence low academic achievement is often associated with dropping out of school, juvenile delinquency, and unemployability or employment in low-paying jobs. When such things happen, the larger society as well as the affected individuals are the "losers." There are enough problems waiting to be solved in society to demand that we encourage the full development of every person's intellectual potential.

EFFECTS OF COGNITIVE MATURATION ON ADOLESCENT PERSONALITY AND SOCIAL BEHAVIOR

As we shall see, distinctions between personality and cognitive-intellectual functioning are superficial. While these two categories can be separated conceptually, in reality they interact with each other. An interesting development in this regard is the emergence of a new area in the study of cognition—that of social cognition.

Social Cognition

Social cognition is the development of observations, inferences, and conceptualizations about our own and others' social roles and relationships, thoughts, feelings and intentions, beliefs and moral judgments (Flavell, 1977). Much research in this area has focused on the development of *role-taking,* that is, learning to take the role of another person. This ability is important in relationships with others. Also, the level of one's moral judgment appears to be related to the ability to understand another person's point of view (Selman, 1971).

Another interesting aspect of social cognition is the development of the various ways we describe other people and explain their behavior. Descriptions of others by children tend to be relatively egocentric in that they will often characterize a person in terms of how the person treats them ("She is nice to me") rather than from a more independent viewpoint ("She has red hair" or "She is quiet"). Young adolescents, on the other hand, frequently use personality concepts to describe others and themselves, with girls appearing to develop these capabilities earlier than boys (Barratt, 1977). Adolescents are also aware of the idea of the "uniqueness" of each individual and their descriptions of others reflect this quality (Peevers & Secord, 1973).

A related aspect of social cognition concerns ideas about the self. The onset of formal operations appears to influence adolescents' conceptualizations (and feelings) about themselves. As might be expected, there seem to be parallels between the quality of the descriptions of "self" and "other." For example, it has been found that characterizations of both oneself and others become more specific with age (Mullener & Laird, 1971).

We turn now to a most interesting problem: "cognitive shortcomings," or the fact that errors, fallacies, and and biases interfere with accurate social cognition, just as they do with nonsocial cognition (Flavell, 1977). Piaget's concept of egocentrism is an example of the operation of a systematic cognitive distortion. We will discuss egocentrism below as it operates in adolescence.

Adolescent Egocentrism

The concept of egocentrism is particularly interesting because it appears to provide a link between personality dynamics and cognitive processes. In each stage of cognitive development, the emergence of new modes of thought gives rise to particular cognitive problems to be grappled with. Ironically, the greater freedom and flexibility in thinking which formal operations brings may also entrap the adolescent in an egocentric "world-view." Formal thought enables adolescents to be conscious of the fact that they are thinking, to be conscious of what and how they are thinking, and to be aware of the thoughts of others. However, adolescents have difficulty understanding that, although they may be preoccupied with their own appearance and behavior (because of the many physical and social changes taking place), others are not (Elkind, 1967a). The operation of egocentrism has been described like this:

> a) The adolescent, now capable of abstract reasoning, can formulate thoughts about thoughts; b) the person often uses this ability to think about others' thoughts; c) further, the adolescent starts thinking about what others are thinking of the adolescent him/herself; and finally, d) the adolescent is thoroughly convinced that what he/she thinks the other is thinking is, in fact, exactly what the other is thinking. In other words, the adolescent believes he or she knows what is going on in another's mind. (Enright, Lapsley, & Shukla, 1979, p. 687)

Adolescent egocentrism is one cause of adolescents' self-preoccupation.

Adolescent egocentrism has several consequences, according to David Elkind (1967a). The first of these he labels the *imaginary audience*. Adolescents often act as if they are continually "on stage" in front of an audience that is focused on them. This belief that they are the center of others' attention operates in actual situations (such as how they think others are evaluating them as they sit in a classroom, for example) or in relation to forthcoming events (such as how they imagine others will react to them at the upcoming dance).

Elkind believes that a great many adolescent behaviors and experiences can be accounted for by the operation of this phenomenon. Most obvious is the characteristic self-consciousness of early adolescence which sometimes takes the form of either unwarranted self-criticism or self-admiration. In both cases self-appraisal is accompanied by input from the imaginary audience. As Elkind has insightfully pointed out, the audience knows exactly which weaknesses to criticize since the audience is constructed by the adolescent himself or herself! It is likely that feelings of self-admiration are also projected onto the audience such that the adolescent plays to an admiring and approving crowd. And, with regard to the operation of the imaginary audience in relating to the opposite sex, who does not recognize himself or herself in the following characterizations?

> The boy who stands in front of the mirror for two hours combing his hair is probably imagining the swooning reactions he will produce in the girls. Likewise, the girl applying her make-up is more likely than not imagining the admiring glances that will come her way. When these young people actually meet, each is more concerned with being the observed than with being the observer. (Elkind, 1967a, p. 1030)

Another example of the operation of the imaginary audience is the fantasies in which adolescents imagine how others will react to news of their death. The adolescent usually views others as recalling, too late of course, what a good person he or she really was (Elkind, 1967a).

The second consequence of adolescent egocentrism discussed by Elkind is the *personal fable*. The personal fable is defined as "a story which . . . [the adolescent] tells himself and which is not true" (Elkind, 1967a, p. 1031). One aspect of the personal fable is the adolescent's view that his or her experience is unique and could not be comprehended by others (especially parents!). The adolescent cannot perceive similarities between his or her emotions and situation and those of others. Examples of the personal fable in this regard come readily to mind: the ecstasy of one's first love and the utter devastation of one's first "breakup."

Elkind suggests that this notion of "personal uniqueness" is also manifested in adolescents' beliefs in their own immortality (in contrast to the mortality of others). This idea may account for the reckless behavior of many young people which results in the high incidence of injury and death by accident, especially among males of this age group. Similarly, Elkind has suggested that the personal fable may be one of the causes of the high incidence of pregnancy among teen-age girls; although they believe that other girls might get pregnant, they believe that they will not and that therefore they do not need to use birth control.

Another outcome of adolescent egocentrism is the emergence of the "idealistic reformer" (Inhelder & Piaget, 1958). This event is directly related to the adolescent's struggle to adopt adult roles (which Piaget sees as the hallmark of adolescence). Not only do young people attempt to find their own place in the world through adapting to societal roles, they also seek to transform the world to meet their needs (without regard for the different needs of others). In their attempts to make the world submit to their views, adolescents often take on the role of reformers who are both idealistic and intolerant (mainly because they have not yet had tested their ideas in the world). (Here, we are not asserting that adolescent idealism is necessarily a "bad" thing; in fact, such idealism can be quite useful to society.)

According to Piaget, egocentrism seems to disappear by the age of 15 or 16. As with egocentrism in other cognitive stages, the modification of adolescent egocentric beliefs takes place by means of realistic feedback from continual reality-testing in the social environment. The most important focus of this process is the adolescent's entry into the world of work or into serious professional training. This change of roles transforms the adolescent "from an idealistic reformer into an achiever" (Inhelder & Piaget, 1958, p. 346).

Similarly, social interaction teaches us that others often have views different from our own. This awareness helps us replace the imaginary audience with a more realistic sense of the reactions of others. Likewise, the ideas of the personal fable are eventually overcome through the establishment of emotionally intimate relationships in which young people come to share deeply personal feelings with a special other person. Through these kinds of interactions, we come to see that our own experiences are not so different from others'. This enables us to integrate the feelings of others with our own and to dispel the personal fable, although it appears doubtful that it is ever entirely overcome.

A recent study compared subjects in the seventh, eighth, tenth, and twelfth grades and college on egocentrism (Enright, Shukla, Lapsley, 1980). It was found that the existence of the imaginary audience and the personal fable were more dominant in early adolescence and declined with age. Also, this research showed that the personal fable

Sharing personal feelings with others helps adolescents overcome the personal fable.

did not decline to the same extent as the imaginary audience. In addition, there was more focus on general self-introspection and self-improvement in late adolescence which did not appear to have the same kind of self-conscious characteristic of the personal fable or imaginary audience constructions. On this latter basis, the authors concluded that adolescent egocentrism may have more than one aspect which may unfold on different schedules during adolescence.

Other Cognitive Influences

The onset of formal thought permits the adolescent to conceive of possibilities (in addition to what is given) and to add a future orientation to the existing past and present perspectives. These new awarenesses are directly tied to adolescents' serious interests in their own futures—fantasies and speculations about careers and life-style options.

In addition, the influence of cognitive changes can be seen in adolescents' heightened interest in political and religious questions, as we shall see in Chapter 10.

We should also mention the use of the defense mechanism of *intellectualization* which Anna Freud suggests is particularly common among adolescents. Intellectualization is a means of draining off the emotion behind anxiety-inducing conflicts by discussing important personal concerns in an abstract and impersonal way. The phenomenon of "bull sessions," in which such issues as abortion, sex, living with someone, homosexuality, and the existence of God are intellectually debated are examples of the operation of this defense mechanism. Clearly, the ability to deal with such abstractions is related to formal operational thought.

SUMMARY

Intellectual abilities appear to mature and peak during late adolescence and early adulthood, and it appears that intelligence declines less rapidly than was once thought. Also, IQ does not necessarily remain constant throughout life.

IQ tests are usually designed to measure intellectual functioning in school and are therefore useful predictors of academic success. IQ tests have been legitimately criticized for discriminating against those who are not middle class and not white. Moreover, there is concern about the possible misuse of intelligence tests. With adolescents, IQ tests are used to ascertain causes of academic performance about which there are questions and in vocational and personal counseling.

Piaget sees thought as progressing through four stages. Adolescence coincides with the advent of formal operational thinking, the last of these cognitive stages. Logical thinking about ideas and abstract concepts begins in this stage.

Sex differences in overall intelligence have not been found. Some differences have been established with regard to specific intellectual abilities, although the cause of these differences is not clear at this time. Because many of the differences in functioning do not appear until early adolescence and because similar differences have not been found in other cultures, there is speculation that differential sex-role expectations may be largely responsible for these differences.

Lower SES is associated with lower intellectual performance. Average IQ scores are lower for blacks and some ethnic minority groups than for whites. There is ample evidence that there are significant discrepancies in environmental conditions between minority groups and white middle-class individuals. Until such differences are equalized, it would be inaccurate to conclude that biological reasons are solely responsible for such differences.

Cognitive functioning also appears related to some adolescent personality dynamics such as self-consciousness, idealism, and feelings of uniqueness.

GLOSSARY

achievement test   A test used to measure how much has been learned in a specific content area.

aptitude test   A test used to determine how well a person might learn new information or skills of a specific nature.

culture-fair tests   Psychological tests which don't favor any particular cultural background.

egocentrism (Piaget)   A cognitive characteristic in which individuals are unable to differentiate their own thoughts and feelings from those of others; diminishes considerably in late adolescence.

formal operations (Piaget)   The fourth and last stage of cognitive development characterized by the ability to think logically about abstract ideas.

imaginary audience (Elkind)   A consequence of adolescent egocentrism in which young people believe that others are paying more attention to them than is really the case.

intellectualization   A Freudian defense mechanism in which anxiety-provoking ideas or problems are discussed in an abstract, rational manner in order to avoid focusing on the unpleasant emotional aspects of problems.

intelligence quotient   A means of measuring intelligence calculated by comparing a given test score with other scores in a standardized sample.

personal fable (Elkind)   A consequence of adolescent egocentrism in which young people believe that they are special and unique.

role-taking   The ability to take the roles of other people so as to understand their thoughts, feelings, and perceptions.

social cognition   The development of people's perceptions and conceptualizations about their own and others' social roles, thoughts, intentions, and feelings.

Chapter 4 Outline

I. Impact of Culture on Personality and Social Development
   A. Socialization Process
   B. Cultural Discontinuity
   C. Social Change
   D. Length and Marginal Status of Transition Period
II. Major Socializing Influences on Adolescents
   A. Parents
   B. Media
   C. Peers
   D. Schools
   E. Religion
III. Developmental Tasks of Adolescence and Youth
IV. Significant Aspects of Adolescent Personality Development
   A. Self-Concept, Self-Esteem, and Identity
   B. Emotional Development
   C. Stressful Events
   D. Styles of Coping with Environmental Demands
   E. Changes in Interests
V. Summary
VI. Glossary

chapter 4

Socialization and Personality Development

In this chapter, we look at adolescent personality and social development. We briefly review the socialization process and the influence of parents, media, peers, schools, and religion on adolescent development. We list the developmental tasks of adolescence and youth and discuss the development of self-concept and identity, the emotions, coping styles, and interests in adolescence.

IMPACT OF CULTURE ON PERSONALITY AND SOCIAL DEVELOPMENT

Socialization Process

Socialization refers to the process by which a culture "teaches" its members to function in socially accepted ways. Socialization is necessary because humans do not have instincts which dictate given behaviors for particular situations; we have to learn how to feel, think, and behave in various settings. This process takes place through the influence of parents, media, peers, schools, and religion. Since roles change as we grow older, socialization is actually a lifelong process, but it is viewed as particularly important during childhood and adolescence because of the relative plasticity in development during this time.

Socialization takes place within a particular cultural and social context, and the adolescent experience varies from one culture to another. Also, we have already seen that adolescents' experiences may be quite different *within* a particular culture. Just as intellectual development is affected by gender, class, and race, so personality and social development is affected by these same variables. Our discussion focuses on the United States, although we will refer to cross-cultural studies to provide perspective when this information is available and seems important. Our discussion reflects mainly the experience of suburban, white, middle-class adolescents (since they have been studied more often), but we will also describe the experiences of minority groups and the lower and upper classes.

We will begin with the question of the role or function of the adolescent period within the larger social structure. In any culture this period (whether weeks or years in duration) is seen as a transition period from childhood to adult status. Obviously, the nature of any given culture will determine the particular competencies adolescents are expected to acquire and the amount of time to be given over to this process. In the United States two basic factors dictate that adolescence will be a lengthy period: (1) the need for young people to acquire the high-level skills required by our technological society and (2) the economic circumstances that create the need to keep young persons from entering an already crowded job market.

What, then, are the particular competencies American adolescents are expected to acquire during this time? First, we expect them to extend their basis of social and emotional support beyond the family to peers and others in the adult world. Second, we assume that young people will formulate a sense of identity—a personally and socially satisfactory answer to the question of "Who am I?" Third, we expect them to develop intellectual and social skills as well as moral standards through preadult experiences, such as attendance at school, participation in extracurricular activities, or work at part-time jobs, which will guarantee them some degree of success in adult society (Campbell, 1969).

Note that these expectations reflect both societal needs and the developmental status of this period. Without certain physical, cognitive, and personality prerequisites, societal expectations would be largely irrelevant or unattainable.

Cultural Discontinuity

Cultural expectations dictate which behaviors are acceptable, who may engage in certain activities, and when they may do so. We live in an *age-graded* society, that is, certain behaviors or activities are assumed to be common to all members of a particular age group (Benedict, 1938). Not all societies are organized this way. For example, not all cultures have a separate stage of adolescence, at least as we know it. It appears that less complex societies than ours as well as cultures in which there is more continuity between childhood and adulthood roles have less need for an extended period of adolescence. Our culture seems to require a more extended "training period" for adulthood.

Ruth Benedict (1938) suggested that adolescence would be a more difficult period to the extent that there was discontinuity between the behavioral expectations for children and adults. She characterized American society as a *discontinuous culture* and discussed three examples of such discontinuity. First, in the passage to adulthood children must move from a *nonresponsible to a responsible status role*. Benedict cited a number of historical examples of other cultures in which children are gradually given more and more responsibility. Consider the Cheyenne Indian culture:

Adolescence serves as a "training period" for adulthood.

At birth the little boy was presented with a toy bow, and from the time he could run about serviceable bows suited to his stature were specially made for him by the man of the family. Animals and birds were taught him in a graded series beginning with those most easily taken, and as he brought in his first of each species his family duly made a feast of it, accepting his contribution as gravely as the buffalo his father brought. When he finally killed a buffalo, it was only the final step of his childhood conditioning, not a new adult role with which his childhood experience had been at variance. (p. 163)

In contrast, American middle-class children generally are not given more and more responsible work as they mature. In fact, we have already noted that the period of adolescence has evolved partly to keep young people out of an already crowded job market. Consequently, there is less continuity in preparing for the assumption of adult roles.

A second aspect of cultural discontinuity in our society is that of *dominance-submission*. American children are expected to be submissive and adults are expected to be dominant. But, how is a submissive child to learn to be a dominant adult when such emphasis is placed on obedience to the authority of adults? In contrast, consider the attitude of the Mohave Indian toward dominance in a child:

The child's mother was white and protested to its father that he must take action when the child disobeyed and struck him. "But why?" the father said, "He is little. He cannot possibly injure me." He did not know of any dichotomy according to which an adult expects obedience and a child must accord it. If his child had been docile, he would simply have judged that it would become a docile adult—an eventuality of which he would not have approved. (p. 164)

A third area of discontinuity in our culture which Benedict discussed is the *contrasted sex role*. Cultural discontinuity exists where a culture teaches its sexually immature children ideas about sex which they will have to unlearn in order to function effectively as sexually mature adults. It exists where cultures prohibit sexual practices among children that are encouraged as adults. In this context the American culture is discontinuous. According to Benedict, Americans have to unlearn not only age prohibitions connected with sex, but also ideas about the "wickedness or the dangerousness of sex" (p. 55). This makes sexuality a difficult aspect of adjustment in our society.

Social Change

According to Margaret Mead (1970), some degree of discontinuity in socialization may be adaptive in a fast-paced, technological society such as ours. Because of rapid change in many areas, adult roles, behavior, or knowledge might be inappropriate or inadequate in situations faced by today's adolescents. Increasingly, Mead suggested, young people in rapidly changing societies would need to rely on their peers and themselves to learn the things they needed to know to function effectively.

More specifically, Mead described the impact of technological and social change on the socialization process in terms of three cultural patterns. The *postfigurative culture* refers to a society characterized by relatively little social change so that young people will live in a world much like that of their parents. It is assumed that adults possess the expertise and values necessary for successful functioning in the world, and it is their role to pass this information to the next generation. An example of this pattern can be seen in the previous descriptions of Cheyenne and Mohave Indian cultural practices.

The *cofigurative culture* refers to a society in which there is moderate social change. Young people continue to learn some things from their elders, but must also look to their peers for guidance in those areas where their parents' views are out-of-date. An example of this pattern would be adolescents whose parents are first-generation Americans who hold to many beliefs which are different from mainstream American attitudes and practices.

The *prefigurative culture* is a society in which there is rapid social change. Young people must learn many things on their own without guidance from adults because adults' skills are outmoded. In the prefigurative culture pattern adults learn about new ideas and practices from the young.

In Mead's view American society is moving toward the prefigurative cultural model while retaining aspects of the other two patterns. If she was correct, it means that children and adolescents will rely less on their parents and other adults for guidance in some areas, but still maintain needs for emotional support. This would change the nature of the parent-child relationship to one in which parents would be more concerned with imparting the value and "hows" of learning, rather than the specific "whats." Also, both parents and the young would be open to learning from each other. In this context, cultural discontinuity is seen as a result of moderate to rapid social change, but this discontinuity can produce adaptive outcomes both for societies in flux and for the individuals coping with social change.

Length and Marginal Status of Transition Period

A related problem associated with discontinuous cultures is the length of the transition period between childhood and adulthood and the status of individuals while they are in the transition period. Benedict suggested that many cultures besides our own are discontinuous in nature. However, many of these cultures minimize the strain of discontinuity by keeping the transition period between childhood and adulthood relatively short and by using rituals to signify to the adolescent and larger society that he or she has attained adult status. The term *puberty rites* (*rites de passage,* or rites of passage) has been given to such rituals or initiation ceremonies in tribal societies. Puberty rites are more common for males than females, but they exist for both sexes.

In our culture adolescence is lengthy. Moreover, we have no rites of passage. On the other hand, we do have certain events which often function as informal initiation ceremonies. Consider, for example, religious ceremonies such as the Jewish Bar (Bas) Mitzvah and Protestant Confirmation, social events such as the debut or sorority or fraternity initiations, high school and college graduations, and legal privileges such as voting, driving, and drinking. But, note the inconsistencies here. These informal events are limited to specific groups. There is no rite in which all members of the culture participate. And their significance in terms of adulthood varies considerably. For example, (male) youth can be required to fight for their country, but are forbidden to

In tribal societies, puberty rites mark the passage from childhood to adulthood.

drink in some states. Consequently, the adolescent experience for most Americans is a lengthy period of role confusion—being neither child nor adult.

This lack of a specific social role led psychologist Kurt Lewin to characterize the adolescent as having "marginal man" (person) status in society. Lewin saw similarities between the plight and reactions of adolescents and those members of minority groups who don't clearly belong to the majority or minority. The consequences of this marginal status are sensitivity, instability, emotional tension, contradictory behavior, and aversion to lower-status members of their own groups (Lewin, 1951). We can see striking similarities between these behaviors and those of some adolescents. According to Kenneth Keniston (1970a), this marginal status has been instrumental in the evolution of an adolescent subculture which provides youth with a basis for group identity.

In this context, we want to mention the impact of living as a member of an ethnic, racial, or cultural minority group in the United States. The experience of growing up for such youth can be particularly hard when the cultural family values are at odds with mainstream American values of individualism and materialism. Differences in skin color and language can also be barriers which are difficult to deal with. Take, for example, Mexican-American adolescents whose culture stresses family ties and dependency, living in the present, and honor as opposed to the values needed for success in this country of independence and achievement, deferred gratification, and utilitarian ethics (Derbyshire, 1979).

Or, consider the even more difficult problem faced by American Indians and blacks who have grown up in a country which has kept them ignorant of their culture and history. Moreover, because of our own ignorance and insensitivity, we have encouraged these and other minority groups to be ashamed of their heritage (Farris & Farris, 1976). Such experiences, of course, can add unnecessary stress to the lives of these adolescents.

MAJOR SOCIALIZING INFLUENCES ON ADOLESCENTS

Parents

Parents appear to be the most influential of the various socializing agents. Contrary to popular notions, most parent-adolescent relationships are not fraught with hostility and rejection. This does not mean that there are not disagreements. Since adolescents need to establish emotional and financial independence from their parents and to evolve an independent identity and values of their own, conflicts with parents are bound to arise. But, these disagreements take place between individuals who have a long history together and in most cases positive emotional commitments keep disagreements under control and serve to restore good feelings.

Disagreements between parents and adolescents appear to peak at about 14 or 15 years of age (Kandel & Lesser, 1972). Most conflicts appear to center on relatively minor issues such as styles of dress, hair length, and music preferences (J. C. Coleman, 1978). Conflicts may occur about more major issues such as sexual behavior, drinking, drug use, family responsibilities, study habits, choice of friends and dating partners, but here, too, most differences are a matter of feeling more or less strongly about an issue rather than having quite different beliefs (Lerner, Karson, Meisels, & Knapp, 1975).

Striving for independence appears to be a more important concern for boys than girls (this no doubt reflects different sex-role expectations). As we shall see, styles of parenting and parents' emotional maturity and their SES are significant factors in parent-adolescent relationships.

Media

Since 1955 television has become a stable fixture of American life, and there is substantial evidence that it performs an important socializing function (Avery, 1979; Comstock, 1978; Liebert, Sprafkin, & Davidson, 1982; Roberts & Bachen, 1981). (Recall our discussion in Chapter 1 of the role of symbolic models in observational learning.)

Recent estimates of adolescents' television-viewing habits suggest that they watch an average of three to four hours a day (Comstock, Chaffee, Katzman, McCombs, & Roberts, 1978). As a group, teenagers watch more television than either younger children or adults, and older adolescents watch less than younger adolescents (Liebert, Sprafkin, & Davidson, 1982).

Television can bring its audience diverse experiences; that is, it makes it possible to see what it would be like to be a member of a different culture, country, religion, socioeconomic status, race, or family. Depending on how the subject matter is portrayed, of course, it is possible for television to foster either accurate or inaccurate perceptions of people and situations which otherwise might not be encountered.

While television has been shown to have some favorable influences on viewers (increases in helping behavior as a result of watching programs with altruistic content, for example), it has been found that many television programs portray stereotypic and discriminatory views which can influence the attitudes and thinking of those who watch a great deal of television (National Institute of Mental Health [NIMH], 1982).

For example, in the area of sex roles, a massive analysis of television programs reported that less than 20 percent of the married women characters with children worked outside the home compared with more than 50 percent in real life ("Life According to TV," 1982). Also, a major survey of research on television and behavior found that males are characterized by "strength, performance, and skill," whereas females are characterized by "attractiveness and desirability" (NIMH, 1982, p. 55). According to this same survey, "male and female sexuality is characterized by a double standard and by stereotyped definitions of masculine and feminine traits and roles. . . . While both male and female roles are stereotyped, there is more stereotyping in the female roles" (p. 56).

On the issue of race, this survey reported that television programs tend to portray blacks as less likely to have jobs than whites. Also, both black and Hispanic characters are likely to work in low-prestige jobs.

Misleading notions about occupations are also portrayed: "Fully one-third of television's 'labor force' is in professional and managerial positions, about three times the number in real life" (p. 59).

Families are often portrayed as more glamorous and successful than is true in real life (NIMH, 1982). In addition, the 1970s saw the emergence of a "dominant upward-mobility theme" among TV families. Some psychologists are concerned that:

This emphasis may suggest that no one should want to stay in the working class but instead should be striving to move out of it. Furthermore, this upward mobility implies that it is easy to attain success. . . . television does not show how many strains accompany such "rising" in the world. (NIMH, 1982, p. 68)

Many psychologists are also concerned about the role aggression portrayed on television seems to play in fostering aggression in children and adolescents (Liebert, et al., 1982; NIMH, 1982; Roberts & Bachen, 1981). In that aggressive impulses are one of the emotions adolescents must learn to control, we would suggest that youth are particularly susceptible to the influence of violent television programs, especially programs in which aggression is glorified and rewarded.

A separate question is, of course, whether program content has any impact on its viewers. While this is a complex issue that needs much more study, the NIMH survey concluded that "On the whole, it seems that television leads its viewers to have television-influenced attitudes" (1982, p. 7). Of course, we don't mean to suggest that television, alone, is responsible for violence or sexist beliefs in American society; nonetheless, it appears that it is not a purely harmless entertainment device either. The role of television as an important socializing agent is now recognized and merits continued study.

Adolescents use other types of media as well. For example, book and newspaper reading increases during adolescence (Avery, 1979). The level of magazine reading, on

Television influences many attitudes today.

the other hand, seems to be similar for adolescents and children. Different types of magazines are preferred by different age groups. Sex differences have been reported also, such that boys prefer "men's" and sports magazines, while girls enjoy "women's" and fashion magazines.

Radio listening and record playing show dramatic increases during adolescence, and listening to music appears to be an important "source of relaxation, entertainment, and relief from loneliness" (Avery, 1979). It is suggested that movie attendance increases during adolescence, but data are lacking on this question.

Peers

One important socializing function of adolescent peer groups is that they provide a social context in which to learn attitudes and skills relevant to adult functioning which cannot necesarily be taught in the family. An important example is learning how to get along with peers of both sexes during a time when physical and sexual maturation increases the complexity of social relationships from childhood.

Also, the peer group and larger adolescent subculture help adolescents cope with their marginal status; that is, they provide a sense of belonging during the period in which youth have left the childhood culture behind, but have not yet assumed the values, interests, and standards of the adult world. Commonly recognized aspects of the adolescent subculture include preferences for certain styles of dress, speech, and music.

A popular but unfounded belief about adolescents is that they exchange closeness to parents for closeness to peers. This notion presumes that adolescents cannot be close to parents and peers simultaneously. In fact, adolescents maintain relationships with their parents *and* develop new ties with peers (J. C. Coleman, 1978).

Schools

Schools have important socializing influences on adolescents in two ways. First, they provide the physical environment in which adolescents spend most of their time and which is the center of the peer culture. Second, schools provide formal education.

Within schools at least two major subcultures can be distinguished: students and teachers. The values of these two subcultures are often different, and this is likely to be more true in college than in high school. Adolescents tend to be more interested in social life and athletics and relatively anti-intellectual, whereas faculty place a higher value on intellectual than social or athletic achievement. We should note that the values of the student subculture are relatively consistent with the anti-intellectual views of adult Americans and, to this extent at least, can be viewed as adaptive.

The college experience appears to have a liberalizing effect on values and religious beliefs. No doubt the exposure to a variety of adult role models, students, ideas, encouragement to question existing beliefs, and increased sophistication in thinking all bear on this fact. Adolescents who attend schools which are either relatively homogeneous in nature or which reinforce the values of parents have fewer opportunities for personal growth. As a rule, greater diversity exists in college and university environments than in secondary school settings.

Religion

In a recent survey of some 1,000 13- to 18-year-olds, it was found that 95 percent indicated that they believed in God and 75 percent believed in a personal God (*Religion in America, 1979–1980,* 1980).

With regard to adolescent attendance at church or synagogue, one study showed that only 29 percent of young people between 18 and 29 years of age attend weekly (Jacquet, 1980). This figure is much lower than that for all adults (41 percent) who attend religious services weekly, although we should note that church attendance typically declines during late adolescence (Johnson, Brehke, Stronimen, & Underwagen, 1974). Many religious dropouts return to the church when they begin their own families.

DEVELOPMENTAL TASKS OF ADOLESCENCE AND YOUTH

Based on the work of Robert Havighurst (1972), Arthur Chickering (1969), and Frederick Coons (1970), we have compiled a list of developmental tasks spanning early through late adolescence and youth. The chapter numbers in this book in which these tasks are discussed are given in parentheses.

1. Accepting one's physical attributes and developing one's physical capacities (2)
2. Accepting one's intellectual abilities and developing one's capabilities (3, 9)
3. Becoming aware of one's emotions and learning to understand and accept one's feelings (4)
4. Achieving a sense of identity, including clarifying sex-role identity (5, 6)
5. Becoming emotionally and financially independent from parents (7)
6. Learning to relate comfortably with peers of both sexes (8)
7. Developing moral values of one's own and a philosophy of life (10)
8. Becoming a sexual person and learning to integrate sexual and emotional intimacy (11)
9. Preparing for a meaningful occupation (12)
10. Successfully negotiating hazards in the adolescent experience (alienation, delinquency, drug and alcohol abuse, psychopathology) (13)

Since it is generally agreed that the assumption of adult roles such as marriage or a full-time job marks the movement of an individual from the status of adolescent to young adult, these facets of development are not included in our list of developmental tasks. Still, we realize that, some "early adults" (teenage husbands and wives, for example) may be developmentally more like adolescents than adults. Consequently, some of these adolescent tasks will still be relevant to them. Again, we see that there are not always clear distinctions in moving from one status to another; development, by definition, is a process. Moreover, development appears to proceed in a spiraling fashion rather than in a straight line (Chickering, 1969). Many adults perform adult roles but still struggle with adolescent or preadolescent developmental tasks when confronted with situations or roles they find difficult.

SIGNIFICANT ASPECTS OF ADOLESCENT PERSONALITY DEVELOPMENT

Self-Concept, Self-Esteem, and Identity

Self-concept refers to those aspects a person identifies as "me" or "mine" and usually includes perceptions and feelings about one's body, personal competencies, values, and interests. While some experts (Erikson, for example) see the self-concept as a view of one's total self (all aspects considered together), others (Kenneth Gergen, Morris Rosenberg) feel that each of us has a number of conceptions of ourselves ("I am funny, intelligent, in good physical condition, politically liberal, impatient," etc.). Also, it seems that some components of our self-concept are more important to us than others. In addition, certain situations may call particular aspects of our self-concept to the forefront. For instance, when we are taking an exam, we are more conscious of our views of ourselves as "intelligent."

We would expect that the cognitive changes occurring in adolescence would cause corresponding changes in the ways young people think about themselves, and research findings bear this out. For example, one study showed that verbal descriptions of the self in concrete operational level children contained more concrete references ("I have brown eyes," "I play hockey," "I love school") than formal operational adolescents (Montemayor & Eisen, 1977). The self-descriptions of adolescents contained more interpersonal references ("I have two girl friends," "I like most people I meet") as well as references to personal beliefs and motivations ("I am a political liberal," "I am an agnostic," "I am kind").

Some psychologists suggest that formal operational thinking is the key to the construction of a self-concept, which is seen as a theory about oneself (Okun & Sasfy, 1977). Formal operational thinking permits adolescents to step outside their own frames of reference and to look at themselves relatively objectively. As egocentrism diminishes, they are able to construct more realistic self-concepts.

Self-esteem refers to how we value or feel about ourselves on an overall basis. Typically, psychological tests measure self-esteem in "global" terms, that is, the sense that we consider ourselves "a person of worth" (Rosenberg & Simmons, 1971).

Identity is related to self-concept and self-esteem. Erikson suggests that realistic self-esteem provides the basis for a firm sense of identity. In Erikson's view, the development of a sense of identity implies at least two things: (1) that we have a basic sense of who we are which is relatively consistent over time and (2) that our view of ourself is relatively consistent with others' views about us (1968). Clearly, the relationship between self and others is a significant aspect of identity.

As we have seen, achieving a sense of identity is viewed by many as an essential task in adolescent development. Research suggests that the identity search is more of an issue during late adolescence (Marcia, 1980).

Because self-concept, self-esteem, and identity are integral aspects of adolescent development, we have devoted Chapters 5 and 6 to these topics.

Emotional Development

Emotional development is particularly significant during adolescence for a number of reasons: (1) the normal changes which occur with physical maturation appear to play a significant role with regard to the intensity of some emotions; (2) cognitive changes enable adolescents to think about their feelings and about what they mean; (3) new social roles force adolescents to cope with new situations which can provoke frustration, fear, exhilaration, and other emotional experiences; and (4) adolescents experience a growing sense awareness of their feelings about themselves, their feelings about others, and others' feelings about themselves. In addition, adolescents carry with them a history of particular emotional sensitivities, fears, and strengths developed during childhood. All of these factors influence the experience of emotions during the adolescent period. We might also note that poor nutrition and fatigue, which are common problems during adolescence, can also contribute to emotionality.

Storm and Stress   G. Stanley Hall's assertion that adolescence is a period of storm and stress has been challenged. Findings from a number of longitudinal studies now suggest that emotional and personality development proceed in a stable and continuous fashion (Dusek & Flaherty, 1981). John C. Coleman (1978) has suggested that the typical pattern is one in which different concerns emerge at different times over a period of years rather than all at once, thus permitting the adolescent time and resources to cope with the many changes in an orderly manner (see Figure 4.1a and b). Only in relatively few cases do the nature and number of stresses exceed the adolescent's resources.

Kinds of Emotional Experiences   Emotions are involved in all our experiences and all our experiences are interrelated. They cannot be divided into separate categories, but we can list certain areas of emotional response.

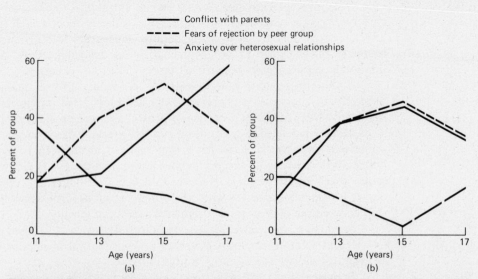

Figure 4.1 Peak ages for the expression of different concerns in **(a)** adolescent males and **(b)** adolescent females. *Source:* Data derived from John C. Coleman (1974). *Relationships in Adolescence.* London and Boston: Routledge & Kegan Paul, Figures 4.2, 5.2, 7.2.

1. Relationship to self (self-esteem, psychological and physical well-being)
2. Relationships with others
3. Attitudes and interests
4. Feeling state at any given time (feeling "good," "bad," etc.)
5. Responses to both familiar and new situations (in academic and social situations, for example)

Adolescents typically experience an increase in the range of their emotional experiences as well as in the depth of their feelings as a result of hormonal and cognitive maturation and exposure to a wider social network. Research indicates that awareness of emotions and expression of feelings in words or behavior increases among college students (Chickering, 1969).

We'll discuss below some of the emotional states which are common among adolescents. Recall, here, the concept of the personal fable as it relates to adolescents' experiences of intensity and uniqueness with regard to their emotions. Also, note that there there are gender differences with regard to the expression of particular emotions: girls are more likely to cry; boys are more likely to express direct anger.

Happiness and joy Adolescents experience euphoria in being alive, the beauty of nature, and the warmth and satisfaction friendships and love can bring.

Love and affection The sense of being loved in childhood appears essential to the development of self-esteem. At adolescence young people begin to move beyond the family for love and affection. In addition, the component of sexuality emerges at adolescence which intensifies and may also confuse the nature of love experiences. For example, it is not uncommon for adolescents to fail to discriminate between sexual attraction, infatuation, and genuine love. Only through experience do we learn to make these distinctions more accurately.

Anger Anger often occurs as a result of frustration, although this is not inevitable. Obviously, a home or school environment which is fraught with frustration is likely to produce anger and resentment. Anger may be directed outward such as in physical assaults on objects or people or in verbal attacks or threats. As adolescents mature, they express their anger more verbally and resort less to physical abuse in keeping with societal expectations. They may engage in vigorous physical activity or work to release emotional tension. They also learn to keep anger "inside"—in which case it may be manifested in moodiness, sulking, or withholding of affection. In a survey among college women (Rice, 1978) it was found that the causes of most anger were the actions of other people (hypocrisy, rudeness, intolerance). Additional causes of anger were treatment by other people (criticism), treatment within the family (favoritism), criticism of or disappointment in self (not doing well on exams when one had studied), and other people's ignoring injustice.

Guilt Guilt arises when individuals feel, think, or do things they have learned to think of as "wrong." Parental attitudes and religious background affect internalized experiences of guilt. One characteristic of adolescence is that it brings young people in contact with a greater variety of ideas, practices, and people than they have heretofore

Adolescents need to learn how to deal effectively with angry feelings.

experienced. Consequently, they are forced to consider values other than those to which they have been exposed at home, at school, and in church. Peers may hold beliefs and engage in behaviors adolescents have been taught are wrong. Yet, it is often a struggle to avoid acting in these ways when status in the peer group is at stake.

Guilt has useful functions in that it offers some internal means of social and personal control. On the other hand, too much guilt can seriously inhibit personal and social development. Usually, through reality testing and reflection, "shoulds" and "oughts" learned early in life can be molded into more appropriate behavioral guidelines so that one becomes less guilt-ridden and more self-directing.

Fear and anxiety   *Fear* is a negative emotional state directed toward a specific object. Intense fears are known as phobias. Fear often causes people to avoid the fear object, for example, getting sick before an exam. Such avoidance may serve to perpetuate the fear and to make it harder and harder to confront the situation. Consequently, the fear may become magnified out of proportion, but by always avoiding the problem, it isn't possible to know this. Girls also express their fears more often than boys. This, too, is no doubt a function of sex-role expectations—the "emotional female" and the "strong, silent male" stereotypes.

Anxiety is the feeling of danger or threat in which the danger cannot be clearly identified. The feeling is not related to a specific object. When we are anxious, we feel generally "on edge" or "jumpy." Anxiety in adolescents may manifest itself in a number of ways—compulsive activity, inappropriate emotional reactions to situations, or in self-righteous dogmatism, among others.

Loneliness   In an average two- or three-week period, over 25 percent of American adults report feeling "painfully lonely," and the rate for adolescents is somewhat higher (Rubin, 1979). Adolescents are likely to be especially subject to feelings of being left out because of their sensitivity about physical appearance and acceptance by their families and peers; egocentrism may heighten feelings of being left out.

It is important to stress that being alone can be experienced as solitude or loneliness, depending on the perceived causes for being alone (Rubinstein, Shaver, & Peplau, 1979). The emphasis American society places on being with others can lead to a fear of being alone and the inability to use "alone time" in a constructive and personally satisfying way. Recall the tendency for some socially withdrawn adolescents to spend considerable time watching television (Hendry & Gillies, 1978). The need for constant companionship is sometimes taken as a symptom of depression in adolescents (Weiner, 1980).

Depressed feelings   Everyone "has the blahs" or "feels down" from time to time. Only when individuals experience feelings of extreme sadness or apathy or when such feelings last for long periods of time are psychologists likely to label such a state "depression." Whether or not adolescents are actually clinically depressed, they can still feel quite bad when their expectations are dashed (not being chosen for a sports team or student government office, not having a date to the dance or breaking off with one's steady, doing poorly in a course). As with other feelings, sadness can be heightened because of adolescent egocentrism. (Clinical depression in adolescence is discussed in Chapter 13.)

Grief   Grief is one of the most difficult emotions human beings must cope with. Children are somewhat shielded from circumstances which cause grief, but adolescents have a broader range of social contacts and a deeper understanding of events and their impacts on themselves and others. Such events as the death of a parent, grandparent, friend, or family pet are common causes of grief reactions among adolescents. Parents' divorce also causes grief. If a close friend moves away or if the adolescent moves away, this can cause feelings of loss and grief.

Regulating Emotions   Learning to be aware of, to understand, and to accept subjective feelings is a significant aspect of personality development during adolescence. Also, young people must learn to negotiate the difficulties inherent in expressing feelings, that is, they must learn when and how to express feelings and what consequences their behavior may have for themselves and others. It takes time and experience to become

Grief is one of the most difficult emotions to experience.

skilled at managing emotions. In the process of learning these skills, it's not uncommon for adolescents to experience mood swings from one extreme to another.

Young people are confronted with two tasks in managing emotions (Chickering, 1969). The first is to loosen lessons of emotional repression learned during childhood. Only after they learn to accept their feelings as legitimate and valuable aspects of their experience can they deal with the second task, that of developing "flexible controls congruent with the self one is and is becoming. . . . Not the controls inherited unwittingly from parents. Not the controls called for by peers or the dominant culture. But controls constructed for oneself, self-control that is truly one's own" (Chickering, 1969, p. 41).

Chickering suggests that emotions related to sexual impulses are probably the most difficult for adolescents to learn to regulate effectively. There are tendencies toward the extremes of sexual gratification or repression and asceticism. It is harder for successful integration to take place so that "sexual behavior becomes a vehicle for expressing complex feelings of affection, nurturance, and respect, and for satisfying a similarly complex network in ourselves" (p. 49).

Stressful Events

Recently, researchers undertook the construction of a scale to measure the events adolescents found stressful and the degree of stress associated with these events (Yeaworth, York, Hussey, Ingle, & Goodwin, 1980). Some 200 white, middle-class, male and female junior and senior high school students were used as subjects. Table 4.1 ranks the events that these adolescents found to be stressful according to the degree of stress associated with them.

They rated events related to death and separation as the most difficult to cope with. Family problems, school problems, and problems with the law (being arrested) also received high ratings. The most commonly experienced events (but not the most stressful) were "hassling with brother or sister" (87 percent), "making new friends" (85 percent), and "hassling with parents" (76 percent). Females reported experiencing only slightly more stressful events than males (9 versus 8).

Another study of adolescent stresses compared black and white, male and female, low-, middle-, and upper-SES, 12- to 14-year-old adolescents (Gad & Johnson, 1980). It was found that black adolescents experienced significantly more stressful events than whites (10 versus 7) and that lower-SES subjects experienced significantly more negative events than higher-SES groups (9 versus 7). Importantly, when SES was controlled, no differences were found in the scores of black and white adolescents.

Other studies have found the following problems to be stressful for adolescents: physical appearance, grades, future schooling, use of free time, relationships with parents, sex-related problems, and peer relationships (Eme, Maisiak, & Goodale, 1979; House, Durfee, & Bryan, 1979).

When stresses are severe or long-lasting, they can negatively affect psychological and physical health. Serious psychological disorders of adolescence will be discussed in Chapter 13.

Table 4.1   ADOLESCENT LIFE CHANGE EVENT SCALE

Rank	Life change event	Life change unit[a]
1	A parent dying	98
2	Brother or sister dying	95
3	Close friend dying	91
4	Parents getting divorced or separated	86
5	Failing one or more subjects in school	86
6	Being arrested by the police	85
7	Flunking a grade in school	84
8	Family member (other than yourself) having trouble with alcohol	79
9	Getting into drugs or alcohol	77
10	Losing a favorite pet	77
11	Parent or relative in your family (other than yourself) getting very sick	77
12	Losing a job	74
13	Breaking up with a close girlfriend or boyfriend	74
14	Quitting school	73
15	Close girlfriend getting pregnant	69
16	Parent losing a job	69
17	Getting badly hurt or sick	64
18	Hassling with parents	64
19	Trouble with teacher or principal	63
20	Having problems with any of the following: acne, overweight, underweight, too tall, too short	63
21	Starting a new school	57
22	Moving to a new home	51
23	Change in physical appearance (braces, glasses)	47
24	Hassling with brother or sister	46
25	Starting menstrual periods (for girls)	45
26	Having someone new move in with your family (grandparent, adopted brother or sister, other)	35
27	Starting a new job	34
28	Mother getting pregnant	31
29	Starting to date	31
30	Making new friends	27
31	Brother or sister getting married	26

[a]Figures rounded to the nearest whole number.

Source: Rosalee C. Yeaworth, Janet York, Maria A. Hussey, Maribeth E. Ingle, and Trena Goodwin (1980). "The Development of an Adolescent Life Change Event Scale." *Adolescence, XV* (57), 91–97. Copyright 1980 by Libra Publishers. Reprinted by permission.

Styles of Coping with Environmental Demands

The complex nature of contemporary American society requires the development of effective coping strategies. While the development of coping styles begins before adolescence, the adolescent period may be critical in the growth of this aspect of personality.

How do adolescents cope with environmental demands? One study (Moriarty & Toussieng, 1976) identified four coping styles among male adolescents: (1) obedient traditionalists, (2) ideological conservatives, (3) cautious modifiers, and (4) passionate renewers. The first two groups comprised 28 percent of the sample and were characterized as *censors,* that is, individuals who cope by limiting sensory experiences and rejecting information that contradicted their traditional beliefs. The other two groups (77 percent) were described as *sensers,* individuals who cope by being receptive to the lessons of experience and even by seeking out new experiences that might change their values.

Adolescents in this study were observed to undergo a brief period of rebelliousness which lasted from puberty to about age 14 or 15. After that point coping styles became quite influential in the adolescents' psychological and social development. Censors tried to discover what adult society found acceptable and tended to adopt these values as their own beliefs. In this process they often rejected the companionship of their peers and discounted school experiences that seemed to contradict their beliefs. Sensers, on the other hand, developed a long-term coping strategy of interacting with others, experimenting, and questioning. Their beliefs were products of their attempts to integrate these ideas and experiences into a set of personally acceptable values that remained open to change in the future.

In a review of research on adolescent coping styles, it was suggested that more studies are needed in this area, especially those using female subjects (Newman, 1979). Nonetheless, it does appear that the adolescent period is important in this regard and has important consequences for further development throughout adulthood. Barbara Newman summarized the implications of these studies to date:

> First, adolescence may well be a period for the consolidation of one's coping style. Second, the articulation of a lifestyle in young adulthood appears to be heavily

Some adolescents cope with new societal demands by becoming more open to new ideas and experiences.

dependent on competences, aspirations, and life choices developed in adolescence. Third, the extent to which maturation continues through adulthood may reflect the ability to experiment and to encounter conflict in adolescence. (1979, p. 260)

Changes in Interests

Psychologists study the topic of adolescents' interests for a number of reasons. For one thing, this information gives us some clues as to what adolescents are like. Also, we want to know if adolescents' interests are more similar to those of children or adults. If we see changes in interests, we want to know when they occur. In addition, psychologists want to know whether the development of adolescents' interests is consistent with particular theories of development. For instance, psychoanalytic theory would predict an increase in sex-related interests in early adolescence.

A comprehensive survey of adolescent interests studied 542 white, middle-class, male and female students in grades 5 through 12 (Dusek, Kermis, & Monge, 1979). Table 4.2 lists interest topics with the average rank for each according to grade level. (Male and female rankings are grouped together so no sex differences are evident in the table.)

The authors reported several findings from this study, most of which can be seen from the data in Table 4.2. First, they suggested that the ninth grade appears to be an important transition period for adolescent interests. This transition occurs in the following categories: (1) arts, crafts, and sports (drops to a lower rank at tenth grade), (2) understanding other people (increases in rank at eighth grade), and (3) future work (increases at ninth grade). They also noted that a number of topics received consistently low rankings across all grade levels: (1) philosophy and religion, (2) venereal disease, (3) teachers and school, and (4) birth control. (The fact of relatively low interest in the topics of venereal disease and birth control led Jerome Dusek and his colleagues to feel

Table 4.2   AVERAGE RANKING[a] OF 14 INTEREST TOPICS AT EACH GRADE LEVEL

Topic	5	6	7	8	9	10	11	12
Arts, crafts, and sports	3.0	3.8	5.0	4.8	4.6	6.0	6.7	8.3
Drugs	6.0	7.4	6.7	6.5	9.3	9.7	7.3	8.7
Future work	6.1	7.6	6.5	6.5	4.9	4.0	5.2	5.1
Ecology	6.3	6.5	5.5	7.2	6.7	8.5	7.2	6.9
Science and math	6.4	6.5	6.3	8.0	8.0	7.1	7.4	7.7
Medicine and health	6.4	6.4	5.8	8.2	7.0	6.6	6.2	6.3
Understanding other people	7.4	7.2	6.7	5.8	5.7	4.7	5.1	6.7
Birth control	8.5	9.8	9.9	9.4	10.1	10.7	7.9	7.8
Teachers and school	8.6	9.6	8.3	9.5	9.1	10.3	10.0	9.7
Venereal disease	8.8	9.0	9.9	8.6	9.5	10.6	9.8	9.0
Philosophy and religion	9.1	10.2	9.0	10.3	10.4	9.2	10.1	8.4
Sexual relations and reproduction	9.3	7.4	8.7	7.5	8.6	8.4	7.6	7.2
Love and marriage	9.4	6.9	9.1	6.8	6.2	6.4	7.0	6.3
Dating and going steady	9.3	6.7	7.7	6.0	7.1	7.8	8.1	7.0

[a]Ranks ranged from 1 through 14. The lower the number, the higher the rank (interest).
Source: Adapted from Jerome B. Dusek, Marguerite D. Kermis, and Rolf H. Monge (1979). "The Hierarchy of Adolescent Interests: A Social-Cognitive Approach." *Genetic Psychology Monographs, 100,* 41–72. Copyright 1979 by The Journal Press. Adapted by permission.

pessimistic about lowering the current epidemic rates of venereal disease and premarital pregnancy among adolescents.)

The authors found significant sex differences in the ratings of some topics (note that ratings are different from rankings). When females were asked to rate their level of interest in a topic on a 7-point scale, their ratings were found to be significantly higher than males' in the following areas: (1) love and marriage (F = 5.2, M = 4.2), (2) teachers and school (F = 3.7, M = 3.4), (3) birth control (F = 4.2, M = 3.4), (4) understanding other people (F = 5.8, M = 4.6), (5) venereal disease (F = 4.3, M = 3.7), and (6) dating and going steady (F = 4.9, M = 4.4). Males' average ratings were found to be significantly higher than females' for the following topics: (1) science and math (M = 4.8, F = 3.9) and (2) arts, crafts, and sports (M = 5.8, F = 5.4). The authors commented that the sex differences found on the topics of sexual relations and reproduction, birth control, and love and marriage do not appear to reflect as much change in the attitudes of the sexes as might be expected from the current focus on human liberation issues.

The authors also noted similarities between their findings and some of Havighurst's developmental tasks for adolescents. In addition, they suggested that changes in interests are related to changes in cognitive abilities which occur during adolescence.

We would expect that adolescents' interests are also governed by cultural and social expectations. The sex differences found by Dusek and his co-workers are consistent with current sex-role expectations in the United States. Additional research with regard to class differences in adolescents' interests would also be useful as a means of studying the impact of societal expectations on this aspect of development.

While biological changes are probably also related to some of the changes in adolescents' interests, this relationship has not been directly studied. Some of the findings listed in Table 4.2 suggest that physical changes may play some role in adolescents' interests. For instance, we can see increases in the rank of the topics of sexual relationships and reproduction and dating and going steady from fifth grade (both ranked 9.3) to sixth grade (7.4 and 6.9, respectively). While we cannot conclude from these data that physical factors are the cause of these changes in interests, the idea is plausible. Additional research would be helpful in clarifying this issue.

SUMMARY

Socialization refers to the complex process of learning how to become a member of a particular society. The socialization process in adolescence is of special importance because young people are moving toward mature physical, intellectual, and emotional functioning and are therefore capable of learning skills which will prepare them to assume responsible adult roles in society. Much of this development occurs in the sphere of personality.

Not all societies have a separate stage of adolescence as we know it. The nature of the adolescent period is determined by the continuity between the roles of children and adults, the rapidity of social change, and the complexity of a particular culture. Benedict characterized American culture as relatively discontinuous. Moreover, the length of the transition period between childhood and adolescence is long and there are no formalized rituals (puberty rites) which signify the attainment of adult status. These factors make adolescence more stressful here than in some other cultures.

Lewin characterized adolescents as holding "marginal man" (person) status because they are neither children nor adults. This role confusion, he felt, led to corresponding emotional instability and a tendency to judge harshly lower-status peers.

A number of socializing agents are important in the adolescent period: parents, media, peers, schools, and religion. Depending on the nature of the interactions between these agents and adolescents, development can be enhanced or thwarted.

The author has integrated the ideas of Havighurst, Chickering, and Coons into a list of 10 developmental tasks for adolescents and youth.

A number of significant developments take place in personality during adolescence. They include changes in self-concept, self-esteem, and identity, emotional maturation, development of coping styles, and changes in interests.

GLOSSARY

cofigurative culture (Mead)   Societies characterized by moderate social change in which youth learn from their peers as well as their elders.

defense mechanism (Freud)   Unconscious reaction to psychological threats to the ego.

developmental tasks (Havighurst)   Attitudes and skills which are best learned at particular stages of development.

discontinuous culture   A culture in which children are taught attitudes and behaviors which they must unlearn to be successful adults.

identity (Erikson)   A stable sense of oneself; the developmental task of adolescence.

marginal man status (Lewin)   Characterization of adolescents based on the fact that they have no designated social role, being neither children nor adults.

prefigurative culture (Mead)   Societies characterized by rapid social change in which young people must learn many things on their own without guidance from adults.

postfigurative culture (Mead)   Societies characterized by relatively little social change in which young people learn from adults.

puberty rites   Formal initiation ceremonies which mark the passage from childhood to adult status; characteristic of tribal societies.

self-concept   An individual's perception of his or her qualities, competencies, etc.

self-esteem   The value placed on oneself; self-worth.

socialization   The process by which a culture imparts socially accepted standards, values, and behaviors to its members.

two

DEVELOPMENTAL ISSUES IN ADOLESCENCE

Chapter 5 Outline

Self-Concept and Identity Development

Adolescents face the challenge of coping with physical, sexual, cognitive, and emotional changes. Their more sophisticated cognitive skills mean that they have much greater flexibility and freedom of thought. This new ability to see things from a broader perspective affects their religious and political beliefs and their evaluations of current social issues as well as their views of themselves. The more visible physical changes, including sexual maturation, provide additional "food" for their introspective musings.

In addition to these significant developments, adolescents in more complex societies must also cope with changing and conflicting societal expectations about appropriate roles and behaviors as they grow toward adulthood. This task is made harder because they lack the security of trust in themselves which repeated testing in the "real world" eventually can bring. Adolescents, then, must deal with both internal changes and external demands.

The achievement of a stable sense of self in a changing society can be difficult. Nonetheless, this is precisely what adolescents need to achieve in order to function effectively in the world. Many psychologists feel that the achievement of a sense of identity is the critical developmental task confronting adolescents.

This chapter concerns the nature and development of the self-concept, self-esteem, and identity during adolescence.

SELF-CONCEPT AND SELF-ESTEEM

Significance of Self-Concept and Self-Esteem

For the purposes of discussing the *self-concept,* we have chosen to define it as those aspects of ourselves which we can consciously identify as "me"—physical attributes, personal characteristics, skills, values, hopes. *Self-esteem* is a related term which we shall define as the value we place on our self-concept and is usually synonymous with feelings of self-worth. Although self-esteem and self-concept are modifiable, they are often difficult to change without concerted effort.

The self-concept has three basic functions: (1) to optimize the pleasure/pain balance of the individual over the course of a lifetime, (2) to facilitate the maintenance of self-esteem, and (3) to organize the data of experience in a manner that can be coped with effectively (Epstein, 1973).

Self-concept and self-esteem appear to play critical roles in general psychological adjustment among adolescents (Offer, Ostrove, & Howard, 1977). Also, there appears to be a positive relationship between self-acceptance and the acceptance of others (R. C. Wylie, 1957).

The self-concept seems to serve as a selective filtering mechanism through which we become sensitized to information which is consistent with our expectations of ourselves and of others in relation to us. It's important to note that although our perceptions of ourselves and others may *feel* accurate, they are not necessarily always valid.

The "power" of self-esteem is illustrated in the following study comparing the self-perceptions of advantaged and disadvantaged youth (Soares & Soares, 1970). Interestingly, the authors found that the disadvantaged adolescents had significantly higher self-concepts than their peers. Even more interesting, however, were the findings from

Self-esteem is an important component of psychological development.

the second part of the study which compared the adolescents' beliefs of their teachers' evaluations of them to their teachers' actual perceptions of them. The students believed their teachers' perceptions to be similar to their self-perceptions: disadvantaged students believed that their teachers looked on them favorably, while the advantaged students believed they were looked on unfavorably. In fact, the teachers' scores indicated that they felt much more negatively toward the disadvantaged students. The teachers' ratings aside, it seemed that the students' self-perceptions were strong determining factors in their perceptions of others' views of themselves. This finding led the authors to suggest that "persons see what they want to see—'selective perception,' perhaps" (1970, p. 457). In a similar fashion, we all develop beliefs which are more or less valid, relatively firmly established, and which influence the ways in which we view ourselves and the social world.

While it is not yet clear exactly how these perceptual sets develop (parental-child interactions seem most important), self-perceptions have considerable influence in our lives. As Kenneth Gergen has aptly stated, "In the final analysis, one's personal conduct is based upon one's conception of 'reality' rather than upon reality itself" (1971, p. viii). Indeed, in some cases beliefs can make the difference between whether individuals choose to live or not.

Recall our earlier mention of the fact that self-perceptions are not usually easily changed. One of the reasons for this is that they have developed over a long period of time and, like most long-standing habits, are difficult to modify. Moreover, although these perceptions may not be valid, they are familiar and therefore provide a basis for security and comfort. Also, it is hard to see inaccuracies when the perception one has is all one has ever known. Unless we hear consistently from others whom we respect and trust that our views are "off," it is unlikely that we will ever realize it or be willing to work toward establishing more accurate perceptions. Parents, teachers, and others who work with children and adolescents need to be aware of the critical roles they play in the development of self-concept and self-esteem.

Developmental Trends in Self-Concept and Self-Esteem

Content of Self-Concept   Four independent dimensions on which adolescents evaluate themselves have been identified: achievement/leadership, congeniality/sociability, adjustment, and masculinity/femininity (Monge, 1973). These dimensions remain relatively stable in both boys and girls from fifth through twelfth grades.

We have already noted that adolescents' self-perceptions are more abstract than those of children. Examples demonstrating this development are given in Table 5.1. Robert Bernstein (1980) found that, compared to 10- and 15-year-olds, 20-year-olds show greater differentiation in their self-concepts in that they are able to give a significantly greater number of causes for their behavior. This same study also found that the oldest group was significantly more able to integrate the various aspects of their self-concepts into a comprehensive system.

Importantly, while significant differences appeared between the 15- and 20-year-olds on these factors, no such differences were found between the 10- and 15-year-olds, suggesting that important cognitive changes occur after age 15. These findings are consistent with others that suggest that the ability to engage in abstract thinking

Table 5.1 DEVELOPMENT OF MORE ABSTRACT SELF-PERCEPTIONS WITH INCREASING AGE

Subject	Description of self
9-year-old boy	My name is Bruce C. I have brown eyes. I have brown hair. I have brown eyebrows. I'm nine years old. I LOVE! Sports. I have seven people in my family. I have great! eye site. I have lots! of friends. I live on 1923 Pinecrest Dr. I'm going on 10 in September. I'm a boy. I have a uncle that is almost 7 feet tall. My school is Pinecrest. My teacher is Mrs. V. I play Hockey! I am almost the smartest boy in the class. I LOVE! food. I love fresh air. I LOVE School.
11½-year-old girl	My name is A. I'm a human being. I'm a girl. I'm a truthful person. I'm not pretty. I do so-so in my studies. I'm a very good cellist. I'm a very good pianist. I'm a little bit tall for my age. I like several boys. I like several girls. I'm old-fashioned. I play tennis. I am a *very* good swimmer. I try to be helpful. I'm always ready to be friends with anybody. I'm not well-liked by some girls and boys. I don't know if I'm liked by boys or not.
17-year-old girl	I am a human being. I am a girl. I am an individual. I don't know who I am. I am a Pisces. I am a moody person. I am an indecisive person. I am an ambitious person. I am a very curious person. I am not an individual. I am a loner. I am an American (God help me). I am a Democrat. I am a liberal person. I am a radical. I am a conservative. I am a pseudoliberal. I am an atheist. I am not a classifiable person (i.e., I don't want to be).

Source: Descriptions taken from Raymond D. Montemayor and Marvin Eisen (1977). "The Development of Self-Conceptions from Childhood to Adolescence," *Developmental Psychology, 13,* 314–319.

(formal operational thought) plays a critical role in self-concept development (Okun & Sasfy, 1977).

Stability of the Self-Concept and Self-Esteem   Since young adolescents are confronted with physical and cognitive changes, we might expect that disturbances in self-image would be more common among this group than among children or older adolescents (recall the storm and stress argument here). A number of studies have supported this view (S. T. Hauser, 1971; Simmons, Rosenberg, & Rosenberg, 1973; Soares & Soares, 1971). For example, a cross-sectional study of urban school children in third through twelfth grades found that 12- and 13-year-olds were more depressed and more self-conscious, had slightly lower self-esteem, as well as more doubts that their parents, teachers, and peers of the same sex viewed them favorably (Simmons, Rosenberg, & Rosenberg, 1973).

On the other hand, other studies provide evidence that self-concept and self-esteem develop in a continuous fashion during adolescence (Bandura, 1964; J.C. Coleman, 1978; Constantinople, 1969; Dusek & Flaherty, 1981; Offer, 1969; Protinsky & Farrier, 1980). In a three-year combined longitudinal and cross-sectional study, Jerome Dusek and John Flaherty (1981) assessed the self-concepts of some 1600 male and female, suburban adolescents from upper-, middle-, and lower-SES families in grades 5 through 12. As did Rolf Monge (1973), they found that individuals evaluated themselves on the four dimensions of achievement/leadership, congeniality/sociability, adjustment, and masculinity/femininity.

Among other things, the investigators were interested in how stable subjects' self-concepts were from middle school through high school. They found that the dimensions of the self-concepts of the younger subjects were quite similar to those of the older subjects. Also, individuals used the same dimensions to describe themselves over a number of years, although they rated themselves differently from time to time.

Dusek and Flaherty also found consistent sex differences each year on three of the four dimensions: Males scored higher than females on the achievement/leadership and masculinity/femininity factors; females scored higher than males on the congeniality/sociability factor. The sexes appear to use the same dimensions in self-evaluation, but differ in terms of the importance of three of these dimensions. This fact is consistent with sex-role expectations and earlier research, which suggests that a central issue in identity development is autonomy for males and interpersonal relationships for females (Douvan & Adelson, 1969). On the basis of their study, Dusek and Flaherty concluded that "one simply cannot consider self-concept without simultaneously considering gender" (p. 41).

On the general question of self-concept stability, Dusek and Flaherty concluded that while there may be some changes in self-concept during adolescence, they appear to take place in a gradual and orderly manner. These findings contradict the persistent notions that adolescence is characterized by storm and stress and "identity crisis."

Factors in the Development of Self-Esteem

Parental Relationships Self-esteem is primarily influenced by those who are important to us and with whom we spend most of our time. Accordingly, parents of children and adolescents are usually the most influential figures. Since self-esteem develops over many years, adolescents' self-regard is dependent not only on the nature of current parent-adolescent interactions, but on earlier interactions as well. Several studies have found that school-age children with high self-esteem had parents who also had high self-esteem (Baumrind, 1975; Coopersmith, 1967). Moreover, parents of these children set firm limits and explained their reasons for doing so. At the same time, they were likely to be warm and accepting toward their children. A study of adolescents found a positive relationship between parental support and adolescents' self-concept, but no relationship between parental control and self-concept (Gecas, 1971).

Minority Group Status Because self-esteem develops in a social context, one's status in a given group would seem to be an important factor in the development of self-concept and self-esteem. In line with this thinking, Morris Rosenberg (1975, 1979) has asserted that one of the most critical determinants in the development of adolescent self-esteem is the extent to which an adolescent is similar to others in his or her social environment. If an adolescent lives in a dissonant environment (is not like others in the group and compares negatively with them), it would be expected that he or she would suffer from lowered self-esteem.

Because of the existence of racial and ethnic prejudices in the United States, it has generally been assumed and sometimes proven that minority group members have lower self-esteem than whites. While some studies have shown that black adolescents generally have had lower self-esteem than white American adolescents (Pierce, 1968; Proshansky & Newton, 1968), there is a good deal of more recent evidence to the contrary (Healey & DeBlassie, 1974; Rosenberg, 1979; Rosenberg & Simmons, 1972; Simmons, Brown, Bush, & Blyth, 1978). A review of studies on the self-concepts of Mexican-Americans reported that inconsistencies in the results of studies and methodological problems made drawing conclusions difficult (Guzman, 1976). A similar situation exists with regard to Puerto Rican adolescents (Rosenberg, 1979). Not enough studies have been done with American Indian and Asian-American adolescents to warrant any definitive statements.

We want to emphasize that not all studies of racial and ethnic minority adolescents have shown a negative pattern of results. Recall the study on the self/teacher perceptions of advantaged and disadvantaged adolescents (Soares & Soares, 1971). The disadvantaged group consisted of over 50 percent black and Puerto Rican youths and the advantaged group was 75 percent white. Still, the disadvantaged youth had higher self-esteem than did the advantaged group. In another study no differences in the feelings of self-worth between Mexican-American and Anglo adolescents were found (Carter, 1968). Gary Healey and Richard DeBlassie (1974) found both Mexican-American and black adolescents to be higher on self-satisfaction than Anglos, although they suggested that the scores of the non-Anglos may have been artificially inflated because of the higher defensiveness (measured on another scale) of these two groups. Or, the authors speculated that the self-satisfaction of the blacks and Mexican-Americans may, in fact, have been higher due to the adolescents' strong identification with the norms of their own ethnic groups.

An interesting question here is why minority group members often appear to have as good and sometimes higher self-esteem than others. Social scientists have logically assumed that minority group members must have low self-esteem because they are looked down on by others, because they internalize society's negative attitudes about them, and because they don't compare favorably with the prestigious majority on socially valued criteria (Rosenberg, 1979). While these principles are important determinants of self-esteem, they appear to have led to false conclusions about minority group status and self-esteem. Rosenberg suggests that this paradox exists because social scientists have falsely assumed that the majority group is the dominant reference group to whom minority group members compare themselves on a day-to-day basis. Instead, it appears that minority group members compare themselves to members of their *own* group and therefore generally feel good about themselves. In those cases when blacks do use whites as a comparison group and do compare unfavorably in terms of SES or academic performance, they do experience lowered self-esteem (Rosenberg, 1979). But, research findings suggest that this does not appear to be the typical experience for most minority group members.

Another answer to this question may lie in the nature of the parent-child relationship. For example, it has generally been found that the self-esteem of Jewish adolescents is much higher than that of either Catholic or Protestant youths. Rosenberg (1965, 1975) suggests that this is true because of the high self-esteem of Jewish parents and the interest which Jewish parents typically take in their children.

Gender Differences

In their comprehensive review of sex differences, Eleanor Maccoby and Carol Jacklin concluded that "the similarity of the two sexes in self-esteem is remarkably uniform through college age" (1974, p. 153). Although data are sparse for postadolescent subjects, some evidence suggests that women's self-esteem may diminish with age. For example, one study of the same male and female subjects at 18 and 26 years of age found that women showed an apparent decrease in abilities to master life problems and cope with emotional issues, whereas men showed increases in those areas over the eight-year period (Nawas, 1971). Other studies suggest that this is less likely to be the case where women have a career role in addition to that of wife and mother (Birnbaum, 1975; L. W. Hoffman, 1972).

Despite a lack of clear-cut sex differences with regard to global self-esteem, there is considerable evidence that girls and women, on the average, lack confidence in their abilities in specific achievement situations, whereas boys and men, on the average, do not (Hyde & Rosenberg, 1980; Lenney, 1977). That is, compared to males, females have lower expectations regarding their performance and lower evaluations of their own abilities and actual performance in certain situations. Girls and women show less self-confidence (1) if they are led to think that the task they have been asked to perform is not an appropriate one for females, (2) if they are given ambiguous feedback about the level of their performance, or (3) if they work with others and expect their performance to be compared with that of others rather than working alone (Lenney, 1977).

These findings are important because there is evidence that people who approach tasks with low expectations of success are less likely to perform as well as individuals with higher expectations (Feather, 1969). Ellen Lenney has concluded that lowered expectations among females result in "a most effective mechanism of self-discouragement" (1977, p. 2).

There is also evidence that sex differences in some aspects of personality work to lower women's self-confidence. Take, for example, the personality variable of "locus of control" which distinguishes between "externalizers" (people who feel that events which affect them are due to chance or luck) and "internalizers" (those who feel that they can control their lives through their own actions) (Rotter, 1966). Research suggests that by late adolescence, women tend to be externalizers, due, no doubt, to differences in sex-role expectations and socialization (Maccoby & Jacklin, 1974). This is true even for college women, whom we might expect to be internalizers.

It is possible that this picture is only partially correct for several studies have shown that males are overconfident (rather than positive and accurate) in their self-estimations (Berg & Hyde, 1976; Eagly & Whitehead, 1972). For example, one study measured subjects' actual as well as estimated performance to ascertain the accuracy of the performance estimates of males and females. It was shown that males tended to overestimate their performance, while females underestimated theirs.

This finding has much different implications than the one that females are less confident than males. Here we are reminded of Carol Gilligan's (1982) warning about the misunderstandings that can develop when male behavior and experience are taken as the standard for all human behavior and one against which female behavior should be evaluated.

In this context Maccoby & Jacklin (1974) have suggested that the components of self-esteem may vary for females and males, with females investing more of their identity in social competence and males in status and power. They also have suggested that because individuals are more likely to be vulnerable to self-doubt in areas which are highly valued—even though these differ for males and females—there is no reason to expect any overall difference in self-satisfaction between the sexes.

We will reconsider sex-role issues as they influence the nature and development of identity in Chapter 6.

Cross-Cultural Findings

Relatively little cross-cultural research has been done on the self-esteem of adolescents. One such study compared young adolescents (13 to 15 years) from three different cultures: the United States, Australia, and Ireland (Offer et al., 1977). It was found that American adolescents had the highest self-esteem, followed by Australians, and then Irish. The same study compared the self-esteem of older adolescents (16 to 19 years) in the United States, Ireland, and Israel. American adolescents scored highest again, followed by Israeli and Irish adolescents (with negligible difference between the two).

A second investigation compared the self-esteem of Indian adolescent middle-class boys and girls from 14 to 18 years of age with the findings of the above study (Agrawal, 1978). The author concluded that Indian adolescents had significantly lower self-esteem than American or Australian adolescents, but significantly higher self-esteem than Irish adolescents.

While it is tempting to conclude that American adolescents have the highest self-esteem compared to adolescents in these three other cultures, the researchers remind us that the instrument they used was constructed and validated in the United States and that there is no guarantee that it has comparable validity in other cultures (even in other English-speaking countries). These results must be viewed as tentative. However, they do represent the beginnings of efforts to make useful cross-cultural comparisons of adolescent personality development.

IDENTITY

What Is It?

Erik Erikson (who contributed the concept of identity) defines identity as having a relatively stable sense of our own uniqueness; that is, in spite of changing behaviors, thoughts, and feelings, we are "familiar" to ourselves in a basic way. In addition, he says, this sense of "who we are" must be pretty consistent with the ways in which other people view us. This fact emphasizes Erikson's belief in the important relationship between self and society.

Carol Guardo and Janis Bohan (1971) have suggested that there are at least four basic dimensions to an individual's sense of identity: (1) humanity, the sense that one is a human being, (2) sexuality, one's feeling of maleness or femaleness, (3) individuality, the recognition that one is special and unique, and (4) continuity, awareness that one is essentially the same person day after day. Thus, developing a sense of identity requires that an individual come to see "that he [she] is one being with a unique identity who has been, is, and will be a male (or female) human person separate from and entirely like no other" (p. 1911).

Erikson saw adolescence as the developmental stage during which a sense of identity must be achieved. Moreover, he conceptualized identity achievement as a single stage of development. On the other hand Barbara and Philip Newman (1976) concluded that adolescence might more appropriately be seen as two separate periods of psychosocial development. They feel that adolescents first must develop a sense of *group identity* with their peers before they can move on to the formation of a unique *personal identity.* The first period extends from the onset of puberty to about age 18 and is characterized by "rapid physical changes and a heightened sensitivity to peer approval. We have called the psychosocial crisis of this period group identity versus alienation" (p. 265). The second period begins at about age 18 and continues to about age 21 or 22. "This stage is characterized by the attainment of autonomy from the family and the development of a sense of personal identity. We have called the psychosocial crisis of this period individual identity versus role diffusion" (p. 265).

In the context of group and personal identity, it has been suggested that role taking—the ability to understand other people and the world in general from other people's points of view—is a critical component of identity formation (Enright & Deist, 1979). The achievement of identity allows the individual to see himself or herself as having both a feeling of solidarity with societal groups (a sense of belonging) and a

Adolescents need to feel that they are accepted members of a social group before they can develop a sense of personal identity.

feeling of individuality (a sense of uniqueness). In order to attain these feelings, the adolescent must engage in social role-taking and this, in turn, seems to require the development of formal operational thought.

According to James Marcia (1976b), ego identity may be viewed on three levels. First, a sense of identity depends on an individual's ability to integrate parental expectations into a relatively congruent sense of self. Even though much of this process is unconscious, the important issue is the *selective creating of one's self,* not the unquestioning assumption of roles and beliefs designated by parents and society. Second, a sense of identity gives the individual the ability to perceive herself or himself as an ongoing entity—a being who has a past, present, and future, all of which feel connected. Third, a sense of identity is manifested in particular social behaviors. For males, these appear to be career and ideological commitments. For females, the issue is more complex, as we shall see in Chapter 6, but relationships seem to be particularly important.

Issues in Identity Achievement

Identity Crisis   A problem with the term *identity crisis* is that it implies that the process of identity achievement is traumatic. Erikson uses the word *crisis* in its sense of "a necessary turning point . . . when development must move one way or another, marshalling resources of growth, recovery, and further differentiation" (1968, p. 16). Thus the identity crisis is seen as a normative decision-making period, not a sudden, out of the ordinary, or necessarily troublesome or intense event. Recent research seems to support the idea that most adolescents have sufficient ego strength to cope relatively well with identity issues (J. C. Coleman, 1978; Dusek & Flaherty, 1981).

Resolving the Identity Crisis   In Erikson's outline of the life-long development of the ego, the psychosocial crisis facing adolescents is that of *identity versus identity diffusion.* (Identity diffusion is typically experienced as not knowing who we are in relation to society or being unable to maintain a relatively stable idea of who we are and want to be.) From this description, it might seem that the resolution of the identity versus identity diffusion crisis must be an either-or solution. A more accurate understanding, however, is given by Marcia: "The ideal resolution of any of the psychosocial crises involves the individual's particular style of achieving a kind of *creative tension* between the polar alternatives, with an emphasis on the more positive pole" (1976b, p. 6).

Another misconception about identity, according to Marcia, is that it must be achieved during adolescence. Clearly, the performance of adult roles is easier if developmental tasks such as identity achievement are successfully negotiated during adolescence. Nonetheless, there is no psychological law which says that if these issues are not resolved by a certain age, they can never be resolved successfully. It seems that individuals past the adolescent years are often able to choose experiences, friends, and lovers who facilitate growth in areas where greater competency is needed. Psychotherapy can also provide this opportunity. The potential for growth seems always to be present, even though sometimes difficult, and individuals may choose, or not, to take advantage of this fact.

Process of Identity Formation

Identity formation has its roots in childhood experiences and identifications and, ideally, continues to develop throughout adulthood. As we have seen, Erikson views adolescence as a period which provides a *psychosocial moratorium,* a time-out before adult responsibilities to be used to answer such questions as "Who am I?" and "What do I want to do with my life?" Others agree with Erikson in this regard:

> Adolescence is . . . a time for examination and testing of self, parents, and society. If all goes well between the adolescent and his elders, the emergent adult knows who he is, who he is not; and he has made differentiated, informed commitments to some aspects of his society and selected those causes which he will continue to support. (Block, Haan, & Smith, 1973, p. 311)

Identity is more likely to be a concern in late adolescence than in early adolescence (Archer, 1982; Marcia, 1980; Meilman, 1979; Newman & Newman, 1976). This later onset of the identity quest is undoubtedly related to the fact that younger adolescents are just beginning to be able to view the world and themselves abstractly. Moreover, in early adolescence significant physical changes are taking place which cause considerable concern about body image. Peer acceptance is likely to be a more important issue for 13- to 16-year-olds (J. C. Coleman, 1978; Costanzo & Shaw, 1966). The achievement of a stable identity is contingent on physical and sexual maturity, competence in abstract thought, and emotional stability. In addition, there needs to be some

The process of identity formation requires adolescents to wrestle with the question "Who am I?"

degree of freedom from the constraining influences of parents and peers. These conditions are more likely to be met in later adolescence.

In this process of unfolding identity, adolescents' task is to integrate their past identifications and future aspirations in such a way as to feel good about themselves and their chances for future success. Erikson theorized that once individuals had achieved a sense of identity, they would move on to the task of young adulthood—that of achieving emotional intimacy versus isolation.

Several studies support this idea, but only for males (Marcia, 1976a; Orlofsky, Marcia, & Lesser, 1973). In females, the issue of intimacy appears to be intertwined in identity development (Hodgson & Fischer, 1979; Josselson, Greenberger & McConochie, 1977; Marcia, 1980). The finding of such sex differences is consistent with Erikson's belief that there are sex differences in the "focus" of identity (which he believes are strongly influenced by the anatomical differences between the sexes). A male establishes who he is in the context of career and achievement, whereas a female establishes who she is in the context of relationships with others. Still, Erikson made no specific references about how these sex differences influence the intimacy-isolation crisis (or other crises in life-span development). We are left, therefore, with the impression that his theory probably best describes the nature and sequence of *male* development. A considerable amount of research needs to be done with female subjects before we have a clear sense of female psychological development.

Identity Statuses

For Marcia, achieving a sense of identity means that an adolescent has made commitments to a vocational goal and to a political and personal ideology. (Note that this conceptualization best characterizes male identity issues.) Marcia is not suggesting that any particular religion (or lack thereof) or particular political view is preferable. Rather, it is the *process* of decision-making and the *commitment* which follows from the process which are the important things, not the particular *content* of the commitment.

Some later studies on identity have expanded Erikson's and Marcia's work by including questions on sexuality and religion (Schenkel & Marcia, 1972; Waterman & Nevid, 1977) as well as on friendships, dating, and sex roles (Grotevant, Thorbecke, & Meyer, 1982). Since the findings of this research take us into gender differences with respect to identity, we will postpone the discussion of these studies until the next chapter.

Marcia has described four states college students may encounter in achieving identity. These are not stages that adolescents pass through, but statuses that characterize an adolescent's identity orientation at a particular time. It is possible that a given adolescent may never be in some of the statuses, including that of identity achievement. The four statuses are briefly described below and are summarized in Table 5.2.

Identity Foreclosure   For some youth, there appears to be no struggle for identity. Adolescents in the foreclosure status have unquestioningly accepted and adopted the expectations of significant others (usually parents) rather than going through the process of questioning and of evolving their own beliefs and vocational choices. An

Table 5.2 MARCIA'S IDENTITY STATUSES

Identity status	Characteristics	Commitment to ideology and vocation?	Role of crisis in identity achievement
Foreclosure	Adoption of parental or societal values	Yes	No independent decision making, crisis bypassed
Moratorium	Active struggling for sense of identity	No	In process of decision making, in state of crisis (which may lead to psychological difficulties in a few adolescents)
Diffusion	Absence of struggling for identity or questioning of values, with no particular concern about this	No	No current decision making, not in state of crisis (although crisis may have been experienced in past)
Achievement	Successful attainment of a sense of identity	Yes	Successful decision making, passage through crisis

adolescent (or adult) who considers himself or herself a Democrat because his or her parents are Democrats would be an example of an adolescent in the foreclosure status. In the words of Edgar Friedenberg in *The Vanishing Adolescent,* "they merely undergo puberty and simulate maturity" (1959, p. 17).

Identity diffusion and alienation are more often discussed as adolescent problems than identity foreclosure. However, recent events (My Lai and Watergate, for example) suggest that the topic of identity foreclosure ought not to be dismissed too quickly. It seems that we could reasonably question whether large numbers of American adults have wrestled seriously with some of the important questions of identity. While a full-blown crisis may not be necessary for identity formation, it seems unlikely that independent thinking and informed commitment can take place without some painful attention to the questions of what we believe in and how our lives reflect these beliefs. The implications of this lack of self-searching are important for individuals and for society as a whole:

> Some societies and some parents cannot afford, and will not allow, the scrutiny involved in establishing fidelity. Some adolescents cannot pose the questions, protecting themselves with the shared code of peer group . . . conformity. . . . Young people who cannot manage this difficult task constructively . . . not only foreclose their own potentialities for growth; they also deprive society of one of its major sources of creative change: the push from each new generation to make society more responsive to its needs. (Block et al., 1973, pp. 311–312)

Moratorium Youth in the process of wrestling with self-definition are classified as being in the moratorium status. These adolescents engage in a variety of identity experiments—trying on different roles, beliefs, and behaviors—as part of the process of evolving a personally satisfying identity. Most move on to the identity achievement status, but some drift into the status of identity diffusion.

Adolescence is a time for "identity experiments"—trying out different roles, beliefs, and behaviors.

It is Erikson's (1968) view that youth who attend college may experience acute identity crises because they are subjected to an artificial prolongation of adolescence. One study looked at this question by comparing college students and working youth of the same age (Munro & Adams, 1977). While both groups had achieved similar rates of occupational commitments, fewer college students had achieved political, religious, and ideological commitments. These findings led the authors to suggest that college environments encourage students to remain in the moratorium and diffusion statuses and to avoid making commitments. (In addition, they noted that different aspects of identity—in this case, occupational and ideological commitments—developed at different rates.) Similarly, another study found that delayed college attendance facilitated identity achievement (Stark & Traxler, 1974).

Identity Diffusion   Identity diffusion is characterized by a failure to achieve a stable and integrated sense of self. Youth in this status experience considerable self-doubt, but don't appear to be concerned about doing anything to change their circumstances. Hence, they are different from those in the moratorium status who, although they haven't yet achieved an integrated sense of self, are struggling to resolve identity conflicts. Adolescents in diffusion give up the struggle for self-definition and remain unfocused and unable to make commitments. Identity diffusion is a serious problem for only a small number of youth, usually in cases where it is prolonged (see Chapter 13).

Identity Achievement   The preferred identity status, of course, is that of identity achievement in which an adolescent successfully passes through the identity crisis and is able to make a commitment to a vocation and to a political and personal ideology.

In Marcia's scheme, both identity achievement and identity foreclosure may be seen as resolutions of the identity crisis because both involve commitments. Adolescents in both the moratorium and diffusion statuses have only vague or no commitments.

An interesting and important finding is that some individuals who were at one point classified in the identity achievement status were later classified in the foreclosure status. The possibility that identity development does not necessarily proceed in one direction has important implications for understanding identity development throughout life (Marcia, 1976a; Raphael & Xelowski, 1980).

Negative Identity   Negative identity refers to a self-concept that is diametrically opposed to dominant parental or societal values. Typically, negative identities evolve because there has been too little support from parents or society for personal success as traditionally defined. Often, labels such as "juvenile delinquent" or "failure" are used to characterize such youth. With no routes to socially accepted achievement available, these adolescents identify with negative labels which, in turn, become self-fulfilling prophecies; that is, they begin thinking and behaving in ways which strengthen and validate their "negative" identities. Marcia classifies such individuals as special cases of identity foreclosure.

Identity and competence in other adolescent developmental tasks are not finally

Some youth adopt a negative identity.

achieved in the sense of reaching an ultimate point on a scale. Although it is possible to evaluate the level of development at a particular time, individuals are always growing toward greater psychological complexity and integration, and this continues throughout life. In the words of an unknown writer, "We know what we are but not what we may be."

Cross-Cultural Perspectives

Identity achievement has been assigned a crucial role in adolescent development by most psychologists. There is some question, however, as to how universal the task of identity achievement is. For example, Myrna Enker (1971) has suggested that children in many cultures (especially children who are poor) are not permitted to experience a psychosocial moratorium because they must begin working at a young age. Such children never have time to try on different roles, beliefs, and feelings in order to achieve a sense of unique identity.

Diana Baumrind (1975) expresses the idea that identity may be a central task only for middle-class Western youth. She argues that the experience of Western youth is atypical of the experience of postpubertal youth in most of the world. In many countries individuals who are 13 years or older take on adult responsibilities and forego the period of psychosocial adolescence that is characteristic of our culture.

Baumrind also suggests that individuals in cultures with a uniform ideology may experience little need for a personal identity as we have described it. Also, during periods of national crisis in cultures that do ordinarily encourage personal identity

The formulation of a personal identity may be a central question only for Western middle-class youth.

achievement, individuals may temporarily renounce personal identity as they come together for a larger purpose.

A lack of cross-cultural research in this area cautions us against generalizing from the experience of Western middle-class adolescents to that of adolescents in different cultural circumstances.

SUMMARY

Self-concept refers to those aspects of ourselves which we can consciously identify as "me"; self-esteem refers to our general feelings of self-worth.

Self-perceptions become more differentiated, less concrete, and more integrated during adolescence, apparently because of increased competence in formal operational thinking and social role-taking. Research findings about the constancy of self-esteem during adolescence are inconsistent, but suggest that changes that do occur are relatively orderly.

Parent-child relationships are the most important factor in the development of self-esteem. Parents who have high self-esteem, who are warm and loving, and who set firm, but fair standards for their children are most likely to foster high self-esteem.

Studies of minority group adolescents do not always show lower self-esteem in such youth compared to those in the dominant majority.

No sex differences in the overall level of self-esteem have been found, but it appears that males may overestimate their level of performance on certain tasks and females may underestimate theirs.

Identity is defined as having a stable and integrated sense of who one is and will become. Adolescents seem to develop a sense of group identity with their peers before they move on to formulating a personal identity. Identity development appears to be characteristic of late adolescence.

Marcia has identified four different identity statuses in college students: foreclosure, moratorium, diffusion, and achievement. "Negative identity" describes those adolescents who see themselves at odds with the dominant values of their parents or community.

It may be that identity achievement is a developmental task only for Western, middle-class adolescents. Other youth may not enjoy the "luxury" of a psychosocial moratorium because they must begin work at a relatively young age.

GLOSSARY

group identity versus alienation (Newman and Newman)   The psychosocial crisis of adolescents from puberty to age 18; feeling that one belongs in a peer group versus feeling isolated.

identity achievement (Marcia)   An identity status characterized by the attainment, after a period of questioning, of a sense of who one is and what one can become.

identity diffusion (Marcia)   An identity status characterized by the failure to develop a stable and integrated sense of self.

identity foreclosure (Marcia)   An identity status characterized by the adoption of the beliefs and goals of parents or the status quo without any serious questioning.

individual identity versus role diffusion (Newman and Newman)   The psychosocial crisis of adolescents aged 18 to 21; attaining autonomy from the family and developing a sense of personal identity versus failing to do so; similar to Erikson's psychosocial crisis of identity versus identity diffusion.

moratorium (Marcia)   An identity status in which a person is actively struggling to achieve a viable identity.

negative identity   The adoption of socially undesirable roles, usually because routes to positive roles are blocked.

psychosocial moratorium (Erikson)   A time of freedom from adult responsibilities granted by many cultures to adolescents in which young people are expected to "find themselves."

self-concept   An individual's perception of his or her qualities, competencies, etc.

self-esteem   The value placed on oneself; self-worth.

GETTING INVOLVED: Exercises, Case Study, and General Questions to Consider

The exercises, case studies, and questions which follow at the end of this and the remaining chapters are designed to be used either on an individual basis or in a group setting. Directions are given for individual use. If your instructor wishes to use the exercises in a group setting, he or she will explain the procedure and may direct you to read the Appendix entitled "Communicating in Small Groups: Learning through Sharing."

EXERCISES: PERSONAL COAT OF ARMS AND TWO IDEAL DAYS

The following exercises are intended to help you think about *your* identity—who you are, where you are going, what is important to you.

Exercise 1: Personal Coat of Arms   To do this exercise, refer to Worksheet 5.1 on the next page and read the instructions printed there.

After you have completed your coat of arms, take some time to reflect on your "answers." Did you learn anything new about yourself and what is important in your life? How might you incorporate what you learned from the answers to questions 5 and 6 into your current life?

Exercise 2: Two Ideal Days[1]   Take about five minutes (or more) and reflect on what you would do during two ideal days; that is, assume that you have 48 hours to do anything you want and that money is no problem. Write down what you would like to do hour by hour. Be as specific as possible so you can get a sense of how your days would really feel.

After you have written out your schedule, think about the following questions. Can you tell anything about yourself from the kinds of activities you planned? For example, did you focus on a particular type of activity or did you include a variety of things in your days? Did you become aware of some aspects of life which are important to you, but which your current life-style doesn't include? Are there ways you could make some aspects of your special days a reality now (or in the near future)?

CASE STUDY: JOHN

John is a first semester college freshman at State University. He comes from an ethnic neighborhood in a large urban area and has strong family ties. While he doesn't attend church regularly, he attended private elementary and high schools in his faith and feels that he is a religious person.

John chose to go to State because the (relatively) low tuition fees made it possible

---

[1]Adapted by permission of A & W Publishers, Inc., from *Values Clarification: A Handbook of Practical Strategies for Teachers and Students.* New Revised Edition by Sidney B. Simon, Leland W. Howe, and Howard Kirschenbaum. Copyright © 1972; Copyright © 1978. Hart Publishing Company, Inc. In cooperation with Sr. Louise, Principal of St. Julian's School in Chicago.

Worksheet 5.1 PERSONAL COAT OF ARMS EXERCISE

Instructions: Draw a coat of arms similar to the one below (make it large enough to draw on). Answer the following questions by drawing a picture, design, or symbol (don't worry about your artistic ability!). Place your answers in the appropriately numbered space on the coat of arms.

1. What do you regard as your greatest personal achievement to date?
2. What do you regard as your family's greatest achievement?
3. What is the one thing that other people can do to make you happy?
4. What do you regard as your greatest personal failure to date?
5. What would you do if you had one year to live and were guaranteed success in whatever you attempted?
6. What three things would you most like to be said of you if you died today?

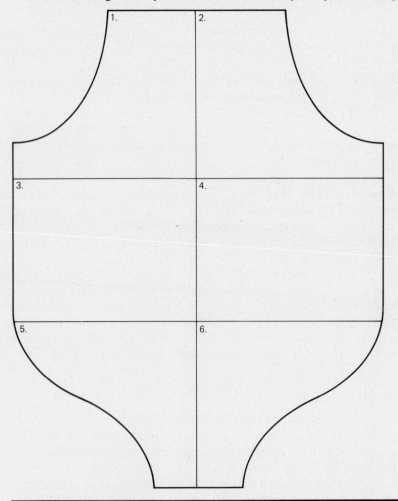

Source: Adapted by permission of A & W Publishers, Inc., from *Values Clarification: A Handbook of Practical Strategies for Teachers and Students.* New Revised Edition by Sidney B. Simon, Leland W. Howe, and Howard Kirschenbaum. Copyright © 1972; Copyright © 1978. Hart Publishing Company, Inc. In cooperation with Sr. Louise, Principal of St. Julian's School in Chicago.

for him to live away from home. His interactions with other students lead him to suspect that some of his attitudes are "out of it" compared to those of other students. For example, John misses his family, but he doesn't hear other students mention their families (or, if they do, it is only to express relief to be away from them).

His religious beliefs, too, seem different from those of most other students. He certainly never considered himself a religious fanatic, but it seems as though most students he talks to think organized religion is passé. They call themselves agnostics, atheists, or existentialists. When he has gotten into "bull sessions" with other students, he has ended up feeling frustrated and foolish because he couldn't articulate or defend his beliefs (even to himself).

In several of his classes, also, there have been discussions which seem to have cast religion in a negative light. For example, if God is good and just, how can one explain all the tragic events in this world? And, on a more personal level, what about birth control, masturbation, and premarital sex? How can he reconcile his actual behaviors here with the teachings of his church? Until now, he just avoided thinking about these contradictions, but now he feels pushed to defend his thinking.

John doesn't feel comfortable talking about these issues; after all, no one at home or in his neighborhood ever questioned these things. He doesn't know what to do. He wishes that it would all go away, but that doesn't seem to be happening. What with being confronted with these issues in class and outside, he is experiencing a lot of conflict and frustration.

Questions for Case Study

1. Assess the situation. What seems to be happening here?
2. Into which of Marcia's identity statuses do you think John falls?
3. Try to explain the nature of the conflict (in relation to identity development) and the causes of it. Pay particular attention to his family, cultural, and religious background and his present need for acceptance by others.
4. What are John's alternatives? What are the implications of his choices for his psychological development with regard to identity achievement?
5. If you were a college counselor and John came to talk to you, how might you advise him?

GENERAL QUESTIONS TO CONSIDER

1. Consider the implications of high and low self-esteem as they affect adolescents' views of themselves, parents, peers, teachers, and the "world outside" in general.
2. What can parents do to help (or hinder) the development of self-esteem in their children and adolescents?
3. How does minority-group status affect self-esteem? How might you account for the inconsistencies in the research findings here?
4. Review the discussion on the impact of gender on self-esteem. What are your feelings about these issues?
5. Which, if any, of the ideas about self-concept and self-esteem did you find particularly interesting? Explain.
6. Does your own experience suggest that identity is an issue grappled with in early adolescence

(11 to 13), middle adolescence (14 to 17), or late adolescence (18 to 22)? What do research findings seem to suggest in this regard?

7. To what extent have you been encouraged to ask identity-related questions (career, moral, sexual, religious and political issues)? Has any one person been especially helpful (or unhelpful) to you? Explain.

8. Has your college experience contributed to or interfered with your own identity achievement? In what ways?

9. Has any single life experience played a critical role in causing you to ask identity-related questions?

10. Review Marcia's identity statuses: foreclosure, moratorium, diffusion, and achievement. Where do you place yourself in his scheme? Why?

11. What do *identity* and *identity crisis* mean to you? Have you ever experienced an identity crisis?

12. Reflect on the role culture plays in identity development. Do you agree with the view that identity may be a developmental task only for Western, middle-class adolescents? Why or why not?

Chapter 6 Outline

chapter *6*

Sex Roles and Identity

The focus of this chapter is on how identity is experienced differently by males and females. Although sex-role norms are changing, it is still true that the traditional social roles which adult men and women are expected to assume are different. Typically, men are expected to identify more with the work they perform than with the roles of husband and father. Women, on the other hand, are usually expected to identify more with the roles of wife and mother than with their work outside the home. Because of this difference in expectation we might anticipate that the nature and process of identity achievement would differ for males and females. In fact, this appears to be so.

Most of the research on identity development has used white, male college students as subjects. And most discussions of identity, until recently, have lumped males and females together with the assumption that identity achievement was similar for both or, perhaps, that the issue was not a particularly important one for females. As more attention is given to women's issues, we find that identity achievement (or lack thereof) is a serious concern for girls and women, and for the larger society as well. But before we can talk about these differences in identity and their evolution, we first need to discuss sex-role identity and its development since it is a critical aspect of identity development.

SEX-ROLE IDENTITY

Defining Terms

Sex-role identity is a specific aspect of personal identity and refers to an individual's conscious and unconscious identification with the traits, attitudes, and interests which social norms dictate to be appropriate for a given sex. Individuals who identify with characteristics that social norms associate with the female gender (gentleness, nurturance, for example) would be considered to have a "feminine" sex-role identity; individuals who identify with the social norms for the male gender (aggressiveness, independence, for example) would be described as "masculine." (We might point out that people may not necessarily act in ways which would be considered consistent with a given sex-role identity—females may act independently and males in a gentle manner.) The process of internalizing these societal sex-role expectations is termed *sex-role identification*.

Gender identity refers to a person's awareness of his or her gender—male or female—and the ability to label others appropriately with regard to gender.

Sexual preference refers to a person's preference for a same- or opposite-sex partner in an emotional and sexual relationship. This topic is not directly relevant to our discussion here, but we mention it because students often confuse sex-role identity with sexual preference. They are not the same, however, as we shall see in Chapter 11.

Theories and Categories of Sex-Role Identification

The social norms that characterize sex roles are based on two assumptions—that all members of the same sex have basically the same traits and that the traits of one sex are different from the traits of the other. Traditionally, sex-role identity has been conceptualized as either "masculine" or "feminine." All males have been expected to develop masculine sex-role identities and females, feminine sex-role identities. Individuals who did not identify strongly with the sex-role expectations for their sex or who identified with the expectations for the opposite sex were judged to be few in number and to have psychological problems.

Recently, there have been significant changes in the ways psychologists conceptualize sex-role identity. One assumption that has been called into question is that males

People don't always act in a manner consistent with traditional sex-role expectations.

are and should be "masculine" and females, "feminine." For one thing, it appears that the number of people who do not conform to sex-role norms is relatively high, as is the amount of strain that accompanies trying to conform to sex-role stereotyping (Pleck, 1981a). Also, research suggests that strong identification with traditional sex-role expectations may produce negative psychological outcomes in males and females. For example, one summary of research findings has reported that highly feminine females are likely to show high anxiety, low self-esteem, and low self-acceptance (Bem, 1975). Also, while highly masculine males are often better adjusted during adolescence, in adulthood they are often characterized by high anxiety, high neuroticism, and low self-acceptance. In addition, greater intellectual development has been consistently related to masculinity in girls and femininity in boys. Highly masculine boys and highly feminine girls tend to have lower overall intelligence, lower spatial ability, and less curiosity (Bem, 1975).

In addition, some sex-role expectations can produce negative effects on the quality of life individuals experience. It has been found that on the average males are more aggressive, less empathic, and less emotionally expressive; they have less intimate friendships, and they die younger than females (Pleck, 1981a). Females on the average have been found to have lower educational and occupational aspirations, to be employed in low-prestige and low-salaried jobs, to be less likely to run for and win political office, to have less self-confidence, and to have a higher incidence of mental illness than males (Hyde & Rosenberg, 1980).

Sandra Lipsitz Bem has suggested: "We need a new standard of psychological health for the sexes, one that removes the burden of stereotype and allows people to feel free to express the best traits of men and women" (1975, p. 59). Bem's concept of *androgyny* (from *andro,* "male," and *gyne,* "female") is an attempt to provide such a standard. According to this concept girls and women could be emotional, gentle, understanding, express tender feelings, and like children *as well as* be independent, good at sports, adventurous, intellectual, self-confident, ambitious, and able to stand up under pressure. Similarly, boys and men could be independent, good at sports, etc., *as well as* be emotional, gentle, understanding, etc. Bem suggests that an individual who has underdeveloped *human* (male *and* female) characteristics is less able to participate fully in all the experiences life offers. Since traditional sex-role expectations limit a person's growth, it is important to move beyond them.

Psychologists have constructed a number of tests that distinguish between androgynous individuals and those who are traditionally sex-typed (Bem, 1975; Spence, Helmreich, & Stapp, 1975). Using such tests, researchers have been able to compare individuals with different sex-role identities.* For example, Janet Spence and her colleagues (1975) found that college males and females could be grouped into four categories on

---

*A distinction between two major theorists in this area, Sandra Bem and Janet Spence, should be made here. Bem theorizes that sex roles (masculinity, femininity, androgyny) are personality traits that can be measured and expressed in gender-congruent attitudes, characteristics, and behaviors. For example, "feminine" individuals are likely to hold stereotypically feminine attitudes and engage in similar behavior. While Spence and her colleagues agree that "masculine" (instrumental) and "feminine" (expressive) traits can be measured, they advance a more conservative theory than Bem's—namely, these personality traits are not strongly related to other attributes and behaviors that are not obviously gender-congruent. For example, high scores on a measure of femininity don't necessarily dictate that a person will engage in stereotypically feminine behavior or have strong feminine interests.

the basis of their self-ratings on gender-related traits (see Table 6.1). Men and women who saw themselves as neither masculine nor feminine (Group 1) were labeled sex-undifferentiated individuals. Men who rated themselves low on masculine traits and high on feminine traits (Group 2) were labeled cross-sex–typed males, while women who rated themselves low on masculine traits and high on feminine traits (also Group 2) were labeled traditional females. Of subjects who saw themselves as highly masculine and not feminine (Group 3), men were labeled traditional males, while women were labeled cross-sex–typed females (Group 3). Men and women who rated themselves high on both masculine and feminine traits (Group 4) were labeled androgynous individuals.

In addition to categorizing these students, the researchers measured the subjects' levels of self-esteem. They found that self-concepts were highest for students who were high in both sex-role qualities (Group 4). The students next highest in self-esteem were Group 3 (high masculine, low feminine), followed by Group 2, and lastly, Group 1. Such studies suggest that there are some demonstrated advantages to breaking out of sex-specific stereotypes, and this appears especially true for females. For example, a number of recent studies have found that while only sometimes do androgynous individuals show higher self-esteem and better personal adjustment compared to masculine males or females, androgynous individuals consistently show such advantages over feminine females (Gilbert, 1981). (This fact suggests that masculinity is the cultural norm for socialization [Block, 1973; Gilbert, 1981].)

Because the androgyny concept supported a philosophy of equality between the sexes and provided a new conceptual framework for research on sex roles, it gained almost immediate acceptance. Its popularity, however, was also instrumental in creating a situation in which its advocates claimed more for it than could actually be demonstrated at the time. With more findings available, it seems that the initial broad-based claims for the desirability of androgyny as a standard of mental health were probably premature (Baumrind, 1982).

Table 6.1 SELF-RATINGS AND SELF-CONCEPT SCORES OF MALES AND FEMALES IN FOUR SEX-ROLE CATEGORIES

Category of self-rating	Sex	Label	Percent	Self-concept score*
Group 1. Low masculine, low feminine	Male	Sex-undifferentiated	31	67
	Female	Sex-undifferentiated	21	70
Group 2. Low masculine, high feminine	Male	Cross-sex typed	13	75
	Female	Traditional	39	75
Group 3. High masculine, low feminine	Male	Traditional	27	87
	Female	Cross-sex typed	11	92
Group 4. High masculine, high feminine	Male	Androgynous	30	94
	Female	Androgynous	30	99

*Average score for men in sample was 82; women, 83

Source: Adapted from Janet T. Spence, Robert Helmreich, and Joy Stapp. (1975). "Ratings of Self and Peers on Sex-role Attributes and their Relation to Self-esteem and Conceptions of Masculinity and Femininity." *Journal of Personality and Social Psychology, 32*(1), 29–39, Table 4. Copyright 1975 by the American Psychological Association. Adapted by permission of the publisher and author.

Most researchers in this area, while tempering some of their initial assertions about androgyny, are continuing to study the concept. There is evidence that sex-role identity can sometimes predict attitudes and behaviors more accurately than gender, and much remains to be learned about androgyny, specifically, and sex-role identity, in general.

Several psychologists have proposed that sex-role identity develops according to stages based on cognitive development (Block, 1973; Kohlberg, 1966a; Pleck, 1975). In the first stage children are confused about their gender and don't have any organized system for understanding sex-role concepts. In the second stage, due to increased cognitive capacities, children become aware of and capable of learning the "rules" that govern the social roles of each sex. In this intermediate stage individuals are likely to be quite rigid in their understanding of these rules and intolerant of deviations from sex-role norms in themselves and others.

In the third stage abstract thought enables individuals to transcend these norms and move on to an androgynous stage in which they feel free to feel, think, and behave in ways which are congruent with their own (non–sex-typed) needs (Pleck, 1975). It may be, then, that once adolescents develop the more sophisticated cognitive processes of formal operations and once they feel adequate in the traditional sex-roles, they can advance to the less rigid and more humanistic third stage, assuming this orientation is a socially valued one. Of course, not all adolescents or adults move to the third stage, no doubt because this orientation is not widely valued in American society.

Not all psychologists agree with this stage theory. They say that children who are reared according to traditional sex-role norms are likely to develop a masculine or feminine sex-role identity and those who are reared according to androgynous sex-role norms are likely to develop an androgynous sex-role identity. Those taking this view agree with the stage theorists that sex-role identity can change over time. However, they feel that the occurrence of a change depends on changes in sex-role expectations and significant sex-role related experiences in an individual's life. Also, nonstage theorists assert that, if changes in sex-role identity do occur, they do not do so in a particular direction (from masculine or feminine to androgynous, for example).

The stage theory of sex-role development remains untested, but it does offer a possible solution to one of the questions that has plagued sex-role research (and some parents). That is, it is not uncommon to find children who have been reared in nonsexist households espousing traditional sex-role norms in their conversations and behaviors. If the stage theory of sex-role development is correct, then the parents of such children could rest more easily, knowing that such a development is a temporary phase determined by cognitive limitations rather than an indication that their parenting practices have not achieved their desired results.

Development of Sex Differences and Sex-Role Identity

Infancy   Learning how to be a boy or a girl begins at birth with the announcement of "It's a boy!" or "It's a girl!" Usually, this exclamation is quickly followed by assigning the newborn a "sex-appropriate" name and by dressing him or her in blue or pink. Such actions imply that we believe that a child's gender is a critical factor in his or her life. It is noteworthy that, besides the more obvious biological differences between boys and girls, few significant sex differences have been observed in infancy (Hyde & Rosenberg, 1980).

Childhood   In early childhood we see the beginnings of gender and sex-role identity. For example, sometime between 3 and 7 years of age children learn that they are either girls or boys and that this is a permanent "condition." They can also label correctly other individuals as girls, boys, men, and women (McConaghy, 1979). By age 5 or 6 children have a good idea of which characteristics and behaviors are stereotypically male or female, even though boys and girls at this age do not act very differently from one another (Bee, 1978). Awareness of the fact that gender is distinguished on the basis of genital differences does not develop until 7 or 9 years of age (McConaghy, 1979).

Lower-class children show clearer and earlier awareness of sex-role patterns than do middle-class children, and lower-class families distinguish to a greater degree between the roles of mother and father than do middle-class families (Rosenkrantz, Vogel, Bee, Broverman, & Broverman, 1968). Also, it seems that small, nuclear families do not emphasize differences between the sexes as much as larger families do. Supposedly, this is because either parent must be able to function in a variety of roles because there are fewer caretakers around.

The nature and process of sex-role identification also varies according to the sex of the child. For boys, there is less ambiguity about sex-appropriate standards, there is more pressure to conform to these demands, and this pressure comes earlier in life than for girls (Hartley, 1959; Lynn, 1959; Pleck, 1981a).

During childhood consistent differences between the sexes are not numerous. Eleanor Maccoby and Carol Jacklin (1974) have found that boys are more aggressive physically, more competitive in children's games, and more resistant to parental demands than girls. Since there is much more sex-typing "pressure" from parents, television, and teachers in childhood than in infancy as well as increased cognitive abilities to "register" these messages, it seems strange *not* to find more clear-cut differences between boys and girls at this age.

Adolescence   At adolescence, however, we do find several significant differences emerging between the sexes (see Table 6.2). Why might this be so? One answer, consistent with Bandura's social learning theory, is that children spend years observing and learning sex-appropriate norms and behaviors, but they are not called upon to demonstrate many of these until adolescence. It is not until adolescence that society begins to insist in earnest that individuals take on sex-appropriate roles and behaviors. The fulfillment of sex-role expectations becomes an important basis for the delivery of reinforcement and punishment. As expectations change significantly at adolescence, we see a corresponding and dramatic shift in adolescent behavior. Adolescents recall and act upon previously learned sex-appropriate behaviors as well as learn new ones.

In addition to these shifts in social pressures, significant changes in physiological and cognitive functioning take place at this time. Hormones (and the accompanying

Table 6.2   SEX DIFFERENCES AND SIMILARITIES

Physical Attributes

Strength	Males taller, heavier, more muscular
Health	Females less vulnerable to illness and disease, live longer
Activity level	Some evidence that preschool boys more active during play in same-sex groups; sex differences for school-age children are qualitative, not quantitative
Manual dexterity	Women excel when speed is important; findings hard to interpret

Abilities

General intelligence	No difference on most tests
Verbal ability	Some evidence that females acquire language slightly earlier; males more often diagnosed as having reading problems; females excel on various verbal tests after age ten or eleven[a]
Quantitative ability	Males excel on tests of mathematical reasoning from the start of adolescence[a]
Spatial-visual ability	Males excel starting in tenth grade, but not on all tests or in all studies[a]
Creativity	Females excel on verbal creativity tests, but otherwise no difference
Cognitive style	Males excel on spatial-visual disembedding tests starting at adolescence, but no general differences in cognitive style

Personality Characteristics

Sociability	No consistent findings on infants' responsiveness to social cues; school-age boys play in larger groups; women fantasize more about affiliation themes, but there is no evidence that one sex wants or needs friends more
Empathy	Conflicting evidence; probably depends on situation and sex of participants in an interaction
Emotionality	Self-reports and observations conflict; no convincing evidence that females feel more emotional, but they may express certain emotions more freely
Dependence	Conflicting findings; dependence appears not to be a unitary concept or stable trait
Susceptibility to influence	Preschool girls more obedient to parents; boys may be more susceptible to peer pressure; no overall difference in adult susceptibility to persuasion across different settings in laboratory settings
Self-esteem and confidence	No self-reported differences in self-esteem, but males more confident about task performance; males more likely to take credit for success; less likely to blame selves for failure
Nurturance	No overall differences in altruism; girls more helpful; and responsive to infants, small children; some evidence that fathers as responsive to newborns as mothers are, but issue of maternal versus paternal behavior remains open
Aggressiveness	Males more aggressive from preschool age on; men more violent, more likely to be aggressive in public, more likely to be physically aggressive in situations not involving anger

Values and Moral Perceptions   Some controversial evidence that males and females approach choice and conflict situations differently. Males seem more likely to emphasize abstract standards of justice, fairness, balancing individual rights. Females seem more likely to emphasize the ethics of care, human attachments, balancing of conflicting responsibilities.

[a] Differences statistically reliable but quite small. *Source:* Adapted from *The Longest War* by Carol Tavris and Carole Wade, © 1984 by Harcourt Brace Jovanovich, Inc. Reprinted by permission of the publisher.

growth of the sex organs) sensitize adolescents to their own and others' sexuality and motivate them to act on their sexual feelings. Cognitive maturation also plays an important role in this regard. Because of these internal changes societal expectations have more immediate relevance to adolescents, and they become more attentive to them.

While it is not exactly clear how hormones, cognition, personality, and social expectations are interrelated, generally we might say that societal expectations function to direct the adolescents' emerging sexual energies and personalities into the prear-ranged social and sex roles within a given culture.

The fact that the adult-role expectations for men and women are different makes it likely that there will be sex differences in the nature and process of personal identity development in adolescence, as we shall see below.

IDENTITY DEVELOPMENT IN MALES

Role Expectations

Although masculine sex-role norms do appear to restrict development in certain areas (emotional responsiveness, for example), little boys who grow up in a society which favors stereotypically masculine modes of behavior develop a clearer sense of self and "naturally" move into positions of political and social power. A boy, more than a girl, grows up with the expectation that he will have control over his life—he will "decide" what kind of work he wants to do and with which level of income he will be satisfied; he will ask a woman to share her life with him, based on his expectations of what he wants in a partner; if he has children, he will assume that their mother will have the major caretaking responsibilities for them.

To function successfully in designated male adult roles, it appears necessary to achieve a sense of identity, to become autonomous from one's family, and to decide upon a vocation, in addition to the other adolescent developmental tasks we have elaborated earlier. In their classic study of adolescents, Elizabeth Douvan and Joseph Adelson (1966) found that *vocational choice* was the central identity issue for adolescent boys: "For most boys, the question of 'what to be' begins with work and the job, and he is likely to define himself and to be identified by occupation" (p. 17). Numerous recent studies have supported this assertion (Marcia, 1980).

Sex-role expectations for boys have remained relatively unchanged for many years. However, it appears that some aspects of the male role are now shifting. In the *traditional male role* masculinity is validated by individual physical strength, aggres-sion, and emotional inexpressiveness (Pleck, 1981a). In the *modern male role* masculin-ity is validated by economic achievement, organizational power, emotional control (even over anger), and emotional sensitivity and self-expression, but only with women (Pleck, 1981a).

The traditional role persists along with the new expectations, so the socialization process for boys may show some inconsistencies. We would speculate that when boys who have been reared more in line with the traditional role reach late adolescence and adulthood, they are likely to find themselves evaluated according to the modern male

Work assumes a central role in the identity and lives of males.

role. Joseph Pleck (1976) explains: "Where childhood socialization valued physical strength and athletic ability and taught boys to shun girls, adulthood confronts males with expectations for intellectual and social skills and for the capacity to relate to females as work peers and emotional intimates" (p. 16).

Clearly, *sex-role strain* would be eased by making sex-role expectations more consistent throughout the developmental sequence. Hopefully, this will happen as the recent changes in social norms regarding sex roles become more widely accepted and integrated into child-rearing practices. In the meantime, however, we can see that many males in late adolescence and early adulthood may experience conflict and confusion if and when they are forced to modify long-standing beliefs, feelings, and behaviors associated with the traditional masculine role.

Identity Statuses in College Males

Recall, now, James Marcia's four identity statuses: foreclosure, moratorium, diffusion, and achievement. Numerous studies suggest that Marcia's identity statuses provide a useful schema for studying identity development in adolescence. A comprehensive review of this research leads to the following generalizations about the identity statuses as they pertain to males (Marcia, 1980).

Compared to foreclosure and diffusion subjects, achievement and moratorium subjects score higher on measures of self-esteem, stability in self-evaluations, moral reasoning, self-direction and autonomy, and cultural sophistication; they score lower on authoritarianism (Marcia, 1980). In addition, achievers and moratoriums are more likely to have intimate interpersonal relationships, whereas foreclosures and diffusions are more likely to have stereotyped relationships with others (see Chapter 8). While no differences in intelligence have been found among the four groups, a number of studies have concluded that foreclosure subjects have relatively "simple" (less elaborated and complex) cognitive systems. In contrast, diffusion subjects have the most complex cognitive systems, possibly suggesting that this factor may be important in the confusion and disorganization characteristic of this status. Achievers and moratoriums have moderately complex cognitive systems (Marcia, 1980).

Other studies have looked at the question of the long-term development of ego identity during adolescence. In a study of white males during their first year of college, there was an increase in the number of students in the moratorium status and a decrease in the number in the diffusion status with regard to vocational commitments (Waterman & Waterman, 1971). (At the same time, the authors found a significant increase in diffusion subjects with regard to ideological commitments, an outcome interpreted as being a function of college pressures to focus on vocational choice, with less emphasis on value issues.)

A study of these same students during their junior year found that 80 percent of the students in the moratorium category had changed their occupational plans (Waterman & Waterman, 1972). This high change rate (higher than in any of the other identity statuses) lends support to Marcia's conceptualization of moratorium subjects as being in a period of crisis (struggling to come to grips with vocational issues).

Fifty-three of the same students were reassessed in their senior year. At this time there were more achievers (in commitments to both vocation and ideology), which provides evidence for a trend toward identity achievement during the college years among white college males. Also, it was found that identity achievement was the most stable status from freshman through senior years. The authors also reported that at least 16 percent of the seniors were still in the diffusion status for both occupation and ideology, a finding which suggests that not all male students experience the college environment in such ways as to be able to consolidate their identities while in college.

Anne Constantinople (1969) has also found a trend toward identity achievement from freshman to senior year and a significant increase in happiness over this same time span among males.

In another study Marcia (1976) interviewed previous subjects six years after college and found indications of backsliding from the achievement and moratorium statuses (considered more mature or high-identity categories) to the low-identity statuses of foreclosure and diffusion. Later research, on the other hand, showed no such backsliding effect beyond the college years (Meilman, 1979). Philip Meilman's study of identity development in male subjects aged 12, 15, 21 and 24 reported signs of a trend toward identity achievement with increases in age.

One finding of particular interest in Meilman's study is that attitudes toward premarital intercourse seem to be related to male identity formation. As we will see in the next section, this issue has been found to be an important component of female identity formation. The question of whether or not it is important in male identity formation was not investigated until recently because of the assumptions of Erikson and others that occupational commitment and ideological beliefs are the key components of (male) identity. (This finding serves as an example of the importance of questioning assumptions—if questions aren't asked, it is unlikely we will find answers to them.)

In conclusion, we find that there is a tendency for college men to move toward identity achievement as they progress from freshman to senior years. Achievement and moratorium men appear to be more autonomous and less conforming, to have higher self-esteem, to be more "advanced" in moral reasoning, and to have more intimate relationships with others compared to foreclosure and diffusion subjects. Hence, there is empirical support for Marcia's and Erikson's interpretation of the nature and process of identity development among late adolescent white males. Here, we should point out that little research has been done with upper- or lower-class adolescents, minority members, and those not in college.

IDENTITY DEVELOPMENT IN FEMALES

Role Expectations

During childhood, girls experience fewer sex-related restrictions than do boys (Hyde & Rosenberg, 1980; Pleck, 1981a). At adolescence, however, they are subject to heavy sex-role constraints and must contend with culturally created conflicts between being a competent person with an independent sense of identity and being "feminine." So-called masculine characteristics and behaviors that were heretofore acceptable are likely to become unacceptable, namely, those of achievement and autonomy (Morgan & Farber, 1982). These pressures on the adolescent girl to move from a more androgynous orientation to a feminine one constitute a form of role discontinuity: achievement is incompatible with traditional femininity (Huston-Stein & Bailey, 1973). This conflict is expressed in a number of aspects of development. One which has received considerable attention is that of women's "fear of success" (Horner, 1969). Recent research in this area suggests that women associate high-level career achievement with social rejection. We will discuss this issue in detail in Chapter 12.

In this context it has been found that female adolescents report greater life stress and significantly poorer emotional and physical well-being than males, even though girls reported that they received greater social support from their peers (Burke & Weir, 1978). The authors suggested that one of the reasons for such findings is the lack of clear definition of roles for adolescent girls. Traditional female sex-role norms dictate that a woman should build her identity around her roles as wife and mother (rather than around a career in the case of males). Also, the girl cannot take the initiative in realizing these roles (she must be chosen as a mate, not do the choosing). Hence, her further psychological development must await the assumption of these roles in adulthood.

Three identity patterns in females have been identified (Dellas & Gaier, 1975):

(1) traditional female role and stereotype: awaiting marriage
(2) achievement and role success: achievement in male-valued areas
(3) bimodal identity: commitment to family and career

Unfortunately, however, none of these patterns is without problems because of the incompatibility between traditional female sex-role norms and achievement. The ado-

Changing sex-role expectations for females are a source of stress for adolescent girls and adult women.

lescent who chooses the traditional pattern may later regret not having been more successful in a job; the one who opts for the second pattern may feel a loss of status without a husband and children; and the girl who chooses the bimodal identity will experience considerable conflict in meeting the often incompatible demands of both roles (Hyde & Rosenberg, 1980).

Assuming that sex-role expectations continue to change such that women have a wider variety of life-style options and career opportunities, increasing numbers of them will be faced with the inherent conflict between family responsibilities and career (a conflict most men do not currently face). However, it is unlikely that large numbers of women will invest considerable identity in occupational success unless and until there is some alleviation of the burden of "role overload" through subsidized child-care programs or fathers' taking equal responsibility in child-rearing and household tasks (Pleck, 1981b). Hence, we would expect the nature and "content" of female identity to be different from that of males.

In addition, because of the discontinuities in the life-styles of most women—from being single and working to being married and working, to stopping work to rear children, to rejoining the work force—it is unlikely that female identity would follow the same developmental course as male identity. We would expect that there would be more movement between identity statuses as a result of attempts to resolve the career-family conflict in different ways as a woman's needs and family circumstances change. This fact is important in understanding female identity development during adolescence.

The life-style subsequently adopted by most college women is a sequential one in which they work and marry, withdraw from employment for rearing children, and return to work at some point after children have been born. Since forming an independent personal identity can make a woman less eligible for marriage, most female adolescents attempt to maintain a "flexible identity" which can adapt to the as-yet-unknown husband (Angrist, 1969; Almquist, Angrist, & Mickelsen, 1980). Given the current sex-role norms, this delay of identity achievement can be seen as quite functional. On the other hand, it may also mean having no distinctive sense of oneself, no commitment to an occupation, or an undeveloped philosophy of life. Therefore, while a flexible identity may be quite functional given some circumstances, it is not clear that it is necessarily advantageous for female development in all respects. In this context, Ronald Burke and Tamara Weir (1978) have observed:

> The net result for females is a delay in evolving a definition of the self, and with this comes a sense of uncertainty and lack of control over their lives. They tend to allow their identities to be defined or molded by their relationships with others which places them in a very vulnerable and unstable position. This process can potentially generate sufficient conflict, ambivalence, confusion, and denial of self so as to affect the health and well being of many women in our society. (p. 287)

We can see, then, that the double bind of femininity and achievement which begins at adolescence causes particular developmental difficulties for women and has important implications for female identity development.

Identity Statuses in College Females

As we have seen, identity for the male is defined largely in terms of occupation, about which adolescent boys have relatively specific and realistic expectations. Research with late adolescent girls, however, shows a different pattern—attitudes toward premarital intercourse and religion are more important to identity achievement in women than are attitudes about occupation and politics (Marcia, 1980; Schenkel & Marcia, 1972). Also, it has been found that religious identity for females (and occupational identity for males) was the most important component of identity that contributed to advanced competence in interpersonal relationships (Fitch & Adams, 1983).

This suggests that Douvan and Adelson (1966) were correct in their conclusions that the components of identity differ for males (occupational choice) and females (social sensitivity, sexual attitudes, and basis for choice of husband-to-be).

A comprehensive review of research on the personality characteristics associated with the different identity statuses in women forms the basis for the following descriptions (Marcia, 1980). Identity achievement and foreclosure subjects have been found to score higher than moratorium and diffusion subjects on measures of self-esteem,

Relationships assume a central role in the identity and lives of females.

masculinity and androgyny, and nonconformity. Also, it has been found that achievers chose the most difficult college majors, had the highest achievement scores, and the highest fear of success scores; diffusion subjects had the lowest scores in these categories and chose the least difficult college majors. The combination of high achievement scores and high fear of success scores for achievers (and also for moratorium subjects) has been interpreted as reflecting the achievement-femininity conflicts encountered by women focused on nontraditional achievement-oriented goals (Orlofsky, 1978). Since foreclosure and diffusion women are less motivated for achievement, they should experience less conflict and less fear of success.

Also, achievers have been found to show more sophisticated levels of moral judgment than either diffusion or foreclosure subjects. Intelligence has not been found to vary among the statuses. Achievers and moratoriums are more likely to have intimate interpersonal relationships, compared to foreclosures and diffusions (Fitch & Adams, 1983; Kacerguis & Adams, 1980).

These findings reveal sex differences in the adaptability of certain identity statuses. That is, among males it was found that achievement and moratorium subjects often showed similar characteristics. Among female subjects, however, achievement and foreclosure subjects appear more similar.

The finding that female achievement and foreclosure subjects were least conforming has led to the speculation that female foreclosures may have developed the ability to resist conformity pressure—even though they have not experienced an identity crisis—because this identity status is the one that has been traditionally reinforced by female sex-role norms. Perhaps, the feeling of security which comes from adopting a socially designated role enables these women to resist pressures to conform (Toder & Marcia, 1973). If female sex-role norms were to change in such a way as to encourage women to explore life-style options, we might expect to see changes here, namely, that moratorium women might resemble achievement women more than foreclosures (Marcia, 1980).

We saw that college males moved toward identity achievement between the freshman and senior years. A similar trend has not always been found for college women. In fact, Constantinople (1969) reported that some women entered college at a more mature level than their male counterparts, but they regressed in greater numbers toward the diffusion status as they progressed in school. These findings led Constantinople to speculate that the college environment may be more conducive to identity achievement in males than in females. However, a more recent study found that college women were significantly more likely to change from a low to a high identity status than from a high to a low status. This study also reported that women showed the greatest change out of the diffusion status and the greatest stability in the moratorium status (Fitch & Adams, 1983).

Taken together, these findings suggest that the process and nature of identity achievement differ for men and women. First, in women it appears that interpersonal relationships, sexuality issues, and religion are more critical components in identity achievement than are vocational and political attitudes (as is true for men).

Second, the process of identity development in women appears to be different from that in men. According to James Hodgson and Judith Fischer (1979), the pathways to identity achievement in women "are both more complex and more conflicted . . . and issues of intimacy are intertwined in female identity development in ways not adequately recognized by Erikson" (p. 49). To more fully understand identity development in women, more information is needed, especially about women in minority groups, those in lower- and upper-socioeconomic statuses, and those not attending college.

IDENTITY AND SEX ROLES RECONSIDERED

As we have seen, Erikson's theory of identity seems to describe male identity and its development, but not that of females. Male identity seems to focus on vocational choice and autonomy, while relationships to others are the paramount identity concern for females, although occupational choice seems to be gaining in importance for college women in recent years (see Table 6.3).

These sex differences seem to reflect current societal sex-role norms, lending credence to Erikson's idea that identity is a psychosocial concept. Now that it has been established that there are sex differences in identity, it would seem wise to heed Carol Gilligan's (1982) admonition to refrain from using male criteria for identity achievement as the standard for evaluating female identity. We need considerable research in this area in order to map out the nature of identity and its development in females. Moreover, the fact that sex-role expectations are in flux makes it imperative to conduct ongoing research to keep abreast of the potential impacts of social change on personality in both sexes.

SUMMARY

Adult social role expectations differ for males and females and this fact affects the nature and development of identity in adolescent males and females.

A high level of identification with the sex-role expectations for either sex can have negative effects on psychological development. Highly masculine males and highly feminine females have lower self-esteem than androgynous males and females. Sex-role

Table 6.3   NUMBER OF COLLEGE STUDENTS IN EACH IDENTITY STATUS IN AREAS OF OCCUPATION, RELIGION, POLITICS, AND SEX

	Occupation	Religion	Politics	Sex
Females				
Achievers	12	16	6	27
Moratoriums	17	12	10	11
Foreclosures	14	14	9	27
Diffusions	27	28	45	5
Males				
Achievers	12	16	14	15
Moratoriums	16	9	4	4
Foreclosures	15	25	7	45
Diffusions	27	20	45	6

Source: Caroline K. Waterman and Jeffrey S. Nevid. (1977). Sex differences in the resolution of the identity crisis. *Journal of Youth and Adolescence, 6*(4), 337–342. Copyright 1977 by Plenum Publishing Corporation. Reprinted by permission.

development may progress from an undifferentiated phase to a stereotyped phase and culminate in an androgynous phase. It is suggested that the greater cognitive flexibility of adolescent thought makes it possible (but not assured) for an androgynous orientation to develop at that time.

According to Erikson, identity achievement is the major developmental task during adolescence and is based primarily on vocational choice. Research has shown that vocational and ideological commitments are the primary bases of male identity. Also, it has been found that male identity achievement and moratorium subjects score higher than foreclosure and diffusion subjects on measures of self-esteem, stability of self-evaluations, moral reasoning, autonomy, and cultural sophistication; they score lower on authoritarianism. There is a trend toward identity achievement from freshman to senior year in college among males.

A significant aspect of the female adolescent experience is the onset of the conflict between femininity and achievement. This fact suggests that the nature of identity and its development will differ from that of males, and research supports this assertion. In women interpersonal relationship, sexuality, and religious issues appear to be more critical components of identity than are vocational and political orientations. Also, the achievement of autonomy (independence from parents and other authority figures) appears to operate by a different process in men and women. Accordingly, Erikson's theory accurately describes identity development in males, but not in females.

GLOSSARY

achievement and role success pattern (Dellas & Gaier)   One of three identity patterns of contemporary American women; entails achievement in male-valued domains.

androgyny (Bem)   A type of sex-role identity which combines positive "masculine" and "feminine" traits.

bimodal female identity pattern (Dellas & Gaier)   One of three identity patterns of contemporary American women; involves a commitment to both career and family roles.

modern male role (Pleck)   A male sex role in which masculinity is validated by economic achievement, organizational power, emotional control, and emotional sensitivity and self-expression displayed only to women.

sex-role identification   The process of internalizing societal sex-role expectations.

sex-role identity   An aspect of personal identity involving the individual's conscious and unconscious identification with the traits, attitudes, and interests that societal norms dictate to be appropriate for a given gender.

sex-role strain (Pleck)   A type of role strain in which individuals feel they can't adequately meet sex-role expectations and expectations are experienced as rigid and confining.

sexual preference   An individual's preference for a same- or other-sex partner in an emotional and sexual relationship.

traditional female role pattern (Dellas & Gaier)   One of three identity patterns of contemporary American women; involves a commitment to the roles of wife and mother.

traditional male role (Pleck)   A male sex role in which masculinity is validated by individual physical strength, aggression, and emotional inexpressiveness.

GETTING INVOLVED: Case Studies and General Questions to Consider

CASE STUDY 1: PAUL

Paul is a college sophomore who is a business major. He has a B+ average and doesn't have to spend a lot of time studying to maintain "decent" grades. He lives at home with his parents and his younger brother and sister.

His mother and father own their own restaurant, and Paul and his parents have always assumed that he would eventually take it over. Recently, however, Paul has begun to question this idea. He doesn't doubt that he could do the job. He has worked part-time in the restaurant since he was 12; he likes most of the people who work there, as well as the clientele.

Still, it seems that lately he has become less interested in his work at the restaurant. He has the vague feeling that he wants "something more" for himself (or at least something different). Paul has begun to develop an interest in computers; he finds this area quite fascinating. He suspects that one of the reasons he has become less interested in his restaurant work is that he would rather be spending the time on computers.

Last week, Dr. Johnson, one of his professors, asked Paul if he would like to assist him on an important computer project and get paid. Dr. Johnson told Paul that he was impressed with his work and felt that he might have some special talent in this area. Paul was quite pleased to have been asked, but accepting the position would mean that he would need to cut back on his hours at the restaurant. This in itself wouldn't be a problem because he could make up the loss in income with the project money and his parents could find someone to take over some of his hours. What he is worried about is how his parents would interpret this change in his plans. He is afraid that they would be upset and take it as an indication of a lessened commitment to the family and the business. He knows that they love him, but they can also be rather rigid and controlling sometimes.

He really wants to work on the computer project to see if he likes computers as much as he thinks he might. And, what if it turns out that he *does* like the work? What might this mean for his major and future job plans? He knows that the field of computers is a growing one and that he could easily find a job when he graduated. He might even want to go to graduate school.

But, if he decided he wanted to switch majors and careers, what would he tell his parents? They have invested a lot in building up the restaurant business and are counting on him to carry on with it. He doesn't want to let them down. On the other hand, he doesn't want to spend his life in a job he doesn't like.

Paul feels conflicted and confused. Sometimes he wishes he hadn't taken the course that opened his eyes to computers—everything was "nice and neat" until then. Still, there's no turning back now.

He has to give Dr. Johnson an answer soon. What should he do?

Questions for Case Study 1

1. Assess the situation. What seems to be happening here?
2. Which of Marcia's identity statuses best describes Paul? Explain your thinking.

3. What do you think Paul might do? Explore the alternatives available to him.
4. Consider the possible short-term and long-term outcomes associated with the alternatives you have outlined.
5. If you were a college counselor, how might you advise Paul?

CASE STUDY 2: ELLEN

Ellen is a junior prelaw major with a 3.4 grade-point average. She is a serious student who spends time on her studies, but she likes to have a good time too. She is in a sorority and is active in campus activities. She has been going with Bill, a junior business major, for the past six months. She attends a college in a different state from the one in which her family lives. She has a younger brother and sister at home.

Recently, she has begun to question her decision to go to law school. She has heard that jobs are hard to find for law school graduates, and wonders, assuming she got into law school, whether she would actually get a job when she graduated. Also, Ellen has found that studying seems to be requiring more of an effort these days, and she has two more semesters to go. Maybe law school just isn't worth the effort?

To make things worse, Bill has begun to be somewhat critical of her career plans. He has more traditional feelings about a woman's role, doesn't like to get into "heavy" discussions, and likes to have a good time. He seems to resent it when she can't go out because she has to study. His behavior is starting to bother her and makes her doubt whether he is the right person for her. (They haven't discussed marriage, but she has toyed with this possibility.)

Ellen also feels in conflict because some of her friends have recently become engaged. Sometimes she wonders whether the idea of going to law school is a big mistake—maybe it would decrease her chances for marriage? She knows that she wants to get married and probably have children, but she is less sure about the latter.

Ellen wonders whether the time and effort spent on her school work and the conflict with her boyfriend are worth it. Maybe she should slack off in her studying. If her grades fell, then she would just have to find something else to do. Also, she suspects that her relationship with Bill is increasing her conflict and confusing her in making this important decision. Maybe she should talk to him, explain her feelings, and see if he could be more supportive? If they can't seem to work this out, maybe she should break off the relationship. Surely, there must be some men "out there" who would be more supportive of her aspirations to combine a career and marriage.

Ellen is not sure what to do about all of this, but it is beginning to bother her more and more. She feels that she will have to make some decisions soon.

Questions for Case Study 2

1. Assess the situation. What appears to be going on?
2. Into which of the three identity patterns of contemporary American women (p. 149) do you feel Ellen falls?
3. Can you place her in any of Marcia's identity statuses?
4. What alternatives are open to Ellen?
5. Consider the possible short-term and long-range outcomes of these alternatives.
6. If you were a college counselor, how might you advise Ellen?

GENERAL QUESTIONS TO CONSIDER

1. What are your feelings about the concept of androgyny? Do you feel that you might be one of the 30 percent who are androgynous? What group do you feel you would be in: 1, 2, 3, or 4 (see Table 6.1 on p. 142)?

2. Consider the issue of androgyny as it relates to mate selection. Would you want an androgynous person for a mate or a person with a more traditional sex-role identity? Why?

3. Consider the issue of androgyny as it relates to the work setting. Would you prefer to work with an androgynous person or a more traditionally sex-typed individual? Does it matter? Why or why not? Do your preferences for androgynous or traditionally sex-typed persons differ depending on the context—marriage, friendship or job? Think about why this may or may not be so.

4. What is your response to the theory that sex roles develop according to a stage sequence based on cognitive development? What are your own experiences in this area? If you believe that such a theory is true, how do you account for the fact that large numbers of adults are not androgynous?

5. Reflect on the findings that a number of sex differences emerge during adolescence, but not before. Can you recall any experiences which might serve as examples of the increased social pressures to conform to sex-role norms during adolescence?

6. Review some positive and negative aspects of the traditional and modern male sex roles. (Males might consider which role they were reared to adopt. Also, they might reflect on any changes in these expectations and how they have coped with these changes.)

7. Review the three female identity patterns (p. 149) and the positive and negative aspects of each. (Women might think about which role(s) they were reared to adopt, and if there have been changes in their role preferences to date. Those who have changed their orientation might reflect on the factors which were influential in bringing about these changes.)

8. Think about the double bind of femininity and achievement. What are the implications for women (and for men) of this conflict? What suggestions do you have for lessening (or eliminating) this conflict?

9. Compare the characteristics of Marcia's four identity statuses for college men and women. How are they similar and dissimilar? Note the difficulties inherent in using male identity development as a standard for female identity development.

10. What are your feelings about the role college plays in facilitating or interfering with identity achievement in males and females? How do you think your college experience has affected your sex-role identity development?

11. Are there aspects of college life you feel could be changed to facilitate identity achievement? Consider this issue in terms of sex-role issues.

Chapter 7 Outline

chapter 7

Relating to Parents and Achieving Independence

Of all the developmental tasks we have set forth for adolescents, perhaps none so clearly captures the desired outcome of psychological maturation as the one we'll discuss in this chapter. Adulthood is characterized by the ability to assume responsibility for oneself. Among other things, this requires that a person be emotionally and financially self-supporting.

Physical, cognitive, and personality factors are all important in the development of independence. Also, culture and class influence the nature and length of adolescence. So, while the achievement of autonomy is a critical feature of adolescence, the criteria for attaining it, the age at which it occurs, the length of time given to the task, and the way the transition to adulthood is marked vary considerably.

In subsequent chapters we will see how interactions with peers and educational and work experiences contribute to the development of autonomy. Here we will focus on the family and its role in this process.

ROLE OF THE FAMILY IN THE SOCIALIZATION PROCESS

The family is generally acknowledged to be the social institution that most significantly influences individual development. Parents are role models, standard setters, and reward dispensers in cognitive and self-concept development, in identity achievement, and in sex-role identification. In the early years the family is more influential than the media, peers, and schools. During adolescence the family assumes a less central role in socialization.

Patterns of Family Organization

Families in almost all societies can be characterized as either extended families or nuclear families (Sussman, 1978). The *extended family,* the more common pattern throughout the world, consists of mother, father, immediate children, grandparents, and sometimes other relatives. The *nuclear family* occurs less frequently throughout the world, but it is the typical family structure in most Western societies. It consists of mother, father, and immediate children. It has been estimated that 85 percent of all North American children live in nuclear families (Keniston, 1975).

Recent Changes within the American Family

During the past 30 years there have been significant general social changes and changes within the family unit which have affected American family life.

Increased Mobility and Urbanization   Over the past three decades families have become more mobile. It is estimated that close to half of American families move every five years (U.S. Bureau of the Census, 1982). Also there are trends toward increased urbanization in the United States—more families are moving to the city.

These changes mean that the contemporary American nuclear family is more isolated than it has been before. This results in stronger demands being placed on family members for emotional support which formerly also came from life-long friendships and the community. Today's parents are in the difficult position of having sole responsibility for the care and discipline of their children, which can be lonely and exhausting.

The extended family is the most common family pattern in the world (but not in most Western societies).

Smaller Family Size   Approximately 200 years ago the number of children in the typical American family was 6 or more (Le Francois, 1981); at the height of the baby boom after World War II the figure was 3.8; according to more recent estimates the number has dropped to 2 (U.S. Bureau of the Census, 1980). This means that today's adolescents grow up in smaller families than has been true in the recent past. And, family size has been found to influence parent-adolescent interactions, as we shall see.

Alternative Family Patterns   The notion that the "average American family" consists of a two-parent family with the father working and the mother at home taking care of the children is a myth (Levine, 1978). In fact, this type of household is characteristic of only 13 percent of all American families (see Table 7.1). Moreover, it has been argued that this myth should be discarded quickly because a growing majority of children and adolescents who don't grow up in families like this believe wrongly that they are atypical and feel stigmatized (Levine, 1978).

Clearly, there appear to be increasing varieties in family organization, although it is not yet apparent whether this trend will continue. Nonetheless, we can say that the family experiences of today's adolescents are different from those of their parents.

Perhaps the most obvious change in the family unit is the increased frequency of divorce. In 1900 1 of every 12 marriages ended in divorce; today, half of all new marriages are predicted to end in divorce (Spanier & Fleer, 1979). While the effects of divorce are numerous and can be positive as well as negative, one obvious outcome of divorce is the breaking up of the family unit. Since 60 percent of divorces involve children, we have seen an increase in one-parent families (Cox & Cox, 1979). In 1948 only 1 child in 14 grew up in a single-parent family (Keniston, 1975), but by 1978 that proportion had increased to 1 in 6 (J. A. Levine, 1978).

Also, divorced parents frequently remarry. Children in these *reconstituted families* have to adjust not only to the initial shift from a two-parent to a one-parent family, but also to the change back to a two-parent family with a new parent and often with new siblings.

Increased Numbers of Working Mothers   The mythical two-parent family with mother at home has become less frequent as the number of mothers who work has steadily increased. By 1980 some 16.6 million mothers were working (U.S. Bureau of Labor Statistics, 1981). More specifically, 54 percent of all mothers with children under

Table 7.1   DISTRIBUTION OF ADULT AMERICANS BY TYPE OF HOUSEHOLD

Household type	Percent of all households
Child-free marriages (childless or after child rearing)	23
Single, separated, divorced, or widowed (no children present)	21
Single-parent families	16
Dual-breadwinner nuclear families	16
Single-breadwinner nuclear families	13
Extended families	6
Experimental families or cohabiting	4
No wage-earner nuclear families	1

Source: Adapted from James Ramey. (1978). Experimental family forms—the family of the future. *Marriage and Family Review, 1*(1), 1, 2–9. Copyright 1978 by the Haworth Press. Adapted by permission.

18 years of age were in the labor force in 1981 (Grossman, 1982). The larger proportion of women workers come from families of average and below-average income who work "not only for fulfillment but because they need the money" (Keniston, 1975).

In our society (as in most), it is expected that mothers will take primary responsibility for childcare. While some may see this as unfair and undesirable, it is nonetheless a fact. Mothers who work necessarily spend less time with their children. In some homes fathers are spending more time on parenting and housecleaning tasks, but the average time increases are quite small (Pleck, 1981b).

Clearly, contemporary American family life is different than it has been in the past. Moreover, this fact is bound to have important effects on the nature of parent-adolescent relationships today.

EFFECTS OF FAMILY STATUS AND STRUCTURE ON ADOLESCENT DEVELOPMENT

Socioeconomic Status

Socioeconomic status has significant influence on adolescent development. This is because there are important differences among upper-, middle-, and lower-SES families with regard to the availability and quality of health care, shelter, food, and clothing as well as educational, cultural, recreational, and occupational opportunities. Also, socioeconomic status is associated with differences in parenting styles, values, and aspirations.

Adolescents in upper-SES families are likely to have many more advantages

More than half of all American mothers work outside the home.

than their middle- and lower-SES peers. They grow up in large and well-cared for homes, often in exclusive areas, have access to excellent health care, and have no worries about basic life necessities. Their parents can afford to send them to the best schools and can provide numerous cultural and recreational opportunities for them. The pressures of having to get a job in order to support themselves are less often present. While it is obvious that such adolescents enjoy important economic and social advantages over their middle- and lower-SES peers, it is difficult to know in more detail about their actual life experiences since few studies have been done with this group.

Youth from middle-class families have parents who have graduated from high school and have often attended or graduated from college. Their parents are often professionals (attorneys, physicians, professors, executives) or work in service and sales occupations. Middle-SES adolescents grow up in families in which education, hard work, and individualism are valued. Middle-SES adolescents are more likely than their lower-SES peers to like and do well in school and to have higher educational and occupational aspirations (S. S. Johnson, 1975).

Adolescents from lower-SES families have parents who may or may not have graduated from high school and who work as skilled and unskilled laborers. The values of obedience, neatness, and conformity to external standards are stressed. A disproportionate number of black and ethnic minority group families fall into this category. This means that youth in these families must fight the double disadvantages of prejudice and socioeconomic deprivation. Compared to their upper- and middle-SES peers, lower-SES youth are more likely to dislike, do poorly, and drop out of school. They also have lower educational and occupational aspirations and marry at earlier ages than their upper- and middle-SES peers.

One study of almost 20,000 subjects researched the relative importance of SES, racial-ethnic group, family size, and birth order on intelligence (Page & Grandon, 1979). It was found that all these variables are important influences on intellectual performance, but SES and racial-ethnic background are much more influential in this regard than family size and birth order. More specifically, it was found that membership in racial and ethnic minority groups and lower-SES families were associated with lower intellectual performance. Given the fact of significant differences in the advantages tied to socioeconomic status and racial and ethnic group membership, these findings, while distressing, are not surprising.

Family Size

Family size interacts with other important factors such as socioeconomic status, a fact which needs to be kept in mind. In larger families both parents and children place greater importance on the needs of the family as a whole than on those of individual family members. Also, larger families are more likely to use authoritarian parenting styles (Elder, 1962; Peterson & Kunz, 1975). One study found that adolescents in middle-class families perceived parental control to increase as family size increased; adolescents in lower-SES families did not have this perception since authoritarian methods are generally more common in such families regardless of the size (Elder, 1962; Peterson & Kunz, 1975). Conflicts between adolescents and parents occur more often in larger families, and parents in large families are more likely to use physical force as a means of discipline (Edwards & Brauberger, 1973).

Research on the effects of family size suggests that adolescents from larger families are likely to be more independent and more oriented toward their peers and peer values rather than toward their families compared to those from smaller families (J. C. Coleman, 1980; Douvan & Adelson, 1966). Those from smaller families are more likely to be superior in intellectual performance, supposedly due to the effects of increased parental attention (Tavris, 1976).

Birth Order and Gender

A number of studies seem to confirm the fact that first-born and only children enjoy a number of advantages over other children. In addition to the obvious economic advantages, it has been found that a greater number of these individuals have a higher need to achieve (Sampson, 1962) and actually attain eminence (Schachter, 1963).

Findings with regard to only children seem to contradict the popular negative stereotypes about this group, that is, that they are self-centered, maladjusted, dependent, and unlikable. For example, in a study of college students it was found that only children were more cooperative, more trusting, and more independent than first- or last-born children, and no more neurotic, unhappy, lonely, or introverted than first-, middle-, or last-born children (Falbo, 1976, 1978). Other research suggests that only and first-born children score higher on intelligence tests than those born later (Zajonc & Marcus, 1975).

On the other hand, second and later children tend to be more easygoing and extroverted than first-borns (V. D. Thompson, 1974). It is believed that this is mainly due to the fact that parents are more relaxed and confident once they have had some parenting experience.

The relationship of birth order to observed differences is not clear because what appear to be the effects of birth order may really be the effects of social-class differences in birth rate or family size (Schooler, 1972). Because middle-class parents not only have fewer children but also are better educated, they can provide their offspring with more economic, educational, and cultural advantages.

Gender will be an important factor determining family role to the extent that sex-roles are emphasized in the family. Sex roles receive more emphasis in lower-SES and larger families (Rosenkrantz, Vogel, Bee, Broverman, & Broverman, 1968). Also, it has been found that most mothers and fathers perceive meals, children, and housework as female responsibilities and odd jobs and chores as masculine activities (Larson, 1974).

When adolescents perceive that there are inequities in household responsibilities due to gender or birth order, legitimate resentments can develop. For example, older children may complain when they are asked to be especially responsible to care for or to set an example for younger siblings; they may resent seeing younger siblings receive privileges at an earlier age than they were awarded them. Adolescent girls often complain of being burdened with household or babysitting responsibilities which their brothers escape (Swanson, Massey, & Payne, 1972).

Where there are two or more children in a family, siblings appear to play a part in sex-role socialization. In particular, the factors of sex and birth order of siblings have been found to produce such outcomes as these: girl-girl dyads are likely to have more highly "feminine" characteristics; boy-boy dyads are likely to have more highly "masculine" characteristics (Sutton-Smith, Roberts, & Rosenberg, 1964); boys and girls with opposite-sex siblings tend to rank high in self-confidence, curiosity, cheerfulness, and kindness and to recover quickly from emotional upset (Koch, 1956).

Working Mothers

Since many people believe that a working mother cannot be a competent mother, it is of interest to know what, if any, effects maternal employment has on adolescents.

In comprehensive reviews of research on maternal employment, Lois Hoffman (1974a, 1979) found that few studies have shown negative effects of maternal employment on adolescents and most have shown positive ones. In fact, Hoffman concluded that "the overall picture suggests that maternal employment is better suited to the needs of adolescents than is full-time mothering" (1979, p. 864). One study compared the effects of working and mothering to the effects of full-time mothering on adolescents. The results indicated that both the sons and daughters of working mothers had higher self-esteem, better personality and social adjustment, better family relations, and better interpersonal relationships at school compared to the adolescents of full-time mothers (Gold & Andres, 1978).

It appears that working mothers can have important positive effects on their adolescent daughters. Girls with working mothers are likely to be more active, independent, and outgoing, do better academically, have higher career aspirations, and show better personality and social adjustment than daughters of nonworking mothers (L. W. Hoffman, 1974a, 1979). On the other hand, one study found that high school girls whose mothers worked outside the home reported greater stress and less social support from their mothers than did other girls. There were no such findings for the male subjects (Burke & Weir, 1978).

A mother's attitude toward her work is an important determinant of her children's responses to the fact of her employment. If she feels positively about her work, her children are more likely to show positive effects; likewise, if a mother feels negatively about working, her children are more likely to show negative effects (L. W. Hoffman, 1979). College women's attitudes toward combining career and family roles have been found to be influenced by whether their mothers had endorsed combining roles and, if their mothers worked, how successfully the mothers were able to integrate the two roles (Baruch, 1972). The daughters of mothers who worked and experienced negative personal consequences because of career-family conflicts had unfavorable attitudes toward the dual-role pattern.

Marital Disruption

Families are disrupted by the death of one or both parents, but more frequently the disruption occurs because of divorce. Of children who grew up in the 1970s, about 9 percent lost one or both parents because of death and about 20 to 30 percent experienced the divorce of their parents (Bane, 1976). The adjustment to a single-parent family, parents' dating activities, and remarriage can all be difficult for children and adolescents (as well as for parents).

Effects of Divorce   Adolescents are better able than younger children to understand the reasons for divorce and to understand that they are not to blame. They are also better able to cope with loyalty conflicts and financial and other practical problems (Hetherington, 1979).

It has been found that divorced mothers are more likely than nondivorced mothers to ask adolescents to function autonomously at an early age. Some of this can be helpful in fostering independence, but inappropriate demands to assume adult responsibilities can lead to "feelings of being overwhelmed by unsolvable problems, incompetence, and resentment about lack of support and unavailability of mothers, and to precocious sexual concerns in some school-aged children and adolescents" (Hetherington, 1979, p. 857).

Findings of studies on the impact of divorce on adolescents' self-concepts are inconsistent. Some report that adolescent self-concepts are negatively affected by divorce (Parish & Dostal, 1980; Parish & Taylor, 1979; Young & Parish, 1977), but others have not found this to be true (Parish, 1981; Parish, Dostal, & Parish, 1981; Raschke & Raschke, 1979). Findings are consistent in regard to adolescents' perceptions of their parents. Parents from divorced families are more negatively evaluated than are parents from intact families (Parish, 1981; Parish & Dostal, 1980, Parish & Kappes, 1980); adolescents hold their parents responsible for the divorce and the problems which result from it (Parish, 1981). It isn't clear whether remarriage alters these perceptions.

Marital discord and divorce seem to have a longer lasting impact on boys than on girls. For example, a study of 13- to 17-year-old girls found that within two years after a divorce, girls showed few disturbances in social and emotional development, although sometimes conflicts about heterosexual relationships did arise (Hetherington, 1972). In contrast, boys from divorced families showed higher frequencies of behavior disorders and difficulties in interpersonal relationships (at home and at school with both teachers and peers) than did girls from divorced families and children from nuclear families (Hetherington, 1979). The causes of these sex differences are not yet clear, but Hetherington speculated that boys may be exposed to more stress and aggression and may have fewer available emotional supports than girls.

Importantly, research findings indicate that children and adolescents may be better off living with one supportive parent than living with two parents who frequently fight or who hold consistently negative feelings toward each other (even though parents attempt to disguise them) (Ahlstrom & Havighurst, 1971; Landis, 1970; Nye, 1957). One study revealed that adolescents from happy, divorced families often showed better personal adjustment, less stress, fewer psychosomatic illnesses, and less delinquency than did their peers in intact, unhappy families (Landis, 1970). Hence, unhappy parents who stay together for "the sake of the children" may not be doing their children any favors.

The immediate and short-term effects of divorce are often quite distressing for children and adolescents. The most common feelings are fear, anger, guilt, depression, and shame (Hetherington, 1979; Wallerstein & Kelly, 1976). Still, most young people seem able to handle the resulting difficulties and adjust to new circumstances within a year or so (Wallerstein & Kelly, 1976).

Effects of Death   The effects of the death of one or both parents are much less well-studied than those of divorce or separation. In one study seventh-, eighth-, and ninth-grade adolescents who were separated from a parent because of death did not differ from adolescents from intact families on measures of self-concept, perception of the mother, occupational aspirations, or school achievement (Rosenthal & Hansen, 1980). Also, parents from families in which the father had died were evaluated less negatively than were parents from divorced families (Parish, 1981).

Single-Parent Families   Recent estimates indicate that one child in five under the age of 18 is living in a single-parent family, almost double the number 25 years ago (Glick & Norton, 1979). Most of them will live about 6 years in a single-parent home (Hetherington, 1979).

Living in a single-parent household is likely to be stressful for both parent and child, and things are made even more difficult when the single parent is poor, which is usually the case. Among families headed by women, almost 50 percent live below the poverty level, compared to about 16 percent of all women with children (Conger, 1981).

The popular stereotype of the child from a single-parent family is an individual with severe problems such as delinquency and psychological disturbances (Bane, 1976). Many studies have supported such a view, but their findings have been called into

The loss of a parent through death or divorce is a painful experience for an adolescent.

question for failing to control for differences in socioeconomic status between intact and single-parent families. When studies have controlled for SES, differences between children from intact and single-parent families have been found to be small or nonexistent.

Also, it's important to consider the possible impact of negative stereotypic attitudes on children and adolescents from divorced families. For example, in one study, researchers showed teachers a videotape of a boy engaging in various social interactions (Santrock & Tracy, 1978). Half of the teachers were told that the boy was from an intact home and the other half were told that his parents were divorced. Teachers in the latter group rated the boy more negatively on two of 11 personality traits (happiness and emotional adjustment) than did teachers in the former group. Also, teachers who believed the boy's parents to be divorced rated him more negatively than the intact-family boy on his ability to cope with stress, one of five behavioral predictions teachers were asked to make.

Effects of Extended Father Absence   Since most single-parent families are headed by the mother, the impact of extended father absence is of interest.

The traditional view of sex-role identity assumes that paternal absence leads to insecure male identity and that this, in turn, leads to poor psychological adjustment (Pleck, 1981a). Girls whose fathers are absent still have a same-sex role model at hand; therefore, it is reasoned that paternal absence will be a less severe problem for girls.

Several studies have shown that paternal absence has a number of negative effects on boys. For example, boys from father-absent homes are more likely than boys from intact homes to score lower on tests of intellectual performance (Blanchard & Biller, 1971; Landy, Rosenberg, & Sutton-Smith, 1969; Santrock, 1972) and general academic achievement (Blanchard & Biller, 1971). It has been found that boys whose fathers are absent often show signs of psychological maladjustment, have some problems in interactions with their peers, and have higher rates of dropping out of school and juvenile delinquency (R. E. Anderson, 1968; Biller & Davids, 1973).

However, not all studies show such negative outcomes. For example, no differences were found in the self-concepts or the quality of relationships with mothers between boys from homes in which the father was present or absent (Feldman & Feldman, 1979). Moreover, a review of studies concluded that on boys' school performance, mental illness, and later marital instability when factors other than father absence were controlled for, the factor of paternal absence appeared to have no effect (Herzog & Sudia, 1973).

Research on the effects of father absence on girls has been minimal. One study investigated its effects on the behavior of lower- and middle-SES white girls aged 13 to 17 years who came from intact families, divorced families, or families in which the father had died (Hetherington, 1972). Father-absent girls and those from intact homes appeared to be relatively similar in sex-typed behaviors, in preference for the female role, and in relationships with other females.

Differences did appear in their interactions with males. Both groups of father-absent girls felt less secure with male peers and adults than father-present girls, but the two groups seemed to respond to their insecurities in opposite ways. Daughters of widows tended to be shy and withdrawn, to be a bit physically tense, and to avoid being near male adults and peers. They also started to date later than other girls and seemed to be sexually inhibited. Daughters of divorcees, however, tended to seek out male peers at the expense of interactions involving other females, to start dating earlier, and to have sexual intercourse at earlier ages.

Single parents can be helpful to their sons and daughters by arranging for or encouraging positive interactions with older, supportive adults of both sexes. For example, it has been found that the presence of a father or a mother substitute can be very helpful in preventing and reducing delinquent behavior in children of the same sex as the substitute (Biller, 1974; Lynn, 1974). Also, parents who attempt to convey positive attitudes about their former spouses to their children can help their children feel less need to take sides with either parent, thus alleviating a common source of stress for them.

Effects of Remarriage   Because remarriage occurs in the majority of cases in which couples have gotten divorces, many adolescents find it necessary to adjust to the situation of a *reconstituted* or *blended family*. Such adjustments are not always easy for adolescents or their parents. Still, several national surveys indicate that there are no significant differences in the psychological characteristics of children and adolescents from reconstituted families compared to those from intact families (Wilson, Zurcher, McAdams & Curtis, 1975).

A study of the stepsibling relationships of children and adolescents reported that approximately 25 percent rated their relationships as "excellent," 35 percent as "good," and 35 percent as "poor" (Duberman, 1973). Some difficulties seemed to arise because stepsiblings saw each other as rivals, usually when they were the same sex or similar in age.

Some of the difficulties in making the transition from a single-parent to a reconstituted family occur because the single parent and child(ren) have been thrown together for support and have become more dependent on each other. The adolescent may assume additional household responsibilities and may even work to help out with family finances.

When the parent remarries, however, the focus of interest shifts in part to the new partner and, possibly, to new stepchildren as well. The young person may now be freed from some of the responsibilities which were previously necessary because there was no second parent in the home, but he or she also relinquishes feelings of pride for performing these tasks competently. Ironically, therefore, a parent's remarriage may mean that life is easier in some ways for an adolescent, but it may also cause him or her to feel less important to the biological parent (Rosenberg, 1965). This situation is further complicated for adolescents whose homes were disrupted by death because a parent's remarriage is often viewed as a betrayal of the memory of the deceased parent.

PARENTING STYLES AND ADOLESCENT DEVELOPMENT

Parental Acceptance and Parental Control

Research suggests that there are two major dimensions underlying parent-child relationships: parental acceptance and parental control (Hower & Edwards, 1979). *Parental acceptance* appears to be the more important of the two factors. High acceptance appears to be positively related to moral development, whereas parental rejection is associated with poor adjustment. *Parental control* refers to the degree of strictness of parental standards. The absence of control is related to higher levels of aggression and maladjustment; too strict and punitive control is associated negatively with moral development and also leads to adolescent rebellion.

Diana Baumrind (1968, 1971) has looked at specific parenting styles as interactions between the two dimensions of acceptance and control. As can be seen from Table 7.2, these styles are *authoritarian, authoritative, neglectful,* and *permissive.* Baumrind argues that it is important to make a distinction between authoritarian and authoritative parenting styles. The authoritarian style involves rigidly enforced rules with low acceptance. The authoritative style combines reasoned control with love and affection; that is, it involves setting firm limits, but demonstrating acceptance by explaining the reasons behind policies and by encouraging verbal give-and-take with the child. In studying the effects of three of these styles, she has found that children reared with the authoritative style were the most autonomous and content with themselves while those reared with the permissive style were judged to be the least well-developed in these areas. The level of development of the children reared by authoritarian parents was in between the first two groups (1968, 1971, 1988).

To a great extent, research on parenting styles focuses on disciplinary practices, the manner in which parental control is employed. Martin Hoffman (1970, 1980) has suggested that parental discipline takes three major forms:

1. *Power assertion:* physical punishment, deprivation of possessions or privileges, or threat of these

Harsh and frequent discipline often results in resentment and rebellion.

Table 7.2 FOUR PARENTING STYLES AS INTERACTIONS OF PARENTAL ACCEPTANCE AND CONTROL

	Parental acceptance	
	Low	**High**
Parental control — High	Authoritarian (low acceptance, high control)	Authoritative (high acceptance, high control)
Parental control — Low	Neglectful (low acceptance, low control)	Permissive (high acceptance, low control)

Source: Table constructed from Diana Baumrind. (1971). Current patterns of parental authority. (Monograph). *Developmental Psychology,* 4(1, Part 2), 1–103. Copyright 1971 by the American Psychological Association. Adapted by permission of the author.

2. *Love withdrawal:* nonphysical expressions of anger or disapproval such as ignoring the child, isolating the child from siblings or friends, refusing to speak to the child, making statements of disappointment or dislike, or threatening to leave
3. *Induction:* reasoning through explanations of harmful consequences of the child's behavior for himself or herself and others, appeals to the child's pride and his or her concern for others

Of course, a parent's disciplinary style may combine these forms. Still, it is usually possible to classify a given technique as predominantly one or another.

Research has shown that power assertion does not facilitate the internalization of moral standards, but rather fosters an externally focused moral orientation such as being careful not to get caught doing something wrong (M. L. Hoffman, 1970; Hower & Edwards, 1979). It is interesting to note that although love withdrawal (psychological control) is widely practiced, research has not shown that it has a clear-cut positive effect on the development of moral standards. Hoffman has explained: "Like power assertion, love withdrawal has a highly punitive quality. Although it poses no immediate physical or material threat to the child, it may be more devastating emotionally than power assertion because it poses the ultimate threat of abandonment or separation" (1970, p. 285). Inductive disciplinary methods have been shown to be positively related to the internalization of moral standards (M. L. Hoffman, 1970; Hoffman & Saltzstein, 1967; Hower & Edwards, 1979).

Power-assertive techniques appear to decrease in effectiveness as children grow older, and inductive techniques increase in effectiveness with regard to the internalization of moral standards (Hower & Edwards, 1979). During childhood and particularly during adolescence, it is important that parents begin to reason with their offspring: "By using reason, the authoritative parent teaches the child to seek the reasons behind the directives and eventually to exercise his option either to conform, or to deviate and to cope with the consequences" (Baumrind, 1968, p. 264).

As we have seen, cognitive development is facilitated by opportunities to test out ideas. The adolescent especially needs to develop his or her own position and may need someone to argue with to do this. This role of "friendly adversary" is one which understanding parents can play for their adolescent children (Baumrind, 1968). In this way young people can learn that others do not necessarily feel the same way they do and why this may be so. This social give-and-take is necessary for them to come to terms with their egocentric orientations.

The nature of parenting during childhood has important implications for parent-adolescent relationships. In the ideal situation, parents will have employed parenting styles that facilitated the child's identification with them, encouraged internalization of their standards, and fostered mutual respect, caring, and good communication. Effective parenting during adolescence requires parents to use less control. For example, it has been found among 18- and 19-year olds, low control and high acceptance seemed to be most highly related to the internalization of moral standards (Hower & Edwards, 1979). Low control is less likely to result in violent disagreements and destructive ways of resolving parent-adolescent conflicts than high control.

Parents' continued use of power alone by which to control an adolescent's behavior can contribute to a number of negative outcomes: inability of the adolescent to make reasonable decisions about his or her own actions, juvenile delinquency, running away from home, and so forth. Under normal circumstances adolescents do not inevitably rebel against all kinds of authority, but rather are more likely to react negatively to either very strict or very permissive parental control (Balswick & Macrides, 1975; Baumrind, 1968). Parents who use authoritative child-rearing practices are more likely to produce adolescents who are autonomous but not blindly rebellious and who can think for themselves.

Social Class Differences in Parenting Styles

Middle-SES parents are more likely to discipline their children with verbal reprimands, while lower-SES parents are more likely to respond with physical punishment and also are more limited in their range of responding to disciplinary situations (Gecas & Nye, 1974; Peterson & Kunz, 1975). Also, adolescents from lower-SES families report more problems than do their peers in higher-SES families (Harper & Collins, 1975). In addition, a study of 16- and 17-year-old lower- and middle-SES males and females found that middle-class adolescents perceived their fathers to be both more supportive and controlling (suggesting more involvement) than did lower-SES adolescents (Gecas, 1971).

It is important to remember, however, that a number of important factors vary with social class: family size, verbal IQ, psychosocial functioning (Henggeler & Tavormina, 1980). A large number of studies have failed to control for the effects of these other variables when investigating the effects of socioeconomic status. Therefore, conclusions about the impact of SES should be viewed with some caution.

Cross-Cultural Findings

A study of American (median age 16 years) and Danish high school students (median age 15 years) investigated adolescents' perceptions of parental authority (Kandel & Lesser, 1969). Three different patterns of parental control were identified: authoritarian, democratic, and permissive. From Table 7.3, it can be seen that fathers were perceived as more authoritarian than mothers. In both countries American parents were perceived to be much more authoritarian than Danish parents, and the permissive style was perceived as being used rather infrequently by parents in both countries.

One of the more interesting findings of this study was that Danish adolescents felt much more independent from parental influence than did American youth. Also the authors reported that Danish adolescents were able to act in a more autonomous manner (did not need to have specific rules to follow) than American adolescents. The authors concluded that Danish parents didn't treat their adolescents as children as long as American parents and that Danish parents subjected their children to stronger discipline than did American parents. They speculated that this may produce children who are much more self-disciplined at adolescence and who can be given additional freedom at that point in development.

PARENT-ADOLESCENT INTERACTIONS

The fact that adult status is approaching is perhaps the most salient characteristic of parent-adolescent relationships. Obviously, the successful achievement of adolescent autonomy requires a joint effort. Adolescents must gradually decrease their emotional dependence on their parents, while maintaining communication with and feelings of affection for them. At the same time parents must gradually relinquish control over their adolescent children while maintaining an appropriate level of emotional support.

It is understandable that there will be conflicts in this process, and research findings suggest that these are most likely to occur around the age of 14 (Kandel & Lesser, 1972). Most adolescents and their parents seem able to cope with the conflicts that arise, but in some cases serious disruptions in parent-adolescent relationships occur, usually a result of a history of difficult parent-child interactions. These are frequently associated with such negative outcomes as delinquent behavior and psychological disorders (see Chapter 13).

Communication and Feelings of Affection

Most adolescents describe their relationships with their parents as positive (Kandel & Lesser, 1969; Niles, 1979; Schvaneveldt, 1973; Sorenson, 1973; Thurnher, Spence, &

Table 7.3   AMERICAN AND DANISH ADOLESCENTS' PERCEPTIONS OF PARENTAL AUTHORITY

Parental authority	Interaction with mother		Interaction with father	
	U.S. (*N* = 983)	Denmark (*N* = 950)	U.S. (*N* = 955)	Denmark (*N* = 936)
Authoritarian	43%	15%	53%	31%
Democratic	40%	61%	29%	48%
Permissive	17%	24%	18%	21%

Source: Adapted from Denise Kandel and Gerald Lesser. (1969). Parent-adolescent relationships and adolescent independence in the United States and Denmark. *Journal of Marriage and the Family, 31*(2), 348–358. Copyright 1969 by The National Council on Family Relations. Reprinted by permission.

Lowenthal, 1974). For example, a survey of 400 American teenagers 13 to 19 years of age revealed that 87 percent of the boys and 89 percent of the girls had a lot of respect for their parents as people (Sorensen, 1973). Similarly, about 80 percent of these youth stated that they had a lot of respect for their parents' ideas and opinions. In contrast, only 21 percent stated that they did not feel any strong affection for their parents, and only 6 percent indicated that they felt that their parents did not really like them. Some 13 percent of the girls and 25 percent of the boys agreed with the statement, "I've pretty much given up on being able to get along with my parents" (Sorenson, 1973, p. 391).

Still, both adolescents and parents frequently complain that neither are willing to listen to others' points of view or feelings (Blood & D'Angelo, 1974; Schvaneveldt, 1973). While this probably does not reflect the intentions of either, there are a number of dynamics operating at this time for both parents and adolescents which can make communication difficult.

Topics of Disagreement

Major conflicts seem to occur over minor issues in most families (J. C. Coleman, 1978; J. C. Coleman, George, & Holt, 1977; Troll, 1972). These include such things as style of dress, hair length, and musical tastes. It has been suggested that this may reflect the displacement of anger to issues which are less likely to disrupt family relationships (Blood & D'Angelo, 1974; Troll, 1972).

Parent-adolescent disagreements occur over a number of issues (Campbell & Cooper, 1975; Chand, Crider, & Willits, 1975; J. C. Coleman, 1978; J. C. Coleman, George, & Holt, 1977; Kinloch, 1970; Schvaneveldt, 1973). We have grouped the various points of conflict into four categories for some coherence.

1. *Beliefs and values:* sexual attitudes and behavior, religious beliefs and church attendance, obeying the law, drinking, smoking, drug use, ethical or moral

Most adolescents report that their relationships with their parents are positive in nature.

principles, social injustice, sex-role issues, music and artistic preferences, earning and spending money

2. *Home and family:* performance of household chores, care of personal belongings and room, use of the family car, use of the telephone, care of family property, relationships with siblings and other family members, eating with the family, use of time, manners, language and speech
3. *School:* attitudes toward and behavior in school, relationships with teachers, grades, study habits, school attendance
4. *Social life:* choice of friends and dating partners, age allowed to date, how often allowed to go out, curfew hours, clothes and hair styles

Causes of Conflicts

Interlocking Identity Issues   Children reach adolescence at about the same time parents may be experiencing identity crises of their own. Such interlocking identity issues increase the likely of disagreements between them (Scherz, 1967). Everyone can get so caught up in his or her own concerns that he or she cannot hear what others are saying. Consequently, both parents and adolescents frequently complain that the other does not try to understand their point of view. Some awareness of the dynamics that are operating at this time can facilitate mutual understanding.

Sexuality   At the same time that adolescents are struggling with their emerging sexuality, their parents are having to cope with a decline in physical attractiveness and vitality. Since a child's physical attractiveness and emergent sexuality reminds parents that they are growing older, it is not uncommon for them to be somewhat jealous or resentful—probably at an unconscious level—of these qualities.

Parents whose lives are relatively satisfying are less likely to respond to this situation in a negative way. Parents who are having more difficulty may react by punishing their children or restricting their social activities, or by pushing their children into social activities and sexual relationships. Such parents may be attempting to live through their children or to prevent their children from repeating what the parents see as their own early unsatisfactory experiences.

Sometimes, too, parents compete with their children for the attention of adolescent friends. This usually causes justifiable anger on the part of the son or daughter as well as conflict and confusion about how to deal with the situation.

Life choices and achievement   While adolescents are starting to consider what to do with their lives, their mothers and fathers may be feeling that the time in which to accomplish important goals is growing increasingly short. Or, they may be feeling that they are not really happy and wonder what types of life changes are possible. Adolescents may criticize the parents' life-style and chosen roles at exactly the time when the parents are feeling particularly vulnerable and confused. Parents may look at their children and wish that they could start all over again. Accordingly, some try to push their children into areas they wish that they had gone into or away from those they have found unsatisfactory. Some adolescents abide by their parents' wishes in order to make their parents happy (even at the cost of their own happiness), while others overreact to such pressures by leaving home or school prematurely.

Changes in communication and power   As the adolescent moves toward adulthood and independence, confrontations with parental (and other) authority are inevitable. It is hard for parents to relinquish the habits of guidance and control they have exercised over many years and they may have difficulty finding an acceptable style of interacting with adolescents. Parents often report that if they show genuine interest in their adolescent's lives, they are seen as "snoopy"; if they retreat and show less interest, they fear being perceived as uncaring.

Changes in attachment   Because of social and emotional needs, adolescents turn more toward peers for support than they did as children. This doesn't mean that adolescents emotionally "exchange" peers for parents; it just means that parents play an increasingly less important role in the children's lives. While parents know that this must happen, they still may feel hurt or resentful when it actually occurs. This is more likely to occur in cases where parents don't have other resources for identity and self-esteem (recall our earlier discussion of the positive effect of working mothers on adolescents).

It is important for parents not to overreact by trying to keep adolescents dependent or by rejecting them. In the first case young people will find it difficult to develop appropriate social skills and may fail to learn to take responsibility for themselves. In the latter case adolescents may be driven to seek emotional support entirely from peers. Ideally, both parents and adolescents will come to see each other as persons and as friends. This often happens after adolescents leave home.

Clashes in values   The process of self-definition requires adolescents to question parental values, and this may cause some parents to become defensive or angry. These reactions are intensified if the parents are uncertain about some of their own values. The fact that adolescents are raising value questions is likely to increase the parents' conflicts and discomfort.

Parental Exploitation   Parental exploitation is another cause of conflicts. Parents may constantly put their own needs before those of their children or may try to use adolescents to gratify their own needs. Examples include demanding unreasonable achievements in sports, school, or the arts so as to be able to bask in the reflected glory or requiring that adolescents take on more than their share of family and household responsibilities.

According to David Elkind (1967b, 1979), adolescents react to parental exploitation in the same way workers might respond to exploitation on the job: quitting, going on strike, sabotaging the work place, or passively submitting. The equivalent of quitting is dropping out of school, running away from home, or becoming incorrigible (quitting the family in a psychological sense). Adolescents on strike defy parental authority by continuing to go to school, but refusing to perform; staying at home, but refusing to do their share of household chores; or associating with peers whom the parents don't like. Examples of sabotage, a more serious reaction, are pregnancy, car stealing, vandalism, drinking, and drug use. According to Elkind, the saddest reaction to exploitation is the youngster who passively submits to the situation with the hope of winning or regaining parental love.

Some adolescents are required to take on more than their share of
family and household responsibilities.

Treating this problem is extremely difficult, because "although the pathology
exists in the parents, the symptoms appear in the children" (Elkind, 1967, p. 83).
Because the adolescent is the one with the observable problem, parents are often
unwilling to accept any more than superficial responsibility for their part in the matter.
And, because the young person feels used and abused, he or she is often unwilling to
take responsibility for his or her own actions.

Adolescent Egocentrism Another cause of conflicts between parents and adolescents
is adolescent egocentrism and its expression in the personal fable and imaginary audience. The operation of the personal fable leads adolescents to believe that their experiences are unique. Consequently, when their parents tease them about their first serious
romantic relationship or suggest that it is "puppy love," young people are convinced
that their parents "just don't understand."

Still, it is only through such experiences that adolescents learn that others' have
similar feelings, thereby diminishing egocentrism. Since younger adolescents are less
likely to be able to understand this phenomenon (because they are caught up in it), it
falls to parents and other adults to display some understanding and forbearance until
some of these lessons are learned.

The operation of the imaginary audience leads adolescents to believe and often
act as if they were "on stage." It gives rise to the self-consciousness and posturing which
are so characteristic of early adolescence. Often, young people will adopt different dress
standards from those their parents prefer or "show off" in an attempt to gain attention.
Because adolescents believe their behavior is acceptable (and worth at least an admiring
glance!), they have a difficult time understanding that others may feel differently and
this can lead to conflicts with parents.

Parenting Styles As we saw earlier, families in which parents used authoritarian
control are more likely to experience conflicts than those where democratic styles are

Table 7.4   ATTITUDE QUESTIONNAIRE ITEMS ON WHICH OLDER ADOLESCENTS AND THEIR PARENTS SHOWED MAJOR DIFFERENCES[a]

Questionnaire item	Adolescents (average rating)	Parents (average rating)
1. Authority of the police must be increased, rather than decreased.	4.4	2.0
2. Marijuana should be legalized.	3.3	5.7
3. Disappointment or concern would overshadow approval if a close friend admitted smoking marijuana.	5.0	2.2
4. Need for strict law enforcement by the police has been justified and generated by the action of troublemakers.	4.1	1.6
5. A school's dress code is a reasonable demand that students should abide by.	5.1	1.9
6. Premarital sexual activities have no place in our present society.	6.3	4.0
7. It is moral to flee to Canada to escape the draft.	3.0	5.5
8. I would not hesitate to experiment with marijuana.	3.4	6.5
9. Premarital sexual activities are and always should be considered immoral.	6.1	3.7
10. Those who use drugs are usually careless about their personal appearance.	5.3	2.6

[a]Major differences are defined as those in which attitudes differed by at least 2 points on a 7-point scale. The rating scale was 1, strongly agree; 2, moderately agree; 3, agree; 4, neutral; 5, disagree; 6, moderately disagree; and 7, strongly disagree.

Source: Adapted from Richard M. Lerner, Michael Karson, Murray Meisels, and John R. Knapp. (1975). Actual and perceived attitudes of late adolescents and their parents: The phenomenon of the generation gaps. *The Journal of Genetic Psychology, 126,* 195–207, Table 1. Copyright 1975 by The Journal Press. Adapted by permission.

employed (Edwards & Brauburger, 1973). Girls reported that family problems made up 22 percent of serious problems they faced. The corresponding figure for boys was only 10 percent, indicating gender differences in family interactions or perceptions of interactions or both (Adams, 1964). Adolescent girls have also reported experiencing much more hostility and arguing than boys who reported that they were dealt with more rationally.

Is There a "Generation Gap"?

The term *generation gap* refers to significant differences in the values and life philosophies of members of different generations. This idea has received a great deal of media attention. It originated because of the more obvious value differences being expressed by some youth in the mid-1960s and early 1970s.

If the generation gap refers not to an age difference, but to a cultural difference between generations, there is some evidence to support the idea. As we have previously discussed, rapid social change is a characteristic of technologically advanced countries. Consequently, parents often find themselves unable to advise their offspring because things have changed so dramatically and rapidly from the time when they were young. As a result, adolescents may look more to their peers than to their parents or other adults for advice about certain aspects of life (Mead's cofigurative cultural pattern).

While some evidence of a cultural gap between generations has been found, differences are not nearly as large as popular stereotypes would suggest. For example, a survey of 225 college students on questions related to religion, sexual freedom, music, dress, drug use, and other social issues revealed that the views of both males and females were in between the values they perceived their parents to hold and those they perceived their peers to hold (Meisels & Canter, 1971–1972). A related study of college students found that major differences in attitudes occurred on only 10 of 36 items (see Table 7.4) (Lerner, Karson, Meisels, & Knapp, 1975). Moreover, most of the differences were more a matter of how strongly they felt about a topic rather than having quite different beliefs.

Adolescents and their parents are most likely to disagree on five issues: drug use and experimentation (Lerner et al., 1975), sexual standards (Lerner et al., 1975), sex-role attitudes (Helmreich, Spence, & Gibson, 1982; Zey-Ferrell, Tolone, & Walsh, 1978), political attitudes (Lerner et al., 1975), and religious values (McAllister, 1981). Typically, adolescents' beliefs in these areas are more liberal than those of their parents, although we should note that some recent studies indicate that the current college population has more conventional attitudes about religion and politics than college students in the late 1960s and early 1970s (A. Levine, 1980; McAllister, 1981).

The facts that there are parent-adolescent value differences in these areas and that these areas are influenced by rapid social change can be interpreted as providing some support for Mead's characterization of contemporary American society as cofigurative.

A comparison of generational attitudes found that both adolescents and their parents significantly misperceived their differences. Adolescents significantly *over*estimated the number of major attitudinal differences between them and their parents, whereas parents significantly *under*estimated such differences.

These findings suggest that our original question, "Is there a generation gap?" might be rephrased, "Do parents or adolescents *perceive* a generation gap?" In fact, the actual generation gap is neither as great as adolescents seem to think nor as small as parents think. Lerner and his colleagues suggest that the differences in perceptions may

Adolescents overestimate the extent of the generation gap, whereas their parents underestimate it.

be related to the nature of parent-adolescent communication. Adolescents may not be open with their parents about issues like sex and drugs (two topics on which there were actual and adolescent-perceived gaps) which might cause parents to misperceive their children's attitudes. Another finding supports this reasoning: while parents did not see a gap existing on the issues of sex and drugs, they did see one with regard to dress. The latter, of course, is quite obvious to any observer, unlike one's privately held attitudes.

Because parents are usually open about their attitudes with their children, adolescents would be expected to have a relatively realistic view of their parents' beliefs. Yet, recall that adolescents overestimated the differences between their values and those of their parents. The authors of this study explain this phenomenon in terms of adolescents' needs to formulate their own sets of values. This may cause them to exaggerate the differences between their own and their parents' values and to perceive parental values falsely.

The perceptions of parents may also be distorted by emotional needs, but in the opposite direction. For example, parents may be unwilling to believe that their son or daughter might fit the negative stereotypes associated with adolescence or they may gain vicarious satisfaction and support by believing that their adolescent's values are similar to their own. Thus, both parents and adolescents may maintain false perceptions about each other in order to reduce the emotional conflict and distress which might otherwise be felt.

There are other explanations of the finding that more of a generation gap is perceived to exist than actually does. For one thing, a number of studies have surveyed the attitudes of a small and unrepresentative sample of adolescents, such as college activists in the 1960s. When these results are assumed to describe *all* adolescents, a rather wide generation gap would be falsely perceived to exist (Conger, 1971).

Also, because we are aware that generational differences have existed throughout history, it is easy to confuse these with the relatively recent culturally based contemporary generational differences (Conger, 1971).

Another cause of the misperception of the nature of the generation gap comes from repeated portrayals of serious and violent generational conflicts in the media. Such programs reinforce the false perception of large generational differences.

In conclusion, we need to consider the idea that generational conflict can provide a useful vehicle for intellectual, emotional, and social development. For example, recall our earlier discussion of the role of parent-adolescent conflicts in breaking down adolescent egocentrism. Also, because interpersonal disagreements are inevitable, it is essential to learn how to cope with them effectively. Parents (as well as other adults and the media) can serve as positive role models by explaining their beliefs and feelings, by being willing to listen to other points of view, and by being able to change their minds or maintain their positions as it seems appropriate.

PHYSICAL AND SEXUAL ABUSE IN FAMILIES

Physical Abuse

Annual estimates of the incidence of child abuse vary widely—from 41,000 to over one million—due to the difficulties of obtaining accurate data. Mothers are more likely to abuse their children than fathers, and abuse occurs more often in lower-SES and larger families (Gelles, 1976; Kempe & Kempe, 1978).

Causes of child abuse are not clearly agreed upon at this time and, no doubt, there are different causes for different types of abuse (Gelles, 1976). A factor that has been frequently cited is the acceptance of violence as a legitimate disciplinary technique in American society. For example, interviews with a national sample of parents revealed that 45 percent of them hit their children regularly (Gelles, 1976).

Other relatively consistent findings on this question suggest that a history of child abuse during childhood predisposes a person to become an abusive parent (Kempe & Kempe, 1978). Parents who have such a history learn abusive interaction styles from their own parents and fail to learn alternative positive parenting strategies. Such a family history is also likely to produce an individual who has low self-esteem and who has particularly strong needs for love and acceptance, but who lacks the skills to make and keep friends. Such a parent may expect more love and affection from children than they are capable of returning, feel betrayed when it isn't forthcoming, and lash out at them.

In this context, Brandt Steele (1980) has suggested that four conditions appear necessary in order for child abuse to occur:

1. A caretaker who is predisposed to child abuse because of a history of neglect or abuse in his or her own life,
2. A crisis that places extra stress on the caretaker,
3. Lack of sources of support for the caretaker, either because he or she is unable to reach out, or because facilities are unavailable, and
4. A child who is perceived as being unsatisfactory in some way.

Taking this view, it is easy to understand why child abuse is more likely to occur in poorer, larger, and less-well-educated families. As we have already seen, the levels of deprivation and stress in such families are much higher compared to higher-SES families.

The short- and long-term effects of child abuse vary depending on a variety of factors such as the age of the child when abuse was experienced, whether abuse occurred rarely or repeatedly, and the severity of the abuse. Those who experience repeated, severe abuse—especially at ages younger than three years—are more likely to have emotional difficulties (Kinard, 1982).

Abused children and adolescents often find it difficult to trust adults and frequently their peers as well (Kempe & Kempe, 1978). They also have been found to have negative views of themselves and feelings that nobody likes them (Kinard, 1982). In addition, it isn't uncommon for abused children and adolescents to believe that they actually deserved the treatment they received from their parents. Yet, the fact that many run away from home or engage in delinquent acts as adolescents suggests that a strong core of (justifiable) anger and resentment exists. Of course, it is important to remember that many abused children grow up to be adequately functioning adults and parents (Kempe & Kempe, 1978). This is more likely to be the case when children (and their parents) can make use of individual and/or family counseling programs.

Sexual Abuse

Experts estimate that the incidence of incest ranges from 48,000 to 250,000 cases a year (Stark, 1984). The most common form of reported incest—75 percent—is between father and daughter. Incest between stepfathers and stepdaughters, which some would not classify as incest, but which therapists consider to be just as psychologically devasting, occurs more frequently than between daughters and their biological fathers. For example, in a study of 930 sexually abused women, one in six had been molested by a stepfather compared to one in forty, by a biological father (Stark, 1984).

Reports of sexual abuse by women are much lower; it is estimated that women are responsible for 20 percent of the sexual abuse of boys and 5 percent of the abuse of girls (Stark, 1984). Although few incidents are reported, it is believed that the most common form of incest is between brothers and sisters while they are growing up. Since this usually takes the form of mutual experimentation between children of younger and similar ages and is usually not exploitive, mental health professionals worry less about its effects.

Incestuous relationships between fathers and daughters typically start when the daughter is between 6 and 11 years of age and continue for at least two years. Most encounters don't involve intercourse; among prepubescent girls, they consist of fondling the breasts and genitals, masturbation, and oral sex (Stark, 1984).

Incest occurs in families across all socioeconomic levels. Its causes are not entirely understood and agreed upon, but mental health professionals believe that it most frequently occurs in families which are socially isolated and controlled by strong, domineering fathers in which the wife is financially and emotionally dependent on the husband or sick, absent, alcoholic, or mentally ill. Frequently, the oldest daughter has taken over the household and childcare responsibilities, and the sexual relationship with her father evolves as an extension of the "little mother" role (Stark, 1984).

Contrary to popular stereotype, incest doesn't usually develop out of a loving father-daughter relationship that has gone too far. The abusers's motives are complex and usually combine sexuality with power, hostility, and the need for a dependent "partner." Daughters usually cooperate with their father's sexual advances so that physical force is seldom used. For this reason, victims of sexual abuse usually suffer considerable guilt and shame, which makes it difficult for them to seek help. Although some victims cooperate with their fathers because they are desperate for any kind of affection, many others do so and remain silent because they believe that they are keeping the family together, that their fathers will go to jail, and that there isn't anyone who can help them (Stark, 1984). Often, not knowing how else to cope with the situation, they run away from home (Brown, 1979). Suicide attempts are also common among victims; one study reported that 38 percent had attempted to kill themselves (Stark, 1984).

As with physical abuse, the effects of incest vary depending on how frequently it occurred, whether or not physical abuse was also involved, the nature of the relationship between the victim and the abuser, and the availability of nonabusing caretakers. Incest victims often suffer from depression, anxiety, feelings of having been exploited or abandoned, helplessness, and an inability to control their lives (Mrazek & Mrazek, 1979).

Also, they have difficulty trusting others, particularly men. Some withdraw totally from sexual relationships, some turn to lesbianism, while others suffer from various types of sexual dysfunction. On the other hand, some victims appear to idealize men and attempt to recapture the "special" relationship they had with their fathers, while others believe that they can obtain love and affection only through sex. Some women, consciously or unconsciously, seek out and marry an abusive man who then molests their children (Mrazek & Mrazek, 1978; Stark, 1984).

Group therapy can be an effective way of helping incest victims. Treatment focuses heavily on convincing the victim that she wasn't to blame for the sexual abuse. Some family therapy programs can aid family members in coming to terms with the problem, whether or not the father returns to the home.

Because of recent widespread publicity about incest and sexual abuse, many schools are beginning to teach children about the problem and how to protect themselves.

DEVELOPMENT OF AUTONOMY

The adolescent's achievement of autonomy is a gradual process in most cases, and one in which the peer group figures importantly. Because adolescents spend more time with their peers and are more emotionally involved with them than they were as children, some mistakenly assume that adolescents reject their parents. As we have just seen, this is not so. Most adolescents feel close to their parents and espouse values similar to those of their parents.

In moving from a state of emotional and financial dependence to one of independence, adolescents must learn to rely less on their parents for support and guidance, while maintaining affection for and communication with them. Peers assume a new significance during adolescence because they are an important source of security in the negotiation of this task. Adolescents need to have some external base of support, independent from parents, in order to feel strong and safe enough to attempt letting go. In the process of achieving autonomy from parents, adolescents may at times exhibit slavish conformity to peer norms. At times they may need to proclaim their opposition to parental views and values in order to "prove" their independence, both to their parents and themselves. Eventually, of course, young people move toward a position of relative independence from both parents and peers.

Parental and Peer Affection and Conformity

Research findings on parent-peer affection and conformity among adolescents shed some light on the nature of the "autonomy process."

Looking first at the question of adolescents' emotional ties to parents and peers, one study has shown developmental trends away from parental dependence, although these appear to vary by race and sex. For example, a study of eighth- and eleventh-grade black and white males and females showed that younger black and white males felt significantly more affection toward their parents than toward their peers (O'Donnell, 1979b). Younger black and white females felt about the same affection for both parents and peers. This suggests that the process of separation from parents may begin sooner in females or that sex-role norms "push" adolescent girls more so than boys toward peer relationships and social competence.

By the eleventh grade, black and white females and white males showed the same affection for both parents and peers, and black males felt more affection toward parents. Since there was no evidence in this study that subjects moved to a position of preferring peers over parents, the author suggested that this change may not occur until young people are out of high school or are living on their own.

With regard to parental-peer conformity, it has been found that conformity to parents' standards decreases with age (Berndt, 1979; Brownstone & Willis, 1971). For example, a study of males and females in the third, sixth, ninth, and eleventh-twelfth grades found that conformity to parents decreased from the third to the eleventh-twelfth grades in both males and females (Berndt, 1979).

The highest levels of peer conformity occur around age 13 to 14 (Berndt, 1979; J. C. Coleman, 1980). This may lead to increased pressures to conform to parental standards and arguments with parents. And, it is around this age that we see the greatest amount of parent-adolescent conflict (Kandel & Lesser, 1972; Musgrove, 1963). By the end of high school peer conformity decreases at the same time that acceptance of conventional standards of behavior increases (Berndt, 1979). Moreover, there is not as much opposition between parental and peer values at this age. Consequently, we see an improvement in the nature of parent-adolescent relationships as the young person moves toward adulthood.

A number of studies have found sex differences on parent-peer conformity and on the intensity of the adolescent struggle for independence from parents. This provides some support for our earlier speculation that the nature and process of achieving autonomy may be different for males and females (Chapter 6). For example, one study showed that girls were less conforming to peers than boys on antisocial behavior and more conforming to parents' standards on issues of neutral behavior (Berndt, 1979). The author of the study concluded, as have others, that adolescent girls are less independent from their parents than boys.

Other studies have found either no sex differences or differences in the opposite direction. For example, two studies of ninth- and twelfth-grade males and females found that ninth-grade males were more influenced by parents and twelfth-grade males more influenced by peers (Emmerich, 1978; Floyd & South, 1972). Both ninth- and twelfth-grade females relied more heavily on their peers than parents. These findings parallel those on parent-peer affectional patterns just discussed. Such sex differences may be due to earlier maturation in girls and may reflect the impact of sex-role norms which place a higher value on the development of social relationships in females.

The lack of consistency in the findings with regard to sex differences and parental-peer conformity makes drawing conclusions unwise at this time. However, it does seem that most adolescent girls are able to establish antonomy without the acute independence conflicts typical of most adolescent boys (Douvan & Adelson, 1966). Clearly, we need to understand better how autonomy develops differently in males and females.

Leaving Home

Recently, there has been an interest in the impact of the adolescent's leaving home on him or her and on the family. Most adolescents want to grow up and become autonomous; at the same time they may feel anxious about being on their own. And, while most parents want their children to grow up, they also want to retain control and to protect their children from hurt and pain.

Daniel Goleman (1980) has reported that leaving home is becoming more difficult for youth. He suggests that there are economic reasons for this; it is harder these days for young people to find jobs and to make enough money to get established. Also, the fact that young people are marrying later (median age in 1980 for men was 24 years, for women 22 years) makes it more likely that they will remain at home.

Parents play an especially important role in making leaving home a positive process. Parents who resent the possibilities open to their children because they perceive that their own options are decreasing can respond to their adolescents with unfair criticism or by emotionally withdrawing in anger. Others may resist letting go of their children because they don't have other sources of satisfaction and self-esteem. This can lead to attempts to get more involved in their children's lives at precisely the time adolescents need to separate from the family. One study found that these kinds of parental reactions resulted in adolescents' engaging in frequent fighting with parents or leaving home but continuing to have hostile interactions with their parents (Levi, Stierlin, & Savard, cited in Goleman, 1980).

There is some evidence that leaving home physically can serve as an important catalyst in the autonomy achievement process. A recent study of college males compared those who commuted to college and those who lived on campus in terms of their interactions with parents and their development of independence (Sullivan & Sullivan, 1980). Those who lived on campus felt that they and their parents had developed better communication and had become more affectionate with each other, they felt more independent, and they were satisfied with these changes in relationships. In contrast, students who lived at home and commuted did not report positive changes in their interactions with their parents, did not feel as independent, and were not as satisfied with the changes which had taken place in their relationships with their parents.

Of course, it is possible for adolescents to move out of their parents' house without leaving home in a psychological sense, that is, without giving some serious thought to the differences and similarities between their own and their parents' values and attitudes. James Marcia has suggested that identity achievers have already left home in the psychological sense, whereas moratoriums are in the process of leaving (packing their psychological bags) because they are questioning their attachment to parental values. Foreclosures, on the other hand, continue to live at home in that they have not yet raised identity-related questions. Sadly, he suggests, those in the diffusion status never had a home in the first place. They talk about being unable to live up to their parents' expectations or feeling abandoned, but speak little of strong positive identities (Goleman, 1980).

American society doesn't have any established norms for the appropriate age to leave home, but high school and college graduation are frequently taken as "markers" in this regard. Other cultures have different norms in this area. This may mean that adolescents in first-generation immigrant families with views at variance with American norms may experience conflicts about leaving home.

Cross-Cultural Perspectives

To give some cross-cultural perspective on the development of autonomy in adolescence, we will briefly review this process in Israel and Uganda.

Parents play an important role in how adolescents experience "leaving home."

Israel (Kibbutz).   Most Israelis do not live in kibbutzim, but psychologists have been interested in those who do because of the different child-rearing methods employed there. The key difference between child-rearing in the kibbutz and in the traditional family is the use of a collective structure to accomplish socialization and educational goals. Children in the kibbutz live apart from their parents, although they visit frequently. Nonparental adults have the day-to-day responsibilities for taking care of children and adolescents. The children are surrounded by the same group of peers until they are 18. At age 18 the adolescents "become" adults (Zellermayer & Marcus, 1972).

Both boys and girls live in the same house (and sometimes in the same room) in groups of up to 20. Strong feelings of closeness and commitment develop among kibbutz members. For example, kibbutz-reared children tend to see their peers as exerting more of a disciplinary influence in their lives than do urban, family-reared Israelis (Devereaux et al., 1974). And, peers often persuade each other to make commitments to kibbutz living (after their army service) which means that they must be willing to give up the potential economic and social luxuries of a noncommunal life (Spiro, 1970).

In contrast to American adolescents, kibbutz youth have a definite place in society and their educational and work efforts are valued by the entire culture. These factors no doubt play a large part in the fact that adolescent turmoil is minimal, major delinquency is highly unusual, and the acquisition of adult roles and behaviors proceeds smoothly (Zellermayer & Marcus, 1972).

Uganda   A study of four different and geographically distant ethnic groups in Uganda revealed that these groups recognized the same age categories of child, youth, adult, and elder (Weeks, 1973). In all four groups youth begins with puberty. For girls, marriage marks the official transition to adulthood in all four societies. In three of the societies, boys become adults when they father their first child (in marriage); in the fourth, adult status comes with circumcision.

The period of youth among these four groups is seen as a time for preparation for adult roles which "are learned through the family and school, from a youth's interactions with . . . peers, through productive work, and from the role models a youth may admire or emulate" (Weeks, 1973, p. 261).

While our rather general statements may suggest that the transition to adult status is relatively straightforward in these four Ugandan societies, considerable variability exists. For example, among one group, the Bagisu, schooling may delay circumcision, as well as marriage because authorities force young couples to drop out of school (Weeks, 1973). Among the Lugbara, where marriage is the criterion for attaining adult status, an educated and employed person who is functionally an adult, but who is not married may be denied full recognition of adult status and participation in society until marriage. On the other hand, full recognition may also be withheld from a couple who marry young and live on the parents' land, until the couple establishes their own home (Weeks, 1973).

It appears that the criteria for attaining adult status are generally more clear-cut in Ugandan societies than in the United States; however, it is obvious that there is also variability in these criteria within a given society.

As can be seen from just two cross-cultural comparisons, adolescence is experienced differently in various societies. Also, we can see a major difference in Israeli and Ugandan youth compared to American youth. In Israel and Uganda there are opportunities for young people to make important contributions to their societies; adolescents feel that they are needed and have a place. Consequently, delinquency and other antisocial behaviors are relatively rare. American youth are less likely to feel they have important and useful roles to play (especially given the current high youth unemployment rates). As one author has expressed it, "Perhaps the heart of the problem of American youth is that there are so few opportunities—indeed there are actually hindrances—for them to make a substantial contribution on any level" (Boocock, 1974, p. 107). While this may oversimplify the case somewhat, it is still true that cultural expectations do play a significant role in the development of autonomy and the transition to adult status.

SUMMARY

The achievement of emotional and financial independence from parents is a critical developmental task for adolescents. This fact has considerable impact on the nature of parent-adolescent interactions.

Recent changes within the American family such as more divorce, smaller family size, and more working mothers have also had important impacts on the nature of contemporary parent-adolescent relationships.

An authoritative parenting style has been found to produce higher self-esteem and autonomy in children than authoritarian, permissive, or neglectful parenting styles. As children grow older, power techniques become less and less effective as a means of control and can produce adolescent rebellion and lower internalization of moral standards.

Most adolescents indicate that they get along well with and feel close to their parents. Still, there are occasions for parent-adolescent disagreement. Such conflicts appear to peak around 14 to 15 years of age. Causes of parent-adolescent conflicts include interlocking identity conflicts, parental exploitation, and adolescent egocentrism.

Reports of a generation gap have been exaggerated. Attitudes of parents and adolescents are relatively similar, although adolescents tend to overestimate the differences between them and their parents, while parents seem to underestimate these differences.

The achievement of autonomy is a gradual process which requires the efforts of both parents and adolescent. Peers provide an important source of security for adolescents in negotiating independence from the family. There is some evidence that boys have more acute independence conflicts with their parents than do girls.

There is considerable variation as to the criteria and time for assuming independence in this country. These norms vary widely across and within other cultures, as well.

GLOSSARY

authoritarian parenting style (Baumrind) A parenting style characterized by low parental acceptance of children and rigidly enforced standards.

authoritative parenting style (Baumrind) A parenting style characterized by high parental acceptance of children and the setting of firm, but reasonable standards.

extended family A type of family unit composed of mother, father, immediate children, grandparents, and sometimes other relatives.

generation gap The idea that parents and adolescents have very different attitudes and values (the nature of the gap is usually greatly exaggerated).

inductive discipline (Hoffman) A disciplinary method that uses reason to induce compliance to parental standards in a child.

love-withdrawal discipline (Hoffman) A disciplinary method that uses nonphysical expressions of anger and disapproval to induce compliance to parental standards in a child.

neglectful parenting style (Baumrind) A parenting style characterized by low parental acceptance of children and low parental control.

nuclear family a type of family unit composed of mother, father, and immediate children.

parental exploitation (Elkind) A condition in which parents put their own needs before those of their children or use their children in order to gratify their own needs.

permissive parenting style (Baumrind) A parenting style characterized by high parental acceptance of children and low parental control.

power-assertive discipline (Hoffman) A disciplinary method that uses physical punishment or deprivation of possessions or privileges as a means to induce compliance to parental standards in a child.

reconstituted (blended) family A family unit made up of two adults, at least one of whom has been divorced, as well as the children of one or both of them from the previous marriage and any children they may have together.

GETTING INVOLVED: Exercise, Case Study, and General Questions to Consider

EXERCISE: COMPARING GENERATIONAL VALUES

The following exercise is intended to focus your attention on the guiding principles in your life and the degree of similarity you perceive between your beliefs and those of your parents. (Students who are parents of adolescents can adapt this exercise to their circumstances.) To do this exercise, first complete Worksheet 7.1 beginning on the following page.

After you have completed the Worksheet, examine your responses, those of others, and your perceptions of others' values. Where are there similarities? Differences? Does it seem that your attitudes are more similar to those of your parents or your best friend? Did you tend to over- or underestimate the differences between your values and those of others? How do you account for your findings?

CASE STUDY: ELIZABETH

Mr. and Mrs. Jackson have three children: Bill (16), Elizabeth (14), and Jimmy (9). Mr. Jackson is an appliance salesperson and Mrs. Jackson is a registered nurse. Their standard of living is comfortable, but there isn't much money left over at the end of every month. With three children and the increases in the cost of living, two incomes are needed to make ends meet.

The Jacksons love their children and their children reciprocate these feelings. The parents have rather traditional views of sex roles so they have different expectations for their boys and girl. For the most part, they use what could be called an authoritative parenting style, but sometimes it runs over into an authoritarian style (especially in the case of Mr. Jackson). After all, with three children, it's hard to be reasonable and explain things *all* the time.

Recently, Mr. Jackson has begun to worry about losing his job. Sales are down and one of his co-workers was laid off about a month ago. He fears that he will be the next to go. Mrs. Jackson isn't worried about losing her job, but they both know that it would be difficult to live on only one income.

They haven't discussed this potential problem with any of the children because they haven't wanted to upset them. Still, it preys on their minds. Recently, Mr. Jackson, especially, has found himself being unnecessarily demanding and critical of the children.

Mr. and Mrs. Jackson made an agreement with Elizabeth about six months ago. Instead of paying an outside babysitter, they agreed to pay her for staying home with Jimmy every day after school for two hours until Mr. Jackson returned from work. Looking for ways to cut back on expenses, Mr. Jackson has just told Elizabeth that he has decided that it is her responsibility to care for her younger brother and that she shouldn't expect to get paid for babysitting. Elizabeth feels this is an unfair demand and says so. At least she and her older brother Bill should split the work so it doesn't all fall to her. Her father says that Bill already has a job (working at the local "ham-

Worksheet 7.1   PARENT-ADOLESCENT VALUE COMPARISION

Instructions: Below is a list of 18 values arranged in alphabetical order. Your task is to arrange them in order of their importance to *you* as guiding principles in *your* life.

Read through *all* of these instructions and the entire list before you begin ranking your choices. Then, under the column marked My Rankings, place a 1 next to the value you feel is most important to you, a 2 next to the value which is second-most important to you, etc. Do this for the 9 most important values for your life. (There is no magic to this number; it just gets difficult to rank long lists of things.)

Then, under the column marked Mother's rankings, rank the values (1–9) as you believe your mother would. Do the same with regard to your father and your best friend under the columns marked Father's Rankings and Friend's rankings.

Note: If you like, you can ask your parents and your best friend if they would do their own rankings and compare these with your perceptions of their values as well as to your own values. If any of them are willing to participate, be sure *not* to let them see your rankings or any one else's responses. Have them use separate sheets of paper. This procedure will prevent them from being influenced by other people's answers.

My rankings	Mother's rankings	Father's rankings	Friend's rankings	
_____	_____	_____	_____	A comfortable life (a prosperous life)
_____	_____	_____	_____	Equality (equal opportunity for all)
_____	_____	_____	_____	An exciting life (a stimulating, active life)
_____	_____	_____	_____	Family security (taking care of loved ones)
_____	_____	_____	_____	Freedom (independence, free choice)
_____	_____	_____	_____	Happiness (contentedness)
_____	_____	_____	_____	Inner harmony (freedom from inner conflict)
_____	_____	_____	_____	Mature love (sexual and spiritual intimacy)
_____	_____	_____	_____	National security (protection from attack)
_____	_____	_____	_____	Pleasure (an enjoyable, leisurely life)
_____	_____	_____	_____	Salvation (deliverance from sin, eternal life)
_____	_____	_____	_____	Self-respect (self-esteem)
_____	_____	_____	_____	A sense of accomplishment (making a lasting contribution)
_____	_____	_____	_____	Social recognition (respect, admiration)
_____	_____	_____	_____	True friendship (close companionship)
_____	_____	_____	_____	Wisdom (a mature understanding of life)
_____	_____	_____	_____	A world at peace (freedom from war and conflict)
_____	_____	_____	_____	A world of beauty (beauty of nature and the arts)

Source: Adapted by permission of A & W Publishers, Inc. from *Values Clarification* by Sidney S. Simon, Leland W. Howe, and Howard Kirschenbaum. (1972). Copyright © 1972 by Hart Publishing Company. (Milton Rokeach, 1967; used with permission of George Spear, Associate Dean for Continuing Education, University of Missouri, Kansas City, Missouri.)

burger joint" Friday evenings and all day Saturdays). Besides, taking care of Jimmy has already been established as her job. She says she won't do it, and he says she will. They end up yelling at each other.

They are both upset. Mr. Jackson is angry with Elizabeth because he feels she is being selfish. When she asked him the reason for the change in the arrangement, he told her that he felt it was time for her to take more responsibility around the house since she was getting older. He didn't tell her the real reason because he didn't want her to worry. Now he wonders if maybe he *should* explain things to Elizabeth and Bill. Also, he wonders if it isn't a bit unfair that he hasn't asked Bill to contribute in some way, too. He speculates about how Bill would react to the idea of babysitting for his younger brother a couple of times a week. Still, Bill already has a part-time job. He feels bad that things have turned out this way and realizes that he probably should have waited to discuss this with his wife before saying anything to Elizabeth. But, that's water over the dam now. His wife will be home soon—he'll see what she thinks.

Elizabeth is hurt and angry. She doesn't mind so much helping out at home (although she would rather get paid for it), but she really resents the idea that she would have to stay at home five afternoons a week while her older brother is free to do what he wants during this time. Even if he works Friday nights and Saturdays, he gets to keep this money for himself—it doesn't go to the household. Besides, boys should have to babysit, too. Also, she doesn't understand why her father suddenly wants to change the agreement they had—everything seemed to be working out fine. She bets her mother will stand by her and waits for her to come home.

Questions for Case Study

1. What is going on here? Spell out the various parts of the conflict.
2. List the possible outcomes of this situation and the possible results of such outcomes.
3. Does Elizabeth have a legitimate right to feel angry? Does her father?
4. Do you feel that Elizabeth or her father is more to blame for things ending up like this? Why?
5. What do you think would be the best way to handle this situation. Should Mr. and Mrs. Jackson explain the real problem to Elizabeth and Bill? Should Elizabeth have to do all the babysitting? Should Bill have to help out?
6. Could this problem have been avoided? If so, how?

GENERAL QUESTIONS TO CONSIDER

1. Consider the issue of birth order and its effects. How do you account for the persistence of the popular negative stereotypes about the only child?
2. Review the impact of gender and sibling position on family interactions. If you have brothers or sisters, can you recall instances in which gender or sibling position was an issue in your family? In your experience, is sibling position a more or less important factor than gender?
3. What are some of the effects on children and adolescents of working mothers. Does your mother work? How do you feel her working or not working has affected you and others in your family?
4. Review Baumrind's four types of parenting styles. Why do you think the authoritative style produces the highest self-esteem and autonomy? What style do (did) your parents use and what are your feelings about it? What style do or would you use with your children? Why?

5. Review Hoffman's three forms of parental discipline and their effects. What disciplinary style do (did) your parents use? What style do or would you use with your children? Why?

6. How would you describe your relationship with your parents? Do you feel you are understood most of the time? Do you feel that you understand them? Can you see your parents as individuals, as well as your parents?

7. What are the three topics you and your parents argue about most frequently?

8. Reflect on the idea of interlocking identity crises of parents and adolescents. Does this idea explain any of the parent-adolescent conflicts you have had?

9. Consider adolescent egocentrism as a factor in parent-adolescent disagreements in your family.

10. When did you and your parents have the most difficulty interacting—junior high school, early high school, later high school, college?

11. Have you experienced divorce first-hand or indirectly (someone close to you)? Reflect on your feelings about it and their evolution. Consider the effects the remarriage of a parent has on a child or adolescent. Why is this such a difficult situation for children and adolescents?

12. If you are not living at home, what types of things do you feel that you have learned as a result of being on your own? If you are living at home, how do you imagine that things might change when you do move out?

Chapter 8 Outline

chapter 8

Relating to Peers

Learning to relate to others begins early in life, but the special combination of developments taking place during adolescence makes peer interactions particularly important at this time.

Perhaps the major function of the peer group is to provide a base of security outside the family. This allows the young person to begin the process of emotional detachment from parents. The separation process takes place over a period of years and doesn't usually mean that adolescents suddenly reject their parents or their parents' values. Instead, they gradually "let go" in order to learn how to be emotionally self-supporting adults.

Adolescents' greater attachment to peers is obvious in the increased amounts of time spent together and their common preferences for particular types of music, styles of clothes, and language. In this context, it has been suggested that the peer group provides an "interim culture" for the young person while status in the adult culture is unattainable (J. S. Coleman, 1961).

Adolescence is a time for identity experiments—for trying on different roles, behaviors, and values in search of the adult person one will become. Peers provide an audience for adolescents in their experimenting.

ADOLESCENT SOCIETY

Is There a Youth Subculture?

Most psychologists would probably agree that there is an adolescent society of sorts because it is possible to identify experiences, activities, values, and attitudes which most adolescents have in common and which are somewhat different from those of the adult culture. However, since there is such wide variability in adolescents' attitudes and experiences according to sex, age, class, and individual differences, it is probably inaccurate to speak of a clearly specifiable youth subculture in anything other than very superficial terms (Weiner, 1970). Moreover, as we saw in the last chapter, most research questions the idea of a generation gap or a clear separation of adolescent and adult culture. Adolescents are likely to have values and attitudes which are similar to those of their parents. And, they are likely to select their friends from neighborhoods and family backgrounds similar to their own.

Some psychologists have concluded that the debate over the existence of a separate subculture is a "pseudo-issue" and really not worth continued discussion (Jahoda & Warren, 1965; Smith & Kleine, 1966). We would agree that support can be found both for its existence and for its absence, depending on the criteria one uses. Its value as a concept depends on its usefulness in exploring other more complex and subtle questions.

> Adolescents share some values uniquely with other adolescents on the national scale; some values are shared uniquely with specific reference groups; and some values are shared with the broader adult cultural fabric. . . . For some research questions, the use of the concept "subculture" may permit examination of certain discontinuous or continuous aspects; for other questions the concept will not be of help (Smith & Kleine, 1966, p. 427).

Aspects of the Adolescent Subculture

Style of Dress   Concern with style of dress and clothing is particularly characteristic of adolescents, especially girls. One reason adolescents place such emphasis on clothing is that it is one way of experimenting with who they are and how they want to be seen. Of course, clothes and style of dress serve as a kind of identification badge for everyone. However, because adolescents are in the process of developing, for the first time, a style of dress which expresses their view of themselves, clothing style assumes more importance for them.

In addition, adolescents learn that clothing plays an important role in social interactions and in how one is viewed by others. Hence, style of dress is an important cue to both peers and adults. For example, one study found that the most fashionable dressers in high school had the highest status and the least fashionable dressers had the lowest status (S. S. Jones, 1976).

Concern with Physical Appearance   Similarly, adolescents are concerned with their physical appearance. As we have mentioned, adolescent egocentrism is an important factor here because young people imagine that "everyone" is looking at them—and usually noticing their most unacceptable characteristics! Younger adolescents are especially likely to be plagued by frustrations and insecurities about their physical appearance: maturing too early or too late, being over- or underweight, having acne, having too large or small a nose. Girls are more likely to have concerns about physical appearance than boys due to sex-role expectations.

Adolescents often experiment with styles of dress as a way of experimenting with who they are.

Over a period of years adolescents become more comfortable with their mature bodies. Too, they begin to see that they have a variety of attributes (sense of humor, intelligence) and can learn to compensate for some negative characteristics with others that are more positively valued.

Language   The language adolescents use to describe their experiences and ideas, like language in general, is influenced by socioeconomic status, geographical location, and specific peer group norms (Leona, 1978). Using particular words or argot is a way of demonstrating to others and oneself that one belongs to a particular group and a way of excluding those who are not members.

A study investigating the functions of slang among seventh- through twelfth-grade girls and boys concluded that the number of slang words used in discussing a certain topic (drugs or cars, for example) reflected the importance of the topic in the youth culture (Nelson & Rosenbaum, 1972). In addition, the authors found differences in slang usage according to the school attended, grade level, and sex. For example, males had more slang terms than females for such things as cars, motorcycles, and money, while females had more slang terms for clothes, appearance, popularity of people, and boys. The authors concluded that such sex differences reflected the different interest patterns and involvements of adolescent males and females.

Music   The themes that appear most often in the lyrics of popular music reflect the concerns of youth at particular periods. For example, one study divided common themes in rock music into seven categories: (1) love, (2) drugs, (3) religion, (4) revolution and social change, (5) area (songs which refer to specific places), (6) type of dancing or music, e.g., the "twist," and (7) other (themes not included in the first six categories) (Kantor, 1974). Table 8.1 shows the relative frequency of these themes from 1955 to 1972. Love is the most important theme in rock music, although it diminished in importance in the early 1970s. References to drugs, religion, and social change increased from 1963 to 1972. Today, popular music seems to be reflecting the 1950s interest in personal rather than larger social concerns.

One study suggests that the songs of the 1960s reflect changing relations between the sexes (Hirsch, Robinson, Taylor, & Withey, 1972). The popular songs of the 1950s depicted a "fatalistic" view of love: "The singer played an essentially passive role, waiting for a permanent love relationship to 'happen' " (p. 89). By 1966 popular songs projected different messages about love relationships between the sexes: music was more sensual and sexy rather than sweet; romantic love was not a prerequisite for a sexual relationship; relationships were not expected to be permanent; both partners in the relationship were "free"; and relationships were actually sought by lovers rather than being passively longed for (Hirsch et al., 1972).

There also appear to be differences between adolescent and adult preferences for the loudness of music. This different orientation is reflected in the oft-heard parental complaint: "Will you please turn that thing down?!"

"Hangouts" Adolescents in a particular neighborhood or school usually have favorite meeting places. These can be particular street corners, video-game arcades, shopping centers, or designated places in parks. These provide places for adolescents to perform before an audience of peers and are considered good places to meet prospective dates.

NATURE AND ROLE OF PEER GROUPS DURING ADOLESCENCE

Types of Adolescent Peer Groups

Cliques and Crowds Two different types of adolescent peer groups have been identified, based on group size (Dunphy, 1963). A *clique* is a small, cohesive group of about

Table 8.1 THEMES APPEARING IN 772 ROCK SONGS, 1955–1972 (PERCENT OF NUMBER OF SONGS SURVEYED)

	1955–1963 (*N* = 366)	1964–1969 (*N* = 275)	1970–1972 (*N* = 131)
Love	73	73	64
Drugs	—	5	7
Religion	—	1	17
Revolution or social change	1	4	7
Area	4	—	—
Dance	7	—	—
Other	15	17	5

Source: Adapted from Irwin Kantor. (1974). This thing called rock: An interpretation. *Popular Music and Society,* *3,* 203–214. Copyright 1974 by Bowling Green State University. Adapted by permission.

Music assumes an important role among adolescents.

6 members (ranging from 3 to 9). A *crowd* is a larger group of about 20 members (ranging from 15 to 30), usually made up from the members of about three cliques. Members of cliques usually live close to one another; the cliques that join together to form a crowd usually come from adjacent residential areas.

Crowds and cliques appear to serve different purposes for their members. While the clique focuses on talking, the crowd is the center of organized, heterosexual social events such as parties and dances. Members apparently use the clique to disseminate information about upcoming crowd activities and to evaluate past crowd events. The crowd is useful because it offers a pool of acceptable peers for dating partners. The clique and crowd are also distinctive in that crowds are most active on weekends, while cliques function more during the week.

Adolescent peer groups progress through five stages (see Figure 8.1) (Dunphy, 1963). In Stage 1, the precrowd stage, peer group interactions are limited to isolated, same-sex cliques. It is characteristic of preadolescence and early adolescence. Activities and interactions are organized around a leader who possesses the "masculine" or "feminine" traits admired by group members. In Stage 2, during the junior high school years, the crowd begins to take shape through the joint participation of different cliques of boys and girls. Heterosexual interactions are viewed as "daring" and take place in the presence of other clique members.

In Stage 3 the heterosexual clique begins to form. Typically, the leaders of the same-sex cliques are the first to begin dating on an individual basis and the other members soon follow. These leaders, however, still maintain membership in their same-sex cliques. Thus, in Stage 3 the crowd is still in the process of developing. The heterosexual interactions of the clique leaders prepare for the emergence of well-

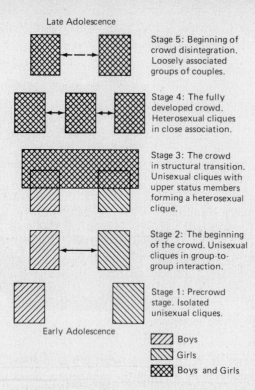

Late Adolescence

Stage 5: Beginning of crowd disintegration. Loosely associated groups of couples.

Stage 4: The fully developed crowd. Heterosexual cliques in close association.

Stage 3: The crowd in structural transition. Unisexual cliques with upper status members forming a heterosexual clique.

Stage 2: The beginning of the crowd. Unisexual cliques in group-to-group interaction.

Stage 1: Precrowd stage. Isolated unisexual cliques.

Early Adolescence

Boys

Girls

Boys and Girls

Figure 8.1 Stages of peer group development in adolescence. *Source:* Dexter C. Dunphy (1963). The social structure of urban adolescent peer groups. *Sociometry, 26,* 236. Copyright 1963 by the American Sociological Association. Reprinted by permission.

established heterosexual cliques which closely interact. These make up the fully developed crowd, which is characteristic of Stage 4. In Stage 5 the crowd slowly disintegrates and is replaced by loosely associated groups of couples who are going steady or who are engaged. Thus, the peer group serves as a vehicle for developing heterosexual social behavior (Dunphy, 1963).

Gangs   Another type of adolescent peer group is the *gang*. In some ways gangs are similar to cliques (Dunphy, 1972). They are usually unisexual, although they sometimes have opposite-sex groups associated with them. Also, they are usually rooted in a specific geographical area, even though their "territory" is much more clearly demarcated and often strongly defended against invasions by other gangs. Gangs differ from cliques in that they are larger in size and are usually more highly organized.

Gangs frequently engage in and promote antisocial and illegal behaviors such as vandalism and robbery. They are usually in revolt against formal social institutions such as the family, school, church, and law (Dunphy, 1972). Gangs provide their members with such benefits as companionship, protection, excitement, and heterosexual contacts (Friedman, Mann, & Friedman, 1975).

Gangs are primarily found in lower-class and urban ghetto areas. This fact has led many sociologists to speculate that adolescent gangs develop because poor youth realize that they lack the means available to middle-class youth to attain economic and social success as defined by the larger society. Consequently, they turn to illegal methods (via the gang) to attain these same goals. Of course, it should be noted that not all poor adolescents are members of gangs or engage in illegal behavior.

Functions of the Adolescent Peer Group

The peer group during adolescence serves a number of useful functions (Hamachek, 1980):

1. *Replacement for family support.* Adolescents need to pull away from parents in order to establish psychological autonomy. In doing so, the support of peers is essential.
2. *Stabilizing influence.* In the midst of the many changes that take place during adolescence, the peer group provides an anchor (as do parents). In addition, adolescents may feel comforted knowing that others are experiencing similar feelings and conflicts.
3. *Social status.* Group membership confers social status. Not being a member may be associated with social stigma.
4. *Source of self-esteem.* Group membership is a sign of peer acceptance. Adolescents who are positively evaluated by their peers have higher self-esteem than youth who are less positively evaluated (O'Donnell, 1979a).
5. *Source of behavioral standards.* Peers influence adolescent decision-making. In families where parent-adolescent relationships are generally good, young people also look to their parents for guidance. In homes where parents do not get along or where parents are unavailable, peer groups assume more importance. However, strong reliance on peer guidance is likely to occur by default rather than by choice.
6. *Source of security.* To some degree, peer groups protect adolescents from demands which parents or other adults attempt to impose on them. It is easier and more persuasive to say "Everyone else is (or is not) doing it" than to have to take a stand alone.
7. *Opportunities for role-taking and feedback.* Participation in group activities and in bull sessions about life, sex, etc., provide opportunities for trying out different roles, practicing skills important in adulthood, and getting feedback about how one's ideas, feelings, and behaviors appear to others.
8. *Opportunities for modeling.* Especially in those cases where parents cannot be useful role models for their adolescents, peers can serve as important models of behavior. This is more likely to be true among lower-SES youth.

Cross-Cultural Perspectives

Research has shown that the role and functions of the peer group vary across cultures. For example, in the Soviet Union family, school, and peer group are brought into a well-defined national program for character education (Bronfenbrenner, 1970). Classroom teachers specify desired behavioral goals set forth in "socialization manuals" and

Interactions with peers provide opportunities for trying out new roles
and practicing useful skills.

monitor and reward appropriate behavior in students. Eventually, students are given
these monitoring functions as a means of teaching them responsibility for each other's
behavior. Parents are asked to monitor their children's progress in character education
and to submit formal reports to teachers. A general thread of social criticism runs
through peer and parent-child interactions such that all are involved in and concerned
about helping to maintain desired behavior.

Hence, we see that the peer group can be used as a means of ensuring obedience
to government-decreed behavioral standards. In the United States there is more emphasis on individual development and less agreement on desirable behavior. Moreover, the
family, schools, and peer group are not involved in an explicit plan of socialization.
Obviously, then, peer groups have different functions in these two countries.

PEER ACCEPTANCE AND SOCIAL ADJUSTMENT

Adolescents, like people at all ages, need to be liked and accepted by others. During
adolescence, however, this need is heightened, especially in girls. The increase in the
desire to be popular with peers is tied to adolescent developmental tasks—gaining
independence from parents, achieving ego identity, and clarifying sex-role identity and
sexual preference. Peer group support plays an important role in these endeavors.

Several studies have confirmed the assertion that popularity with peers is important to adolescents (J. S. Coleman, 1961; Sebald, 1977; Sebald, 1981). Hans Sebald
(1981) compared the responses of suburban high school students in Columbus, Ohio,
and Phoenix, Arizona, to the question "How important is it to be liked and accepted
by other teenagers?" (See Table 8.2). Despite an apparent decline in the importance
attached to being popular between 1960 and 1976 (perhaps due to sample differences
between Ohio and Arizona), still 84 percent of high school students in 1976 responded
that peer acceptance was either of "very great" or "great" importance.

Table 8.2   SUBURBAN HIGH SCHOOL STUDENTS' RESPONSES TO THE QUESTION "HOW IMPORTANT IS IT TO BE LIKED AND ACCEPTED BY OTHER TEENAGERS?" IN 1960 AND 1976 (BY PERCENT)

Response	1960 (Ohio)	1976 (Arizona)
Very great importance	67	47
Great importance	27	37
Some importance	6	14
No importance	0	2

Source: Table compiled from data given in Hans Sebald. (1981). Adolescents' concept of popularity and unpopularity, comparing 1960 with 1976. *Adolescence, 16*(6), 187–193. Copyright 1981 by Libra Publishers, Inc. Adapted by permission.

Correlates of Popularity

Conforming to Peer Group Norms   The Sebald (1981) study also looked at high school students' responses to an open-ended question about the criteria for popularity. Of course, the criteria vary somewhat with socioeconomic status, ethnic group, and sex. As can be seen from Table 8.3, conforming to the peer group was the most frequently reported criterion for being popular by the 1976 sample (47 percent). A significantly larger proportion of girls than boys mentioned peer group conformity as a criterion (55 percent and 37 percent respectively). Of course, these results don't demonstrate that girls actually are more conforming to peer standards than are boys; as we have seen, there are inconsistent findings on this issue.

Other sex differences that appear in Table 8.3 and Table 8.4 suggest that the popularity concerns of boys and girls are tied to traditional sex-role expectations and

Table 8.3   SUBURBAN HIGH SCHOOL STUDENTS' RESPONSES TO THE QUESTION "WHAT IS EXPECTED OF A TEENAGER BY HIS OR HER FRIENDS IN ORDER TO BE POPULAR WITH THEM?" IN 1976 (BY PERCENT)

Response	Males	Females	Total
1. Conforming (in activity, argot, attitude, dress, interests)	37	55	47
2. Being friendly and courteous, getting along with others	40	40	40
3. Being oneself, being an individual	18	20	19
4. Having a good personality	10	20	14
5. Having a sense of humor, being cheerful, being fun to be with	11	12	11
6. Being cool	11	8	9
7. Helping, caring about, taking an interest in others	0	17	8
8. Being trustworthy, honest	11	5	8
9. Being good looking	4	10	7
10. Having money	4	0	2
11. Having a good reputation	2	2	2
12. Not being gay	0	4	2
13. Keeping up with fashions	0	2	1
14. Engaging in antiestablishment behavior	2	0	1

Source: Adapted from Hans Sebald. (1981). Adolescents' concept of popularity and unpopularity, comparing 1960 with 1976. *Adolescence, 16*(6), 187–193. Copyright 1981 by Libra Publishers, Inc. Adapted by permission.

Table 8.4   SUBURBAN HIGH SCHOOL STUDENTS' RESPONSES TO THE QUESTION
"WHAT SORT OF TEENAGER MIGHT BE CONSIDERED AN 'ODDBALL' OR
'SQUARE'?" IN 1976 (BY PERCENT)

Response	Males	Females	Total
1. Someone who doesn't conform (in activity, belief, dress, interests, values)	31	34	33
2. Someone who is too straight (Jocks, Mormons, those following the older generation)	27	20	24
3. Someone who does not socialize, does not show interest in others	30	17	24
4. Someone who wears unfashionable clothes	2	25	13
5. Someone who studies too much	12	13	13
6. Someone who does not drink, smoke, have sex, use "dope"	8	13	11
7. Someone who is ugly, not good looking	6	13	10
8. Someone who is not friendly, does not get along with others	6	10	8
9. Someone who is arrogant	6	5	6
10. Someone who is gay	8	2	6
11. Someone with a bad personality	3	7	6
12. Someone who is too shy, too quiet	2	10	6
13. Someone who does not date	3	5	4
14. Someone without athletic ability or interest	3	2	3
15. Someone who is a "cowboy"	2	2	2
16. Someone who smokes pot, uses drugs	2	2	2
17. Someone who does not study at all	0	2	1
18. Someone who is stupid	2	0	1

Source: Adapted from Hans Sebald. (1981). Adolescents' concept of popularity and unpopularity, comparing 1960 with 1976. *Adolescence, 16*(6), 187–193. Copyright 1981 by Libra Publishers, Inc. Adapted by permission.

parallel other findings that indicate that relationships are more salient in the lives of females than in the lives of males (Douvan & Adelson, 1966; Gilligan, 1982).

Personality and Social Skills   Personal qualities are among the most important factors influencing social acceptance in adolescence. As we saw in Chapter 3, the ability to perceive others in terms of personal qualities develops in early adolescence, with girls appearing to show earlier development in this area than boys (Barratt, 1977).

Physical Attractiveness   High positive correlations between physical attractiveness and popularity have been found from age 6 through college age (Cavior & Dokecki, 1973). The fact that 10 percent of girls and 4 percent of boys mentioned good looks as an important criterion in the Sebald study suggests that attractiveness is more salient for adolescent females.

Participation in Athletics   Participation in athletics appears to be an important factor among boys. Although athletes are generally more popular than scholars, athlete-scholars are the most popular (J. S. Coleman, 1961; Eitzen, 1975). High schools and communities vary considerably in their view of athletics. For example, one study found that the strongest supporters of athletics lived in small, rural communities, were sons of the undereducated, and attended schools with a strict authority structure which encouraged sports. The weakest support for athletics came from the wealthier sons of college-educated fathers from large urban or suburban permissive schools. However, even in these schools, athletic participation was still seen as the single most important criterion for popularity for boys (but to a lesser extent than in the other schools) (Eitzen, 1975).

Participation in Extra-Curricular Activities   Being a leader in activities has been found to be an important factor related to adolescent popularity (J. S. Coleman, 1961; Eitzen, 1975; Snyder, 1972). This is especially true for adolescents from higher income families (Hartup, 1970).

Intelligence   Intelligence is positively and significantly correlated with popularity among adolescents (Hallworth, Davis & Gamston, 1965).

Academic Achievement   Academic achievement by itself doesn't seem to be related to acceptance or rejection. Rather, other factors—participation in extracurricular activities and athletics—interact with academic achievement to influence popularity. For example, a study of 11- and 17-year-old male and female adolescents reported that physical attractiveness and perceived attitudinal similarity were positively correlated with popularity, but that academic performance was not (Cavior & Dokecki, 1973).

Correlates of Peer Neglect and Rejection

The characteristics that are least admired among adolescents are often, but not always, the opposites or negatives of those listed above. Table 8.4 lists the responses of high school males and females to the open-ended question "What sort of teenager might be considered an 'oddball' or 'square'?" Such things as not conforming, appearing too much like adults, not being sociable, or studying too much are considered to be grounds for peer rejection. Again, there are variations with sex, socioeconomic status, and ethnic group.

Of course, all adolescents can't be classified as either "popular" or "rejected." Both of these designations indicate strong feelings (positive or negative) toward a peer. Some adolescents are neither actively liked nor disliked and have been classified as "socially neglected" and described as "the neutral personalities who were over-looked, rather than disliked, by their classmates. . . . They were characterized as being quiet and not talkative" (Gronlund & Anderson, 1957, (p. 251).

Socioeconomic Status and Ethnic Group Membership   Youth who belong to the culturally and economically dominant majority in their peer groups are more likely to be accepted by their peers. This is probably due to the fact that norms and standards for behavior are most often set by those in the majority (Conger & Petersen, 1984).

In the past research has supported the idea that adolescents from ethnic minorities also had a more difficult time achieving social acceptance (Peck & Galliani, 1962). More recent research suggests that the acceptance and pride of such adolescents in their culture and traditions is increasing. This, in turn, is correlated with more positive feelings toward other members of one's ethnic group (Hraba & Grant, 1970; Ward & Braun, 1972).

One of the causes of class and racial prejudice is the discrepancy in values of various groups. For example, one study reported that lower- and middle-SES adolescent boys stress the importance in peer popularity of common interests, minding one's own business, and the ability to talk well (Feinberg, Smith, & Schmidt, 1958). Higher-SES boys, on the other hand, stressed leadership, scholarship, cooperativeness, and participation in activities as important for peer acceptance. Young people may find it more comfortable to interact with people who have the same values. Unfortunately, this kind of selectivity makes it easier for misunderstandings to develop and can also perpetuate negative stereotypes and prejudice.

Effects of Peer Group Acceptance and Rejection

Being popular with one's peers is an important factor in adolescents' feelings about themselves. For example, a study of eighth- and eleventh-grade youth found that adolescents whose peers rated them as having high self-esteem were significantly more likely to have high self-esteem than were adolescents whose peers rated them as having low self-esteem (O'Donnell, 1979a).

It has been suggested that the peer group provides an interim culture for the young person while status in the adult culture is unavailable (Coleman, 1961). As such, the peer group and its culture can serve as a training ground for learning and refining adult social skills, as a source of self-esteem, and as a source of security. This is true for those who are accepted by their peers, but it is not so for those who suffer from neglect and rejection. Being neglected or rejected by one's peers is important not only

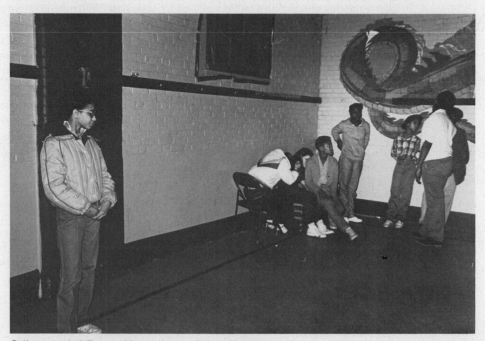

Self-esteem is influenced by one's popularity with peers.

because it feels awful, but also because it means being deprived of opportunities for learning adult social skills. And, while deficiencies in social skills during adolescence can cause emotional distress, in adulthood they can result in such negative outcomes as not getting or losing a job and not being able to start or maintain friendships and romantic relationships.

In addition, a circular effect can begin to operate. Those who lack confidence avoid interacting with others, fail to learn important social skills, feel even less self-confident, and withdraw even further. Because adolescents are somewhat insecure, they may find it easier to ridicule and reject peers who lack self-assurance than to include them in activities. Consequently, it is important for parents, teachers, coaches, and counselors to encourage what may be initially awkward attempts at interaction and to be generally supportive.

It has been suggested that more positive interactions between neglected adolescents and their peers can be facilitated by teachers through classroom seating arrangements, small group work, and sports team assignments so that the neglected ones come into contact with others, learn skills related to social acceptance, and learn to be more assertive (Gronlund & Anderson, 1957). Rejected adolescents also need to unlearn some of the negative behaviors they engage in before they can gain peer acceptance. Sometimes, this is a relatively simple problem, but in other cases it is more complex and may require individual counseling.

CONFORMITY DURING ADOLESCENCE

Conformity concerns the degree to which a person's attitudes and behaviors are influenced by others. As we have seen, adolescents conform to both parental and peer standards and eventually move to a position where they are more self-reliant in this regard.

Research on identity development is relevant to adolescent conformity. Recall that males in the identity foreclosure and moratorium statuses were high in conformity to parental values and were particularly vulnerable to attempts to manipulate their self-esteem (a factor found to be associated with conformity). In females, conformity and vulnerability to self-esteem manipulation were highest among moratorium and diffusion subjects. It was suggested that female foreclosure subjects may have developed the ability to resist conformity pressures, in spite of not having experienced an identity crisis, because they may gain a sense of security from taking on socially designated roles.

Developmental Trends

We have seen that conformity to peer standards is greater in early and middle adolescence than it is in childhood and later adolescence (see Figure 8.2). Fears of rejection appear to peak around the age of 15.

These findings correspond, in general, with Barbara and Philip Newman's (1976) division of adolescence into two periods of psychosocial development, as we discussed in Chapter 5. The first period, characterized by the psychosocial crisis of group identity versus alienation, begins with the onset of puberty and ends with graduation from high

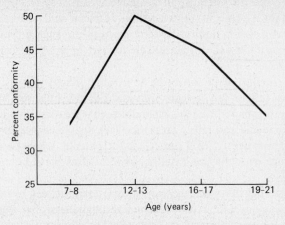

Figure 8.2   Peer conformity peaks in early adolescence. *Source:* Philip R. Costanzo (1970). Conformity development as a function of self-blame. *Journal of Personality and Social Psychology, 14*(4), 370. Copyright 1970 by the American Psychological Association. Reprinted by permission of the author.

school. Heightened sensitivity to peer approval is one of its salient features. The second period, beginning at about age 18 and continuing for about four years, is characterized by the psychosocial crisis of individual identity versus role diffusion; that is, struggling for autonomy from the family and developing a sense of personal identity.

The most likely reason for the decrease in conformity from middle to late adolescence is that "the importance of self increases relative to the importance of the group. Therefore, the adolescent and young adult become more able to resist the pressures of the group" (Costanzo, 1970, p. 372).

Gender Differences

Traditional sex-role expectations dictate that females should be dependent and submissive and that males should be self-sufficient and independent. Early studies did find such sex differences in peer conformity (Crutchfield, 1955). More recent research findings have demonstrated that females do not conform to peer standards significantly more than do males when there is no group pressure to do so (Brownstone & Willis, 1971; Collins & Thomas, 1972; Costanzo & Shaw, 1966; Eagly, 1978; Purnell, 1970; Sistrunk & McDavid, 1971). When group pressure exists, females are more likely to conform than males (perhaps to preserve social harmony) (Eagly, 1978). Also, it appears that girls are less susceptible than boys to antisocial peer influence (Berndt, 1979).

Importantly, a review of research on this issue noted that gender differences in conformity favoring males seem to appear only in research conducted by males. In conformity studies conducted by female experimenters, the two sexes have usually shown equal levels of conformity (Eagly & Carli, 1981). This raises the question of sexist bias in experimentation.

Also, the settings and types of conformity tasks used in these experiments differed. Task familiarity has been found to influence self-confidence and conformity behavior, and some studies that reported sex differences in conformity used tasks that were more familiar to males than to females. When males and females felt equally confident about how to perform a conformity task in an experiment, sex differences weren't found (Sistrunk & McDavid, 1971).

Some Consequences of Adolescent Conformity

Conformity has both positive and negative consequences. Acting, talking, and dressing like others makes adolescents feel that they "belong" and a certain amount of security is essential in order to function effectively. To the extent that peer groups encourage an adolescent's social, emotional, and cognitive development, we would suggest that the consequences of peer group membership and conformity can be positive.

Peer group conformity can be seen as negative, however, when it hinders the development of autonomy and encourages beliefs and behaviors that are clearly not in the best interests of either the young person or society. By the latter, we are referring to antisocial and illegal acts, dropping out of school, life-endangering acts ("playing chicken"), and similar behaviors. For example, adolescent gangs encourage their members to engage in antisocial and illegal behaviors (Friedman, Mann, & Adelman, 1976). Also, peer group norms work against serious intellectual involvement and, to a lesser extent, high academic achievement, particularly in high school (Braham, 1965; J. S. Coleman, 1961; Eitzen, 1975; Sebald, 1981).

A small number of adolescents consciously choose not to conform to social norms or rebel against them. Such behavior may be judged positively or negatively depending upon adolescents' values or reasons for engaging in such behavior—for example, the numerous student demonstrations against the Vietnam War.

INDIVIDUAL FRIENDSHIPS IN ADOLESCENCE

Importance and Development of Adolescent Friendships

Adolescence is a time for moving beyond the family into the larger world and for developing a new orientation toward oneself. Relationships with friends play important roles in both of these transitions. As we have said, friends provide support and security

Peer-group conformity can sometimes have serious negative consequences.

to help the adolescent negotiate emotional independence from the family. Peers serve as an important source of feedback on the adolescent's ideas and behavior. Also, exchanging information and verbalizing beliefs and feelings force adolescents to step back from themselves. This process can lead to the development of new and different perspectives on themselves—an important aspect of achieving identity (Douvan & Adelson, 1966). In addition, hearing what others are thinking, doing, and feeling helps reduce anxiety associated with issues which may be threatening (sex or drugs, for example).

Several developments in adolescence heighten the potential impact friends may have on each other at this time. First, adolescents have just recently come to realize their own power in actively directing their personal development (Douvan & Adelson, 1966). Children tend to accept things as they are because they feel they are powerless to change them. Adolescents, on the other hand, relate to new experiences, relationships, and ideas in different, more "open" ways. Sometimes this openness is manifested in receptiveness and, at other times, it takes on a more active, intentional quality.

Second, important cognitive and personality changes are in process which work both for and against the young person. On the one hand, the operation of egocentrism can distort their perceptions of others and interfere with mutuality in relationships. On the other hand, social interaction is exactly what is needed for growing beyond egocentrism and narcissism.

Third, the physiological and hormonal changes which take place in adolescence heighten emotional and sexual sensitivity to others. These factors taken in combination, then, increase the developmental significance of adolescent friendships.

There is some evidence that friendships become more stable from age 5 through 18, that is, people are more likely to keep the same friends over a period of time. From about 18 to 21 there are increased fluctuations in friendships, probably due to the fact that young people leave their neighborhoods and go on to work, college, marriage, or service in the armed forces (Skorepa, Horrocks, & Thompson, 1963).

Several longitudinal studies on the development of adolescent friendships have found that the greatest insecurity and fears of rejection occur around 15 years of age (J. C. Coleman, 1974, 1980; Douvan & Adelson, 1966; Powell, 1955). This finding, coupled with the high levels of peer conformity at this age, suggests that adolescents feel particularly dependent on their peers during middle adolescence. The fact that the highest levels of parent-adolescent conflict also occur at this time gives rise to the speculation that middle adolescence is a critical time for decreasing emotional dependence on parents and that peers are assigned a critical role of providing emotional support in this process.

Peter Madison (1969) has contributed the term *developmental friendship* to describe a special kind of friendship in which there are strong emotional ties and in which one of the friends has personal qualities that are lacking in the other and are needed for the other's development. This idea is illustrated in the following excerpt from one of Madison's case histories:

Fred had certain qualities particularly lacking in Bob and required by him for his own development. Two of these qualities are prominent: Fred's interest in and evaluation of ideas and all that we mean by the "liberal arts" in education and his freedom to oppose and criticize authority. Bob was badly in need of being opened up to intellectual, cultural, and human values and freed from the overly technical and materialistic outlook he had on education when he came [to college]. Bob needed to break out of the constraints of parental obligation and to oppose such authority. Fred was an expert at rebellion of this kind. (Madison, 1969, pp. 117–118)

Such friendships are especially likely to develop in high school or college. While most friendships are not of this type, developmental friendships can exert a significant influence in a young person's life, bringing about changes which would not otherwise happen.

Gender Differences

As we have seen, traditional sex-role expectations dictate that relationships, social skills, and the capacities for intimacy and dependency will be highly valued in females and that those for males will stress independence and competence, an orientation which doesn't facilitate the development of close emotional relationships. Consequently, friendships appear to serve different functions for and to develop somewhat differently in males and females (J. C. Coleman, 1980; Douvan & Adelson, 1966).

Girls' Friendships   The development of friendships in girls has been traced throughout the adolescent period by Elizabeth Douvan and Joseph Adelson (1966). In early adolescence (11 to 13 years in this study), girls' friendships don't appear to be "emotionally relevant," that is, their emotional commitments are still very much based in their families. The focus of the friendship is common activities rather than the relationship itself. The quality of early female friendships is generally superficial and narcissistic in nature, friends should be "amicable, easy to get along with, cooperative, and fair. The friend ought not to be a crab, grouchy, mean, selfish or a showoff" (Douvan & Adelson, 1966, p. 186). Friendships at this age are predominantly same-sex. Interactions with boys take place primarily in play, and the sexes judge one another by skill rather than by gender.

In midadolescence (14 to 16 years) girls' friendships appear to be the most difficult. Girls of this age appear quite anxious about being rejected or excluded from a same-sex friendship (J. C. Coleman, 1980). Sexual references in interviews are more common in this period than either before or after, suggesting that there is considerable anxiety, confusion, and doubt about sexuality (Douvan & Adelson, 1966). No doubt this is related in part to the fact that girls typically begin dating at this age.

Girls' friendships in middle adolescence are less egocentric and superficial and focus more on the other's personal qualities than they did earlier. There is strong emphasis on loyalty and support, suggesting that there is still some narcissism operating. Girls seem to use same-sex relationships as a secure base from which to make the transition to heterosexual relationships.

By late adolescence (17 to 18 years) friendships are easier for girls. This is probably because the girl has more of a sense of her identity and is more familiar with her sexuality, more secure in her interactions with boys, and more adept socially. In addition, for most girls, much of the emotional energy that was previously invested in same-sex friendships is now invested in relationships with boys. These changes permit each person to see the other more as a separate person than as an extension of herself. Douvan and Adelson report that late adolescent girls' descriptions of friends stress the other's individuality and show a greater ability to tolerate differences in the other.

Boys' Friendships   In general, it has been found that boys are less likely to have close same-sex friendships than girls (Coleman, 1980). Moreover, boys' friendships do not usually achieve the depth of intimacy typical of girls' friendships.

Douvan and Adelson's survey of adolescents included boys only from age 14 to 16. Therefore, it is impossible to compare the development of male and female friendships across the entire span of adolescence. The authors do report, based on the 14- to 16-year-old males they studied, that the larger peer group appears to be more important to males than individual friendships. Also, they found that boys seemed to lag behind girls in the development of close friendships. Other researchers have described adult male friendships similarly, suggesting that emotionally intimate friendships between males are less common than among females: "When men meet, the result is essentially a 'noninteraction,' either a glad-handing, back-slapping superficiality or a self-conscious exchange of monosyllables" (Crites & Fitzgerald, 1978, p. 12). Of course, this is not true for all men, but the cultural press definitely pushes men in this direction (Pleck, 1981a). Perhaps the recent emphasis on men's developing friendships with other men will eventually prevail so as to allow them their share of supportive interactions with each other.

Boys in middle adolescence describe their friends in terms similar to those used by preadolescent girls. In contrast to girls of the same age, boys do not see emotional support, closeness, or security as being important qualities of a friendship. They do, however, expect a friend to stand by them in times of trouble. Generally, a boy prefers to interact with a group of friends rather than with one or two peers. This group orientation facilitates less intimate interactions, which boys appear to prefer, and gives them a base from which they can collectively (and more safely) confront adult authority.

A classic study conducted in a college rooming house investigated the development of late adolescent male friendships and found that those who had similar attitudes and values were more likely to be friends (Newcomb, 1961). This suggests that by college age males can relate to each other on the basis of personality characteristics rather than activities.

One of the criteria of emotional closeness in a relationship is the degree of *self-disclosure* (or openness and honesty) shared by two people. A number of studies have found females to be more self-disclosing than males (Rivenbark, 1971; Snoek & Rothblum, 1979). Other studies have found more subtle differences between the sexes in this area (Komarovsky; 1976; Morgan, 1976; Pleck, 1981a). For example, one recent study found that high school girls disclosed general information, such as types of recreation enjoyed, and personal information, such as things most feared, but disclosed less about sexuality to parents and peers, such as questions about sex and reproduction (Davidson, Balswick, & Halverson, 1980). The pattern of boys' results was the opposite. Although high school girls may use their friends for feedback and support in personal development, they do not include highly personal and explicit revelations about sex in these interchanges. For some, this may come later—in college, perhaps—but others may never feel comfortable discussing sex-related issues in a personal way.

Opposite-Sex Friendships

Friendships between males and females during adolescence can have both positive and negative effects. On the positive side, they can teach boys and girls what the other sex is like. This is particularly important for those who have not grown up with siblings of the other sex.

Opposite-sex friendships among black college students were found to be characterized by more sharing of information about the self, more participation in shared activities, and greater feelings of reciprocity than same-sex friendships (Peretti, 1976). In addition, there is some evidence that college males may find it easier to engage in self-disclosure with a woman than with another man, consistent with Pleck's description of the modern male sex role discussed in Chapter 6 (Komarovsky, 1976).

Females, too, may benefit from opposite-sex friendships. Sandra Schwartz Tangri (1972) studied college women who had selected male-dominated careers; she called them *role innovators*. Tangri found that these role innovators listed more males among their 10 closest friends than did *traditional* women (those who had chosen occupations with 50 percent or more women). The role innovators' male and female friends were both supportive of the innovators' career goals, and the male friends were found to be quite supportive of the idea of having a wife who had a strong investment in her own career.

On the negative side, some evidence suggests that opposite-sex friendships may work to impede development. This is most likely to occur when sex-role stereotypes interfere with opposite-sex friends' perceptions of each other. We know that most males and females are likely to view females as less competent and independent than males

Opposite-sex friendships allow adolescents to learn about each other.

(Broverman, Vogel, Broverman, Clarkson, & Rosenkrantz, 1972), and most males do not have as strong feelings as most females about the equal participation of women in society (Komarovsky, 1973; Roper & Labeff, 1977; Zey-Ferrell, Tolone, & Walsh, 1978). Also, many males have difficulty with heterosexual relationships in which they do not feel superior (Komarovsky, 1973). Therefore, a girl or woman with nontraditional views about sex-roles might find it difficult to find male friends who would encourage her ideas and encourage her to raise her expectations. She might be tempted to lower, disguise, or change her aspirations in order to be accepted. (The Tangri study indicates that this is not invariably so, but the women chosen for the study were a special group in terms of views and actions and they may have been very selective in their friendships. Less unusual women, even if they hold nontraditional views, might not come in contact with or seek out such men; they would be more likely to seek or fall into friendships with traditional males. In such relationships the problems arising from sex-role stereotyping would be apparent.)

Females who believe in the stereotype of the "strong, silent male" may encourage this behavior in male opposite-sex friends and not be able to see that other qualities (nurturance, dependency) are also present. In this case, males would lose opportunities to develop these aspects of their personality.

Sources of Difficulty in Adolescent Friendships

It has been suggested that there has been a "studied neglect" of the negative and distressing aspects of friendship (Roll & Millen, 1979). One study investigated the prominence of negative themes related to friendship in the dreams of 19-year-olds and found that almost half of the dreams of both males (45 percent) and females (46 percent) contained negative interactions with friends. Although the percentage of positive interactions was higher, such a high percentage of negative interactions was unexpected, say the authors, given the almost universal positive associations with friendships. Also, the authors found that the friends in dreams were described as being supportive, helpful, or loving in a minority of dreams (24 percent of males and 18 percent of females).

Of course, young people aren't alone in having problems with friendships. Still, the psychological issues that confront adolescents ensure that such difficulties are likely to occur for unique reasons. Egocentrism makes it difficult for the adolescent to focus attention on other people, to perceive others accurately, and to grasp what others are saying or implying. Douvan and Adelson describe another consequence of such self-centeredness on adolescent friendships:

> There is the well-known adolescent touchiness, a hypersensitivity to rejection which in some cases can assume an almost paranoid intensity, in the conviction that friends are talking about them, or are out to exclude, wound, and humiliate them. . . . casual happenings . . . will be magnified into events of major interpersonal significance. (1966, p. 181)

Difficulties with friends are also related to undeveloped social skills. With practice and the self-confidence growing out of such practice, most adolescents grow into adults who are skilled at and comfortable with interpersonal interactions.

Intimacy and Identity

As you recall, Erikson has theorized that identity achievement precedes the ability to establish intimate relationships. Jacob Orlofsky and his colleagues (1973) constructed interview questions to measure intimacy development based on the criteria of depth and mutuality of interpersonal relationships with same- and other-sex peers.

Elaborating on Erikson's concept, they established five statuses of intimacy: intimate, preintimate, stereotyped, pseudointimate, and isolate. Individuals in the *intimate* status form close and open relationships with male and female friends and are involved in a committed relationship. *Pre*intimate individuals are also capable of mature, reciprocal relationships, but because of ambivalence about commitment, they have not yet had a relationship to which they are strongly committed. Individuals in the *stereotyped* status have relationships that are superficial. That is, there isn't much openness or closeness, and others are often seen as objects to manipulate rather than persons to share with. Those in the *pseudointimate* status are typically involved in a relatively permanent relationship, but it is one that resembles the stereotyped relationship in quality. *Isolates* avoid social situations and appear to be loners whose social interactions consist of casual conversations after class with a few acquaintances.

In keeping with Erikson's theory that one must have a sense of oneself before being able to relate on an intimate basis to another person, a number of researchers have investigated the relationship between identity and intimacy statuses. Findings support Erikson's theory that the two are related. For example, it has been consistently found that college males and females in the more advanced identity statuses (achievement and moratorium) are most likely to be in the more advanced intimacy statuses (intimate and preintimate) (Fitch & Adams, 1983; Kacerguis & Adams, 1980; Marcia, 1976a). Likewise, foreclosures and diffusions are predominant in the three less advanced intimacy statuses (stereotyped, pseudointimate, and isolate).

While these studies demonstrate that intimacy is a correlate of identity status, much more research is needed to determine whether identity achievement is a precursor to intimacy and how this process may differ in males and females.

DATING

Pattern and Functions of Dating

The practice of dating is a twentieth-century North American phenomenon (Feinstein & Ardon, 1973). Initially, dating was presumed to lead to marriage. As we shall see, adolescents today see dating as a way of socializing with the opposite sex rather than as a precursor to marriage (Place, 1975).

Psychosexual development and dating patterns have been described as following a four-stage sequence (Feinstein & Ardon, 1973):

Stage 1. Sexual awakening (ages 13 to 15). Both sexes become aware of their emerging sexuality. Since girls are more mature than boys their own age, they may date older males. This may cause some insecurity in boys.

Stage 2. Practicing (ages 14 to 17). Boys and girls engage in numerous short-term relationships, usually with the opposite sex. Dates may often take place in groups, as adolescents learn to feel comfortable in these interactions. The solidifying of sex-role identity and sexual preference issues is an important aspect of this stage.

Stage 3. Acceptance of the sexual role (ages 16 to 19). Having accepted their emerging sex-role identities and sexual preference, adolescents begin engaging in longer-term dating relationships, including experimenting with sex.

Stage 4. Development of a permanent object choice (ages 18 to 25). Once adolescents have a secure sense of identity, they are more able to incorporate emotional intimacy into sexual relationships and to make a commitment to another person for a long-term relationship.

This pattern of psychosocial development appears consistent with the development of adolescent peer relationships (unisexual cliques, heterosexual crowds, and cliques of loosely associated couples) described by Dexter Dunphy (1963).

Several studies have surveyed adolescents in order to understand why they date (Grinder, 1966; Hansen, 1977; D. W. Jackson, 1975; Place, 1975; Skipper & Nass, 1966). Some of these reasons are listed below.

1. *Socialization.* Dating helps young people learn to interact with others and to develop social skills and etiquette.
2. *Recreation.* Dating is fun and a source of enjoyment.
3. *Social status.* Dating plays an important part in young people's social status and in their own evaluation of themselves with regard to social achievement.
4. *Independence assertion.* Dating provides a means of achieving autonomy from parents and other adults. It involves relationships and activities separate from the adult world, and it can serve as a way of defying adult authority, for example, by dating people parents consider undesirable for religious, political, or social reasons and by violating curfew restrictions.
5. *Intimacy development.* Dating provides a setting for the development of mutual affection, openness, trust, respect, and loyalty, the precursors to close and committed relationships.
6. *Sexual experimentation and gratification.* Dating provides socially acceptable opportunities for varying degrees of sexual intimacy which facilitates learning about sex and sexuality.
7. *Mate selection.* Dating offers opportunities to interact with others for the purpose of selecting a mate.

While the American dating system serves a number of useful functions, it has been severely criticized, mainly on the grounds that it contributes to the development of superficial relationships (Husbands, 1970). Some critics feel that dating encourages role playing or acting in ways which are socially acceptable, but don't represent adolescents' true feelings—pretending to be happy all the time, for example. Adopting such an interaction style can mean that adolescents don't learn to be comfortable with "being themselves" for fear that others won't like them. Also, young people can get so concerned about making good impressions on others that they fail to learn who they really are; they become identified with the roles they play.

Dating also encourages "playing the field," which can lead to competitive and manipulative practices that discourage trust between two people (Place, 1975).

In addition, it's possible for adolescents to get caught up in the dating game to the degree that they don't learn how to make a commitment to a long-term, meaningful relationship.

Qualities Adolescents Look for in a Date

Research findings have consistently shown that physical attractiveness is a key factor in individuals' choices of *potential* dating partners, especially among young people (Curran & Lippold, 1975; Folkes, 1982; Walster, Aronson, Abrahams, & Rottman, 1966). And, although people tend to choose *actual* dating partners who are similar to themselves in physical attractiveness (Berscheid, Dion, Walster, & Walster, 1971), attractiveness is a major criterion by which others are evaluated. These findings reflect the American cultural norm of "attractiveness prejudice" which associates positive qualities with good looks (Dion, Berscheid, & Walster, 1972). This stereotype appears to be held even more strongly for females. For example, one study found that physical attractiveness is highly correlated with the number of dates female adolescents have in a year, but is less strongly related to the frequency of dating of adolescent males (Berscheid et al., 1971).

Attractiveness prejudice exerts considerable influence on adolescents, especially girls, as can be seen by their preoccupation with their bodies and physical characteristics. In this context, recall that 25 percent of high school girls and only 2 percent of boys considered being "ugly or not good looking" as a criterion for being rejected by peers (Sebald, 1981).

Personality characteristics are not irrelevant in interpersonal attraction, but they seem to assume significance mainly after a couple gets to know each other. Then, factors such as similarity in attitudes become important.

Age Trends in Dating

Young people begin dating earlier now than in the past. In 1924 the average age for a girl's first date was 16 years (G. F. Smith, 1924). Since about 1950 the age seems to have fluctuated between 13 and 14 years (Dickinson, 1975; Douvan & Adelson, 1966; Hansen, 1977). A study of black and white senior high school students indicated that among white students the average age for the first date remained relatively constant at 13.59 years in 1964 and 13.88 years in 1974 (Dickinson, 1975). Among black students, however, the age declined from 14.91 years in 1964 to 13.93 years in 1974. A later study of black and white adolescents suggests that dating may be starting somewhat later (14 or 15 years). However, the difference in ages may be due to regional practices since the first study was conducted in Texas and the second in Florida (Hansen, 1977).

While it is important for young people to wait to date until it feels "right," dating out of phase with peers may have negative consequences. For example, there is some feeling that same-sex relationships in preadolescence and early adolescence play an important role in the beginnings of identity consolidation and in the development of the ability to trust, understand, and care deeply about another (Douvan & Adelson, 1966; Sullivan, 1953). If young people begin dating so early that they skip this stage

Today, most American adolescents begin dating at about age 14.

in the developmental process, it is possible that they may miss out on this essential learning. If so, there is a possibility that the adolescent may not feel secure enough to share deep feelings with the opposite sex, which can lead to a series of superficial relationships.

Getting a late start in dating can also be a problem because adolescents may lose opportunities to develop their social skills and confidence. At worst, they may develop into adult loners or isolates who never really learn to trust and enjoy others.

Dating Practices

Frequency   About 50 percent of high school students average one or more dates per week, close to 20 percent date once a month or less, and about 13 percent don't date at all (Bachman, Johnston, & O'Malley, 1980; Dickinson, 1975; Hansen, 1977). Those who date most frequently are likely to be involved in a steady relationship.

A survey of black and white high school students revealed that about a third were dating either randomly or only two or three people, a third were dating only one person, and the remaining third either never or almost never dated (Hansen, 1977). The number of dating partners increases up to about the twelfth grade. After that time, the number of partners decreases (Feinstein & Ardon, 1973).

Socioeconomic status appears to influence the number of dating partners. For example, middle-class adolescents are more likely than lower-SES youth to "play the field" before settling on a steady dating partner.

Activities   A survey of black and white high school students reported that white students preferred, in order, going to movies, driving around, and going to parties (Dickinson, 1975). Black students indicated that they liked, in order, driving around, going dancing and going to the movies. About three-fourths of both blacks and whites reported that they "parked" on dates.

Sex-Role Issues   The recent trends toward more liberated sex roles have had some limited impact on dating practices. Traditional sex-role stereotypes hold that males take the more dominant and assertive role in dating: asking for the date, deciding where to go, supplying the car, initiating sexual activities, and paying the bills. Adolescent females, and especially college women, have more liberal sex-role attitudes than males. Consequently, females are most likely to feel the need to make changes in traditionally structured male-female relationships. This imbalance in beliefs puts an additional strain on individuals as well as on relationships.

Despite the fact that females have more liberal sex-role attitudes than males, on the question of girls asking boys out females appear to hold more traditional views than males. For example, a national survey of adolescent girls found that 64 percent had "never" asked a boy out first, nearly 25 percent "seldom" did, and only 2 percent did so "frequently" (Gaylin, 1979). Among female college students, a majority reported that they had "never" asked a boy out first and only slightly more than 10 percent indicated they "sometimes" did (Gaylin, 1979). On the other hand, a national survey of adolescent males found that 44 percent would react "positively" if a girl asked them for a date and 43 percent said that it "didn't matter" to them; only 13 percent indicated that it would "turn them off" (Gaylin, 1978).

Going Steady   Most high school students have gone steady at least once and approximately a fourth of high school students are going steady at any given point in time (Dickinson, 1975). A study of dating patterns among Kentucky high school students found that 53 percent of the teenagers indicated that the most important advantage in going steady was "being with someone you enjoy" (Wittman, 1971). Less than 1 percent of students reported that they went steady for prestige, while 11 percent said that "security in always having a date" was the most important advantage of going steady. They felt that the most important disadvantage was that "you can't date others." Ideally, interacting as a couple over an extended period of time allows young people to get to know each other on an emotionally intimate basis and encourages the development of mutual trust and self-disclosure. If this happens gradually, and if the level of involvement in a relationship is matched by the couple's emotional development, then going steady may be seen as having some advantages. A study of factors related to dating adjustment in college students found that recent dating frequency and involvement in a committed relationship were the variables most strongly related to dating adjustment (Herold, 1979).

The disadvantages of going steady are more numerous, which is why many parents and other adults have negative feelings about the practice. For one thing, it is been found that people who have had numerous friends of both sexes prior to marriage are more likely to have successful marriages. Since dating the same person steadily limits the number of friends a young person has, this practice might turn out to be detrimental to the formation of a good, long-term relationship. Second, going steady can lead to marriage during the teenage years, and research quite consistently shows that such marriages are much more likely to be unhappy and result in divorce.

Third, going steady appears to present greater opportunities for increased sexual intimacy than does "playing the field" and therefore greater risk of pregnancy and sexually transmitted disease. Several studies have reported that teenagers are engaging in sexual intercourse at earlier ages than before (Vener & Stewart, 1974; Zelnick & Kantner, 1979). Since the use of birth control among teenagers is notoriously lacking, the probability of pregnancy among those who engage in sexual intercourse is quite high (Zelnick & Kantner, 1972). Coping with decisions about abortion, adoption, marriage, and child rearing is extremely difficult for young people, especially those who may not want to involve their parents or other adults because of guilt, fear of rejection, or needing to prove their independence. And the choices they make affect the rest of their lives. Sexually transmitted disease among adolescents has reached epidemic proportions in recent years (Carroll, Miller & Nash, 1976).

Of course, not all adolescents go steady; estimates range from 25 to 40 percent (Dickinson, 1975; Herold, 1979; Poffenberger, 1964; Wittman, 1971). Moreover, one study indicated that approximately 40 percent of the high school students who have gone steady reported that they had done so with three or more people (Poffenberger, 1964). This suggests that going steady is more likely to be a short-term "affair" and need not necessarily result in premature commitments.

SUMMARY

Similarities in adolescents' interests in clothes, styles of dress, choice of music, use of language, and other behavior suggest that there is an adolescent subculture in these respects. To conclude that there is an adolescent subculture based on strong and numerous value differences between adolescents and adults would, however, be inaccurate.

The adolescent peer group serves as a stabilizing influence and a source of self-esteem, standards, and security during the time adolescents are undergoing personal changes and reducing their emotional dependence on the family. In addition, the peer group provides opportunities for practicing new behaviors and developing the necessary social skills for same- and opposite-sex interactions.

Popularity with peers in adolescence is related to conforming to peer norms, personality attributes, physical attractiveness, and intelligence. Peer group acceptance has been found to be important with regard to self-esteem, the learning of social skills, and conformity. Conformity reaches its peak during early adolescence and declines thereafter.

Girls' friendships appear to be more intimate than boys' friendships, and adolescent girls are more advanced in their social development than boys at any age. Both boys and girls appear to pass through stages in their friendships, first focusing on the activities the two people share and later on the relationship and personal qualities.

Dating in adolescence can serve a number of useful purposes, but it can also encourage the development of superficial relationships and competitive and manipulative interaction styles. More than half of senior high school students average one or more dates a week, and about three-quarters have gone steady at least once. Going steady can provide a sense of security, but its disadvantages are numerous.

GLOSSARY

clique (Dunphy)   A type of adolescent peer group characterized primarily by its small size (approximately 6 members).

crowd (Dunphy)   A type of adolescent peer group composed of about 20 members from different cliques.

egocentrism (Piaget)   A cognitive characteristic in which individuals are unable to differentiate their own thoughts and feelings from those of others; diminishes considerably in late adolescence.

gang   A type of adolescent peer group characterized by antisocial and illegal activities.

intimate (Orlofsky)   A more advanced intimacy status characterized by individuals who have close and open relationships with others and who are involved in a committed relationship.

isolate (Orlofsky)   A less advanced intimacy status characterized by individuals who are loners and who cannot engage in committed relationships.

preintimate (Orlofsky)   A more advanced intimacy status characterized by individuals who have close, open, and reciprocal relationships with others, but who have not yet engaged in a committed relationship.

pseudointimate (Orlofsky)   A less advanced intimacy status in which individuals are involved in relatively permanent relationships, which are characterized by superficiality and manipulation.

self-disclosure   Revealing one's private thoughts and feelings to another person.

stereotyped (Orlofsky)   A less advanced intimacy status in which individuals usually see others as objects to be manipulated and cannot make long-lasting commitments.

GETTING INVOLVED: Case Study and General Questions to Consider

CASE STUDY: NANCY

Nancy is a first-semester freshman at State University, an institution of approximately 20,000 students. She is from another part of the state and lives in a residence hall on campus with other freshman. She works 15 hours a week in the Student Union cafeteria to pay for part of her educational expenses.

Nancy is thinking about a career in photojournalism, working in business, or doing free-lance photography when she graduates. Because she is unsure of her career goals at this point, she has not chosen a major and is taking courses which fulfill liberal arts requirements. This first semester she is enrolled in English, biology, math, psychology, and history courses.

In high school Nancy was a B— student and worked on the school newspaper. Although she made an effort to get along with others, she never felt very much accepted by her peers. While they usually didn't reject her, she was never sought out. Also, she didn't date much. Now, for the first time since grade school, Nancy has found friends she can relate to. Consequently, she has been spending more time talking, going out, partying, and playing cards than studying.

Nancy feels relieved that her courses are not as demanding as she expected they would be. She goes to her classes once or twice a week, takes notes, and tries to study several hours a week. When mid-semester exam time comes, Nancy hits the books the night before each exam to cram. On her mid-terms, she gets two C's (English and history) and 3 D's (biology, psychology, math). She is stunned—she didn't expect to get all A's, but she certainly didn't expect D's!

Most of her friends didn't do particularly well on their mid-terms either, but they say not to worry because they've heard that professors always try to scare freshmen with mid-term exams and finals will be easier. But Nancy is scared. Part of her wants to believe her friends and enjoy her newfound companionship and freedom; another part of her is worried that she will flunk out or be put on probation. How humiliating —and what would they say back home?

If she starts now, she feels that she may be able to redeem the semester. On the other hand, since she has to work, if she spends more time studying, she will have less time to spend with her friends. She is afraid that they will "ditch" her. She enjoys their company and this is a big campus; it can get very lonely, and she knows what loneliness is like. What can she do?

Questions for Case Study

1. What seems to be happening here? Identify the conflict(s). Then, try to isolate the factors contributing to the conflicts.
2. What characteristics of the college environment appear to be significant in this situation? Do you feel that this is a common problem at your school? What might be done by the students, faculty, administrators to improve the campus social climate?
3. Does Nancy seem to have any problems related to personality development? If so, what are they and how might she deal with them?

4. What are Nancy's options? Briefly discuss the short- and long-term outcomes of the most "likely" options.

GENERAL QUESTIONS TO CONSIDER

1. In which ways is it appropriate to speak of a youth subculture in the United States. In which ways, not?
2. Consider some of the aspects of the adolescent subculture in the United States (styles of dress, physical appearance, language, music, "hang-outs"). What have your personal experiences been with these aspects? What function(s) do you feel such things play(ed) in your life?
3. Why does peer group pressure seem to be particularly important for adolescents compared to other age groups?
4. Are there any areas in which you did or do find peer pressure very strong (drinking, drugs, smoking, sex, dress, vocational choice, or others)?
5. What characteristics do you look for in a friend? What kinds of things might a friend do which might cause you to break off the friendship? Compare your current feelings to those when you were younger.
6. Consider the problems of peer neglect and rejection in adolescence. What might be done to help adolescents learn to get along better with their peers? Based on your experience, what are the chances that peers would help here?
7. Reflect on the role of egocentrism in adolescent friendships. Can you recall examples in your own life when egocentrism interfered with your perceptions of others?
8. What role do friends play in your life? Why are they important to you? How can friendships facilitate adolescent development? How can friends stand in the way of adolescent psychological growth?
9. Consider gender differences in adolescent friendships.
10. How can other-sex friendships help and hinder adolescent personal development?
11. Consider sex-role issues in dating. Should girls and women be more assertive in asking and paying for dates, in deciding where to go, in initiating sexual activities? Why or why not?
12. In what ways do you feel going steady is a good idea for adolescents? What are some negative aspects of going steady? Recall your own experiences.

Chapter 9 Outline

I. Junior and Senior High School Setting
   A. Impact of School Structure
   B. Current Status of Elementary and Secondary Education
   C. Conflicts Between Academic and Social Forces
   D. Factors Influencing Adolescents' Academic Achievement and Aspirations
   E. School-Related Problems of Adolescents
II. College and University Setting
   A. Who Goes to College?
   B. Types of Colleges and Student Satisfaction
   C. College Student Subcultures
   D. Impact of College on Students
   E. Problems of College Students
III. Postsecondary Vocational Program Setting
IV. Summary
V. Glossary
VI. Getting Involved: Exercise, Case Study, and General Questions to Consider
   A. Exercise: College Student Subcultures
   B. Case Study: Patrick
   C. General Questions to Consider

chapter 9

Educational Experiences

Educational institutions have the role of educating and socializing citizens so they can be productive members of society. They have the following general functions in a society (Johnston & Bachman, 1976):

1. Caretaking and managing students
2. Teaching required skills and knowledge
3. Transmitting cultural values, beliefs, and traditions
4. Sorting, classifying, and evaluating students

The specific functions of educational institutions vary from one society to another because of differences in the societies' structures, needs, and values. For example, the United States' policy of public education is based on a belief that every citizen is entitled to a free education at least through the twelfth grade. Some industrialized countries provide a free general education through only the sixth or seventh grade. In many countries students then take an examination, the outcome of which determines whether they are to continue with a vocational or academic education. Further examinations are required of those in the academic "track" for admission to a university.

In developing nations which are struggling to achieve even a basic standard of literacy, institutionalized systems of general education are not yet entirely in place. Consequently, formal education, at least at the junior high and high school levels, is available only to those in the privileged classes who can afford to pay for such schooling or to those bright individuals who earn scholarships. Children and adolescents unable to attend school learn useful skills at home which enable them to be productive members of society.

Adolescents experience educational institutions in terms of peers, teachers, coaches, classes, homework, social activities, and athletics. In this chapter we will focus on the experiences of American adolescents in three different educational settings: junior and senior high schools, colleges and universities, and postsecondary vocational programs.

JUNIOR AND SENIOR HIGH SCHOOL SETTING

Impact of School Structure

Grade-Level Organization   Research suggests that grade-level organization (that is, whether a school is kindergarten–eighth grade or kindergarten–sixth grade) may influence the nature of the transition of early adolescence. One study compared sixth-grade students in schools with either a K–8 or K–6 organizational pattern (Blyth, Simmons, & Bush, 1978). The researchers looked at eight K–6 and six K–8 public schools in a large Midwestern city which were quite similar on a number of social characteristics such as average family income, average minority population, and the like, thus ensuring that any differences observed between students from the two types of schools were actually due to grade-level organization. It was found that the sixth-grade students in the K–8 setting were more likely than the sixth-grade students in a K–6 setting to be influenced by their peers. They dated more and preferred to be with their close friends more than with their parents. Also, they were more likely to be a victim of an assault, robbery, or theft. On the other hand, the K–6 students were more likely than their K–8 peers to be academically oriented and to have internalized a greater sense of responsibility.

When these same students were retested as seventh graders, it was found that the K–8 students had developed more positive attitudes about themselves, participated more frequently in activities, and felt less anonymous in their schools. The seventh graders who switched to junior high schools felt less positively about themselves, participated less in activities, and felt a degree of anonymity in school. Also, it seemed that the junior high school males were more likely to be a victim of an assault, robbery, or theft.

This study doesn't answer the question about how the transition to senior high school from K–8 versus junior high affects students. Also, we don't know whether a transition between schools is easier for students at a younger or an older age.

School Size   School size has been found to influence students' educational experiences. One recent study looked at the impact of size on five areas of school activity—academics, social life, athletics, clubs, and fine arts (Grabe, 1981). (Large schools were defined as those whose total enrollment in the tenth through twelfth grades exceeded 580.) The study reported that students in small schools were involved in more activities in all five areas. As might be expected, males participated in significantly more athletic activities than females, and females listed more academic accomplishments and greater participation in fine arts and club activities. Also, ninth and tenth graders reported higher levels of participation in athletic activities, while eleventh and twelfth graders listed more academic accomplishments and higher levels of participation in social activities and clubs.

Curricular Tracking Because of compulsory attendance laws, there is a wide range in the academic abilities of students. One attempt to deal with varying abilities and interests has been academic tracking. Three curricular options commonly offered at the high school level are college preparatory, vocational, and general. An honors curriculum is sometimes also available. While many high schools offer all three of these curricula, some specialize in one or another, for example, vocational and technical high schools.

The *college preparatory curriculum* is designed to prepare students for entrance into and successful academic performance in college. Approximately 39 percent of 1980 high school seniors were enrolled in this track, which is usually perceived by students and teachers as the most prestigious curriculum (Peng, Fetters, & Kolstad, 1981).

The *vocational curriculum* is designed for students who want to work immediately upon high school graduation. In 1980 24 percent of high school seniors were enrolled in this curriculum (Peng et al., 1981). Students are prepared for jobs in such fields as automobile mechanics, accounting, secretarial office work, and food services. They usually spend about half their time in general education courses and half in courses geared to their anticipated jobs and in on-the-job training.

The *general curriculum* is designed for students whose current plans include neither college preparation nor vocational training. Often, students with the lowest academic ability and motivation enroll (or are encouraged to enroll) in this curriculum. Among 1980 high school seniors 37 percent were enrolled in the general curriculum (Peng et al., 1981).

Because it has been observed that adolescents from minority and lower-SES families are less frequently assigned to the college preparatory track and drop out of school in greater numbers, it has been suggested that tracking may encourage such students to set lower academic standards and to have lower academic and occupational

The vocational curriculum is designed for students who want to work immediately upon high school graduation.

aspirations. One study statistically controlled for differences in students' IQ and family background so that the impact of tracking could be isolated and assessed (Schafer, Olexa, & Polk, 1970). The findings indicated that almost 40 percent of the non-college-preparatory students placed in the lowest quarter of the class, based on grades (remember that this couldn't be explained on the basis of ability or family background). In addition, these students were less involved in school activities and had four times the dropout rate as did college-preparatory students. These findings suggest that tracking can have important negative effects on some students and that alternative strategies for dealing with the problem of varying student ability levels are needed.

Current Status of Elementary and Secondary Education

American elementary and secondary schools have come under strong attack recently. Two concerns have received the most attention: declining academic achievement and school crime and violence.

Declining Academic Achievement   As we saw in Chapter 3, there has been a steady decline in Scholastic Aptitude Test scores of high school seniors since 1963. Between 1963 and 1983 the national average of verbal SAT scores fell 53 points, from 478 to 425 and math scores decreased 34 points, from 502 to 468 (College Entrance Examination Board, 1983). Also, the number of students scoring at the highest levels (650 or better out of 800) on the verbal section of the SAT fell by 45 percent between 1970 and 1980. The number of students scoring at the highest levels on the math section fell by 23 percent ("Fewer score high," 1983).

Additional evidence of a decline in academic achievement comes from the National Assessment of Educational Progress, a national evaluation of the academic performance of American students aged 9, 13, and 17 years of age. Between 1972–1973 and 1977–1978 there were decreases in the math and science performance of students at all of these ages (National Assessment of Educational Progress [NAEP], 1979, 1980).

In 1981 the Secretary of Education created the National Commission on Excellence in Education for the purpose of assessing the quality of American education. In April 1983, the National Commission reported its findings in the form of an open letter to the American people, entitled *A Nation at Risk: The Imperative for Educational Reform*. The Commission concluded, among other things, that for the first time in American history the educational skills of the current generation will not even approach the skills of their parents. In its report the Commission identified four serious problem areas:

1. *Curriculum content.* The high school curriculum has no coherent focus, consists of too many watered-down courses, and allows students too much choice (electives). For example, although intermediate algebra is widely offered, only about 31 percent of recent high school graduates complete the course.
2. *Academic expectations.* Standards for classroom performance and requirements for both high school graduation and college admission are inadequate. For example, high school students in many other industrialized countries spend three times the amount of time in class that their American counterparts

do in subjects such as advanced mathematics, biology, chemistry, physics, and geography.

3. *Time in school.* The amount of time students spend in school is too little and what time is spent is used ineffectively. For example, high school students in other industrialized countries spend 2 more hours each day and 40 more days per year in school than do American students.

4. *Teaching.* Teacher preparation programs are poor, the rewards of teaching are insufficient to attract the most able students to the field, and there are serious teacher shortages in mathematics and science. More specifically, the Commission reported that half of the newly employed teachers of English, mathematics, and science are not qualified to teach these subjects.

To combat these quite serious problems, the Commission made a series of recommendations:

1. All students seeking a high school diploma should be required to take the following curriculum: four years of English, three years of mathematics, three years of science, three years of social studies, and one semester of computer science. For college-bound students, two years of a foreign language are strongly recommended.
2. Schools, colleges, and universities should adopt more rigorous performance standards, and college admissions standards should be raised.
3. State legislatures and school districts should strongly consider adopting a 7-hour school day and a 200- to 220-day school year.
4. The preparation of teachers must be improved considerably and the rewards for teaching substantially increased.

Students seem aware that there is a problem in American education today. As shown in Table 9.1, a 1980 national survey of high school seniors found that 67 percent agreed that schools should have placed more emphasis on academic subjects, whereas "only" 50 percent of 1972 seniors felt this way (Peng et al., 1981). This same survey reported that 1980 high school seniors received somewhat higher grades than 1972 seniors *and* spent less time on homework (68 percent of the 1980 group versus 54 percent of the 1972 group spent less than five hours a week on homework).

It is generally agreed that American education is in serious trouble. Unfortunately, there is more agreement about the fact that there is a problem than about the causes or cures of the problem. While there is probably no single cause of low academic achievement among today's youth (and causes vary from one school to another), several factors stand out: lowered academic standards, low levels of teacher competency and academic instruction, increased time spent by students watching television, disruptions in family life which interfere with parental supervision of children and adolescents, and changes in the proportions of students from various socioeconomic statuses (Advisory Panel, 1977; Handleman, 1980).

One response to the problem has been the "back to basics" movement. This approach focuses on developing basic skills in reading, writing, mathematics, science, and social studies.

Approximately two-thirds of the states have gone further and established some form of *competency-based education* (CBE) (Gorth & Perkins, 1980). This approach

Table 9.1   PERCENTAGE OF 1980 SENIORS AGREEING WITH VARIOUS STATEMENTS ABOUT HIGH SCHOOL EDUCATION OR PRACTICE BY CURRICULUM AND SCHOOL TYPE

Statements	All seniors	Curriculum			Type of school[a]	
		Academic	General	Vocational	Public	Private
School should have placed more emphasis on vocational and technical programs.	70	57	75	81	55	63
School should have placed more emphasis on basic academic subjects.	67	67	67	65	72	48
School provided me with counseling that will help me continue my education.	64	67	58	61	66	69
School did not offer enough practical work experience.	59	52	63	60	50	65
School provided me with counseling that will help me find employment.	44	35	43	57	36	30

[a]Only academic students were included in the computations.
Source: Samuel S. Peng, William B. Fetters, and Andrew J. Kolstad. (1981). *High School and Beyond, A National Longitudinal Study for the 1980s: A Capsule Description of High School Students.* Washington, D.C.: National Center for Education Statistics, p. 16. Copyright 1981 by the National Center for Education Statistics. Reprinted by permission.

requires all students to demonstrate that they are competent in a given set of academic skills in order to pass from one grade to the next. About one out of five American high schools in 1980 required seniors to pass a minimum competency exam for graduation, although there is considerable variability by geographical region (see Figure 9.1). High school seniors who are unable to pass the competency test receive a certificate of attendance. About two-thirds of the high schools with a competency exam graduation requirement had specific remedial programs for students who failed the tests (Peng et al., 1981).

The CBE approach, however, does have some important drawbacks. One problem is that if competency testing isn't instituted before high school, it's difficult to do much to help improve the performance of students who don't pass the tests. A second problem is determining in which areas competencies will be required. Since there are limits on the amount of time available for academic instruction, time spent on one subject will mean less spent on others.

Other questions remain to be answered. What constitutes minimally acceptable levels of performance, how should these be tested, and who will make these decisions? Is the student or the school responsible when the student doesn't pass the tests? At least one lawsuit based on this question has been brought to the courts already. Do the schools have an obligation to provide remedial instruction for students who fail? If so, how much instruction and for how long?

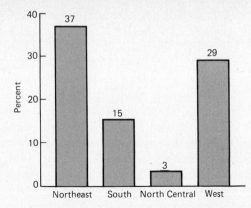

Figure 9.1 Percentage of schools requiring minimum competency tests for high school graduation in 1980, by geographic region. *Source:* Samuel S. Peng, William B. Fetters, and Andrew J. Kolstad (1981). *High School and Beyond, A National Longitudinal Study for the 1980's: A Capsule Description of High School Students.* Washington, D.C.: National Center for Education Statistics. Copyright 1981 by the National Center for Education Statistics. Reprinted by permission.

Clearly, there are problems with competency-based education, but at the present time it is an approach that has widespread appeal among educators.

School Crime and Violence   The other most frequently cited crisis facing the junior and senior high schools is violence. The past 20 years have seen substantial increases in school crime (see Table 9.2). Indeed, in 1975 the U.S. Senate Sub-Committee on Juvenile Delinquency concluded that school violence and vandalism had reached crisis proportions (Bayh, 1975). More recent statistics indicate that the levels of school violence are beginning to decrease in the larger cities. Unfortunately, these same reports show that school violence is increasing in small towns and suburbs ("Now it's suburbs," 1979).

We should note that there is considerable underreporting of school crime, often for fear of reprisal. One recent study has suggested that the actual rate of student victimization in schools may be at least five times higher than the official rate (Blyth, Thiel, Bush, & Simmons, 1980). Victims and offenders are usually of the same age, the same sex (usually male), and in a majority of cases the same race (National Institute of Education [NIE], 1978).

Clearly, school violence is a serious problem with complex causes. The inability of educational institutions to meet some students' needs results in student alienation which increases the likelihood of school violence. Also, school officials may fail to signal faculty and students that personal assaults and destruction of property will be dealt with. One national survey of schools reported that the single most important difference between safe schools and violent schools was "a strong, dedicated principal who served

Table 9.2   CRIME IN AMERICAN SCHOOLS

1. Approximately 8 percent of U.S. schools (6,700) have serious crime problems.
2. Over 25 percent of all schools reported incidences of vandalism in a given month.
3. About 10 percent of schools are burglarized each month.
4. Some 282,000 students (1.3 percent) reported being attacked in a month.
5. About 5,200 teachers (less than 1 percent) are physically attacked in a month.

Source: Adapted from *Violent Schools—Safe Schools: The Safe School Study Report to the Congress, Volume I.* (1978). Washington, D.C.: National Institute of Education; pp. iii–iv. Copyright 1978 by the National Institute of Education.

as a role model for both students and teachers, and who instituted a firm, fair, and consistent system of discipline" (NIE, 1978, p. iv).

Still, not all of the problem resides with the schools. The behaviors and values of the larger community are important factors. Television programs that model aggressive and violent solutions to problems encourage adolescents (and adults) to view aggression as an acceptable means of conflict resolution. Parents, especially, play an important role. Consider the following statement by a school social worker: "When I come home from meetings at 2 in the morning, I see 12-year-olds in the street who tell me their parents don't demand that they be at home. . . . This sort of parental abdication is a root cause of disruption in the schools" ("Now it's suburbs," 1979, p. 64).

Since violence has been recognized as a serious problem in the schools, more attention is being given to the development and implementation of effective intervention strategies. For example, one research team worked on the assumption that school vandalism results from hostile feelings which students develop as a result of punitive educational experiences (Mayer & Butterworth, 1983). To make school a more pleasant place in an attempt to reduce vandalism, these researchers trained teachers in 10 Los Angeles high schools to praise students more often in the classroom. Students were also rewarded for appropriate behavior in the cafeteria and during recreational activities. In addition, there were some nonschool programs directed toward reducing vandalism such as youth group activities and discussions with members of the communities. Over a three-year period, it was found that inappropriate behaviors such as hitting others, throwing objects, and not doing assigned work decreased and that school vandalism costs decreased by an average of 79 percent when these 10 project schools were

Vandalism is a serious problem in many schools.

compared to 10 similar schools which didn't have these programs. Hence, it appears that some recent attempts to reduce vandalism and antisocial behavior have been effective.

Conflicts Between Academic and Social Forces

As we saw in Chapter 8, social interactions with peers become increasingly important for adolescents. Since most adolescents spend most of their time in school, educational institutions become the primary setting for peer interactions. So, although adolescents attend school to develop cognitive skills, they often focus more on the social than the academic aspects of education. Hence, there appear to be built-in conflicts between the goals of educational institutions as currently designed and some developmental needs of adolescent students.

In this context, however, it is important to point out that the orientations of peer groups within a given high school vary. Some place positive values on academic achievement, some on athletics, and some on social activities or popularity. Jere Cohen (1979) has identified three different subcultures in American high schools.

The *fun subculture* focuses on extracurricular activities such as informal clubs, school dances, and athletic events. While educational attainment isn't rejected, it is not as strongly supported as are social activities. This group is comprised of a large number of students and typically includes those who are most popular. Many of these students go on to college, but not solely for intellectual reasons.

The *academic subculture* is composed of those students who place major emphasis on acquiring knowledge and on intellectual and academic achievement. Most students in the academic subculture are college-bound.

The *delinquent subculture* is composed of the youth who actively rebel against the school's educational program and social activities. According to Cohen, this group can be divided into the *greasers* (those interested in drinking, fighting, cars, toughness) and the *hippies* (those who rebel against the values of the status quo and who refuse to prepare for adult responsibilities).

So in examining conflicts between academic and social forces, we must keep in mind the orientation of particular peer groups. For example, one study found that clique membership was a better predictor of high school grades than aptitude test scores, sex, or race (Damico, 1975). Of course, the amount and kind of influence a peer group has on an adolescent depends not only on its orientation, but also on its stability and the extent to which members identify with the group.

An interesting study of the academic and social forces operating in high schools surveyed some 2,000 boys and teachers (Johnston & Bachman, 1976). In Figure 9.2 it can be seen that both boys and teachers agreed that "developing athletics" was an important *actual* objective of the schools and that boys saw this as being stressed more than "transmitting subject matter," whereas teachers had the opposite perception. As *ideal* objectives, boys would like to see considerably more stress on academic matters and teachers felt even more strongly about this issue.

Ironically, while parents appear concerned about declining academic achievement of their sons and daughters, they also appear to contribute, albeit unwittingly, to many schools' overemphasis on athletics. David Elkind (1981) suggests that middle-

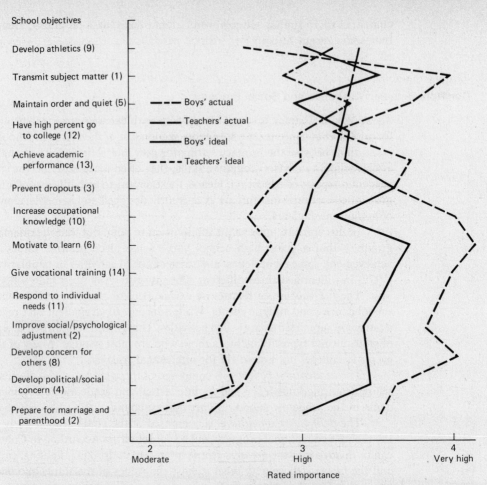

Figure 9.2 Ideal and actual objectives as reported by boys and their teachers. *Source:* From James F. Adams, *Understanding Adolescence: Current Developments in Adolescent Psychology.* Copyright © 1976 by Allyn and Bacon, Inc. Reprinted by permission.

class parents have begun to push children at younger and younger ages into athletics, making participation in sports even more competitive in junior high and high schools.

In the United States there appears to be considerable ambivalence about intellectual development (but less about achieving good grades), coupled with strong support for social activities and athletic prowess. Therefore, the lack of a strong academic orientation among many of today's adolescents is probably a reflection of cultural values as well as a reflection of their own developmental needs for social support.

Formal extracurricular activities and informal peer interactions provide many opportunities for young people to develop adult social skills as well as useful organizational and leadership skills. In addition, participation in extracurricular activities brings social status (J. S. Coleman, 1961; Eitzen, 1975) and is associated with feelings of personal worth (Grabe, 1981). Hence, participation in such activities is seen as an essential aspect of social development—provided that such interactions do not negatively affect academic performance.

Factors Influencing Adolescents' Academic Achievement and Aspirations

Many factors combine to produce individual differences in adolescents' levels of academic achievement and educational aspirations.

Socioeconomic Status   Membership in a particular socioeconomic status affects adolescents' value orientations and their opportunities for achievement and success in the adult world. For example, upper-middle- and upper-class youth do better in school (S. S. Johnson, 1975; National Assessment of Educational Progress [NAEP], 1981–1982). From Figure 9.3, it can be seen that adolescents who come from the inner city

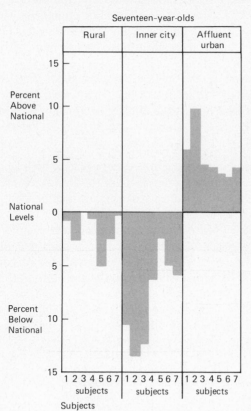

Figure 9.3 Typical educational achievement of 17-year-olds by type of community. *Source:* Figure constructed from National Assessment of Educational Progress data reported in Table 20, page 27, of the *Digest of Education Statistics, 1982.* Copyright 1982 by the Education Commission of The States. Adapted by permission.

(predominantly lower SES) are far below national levels and even farther behind adolescents from the affluent suburbs in a variety of academic areas. More recent NAEP findings, shown in Table 9.3, suggest that the reading, science, and math scores of low-achieving black and white 9- and 14-year-olds are improving (Martin & Ward, 1983). Still, Table 9.3 indicates that these gains are not necessarily maintained at the high school level.

The causes of SES differences in academic achievement are many and complexly interwoven. Among other problems faced by those in the lower socioeconomic statuses are hunger and inadequate nutrition, inadequate health care, substandard housing, poor academic preparation in elementary schools, and high levels of stress. Also, lower-SES parents usually have lower levels of educational attainment than middle- and upper-SES parents and may often have low interest in the educational achievement of their children because of realistic doubts as to the ability of the schools to help their children in any significant way.

Socioeconomic status has also been found to be related to students' educational aspirations (S. S. Johnson, 1975; Peng et al., 1981). For example, a national survey (Table 9.4) reported that almost three times as many high-SES seniors (76 percent) as low-SES seniors (26 percent) planned to finish four years or more of postsecondary education (Peng et al., 1981).

Teachers, too, may have different expectations for students from different socioeconomic statuses. One national survey found that high school teachers were more likely to encourage students from higher-SES families to attend college, but to encourage those from lower-SES families to attend vocational schools (Fetters, 1976).

Parents   Adolescents whose parents had either no or only some high school education were considerably below the national average in all of the NAEP test areas compared to their peers whose parents had graduated from high school or who had attended college (Johnson, 1975; NAEP, 1981–1982).

Also, parents who place a high value on achievement and competence and who encourage emotional independence are more likely than parents who don't do these things to have adolescents with higher academic achievement and educational aspirations (Baumrind, 1974; L. W. Hoffman, 1974b; McClelland, 1961).

Parents who are able to create a home atmosphere which fosters learning—reading to their children, encouraging them to go to college, taking them to the library and to cultural events—are likely to have adolescents with higher levels of academic achievement than parents who don't create such an atmosphere (K. R. White, 1982).

Peers   High school students in the academic subculture have strong interests in academic work and attending college. Students in the fun subculture don't have as studious an orientation as those in the academic subculture, but do place importance on attending college. Members of the delinquent subculture reject any interest in studies or in attending college (Cohen, 1979).

In most cases parents and peers are likely to hold similar values with regard to academic achievement and educational aspirations (Lesser & Kandel, 1969; Offer & Offer, 1975). This is because parents and peers usually share common backgrounds—

Table 9.3 NATIONAL REPORT CARD ON EDUCATION DURING THE 1970s

Group	Reading	Science	Mathematics	Educators' comments
Junior High Level: 13-Year-Olds in the Eighth Grade				
Black low achievers	Improvement: gain of 3.5 percentage points	No significant change in performance	Improvement: gain of 2.6 percentage points	Gains of low achievers may be follow-up effect of compensatory education begun at elementary level. Declines of high achievers in mathematics, coupled with decline of white high achievers and downward trend of black high achievers in science are especially worrisome; they may be indicative of lack of challenge in both areas for high achievers.
White low achievers	Improvement: gain of 1.5 percentage points	Improvement: gain of 2.0 percentage points	No significant change in performance	
Black high achievers	Improvement: gain of 2.5 percentage points	No significant change in performance	Decline: loss of 2.5 percentage points	
White high achievers	No significant change in performance	Decline: loss of 4.1 percentage points	Decline: loss of 3.2 percentage points	
Senior High Level: 17-Year-Olds in the Eleventh Grade				
Black low achievers	No significant change in performance	No significant change in performance	Improvement: gain of 1.6 percentage points	Declines of white low achievers are puzzling in view of minimal competency testing programs in many areas which emphasize reading and mathematics skills. Declines of high achievers (both black and white) in mathematics and science may be result of relaxing course requirements for graduation in both areas. This may prevent them from pursuing careers in technical fields.
White low achievers	Decline: loss of 1.7 percentage points	No significant change in performance	Decline: loss of 1.8 percentage points	
Black high achievers	No significant change in performance	Decline: loss of 3.9 percentage points	Decline: loss of 5.5 percentage points	
White high achievers	No significant change in performance	Decline: loss of 4.2 percentage points	Decline: loss of 4.3 percentage points	

Source: Adapted from Wayne H. Martin and Barbara J. Ward. (1983, February 8). Educational "winners and losers," The "whos" and possible "whys." *NAEP Bulletin.* Copyright 1983 by the National Assessment of Educational Progress. Adapted by permission.

Table 9.4   POSTSECONDARY EDUCATIONAL ASPIRATIONS OF 1980 HIGH SCHOOL SENIORS (BY PERCENT)

"How far in school do you think you will get?"	All seniors	SES		
		Low	Middle	High
High school graduation only or less	20	34	19	5
Vocational, trade, or business school				
Less than 2 years	8	11	9	2
2 years or more	11	14	13	6
College program				
Less than 2 years	3	3	3	1
2 years or more	12	12	14	9
4- or 5-year degree	26	16	25	37
Master's degree or equivalent	11	5	9	22
Ph.D., M.D., etc.	9	5	7	17

Source: Adapted from Samuel S. Peng, William B. Fetters, and Andrew J. Kolstad. (1981). *High School and Beyond, A National Longitudinal Study for the 1980s: A Capsule Description of High School Students.* Washington, D.C.: National Center for Education Statistics, p. 30. Copyright 1981 by the National Center for Education Statistics. Reprinted by permission.

SES and ethnic group membership, for example—which results in similar orientations. In cases of strong parent-adolescent conflicts, adolescents turn to peers for support.

Gender Differences   The average school grades of girls surpass those of boys in English, foreign languages, biological sciences, and social studies; the average grades of boys and girls are the same in the physical sciences; and boys' grades are slightly higher than girls' in mathematics (College Entrance Examination Board, 1982).

Parents who can create a home environment that encourages learning are more likely to have adolescents with higher academic achievement.

As we have seen, traditional sex-role stereotypes operate in such a way as to make it more likely that females will have lower educational aspirations than males. School experiences are only one of many socializing influences that work to inhibit the educational achievements and aspirations of girls. The expectations of teachers, guidance counselors, coaches, and peers as well as course and textbook content are important factors in this regard. For example, an analysis of high school courses and textbooks reported the following (Trecker, 1973):

1. An "overwhelming majority" of females are steered toward homemaking, health, and clerical occupations.
2. Males predominate in agriculture, the skilled trades, and the industrial and technical fields.
3. In history textbooks only 1 out of 500 to 800 pages is devoted to women's contributions and problems.
4. Most science textbooks portray males using scientific equipment and often use examples which are unfamiliar to girls, but familiar to boys.

Recently, considerable attention has focused on the fact that many female students choose not to enroll in more advanced math courses or to pursue math-related college majors. Unfortunately, when they make such choices, they are automatically restricting themselves from certain college majors and career options which can have long-term negative consequences (Meece, Parsons, Kaczala, Goff, & Futterman, 1982).

Parents, teachers, and guidance counselors need to become sensitive to their own attitudes in order to avoid perpetuating stereotypical views of math achievement or ideas that math-related careers are inappropriate for women (Meece et al., 1982). Girls need to be encouraged in math achievement in junior and senior high school and need to be made aware of the long-term consequences of avoiding higher level math courses.

Intelligence   Research findings show that intelligence is strongly and positively related to academic success. It has also been found that more intelligent adolescents have higher educational aspirations than their less intelligent peers, although this is less likely to be true for girls (Marini, 1978). Of course, not all bright adolescents do well in school and some less bright youth perform at higher levels than we might expect. In such cases we look to factors such as SES, parental, teacher, and peer influences, sex-role expectations, and personality factors such as self-esteem, academic orientation, achievement motivation, and control over anxiety (Taylor, 1964).

School-Related Problems of Adolescents

School Phobia   Like school phobia in younger children, adolescent school phobia is characterized by refusal to attend school accompanied by complaints of physical illness (nausea, headache) or about the school situation (often focused on a teacher) (Weiner, 1980). Physical symptoms usually disappear while the young person is allowed to stay at home, but reappear when he or she is told to return to school. School phobics are likely to have at least one parent who is overprotective and who reinforces the strategy of retreating to the home when difficulties in the "outside world" develop.

In contrast to school phobia in younger children, adolescent school ph more likely to be a response to difficulties in school rather than with parents. In junior high school these difficulties include the shift from a one-room or one-teacher setting, the lack of privacy in locker rooms (a particular problem for boys and girls who are early or late maturers), and competitive sports situations in which failure is humiliating. In high school stresses are more likely to be focused on social interactions and fears of rejection.

Adolescent school phobia is likely to signal the development of a particular style of coping (retreat) with external stresses, that is, withdrawal from intellectual and social activities.

In adolescence the school phobic response is more likely to be only one aspect of a larger and ongoing problem of adjustment. Consequently, it is seen as a more serious problem than when it occurs in childhood (Weiner, 1980).

Academic Underachievement It has been estimated that at least 25 percent of school youth perform at levels lower than their abilities (Weiner, 1980). Causes for unexpectedly low academic performance may be either school-based, sociocultural, or psychological in nature. One school-based cause is an insufficiently challenging school program, especially for bright students. For example, one study of underachievers found that 78 percent of them were highly intelligent and that they were significantly more creative than "normal achievers" of similar intelligence (Eisenman & Platt, 1968). These authors speculated that the underachievement problem developed because achievement seemed to be based on conformity to the teacher's expectations and had less to do with critical thinking, imagination, or self-improvement.

Sociocultural causes of academic underachievement include family and neighborhood values which minimize the importance or utility of formal education, peer group attitudes which equate academic success with lack of masculinity or femininity, and school policies and attitudes which are insensitive and unresponsive to the needs of non-middle-class youth (Weiner, 1980). Neither school-based nor sociocultural underachievement is viewed as a psychological disorder (even though it reduces a young person's chances for success in the adult middle-class world).

Psychological causes can usually be traced to neurotic family interactions which produce a syndrome of passive-aggressive underachievement (Weiner, 1980). Anger is expressed passively through purposeful inactivity (not studying, pouting, etc.). Parents who make too heavy demands for academic success or those who discourage their children from surpassing the parents' level of education may produce hostility in adolescents which can't be directly expressed. Unfortunately, in the process of underachieving "to get back at" parents, adolescents can also ruin their own chances for later academic and occupational success.

Dropping Out Most adolescents do graduate from high school (74 percent in 1980). Still, in 1980 almost 2 percent of 14- and 15-year-olds dropped out and this number rose to almost 9 percent among 16- and 17-year-olds. As can be seen in Figure 9.4, there was a sizable decrease in the dropout rate among 16- and 17-year-old blacks between 1979 (12.8 percent) and 1980 (6.9 percent). During this same period the dropout rate for 16- and 17-year-old whites rose from 7.3 percent to 9.2 percent (Grant & Eiden, 1982).

Most boys and girls drop out of high school because they do poorly, feel frustrated

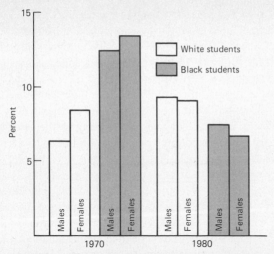

Figure 9.4   Percent of high school dropouts ages 16 and
17 by race and sex from 1970 to 1980. *Source:* W. Vance
Grant and Leo J. Eiden. *Digest of Education Statistics.*
Washington, D.C.: National Center for Education Statistics, 1982, p. 68. Reprinted by permission.

and alienated, and dislike school. Many girls drop out because of early marriage or
pregnancy. While leaving school under such circumstances is understandable, it usually
only presents the dropout (and society) with other problems: increased likelihood of
delinquency and unemployment.

Studies have shown that in adulthood high school dropouts are more likely to
marry earlier, have more children, have more marital problems, and die earlier. Also,
it has been estimated that the average high school graduate will earn 48 percent more
in his or her lifetime than a dropout and that a college graduate will earn 98 percent
more than a dropout (U.S. Bureau of the Census, 1978; U.S. Bureau of Labor Statistics,
1982).

Staying in a traditional school may be an untenable option for potential dropouts,
but leaving school is an unsatisfactory solution. Such students need alternative education programs that can build their self-esteem and competence by offering them opportunities for increasing autonomy and responsibility. The most successful programs for
dropouts include teaching some academic skills and preparing them for adult work
(Gold & Petronio, 1980).

COLLEGE AND UNIVERSITY SETTING

Who Goes to College?

Approximately half of those who graduate from American high schools continue their
education in colleges and universities (Grant & Eiden, 1980). As might be expected,
those who do go to college are likely to be those high school students with higher
academic averages and higher educational and occupational aspirations.

College students are on the average more advantaged than those who do not
attend college, at least with respect to family income and scholastic aptitude and

achievement (Grant & Eiden, 1980). This remains true despite the increased enrollment of lower-SES youth, women, and ethnic and minority group members. Obviously, the steadily rising costs of college attendance and the recent cutbacks in financial aid make it increasingly difficult for qualified students to finance a college education, and this is a particular problem for those who are poorer.

One of the major decisions confronting American high school students who plan to go to college is the selection of the most appropriate collegiate experience. This is a complex issue with many implications and ideally requires the assistance of knowledgeable adults (teachers, guidance counselors, college admission counselors, and some parents). Unfortunately, many high school students report that they are not getting the kind of assistance they need from their guidance counselors (Noeth, Roth & Prediger, 1975; Peng et al., 1981). Girls are likely to experience special difficulties in academic and career planning because of sexist attitudes of many guidance counselors (Harway & Astin, 1977).

Colleges are not as helpful as they could be to incoming students. College catalogs and admissions brochures naturally attempt to portray the institution in the most positive light. However, information that may be specially relevant to potential students is often not available. Hence, various "guides" to colleges and universities edited by students have come into being that attempt to answer their peers' important questions.

Types of Colleges and Student Satisfaction

The number of colleges and universities in the United States is quite high compared to other industrial countries. In 1981–1982 there were 3,253 institutions of higher education in the United States, including universities, four- and two-year colleges, and

Choosing an appropriate school is an important decision for college-bound adolescents.

other institutions (Grant & Eiden, 1982). These institutions are quite diverse. For example, some colleges enroll a few hundred students, while others enroll many thousands; some select their students from among the best in the nation, while others admit those whose academic competence is mediocre; some are residential, while others are not.

There are different types of students as well as different types of colleges. These two factors interact to produce an individual educational outcome. As might be expected, a student's satisfaction with a college depends on a good match between student needs and collegiate climate. One study attempted to discern whether particular institutional characteristics were more or less likely to be associated with student satisfaction (Astin, 1977). Students in highly selective and prestigious institutions rated these colleges very high on an overall evaluation, as well as on the academic reputation of the school, the curriculum, and classroom instruction. Students in large universities gave high ratings to social life, academic reputation, and curriculum variety, but reported that they were dissatisfied with faculty-student contacts. At teachers' colleges (and, we would infer, at 4-year nonprestigious colleges), students were very satisfied with peer relationships, but dissatisfied with intellectual climate, classroom instruction, and student-faculty contacts. Satisfaction was lowest at technological schools.

Students who attended residential schools were more satisfied than those who commuted and lived at home. Interestingly, students who attended single-sex institutions were considerably more positive about many aspects of their college experiences than their peers in coeducational institutions. The only area in which this was not true was social life, where males (but not females) expressed strong dissatisfaction.

Overall, students were most pleased about the friends they had made in college and least pleased about the variety of courses they could take and about the college administration.

College Student Subcultures

As is true in high schools, student subcultures have been identified in colleges. Probably the best-known model is the Clark-Trow typology which is based on two variables: (1) the extent to which students are involved with ideas and (2) the degree to which they identify with their college (Clark & Trow, 1966).

The *collegiate* orientation most closely approximates the popular stereotype of college students and is similar to the fun subculture in high schools (Cohen, 1979). These students are primarily interested in social and athletic events and are relatively indifferent to intellectual issues. This group consists predominantly of middle- and upper-middle-SES students since it takes money and leisure time to keep up a busy schedule of such activities. This subculture is quite common at large, residential state universities.

Students in the *vocational* typology come to college in order to get a better job and make more money than they could otherwise expect. These students are not intellectually oriented; rather they see their courses as steps toward getting a degree. Most of them are from the lower-middle class, and they often work while in school to pay for their college expenses. Such students are often found in urban institutions.

Students in the *academic* subculture are eager to get involved with intellectual ideas. They identify strongly with faculty members and want to do more than is required to pass a course. They are likely to be interested in attending graduate or professional school. They may have some concern about a career, but don't see a job as being so directly related to college work as those in the vocational subculture. The number of such students is generally small, except at those institutions which have high academic reputations.

The *nonconformist* subculture is generally a small one and is more common in the small, elite liberal arts colleges and leading universities. These students are aggressively and self-consciously nonconforming. While they are often deeply involved with ideas and issues in classroom and in the larger society, they are more likely to identify with off-campus groups and social trends as points of reference than with faculty members.

Impact of College on Students

Intellectual and Cognitive Development Most studies of the impact of college on students' intellectual development have found positive changes. One survey of 40 years of research on the impact of college on students concluded: "Generally speaking, seniors, as compared to freshmen, have more liking for reflective thought, are more intraceptive (referring to an inner, subjective life), show more independence of thought, are more creative, and are more critical and analytic" (Feldman & Newcomb, 1969, pp. 28–29).

A more recent summary of research in this area reported that students made modest gains in the abilities to think logically, critically, and independently and showed gains in substantive knowledge during the college years (Bowen, 1977). Also, studies measuring students' interests in academic activities, abstract thought, and the ideas typically expressed in literature, art, and philosophy indicated that adolescents who attended college made greater gains in these areas than did those who were employed or became homemakers. The gains in these areas for men were greater for those of low ability and low socioeconomic status than for those of high ability and high socioeconomic status. Homemaking was found to have strongly negative impacts in these areas on young women (Bowen, 1977).

College students are more likely than those at lower levels of education to be confronted with the need to solve abstract and complex intellectual problems. This situation would be likely to produce the cognitive disequilibrium necessary to stimulate movement toward formal operational thinking. Whether college attendance actually encourages the development of formal operational thought isn't known at this time (K. M. White, 1980). One of the few studies related to this question found that 67 percent of the problem-solving responses of college women could be scored at the formal operational level, while only 54 percent of older women's (average age 54) responses and 32 percent of sixth-grade girls' responses could be scored at this level (Tomlinson-Keasey, 1972). While more college women than other-aged females scored at the formal operational level of thinking, still this percentage (67 percent) wasn't as high as might be expected or desired.

College students are exposed to many new ideas.

Personality and Social Development   Many studies have investigated the impact of college on students' personal and social development. One major review of research reported freshman-senior differences in the direction of:

> increases in "open-mindedness" (reflected by declining authoritarianism, dogmatism, and prejudice), decreasing conservatism in regard to public issues, and growing sensitivity to aesthetic and "inner" experiences. In addition, a majority of studies show declining commitment to religion . . . and increases in independence, dominance, and confidence as well as in readiness to express impulses. (Feldman & Newcomb, 1969, p. 48)

What happens in college to bring about these changes? Both student characteristics and campus climate need to be considered. For one thing, it appears that students who come to college more open to intellectual and personal change are more likely to develop in these areas (Tavris, 1974). Other specific student characteristics which have been found to be associated with increased liberalism include having Jewish parents, being black, having high academic ability, majoring in the social sciences rather than the natural sciences, and having high test scores on such personality dimensions as artistic interest, altruism, and hedonism. Students who become more conservative in personal ideology were likely to be female, to be older than average freshmen, to have high scores on "religiousness," and to have strong business interests (Astin, 1977).

Characteristics related to the college setting that were associated with increases in a liberal ideology included attendance at more selective and prestigious four-year colleges, living in a residence hall, and participation in student activities. In contrast, students who participated heavily in academic or athletic activities developed more conservative ideologies during their college years (Astin, 1977).

Another important aspect of personality development is identity formation. As we saw in Chapters 5 and 6, research has shown a tendency for college students to move toward identity achievement between the freshman and senior years, although the trend appears more pronounced among males (Cauble, 1976; Constantinople, 1969). A previously mentioned study of identity development in same-aged Canadian college students and working youth found that both groups had achieved similar rates of occupational commitments (Munro & Adams, 1977). However, fewer college students had achieved political, religious, and ideological commitments compared to working youth. These findings led the authors to conclude that college environments encourage students to remain in the moratorium and diffusion statuses and to avoid making commitments. Based on Newman and Newman's conceptual framework, we would predict that this might be true in some cases, but not on all.

While it does appear that college experiences do have a positive impact on some aspects of personality development, it is important to remember that adolescents who don't go to college also change in similar ways, although these changes occur less consistently (Tavris, 1974).

Living Arrangements in College   A recent study found that male and female college freshman and sophomores who lived at home perceived their parents and friends as viewing them less favorably than did a similar group who lived in college residence halls (Lundgren & Schwab, 1979). Of course, since it is not clear whether the students who lived at home were initially different from those who lived on campus, we can't tell whether the differences in students' feelings were due solely to their living arrangements.

The impact of college living units has been studied in terms of the physical and architectural features of buildings. For example, one study involving 87 different living groups on 16 different college campuses found that in living groups with a high proportion of single rooms, there was less emphasis on social interaction, intimate communication, spontaneity, and student activities (Moos, 1978). Also, in living units that were not centrally located on campus, there was more emphasis on social interation and on student control of house rules. These students placed less emphasis on dating, partying, and academic accomplishments and more on closer relationships among residents. Differences between larger and smaller living units seemed to balance out. For example, the larger groups were less cohesive and friendly than the smaller groups, but they were also more heterogeneous, making it likely that everyone could find someone to relate to.

Problems of College Students

A recent study of 7,000 undergraduates at 34 New England colleges revealed that the most commonly reported problem was pressure to do well in school (Wechsler, Rohman, & Solomon, 1981). Other major concerns were difficulties in concentrating, depression, anxiety, and loneliness. Female students reported a significantly higher incidence of problems than males, although this apparent difference may be due to less defensiveness in reporting problems. Weight control was a major concern for 23 percent of college women, but only 5 percent of college men.

Academic Problems   As reported above, concern about doing well was the most frequently listed problem in the survey of New England college students. Freshmen are more likely than upper classmen to have academic problems simply because they are not yet adjusted to the new pressures and freedoms of the college environment. A common problem is time management—balancing time for classes, studying, social activities, and work.

Students who have never had to take responsibility for themselves find it easy to get involved in the swirl of social activities only to find themselves suddenly sobered (and panicked) by poor grades on mid-term exams. Such panic often become manifested in test anxiety (although many students confuse the realistic anxiety caused by poor preparation for exams with actual test anxiety). It has been estimated that concerns about study habits and grades account for over half of student requests for counseling in college counseling centers (Weiner, 1980).

Underachievement also plagues college students; the dynamics of this problem are similar to those we have already discussed in high school students. Related to under-achievement is the phenomenon of "big league shock." It is likely to be a special problem for freshmen and some transfer students (McArthur, 1971; Weiner, 1980). "Big league shock" is triggered by the transition from a less to a more competitive school and produces anxiety and heightens fears of failure. (This phenomenon can also occur in the transition from junior high to high school.)

Most students struggle, at least to some degree, with choosing a major field of study. The fact that most students have a rather functional view of education means that a student's career choice will usually determine the choice of a major. While we would argue that such a practical orientation may work against the ideal purposes of a college education, it is also understandable that students expect that the college experience will prepare them for adult work.

Colleges and universities have recently begun to be more helpful to students who have conflicts about academic major and career choices (historically, this has not been their function). In most cases academic advising is separate from career counseling and is handled by different people. As a result, students often find themselves confused about making college major and career-related decisions. This is a particular problem for today's students because of the increasing specialization of jobs and their rapid obsolescence in our postindustrial society. Consequently, young people must take more initiative to seek out career-related information.

Personal and Social Problems   For college freshmen who live on campus, the stresses of making independent decisions about such things as courses, what hours to keep, and how to meet people are increased by the experience of leaving home (Margolis, 1981).

Coping with peer pressure on the college campus (where there are few restrictions on a student's personal behavior) can be a problem for some. Those whose parents allowed them some independence and personal responsibility have fewer problems in this area. Typically, college students find increased peer pressure in the areas of party-

Choosing a major can be a problem for college students.

ing, sexual activities, and drug experimenting or usage (especially tobacco, alcohol, and marijuana).

For many students feelings of loneliness and social isolation may be a problem. Those who join sororities and fraternities or live in residence halls which encourage social interaction are less likely to experience these feelings. However, for students who have minimal opportunities for interaction, such as commuters and evening and part-time students, this can be a painful problem. Institutions serving these populations are becoming more sensitive to their needs, but progress is slow. In some cases students have taken the matter into their own hands and have been quite successful in stimulating needed programs and services on campuses; the United States Association of Evening Students (USAES) has been quite effective in this regard.

Sometimes, loneliness turns into depression. One study has estimated that 25 percent of the total college student population suffers from some symptoms of depression (Beck & Young, 1978). Depression in college students is usually related to typical campus pressures such as failing to meet personal academic standards, confusion about career and life goals, and lack of friends (Beck & Young, 1978). Also, the breakup of intimate relationships often triggers depression. Close to half of those experiencing depressed feelings seek professional assistance. Usually, talking with a helpful person enables students to get a more realistic perspective on their problems. But sometimes, seeking the advice of a campus mental health professional may be the best option, especially in cases where depressed feelings are chronic.

In some cases depression leads to suicide, which is 50 percent more frequent among college students than nonstudents of the same age (Beck & Young, 1978).

Dropping Out   Almost 50 percent of students withdraw from four-year colleges at sometime, although there is considerable variability among institutions. Research findings suggest that dropout rates for high ability students are much lower in private colleges than public colleges.

Most withdrawals occur during the first two years of school. Academic and financial difficulties and personal problems are the most common causes of dropping out. Also, many students who withdraw from school reenroll later; perhaps 66 to 91 percent (Timmons, 1977). It seems that a period of time away from college provides students with an opportunity to reflect on their goals or to organize their lives so that they are able to return to school with a renewed sense of purpose and graduate.

POSTSECONDARY VOCATIONAL PROGRAM SETTING

Increasing numbers of young people are choosing to attend vocational schools rather than going on to college or looking for jobs upon high school graduation. It has been estimated that there has been an increase of 16 percent in the enrollments (all ages) of noncollegiate vocational schools between 1976 and 1980 (Grant & Eiden, 1982). The most numerous of these institutions were cosmetology and barber schools and business and commercial schools. Other types of noncollegiate schools include hospital and allied health, flight, arts and design, trade, and vocational/technical institutes. Numerous occupational programs are also offered by junior and community colleges (Grant & Eiden, 1982).

Vocational schools have become more popular for several reasons. For one thing, many of the fastest-growing areas of employment don't require a college degree, and many people who might have considered college have come to realize that a college degree isn't a guarantee of high-paying and secure employment ("Vocational schools," 1983). Also, vocational programs generally take less time to complete than a four-year degree. They may not be less expensive, however. For example, in 1979–1980 the average annual tuition of aeronautical technician programs in private vocational schools was almost $5,400, or $630 for the same programs in public vocational schools (Grant & Eiden, 1982).

Vocational programs are useful options for many students. Still, it is important to note that they usually prepare people for short-term careers. Job obsolescence and turnover have become much more common today and this pattern will continue in the future. This means that most people will change careers several times during their lifetime and will need to develop new skills as they change jobs. Hence, today's youth need to view education as a life-long process.

SUMMARY

Educational institutions have the role of educating and socializing individuals so they can be productive members of society. In recent years considerable concern has been expressed about how well schools are doing this job. Most criticism has been directed to the problems of declining academic achievement and school violence.

American high school students seem to view the high school experience as a social

Today, many high school graduates are attending vocational schools.

rather than an educational one. Both teachers and students agree that more emphasis should be placed on academic matters and less on athletics.

A variety of factors combine to influence a student's academic achievement and educational aspirations. These include socioeconomic status, parental educational level and aspirations, teacher expectations, peer group influences, intelligence, and certain personality factors.

Several types of problems are often found among today's high school students: school phobia, academic underachievement, and dropping out.

Approximately half of American high school graduates go on to college and half of this number eventually graduate from college. Those who continue their education beyond high school tend to be brighter, to have higher educational and career aspirations, and to come from higher income families.

Colleges and universities have been shown to have positive effects on students' cognitive and intellectual abilities. In addition, changes in personality characteristics are often reported, especially with regard to increases in esthetic appreciation and liberalism and decreases in authoritarianism. Also, progress toward identity achievement has often been noted, but seems to appear more consistently in men than in women.

Problems encountered by college students include coping with academic pressures, managing time effectively, underachievement, choosing a major, making career decisions, coping with peer pressures, loneliness, and depression.

Recently, there has been a considerable increase in the number of high school graduates choosing to attend vocational schools.

GLOSSARY

academic subculture (Clark & Trow; Cohen)   A high school subculture oriented toward intellectual and academic achievement; a college subculture oriented toward serious involvement with intellectual ideas.

academic underachievement   Performance at levels lower than expected on the basis of academic abilities.

big league shock (McArthur)   Anxieties triggered by the transition from a less to a more competitive school setting (from junior high to senior high school, from high school to college).

collegiate subculture (Clark & Trow)   A college subculture oriented more toward social and athletic events than toward intellectual pursuits.

competency-based education (CBE)   An educational approach that requires students to demonstrate minimal competence in designated areas to pass from one grade to another and to graduate.

delinquent subculture (Cohen)   A high school subculture whose members actively rebel against the school's academic program and social activities.

fun subculture (Cohen)   A high school subculture oriented more toward participation and success in extracurricular activities than toward academic achievement; similar to the collegiate subculture.

nonconformist subculture (Clark & Trow)   A college subculture whose members are deeply involved with intellectual ideas and social issues, but who tend to identify with off-campus groups rather than faculty members.

passive-aggressive behavior   Passive expression of anger through inactivity.

school phobia   Refusal to attend school apparently because of sickness or complaints about the school situation, but actually because of psychological conflicts.

vocational subculture (Clark & Trow)   A college subculture oriented more toward job-related pursuits than toward intellectual or social activities.

GETTING INVOLVED: Exercise, Case Study, and General Questions to Consider

EXERCISE: COLLEGE STUDENT SUBCULTURES

This exercise is intended to help you determine which of four college student philosophies most closely represents your own. You will need to use Worksheet 9.1 on the following page. Write your answers in the appropriate spaces on the worksheet.

After you have finished the worksheet think about your responses. How do you think college students in general are distributed among the four philosophies or subcultures? How would you characterize your campus? Where do you fit? How does the pattern of subcultures (particularly the dominant one) influence the nature of academic, social, and political life on your campus? Do you wish your campus were different? How?

CASE STUDY: PATRICK

Patrick Murphy is a high school student nearing the end of his freshman year in a regional vocational-technical high school. He lives in a lower-middle-class suburb with his parents and five brothers and sisters. His father completed high school and drives a cab. His mother dropped out at the end of her junior year and works part-time as a clerk at the neighborhood dry cleaning store.

Pat has a slightly above average IQ, but because his grade school academic record was mediocre, he was encouraged to enroll in the regional vocational-technical high school. Since most of his friends did the same, this seemed the reasonable thing to do. He has been getting B's and C's in his courses, but thinks that he could do better if he felt more challenged.

Several months ago, Pat joined his church's youth organization and has developed a friendship with one of the youth leaders, Bobby, a college sophomore. Bobby has been encouraging Pat to think about going to college. This idea brings up conflicting feelings in Pat. On the one hand, it sounds exciting and seems to offer a possible way to a better life. On the other hand, he wonders whether he could "cut it" academically and socially. Also, he worries that his parents and friends might think that he was trying to show them up. And, where would he get the money for tuition?

Bobby has told Pat that if he wants to go to college, he will have to transfer to a college preparatory high school next year. He will have to make this decision soon and he doesn't know whom to talk to besides Bobby. He's afraid that his teachers and the guidance counselor will discourage him and that his buddies will laugh at him. If he did change schools, he worries that he would lose the friends he has and wouldn't be able to make new ones because he would be a late-comer.

He knows that his parents don't expect him to go to college. He fears that if he talked to them about this idea they would discourage him because it would cost too much. He knows that they expect him to get a job when he graduates so that he can support himself and contribute something to the family's finances.

Worksheet 9.1   COLLEGE STUDENT SUBCULTURES

Instructions: On every college or university campus, students hold a variety of attitudes about their own purposes and goals while at college. Such an attitude might be thought of as a personal philosophy of higher education. Below are descriptive statements of four such "personal philosophies" which there is reason to believe are quite prevalent on American college campuses. As you read the four statements, attempt to determine how close each comes to *your own* philosophy of higher education.

Philosophy A. This philosophy emphasizes education as preparation for an occupation. Social or purely intellectual phases of campus life are relatively less important, although certainly not ignored. Interest in extracurricular activities and college traditions is relatively small. Persons holding this philosophy are usually quite committed to particular fields of study and are in college primarily to obtain training for a career in their chosen field.

Philosophy B. This philosophy, while it does not ignore career preparation, assigns greatest importance to scholarly pursuit of knowledge and understanding wherever the pursuit may lead. It entails serious involvement in course work or independent study beyond the minimum required. Social life and organized extracurricular activities are relatively unimportant. Thus, while other aspects of college life are not forsaken, this philosophy attaches greatest importance to interest in ideas, pursuit of knowledge, and cultivation of the intellect.

Philosophy C. This philosophy holds that an important part of college life exists outside the classroom, laboratory, and library. Extracurricular activities, group functions, athletics, social life, rewarding friendships, and loyalty to college traditions are considered important elements in the college experience and necessary to the cultivation of the well-rounded person. Thus, while not excluding scholarly endeavor or occupational training, this philosophy emphasizes the importance of the extracurricular side of college life.

Philosophy D. This is a philosophy held by the student who either consciously rejects commonly held values in favor of personal values or who has not really decided what is to be valued and is in a sense searching for meaning of life. There is often deep involvement with ideas and art forms both in the classroom and in sources (often highly original and individualistic) in the wider society. There is little interest in a business or professional career; in fact, there may be a definite rejection of this kind of aspiration. Many facets of the college, such as organized activities and the administration, are ignored or viewed with disdain. In short, this philosophy emphasizes individual interests and styles, concern for personal identity, and often contempt for many aspects of organized society.

When you have finished reading the four descriptions, rank them below in the order in which they portray *your* point of view.

_____   1. Most accurate

_____   2. Nearly accurate

_____   3. Somewhat accurate

_____   4. Least accurate

Note: These philosophies represent the four college subcultures we discussed in the chapter. They are A, vocational; B, academic; C, collegiate; and D, nonconformist.

Source: Adapted from *College Student Questionnaires—Part I.* Princeton, N.J.: Educational Testing Service, 1965. Copyright 1965 by the Educational Testing Service. Adapted by permission.

Questions for Case Study

1. Summarize the essential aspects of this situation.
2. Compare the various social influences operating here: parents, peers, teachers, guidance counselor, youth leader.
3. Do you think Bobby made a mistake by encouraging Patrick to think about college?
4. Does Pat have a responsibility to his family to get a job to support himself and to contribute to the family? How could he justify going to college to his parents?
5. What do you think Pat might do in this situation? Explore the various alternatives and their consequences.

GENERAL QUESTIONS TO CONSIDER

1. What factors do you feel contribute to the declining academic achievement among today's high school students? What solutions would you recommend?
2. Have you had any experience with CBE? Do you think that it's a good idea to require students to pass a competency exam to qualify for a high school diploma? Why or why not?
3. Have you had any experiences with school crime? What factors do you think contribute to this problem? What solutions can you pose?
4. With which of the three high school subcultures did you identify? Was one of them dominant at your high school? What role(s) did the subcultures play in your school's academic and social life?
5. How have such factors as SES, parents, teachers, peers, and gender influenced your academic achievement and aspirations?
6. Review the problems of school phobia and academic underachievement. Do you have a basic understanding of their causes?
7. What are some common causes of dropping out in high school? What are some consequences of dropping out for adolescents and the larger society? Do you have any suggestions for reducing the number of high school dropouts?
8. How helpful was your high school guidance counselor in advising you about your college plans?
9. With which of the four college student subcultures do you most identify? (See Worksheet 9.1 on p. 253). What is the dominant subculture on your campus? Do you think your campus is similar to other colleges in this respect? How does the dominant subculture influence the nature of academic, social, and political life on your campus?
10. Review the impact of college attendance on intellectual and personality development. In what ways, if any, do you feel that college attendance has influenced you?
11. Compare different types of college living arrangements (fraternity and sorority houses, types of residence halls, off-campus apartments, living with parents) in terms of their influence on college students' experiences.
12. Reflect on your choice of academic major. Why did you choose the one you did? Did you receive the help you felt you needed in making this decision? Could your university be more helpful in its academic advising? How?
13. What are some typical problems college students must learn to cope with?

Chapter 10 Outline

chapter 10

Establishing Personal Values and a Philosophy of Life

A major task of adolescence is the development of a coherent set of principles by which to make important life decisions. Although many values are learned prior to adolescence, the increased flexibility of thinking which comes with formal operations gives adolescents new cognitive tools with which to evaluate standards and behavior. And, as we have seen, struggling with questions of values is a key component of identity achievement.

This chapter focuses on the establishment of values and a philosophy of life during adolescence. We will discuss several theories of how "moral rules" are learned and examine how parents, peers, media, and schools influence moral development. In addition, we'll discuss contemporary trends in the religious and political values of youth.

Before discussing moral development, we want to make our use of some terms clear. *Moral judgment* refers to an individual's evaluation of the "rightness" or "justness" of an act. *Moral feelings* are an individual's emotional reaction to his or her thoughts or behaviors (for example, guilt). *Moral behavior* refers to the way an individual actually behaves (for example, helping others or cheating).

We emphasize these distinctions for two main reasons. First, even though a person knows what is "right" (moral judgment), he or she may not always act (moral behavior) in accordance with these beliefs, in spite of feeling guilty (moral feeling). Second, a given theory may focus on only one of these aspects of moral development, and since the three are not necessarily consistent, it is important to recognize which factor is being discussed.

THEORIES OF MORAL DEVELOPMENT

Psychoanalytic Theory

Recall from our discussion of psychoanalytic theory in Chapter 1 that Freud conceptualized the personality as consisting of three structures: id, ego, and superego. The id consists of instinctive, human urges (sex and aggression) and has no awareness of the external world; it controls the infant's behavior during the first year of life (oral stage). The ego distinguishes between "self" and environment and functions to bring the reality of the outside world to the id (anal stage).

The superego is the last personality structure to develop, through the resolution of the Oedipal complex during the phallic stage. The *superego* represents the moral aspect of the personality. According to psychoanalytic theory, as boys and girls identify with the same-sex parents, they internalize parental values. Children also develop the capacity to punish themselves through feelings of guilt when they think about acting or actually do act contrary to internalized parental standards.

Psychoanalytic theorists view moral development as a process whereby the child's moral behavior, initially dependent on external (parental) prohibitions, comes under self-control through the superego. The basic development of the conscience takes place in the phallic stage (age 3 to 6). In the latency period (age 6 to 11) the conscience is further developed. During the genital stage (adolescence), the Oedipus conflict is reawakened. Psychoanalytic writers disagree about the implications of this event, but it appears that the conflicts during adolescence impel young people to consciously reformulate beliefs and values which previously operated unconsciously (Settlage, 1972).

Although psychoanalytic theory has fostered extensive research on moral development in childhood (particularly on the effects of parenting styles), there is not substantial empirical support for many Freudian concepts (M. L. Hoffman, 1980).

Relatively little has been written about moral development during adolescence from the psychoanalytic standpoint since primary development in this area is seen as taking place prior to adolescence. Moreover, many psychoanalytic ideas are somewhat vague. For example, what precisely is the mechanism by which identification operates and how does it come about? Consequently, other theoretical formulations appear to be more useful in explaining moral development.

Cognitive-Developmental Theory

Cognitive-developmental views maintain that a person's level of cognitive development determines his or her level of moral reasoning. Typically, these theorists focus on the development of moral judgment rather than on moral behavior.

Perhaps the most fully developed theory of moral development at this time is Lawrence Kohlberg's. His theory is based on Jean Piaget's work in cognitive and moral development. Like Piaget, Kohlberg believes that a person's level of moral reasoning is based on his or her level of cognitive development and that a stage theory best explains moral development.

Kohlberg uses a series of hypothetical moral dilemmas by which to evaluate an individual's moral reasoning. A well-known one is the "Heinz dilemma." A woman is dying of cancer. A druggist has just discovered a new drug that could save her life. He is selling the drug for ten times what it cost him to make it (about $2,000). In order to purchase the drug, the sick woman's husband tries to borrow money from friends, but is able to raise only $1,000. The husband talks to the druggist and asks if he will sell the drug for half price or let him (the husband) pay the balance later. When the druggist refuses, the desperate husband breaks into the store and steals the drug. Subjects are asked whether he should have done so and why or why not.

It is important to remember that Kohlberg focuses on the *reasoning* behind the moral choices a person makes, not on the particular choices. In this dilemma, then, the emphasis would not be so much on the subject's judgment as to whether the husband was right or wrong, as on the reasons given to justify the judgment.

Kohlberg's initial research consisted of intensive two-hour interviews of boys from 10 to 16 years of age (Kohlberg, 1958). The interviews focused on nine moral dilemmas like the one described above. From these data, Kohlberg postulated that there were three basic levels of moral development, each with two subcategories, yielding six stages (see Table 10.1).

Kohlberg suggests that progression through these six stages follows an invariant sequence, but since one level never entirely replaces another, adults are capable of making moral judgments similar to those made by young children. However, children cannot move ahead to make adult judgments. He proposes that the level of reasoning characteristic of any given stage is applied to a variety of situations. In addition, he believes that this sequence of stages of moral development is the same in all cultures. Kohlberg stresses that his stages are not an attempt to evaluate the moral worth of individuals; they merely reflect ways people think and make moral judgments (Kohlberg, 1976).

The specific "mechanism" which enables individuals to progress from one stage to another is that of role-taking, the ability to take the perspective of another person (Kohlberg, 1976). Both parents and peers expose the adolescent to points of view different from his or her own and thereby provide the young person with opportunities for role-taking. Hearing information that is contradictory to one's own beliefs produces a state of *cognitive disequilibrium.* This state is experienced as conflict and motivates individuals to adjust their views in such a way as to resolve the contradiction and return to a state of equilibrium. Kohlberg maintains that such adjustments automatically proceed in the direction of higher levels of moral development. Here, we can see the influence of Piaget on Kohlberg's ideas.

In discussing Kohlberg's theory, we should first note that his work is valuable both for the theory itself and for stimulating considerable research related to it. Still, a number of findings pose problems for Kohlberg's original formulations:

1. The theory was developed from data from only male subjects.
2. Some individuals appear to "skip" stages or revert to earlier moral orientations, rather than to follow an orderly sequence (Holstein, 1976).
3. When 5 different moral dilemmas were presented to 75 subjects, not a single subject appeared to function at the same stage on all five problems (Fishkin, Keniston, & MacKinnon, 1973).
4. Very few adolescents or adults engage in Stage 5 or Stage 6 reasoning (Turiel, 1974).

5. The theory doesn't adequately account for the fact that situational influences are a powerful determinant of moral judgments and behavior.

Many of these criticisms are related to a serious lack of standardization in both the administration and scoring of moral reasoning levels in his moral dilemmas. In response to these problems, James Rest, a former student of Kohlberg's, has developed

---

Table 10.1 KOHLBERG'S STAGES OF MORAL DEVELOPMENT

Level I. Preconventional level
Concepts of right and wrong are based on external punishment and reward. Level I is characteristic of children functioning at concrete operational level.

Stage 1. Punishment and obedience orientation
"Good" or "bad" is determined by obedience to rules and authority. There is unquestioning deference to authority figures.

Stage 2. Naive instrumental hedonism
Behaviors which satisfy oneself (and occasionally others) are defined as "right." There is evidence of a kind of reciprocity, but it takes the form of "you help me and I'll help you" rather than being based on any idea of justice.

Level II. Conventional level
Concern for maintaining the accepted social order and living up to the expectations of others; characteristic of older children and younger adolescents functioning at formal operational level.

Stage 3. Morality of maintaining good relations
Goodness is based on pleasing and helping others. The intentions of others ("meaning well") are considered in making moral judgments.

Stage 4. Authority and social order orientation
"Rightness" is defined as doing one's duty, showing respect for authority, and maintaining the social order for its own sake ("law and order" viewpoint). Individuals can see that others have legitimate rights and expectations.

Level III. Postconventional level
Morality is defined as conformity to shared standards; but only insofar as they serve human ends; it is acknowledged that conflicts can exist between two socially accepted standards; Level III is reached by very few, although theoretically is attainable by adolescents at formal operational level.

Stage 5. Contractual legalistic orientation
Right and wrong are defined in terms of mutually agreed upon rules or laws (contracts). Such rules are acknowledged to be arbitrary and sometimes unjust, but are generally accepted as the ultimate criterion of what is right.

Stage 6. Conscience or principle orientation
Right is defined in terms of universal principles of justice, equality, and human rights which go beyond laws, agreed upon rules, or social standards. Actions are based on these principles of conscience, regardless of the reactions of others, in order to avoid self-condemnation and guilt. Unjust civil laws may be broken when a higher morality than the existing law is recognized

---

Source: Adapted from Lawrence Kohlberg and Richard Kramer. (1969). Continuities and discontinuities in childhood and adult moral development. *Human Development, 12,* 93–120. Copyright 1969 by S. Karger, AG. Adapted by permission.

a standardized test for measuring moral judgment levels—the Defining Issues Test (DIT).

Research findings suggest that the DIT and Kohlberg's interview method yield similar, but not identical results (Froming & McColgan, 1979; Rest, Cooper, Coder, Masanz, & Anderson, 1974). For example, a review of cross-sectional and longitudinal studies which used the DIT reported general trends toward higher levels of moral judgment with age (Rest, Davison, & Robbins, 1978). This same study also found evidence that high school and college students showed the most dramatic changes in moral judgments and that moral development appears to slow down after age 20 and to reach a plateau upon leaving school.

It is undeniable that Kohlberg's theory is an exciting one, that it has stimulated valuable research, and that its developmental perspective has obvious relevance to the study of children and adolescents. It remains to be seen, however, whether the theory will withstand the criticisms that have been leveled against it.

Social Learning Theory

Social learning theory is not a developmental theory since it doesn't view human behavior as evolving according to distinct stages. Rather, the same principles (observational learning, operant and classical conditioning) are used to explain human behavior at any age.

Social learning theorists believe that moral behavior is learned like any other social behavior. From our earlier discussion in Chapter 1, recall that significant figures (including parents, teachers, siblings, peers, and television characters) serve as models of appropriate and inappropriate behavior. Those behaviors that are modeled and rewarded are more likely to be imitated, whereas those that are modeled and punished are less likely to be imitated. The consequences of the observer's actual behavior are important factors also. Moral behaviors that are rewarded are likely to occur more frequently, and those that are punished, less frequently.

In addition to learning moral behaviors, children also learn rules that govern moral behavior in particular situations (these become a basis for self-control). The learning of these moral rules is an extremely complex process because children are exposed to and observe many inconsistencies and conflicting standards. There is likely to be considerable inconsistency in the moral judgments of a single individual as well as differences between people's moral judgments (Rosenthal & Zimmerman, 1978). And, in contrast to Kohlberg's view, moral judgment and behavior are not necessarily consistent—people say one thing and do another. This is because situational factors such as the presence of other people and consequences of behavior have considerable influence on behavior and may "override" the moral rules one has learned. For example, one-third of Stage-6 subjects who were asked to participate in an experiment requiring them to shock another person actually did so (in fact, no one received any shocks, but the subjects thought they were shocking another person) (Milgram, 1965). Such behavior is obviously inconsistent with Stage-6 reasoning.

For these reasons, social learning theorists claim that there is too much variability in moral judgments and behavior to justify the formulation of uniform moral stages of development like those of Kohlberg (Bandura, 1977; Rosenthal & Zimmerman, 1978).

GENDER, CLASS, AND CROSS-CULTURAL DIFFERENCES IN MORAL DEVELOPMENT

Gender Differences

In Freud's view, females are less able to internalize moral principles and to act autonomously than males. (This is supposedly because they don't resolve the Oedipal conflict as quickly and dramatically as males.) Contrary to this assertion, most research suggests that female adolescents and adults are more "internalized" than are males (M. L. Hoffman, 1980), that is, moral transgressions are more likely to be associated with guilt in females and with fear of detection and punishment in males.

As we have already noted, Carol Gilligan has suggested that developmental theories haven't adequately reflected the experiences and concerns of females (1977, 1979, 1982). For example, Kohlberg's theory is based on research on only male subjects. Also, when both male and female subjects have been tested, males are more likely to be classified in Stage 4 (maintaining the social order) and females in Stage 3 (wanting to please others) (Kohlberg & Kramer, 1969; Gilligan, 1977). Gilligan asserts that Kohlberg's emphasis on abstract reasoning favors male sex-role values and diminishes the importance of female sex-role values which stress relationships with others.

Gilligan has developed an alternative theory of moral development as an example of correcting the male bias inherent in many developmental theories. In order to study how women perceive moral issues, she conducted interviews with women who were pregnant and who were contemplating abortions. She interviewed 29 women of diverse ages, races, and social classes who were referred to her by abortion and pregnancy counseling services. Gilligan observed that the distinguishing characteristic of these women's judgments was a "relational bias," that is, a tendency to see themselves and moral issues in terms of themselves in relation to other people. This conceptualization of the feminine perspective is not new. What is new is Gilligan's suggestion that this relational bias reflects a *different* social and moral understanding rather than a developmental deficiency (as it often has been characterized). Gilligan, like Kohlberg, focuses on the reasons for making moral choices, not on the actual choices, themselves (see Table 10.2).

Based on her research, Gilligan concludes that the moral imperative for women appears to be "an injunction to care, a responsibility to discern and alleviate the 'real and recognizable trouble' of this world" (1977, p. 511). On the other hand, she suggests that the moral imperative for men (based on Kohlberg's interview data) appears to be "an injunction to respect the rights of others and thus to protect from interference the right to life and self-fulfillment" (1977, p. 511).

According to Gilligan, the masculine orientation (abstract principles of justice) and the feminine orientation (compassion and care) represent different ways of viewing moral issues, and it has not been demonstrated that the masculine orientation is the better one. In fact, one might argue that the masculine conception has a serious weakness in that it gives

> lip service . . . to the interdependence of intimacy and care but constantly stressing, at their expense, the importance and value of autonomous judgment and action. To admit . . . the truth of the feminine perspective is to recognize for both sexes, the

Table 10.2   GILLIGAN'S LEVELS OF MORAL DEVELOPMENT IN FEMALES

Level I. Orientation to individual survival

Moral issues are viewed only from an egocentric, pragmatic point of view. For example, one of the subjects decided to have an abortion because she did not want a child. Another subject decided to go through with her pregnancy because having a baby would enable her to get married and to move out of her parents' house.

First Transition. From selfishness to responsibility

When a woman can make a distinction between what she wants to do (selfishness) and what she should do (responsibility), she has moved out of Level I and is on her way to Level II. This requires a more positive self-concept than is present at Level I.

Level II. Goodness as self-sacrifice

Self-worth is based on a woman's ability to care for and to protect others. The ability to take care of oneself (self-assertion), on the other hand, is seen as dangerous because it can hurt others and because one risks being criticized and abandoned by others. Women at this level are not able to make a distinction between self-assertion (acting responsibly toward oneself) and selfishness (taking only one's own needs into account).

Second Transition. From goodness to truth

Women at the second transition start to question whether it is responsible or selfish to consider their own needs (not only the needs of others) as part of their commitment to caring and helping. A woman cannot move from Level II to Level III if she is so uncertain about her own self-worth that she cannot allow herself to claim equality with others.

Level III. Morality of nonviolence

A woman understands that she has a responsibility to herself as well as to others and therefore is able to transcend the Level II conflict between selfishness and responsibility. She is able to apply the principle of nonviolence—the obligation not to hurt—to herself as well as to others. Moral judgments take into consideration the real physical and psychological effects of possible outcomes (the feminine perspective) rather than being based on abstract ethical principles (the masculine perspective) which dismiss such considerations as being of a lower order.

Source: Table constructed from Carol Gilligan (1977). In a different voice: women's conceptions of self and of morality. *Harvard Educational Review, 47*(4), 481–517. Copyright © 1977 by President and Fellows of Harvard College.

central importance in adult life of the need for compassion and care. The concept of the separate self and of the moral principle uncompromised by the constraints of reality is an adolescent ideal. . . . (1977, p. 509)

In order to develop a more fully human conception of moral development, Gilligan argues that the masculine and feminine orientations are complementary and need to be integrated. (This idea of integrating complementary characteristics of the masculine and feminine sex role is similar to the earlier discussed concept of androgyny.)

Some men probably have a so-called feminine moral orientation and some women a masculine one. Also, some individuals may have both masculine and feminine orientations and may use one or the other depending on the situation. Clearly, additional research on this and related issues is needed.

Social Class Differences

According to Kohlberg's method of measuring moral development, middle-class adolescents reach higher levels than lower-class adolescents, and middle-class adolescents appear to move from one stage to another more quickly than lower-class adolescents (Kohlberg, 1966b; Kohlberg & Kramer, 1969; Weinreich, 1974).

Kohlberg suggests that these differences occur not because lower-class adolescents hold values which are different from middle-class values, but because lower-class adolescents participate less in the larger social order and have less understanding of it.

Cross-Cultural Differences

Kohlberg asserts that individuals in all cultures employ the same basic moral concepts (liberty, authority, love, and so forth) and that *all* individuals, regardless of culture, pass through the same invariant sequence of stages of reasoning about these concepts.

In order to test these assumptions, Kohlberg studied 10-, 13-, and 16-year-old boys from six different cultures: villages in Yucatan (Central America) and Turkey and cities in Taiwan, Mexico, and the United States (Kohlberg & Kramer, 1969). He maintains that these findings show a similar sequence of development across all cultures (a decrease in the number of subjects in the lower stages and an increase in the number of subjects in the higher stages as age increases). Such general trends can be seen in Figures 10.1a and b. Note also, however, that there is hardly any growth toward Stages 5 and 6 in the preliterate villages in Yucatan and Turkey. Moreover, relatively few subjects in other countries, including the United States, appear to reach Stages 5 and 6. Such findings have led a number of psychologists to challenge Kohlberg's "universality" assumptions (Harkness, Edwards, & Super, 1981; Simpson, 1974; Stanton, 1980). These criticisms can be summarized as follows:

1. His claims of universality are based on limited cross-cultural samples.
2. His moral dilemma and verbal interview techniques require analytical thinking and language not valued by or developed in many cultures.
3. Value categories meaningful to American subjects (such as property rights) are used as a basis for scoring responses of subjects from cultures which may not hold such values in esteem.

When Kohlberg has found greater numbers of non-American subjects to fall at lower levels of moral reasoning, his conclusion has been that the subjects come from cultures which are less well-developed morally than the United States. Recall here Gilligan's comments about male bias in developmental theories which has led to the conception of women as deviant or less well-developed compared to men. Because of the ethnocentric bias in Kohlberg's theory, similar criticisms can be made with regard to his findings that subjects in different cultures are less well-developed than Americans.

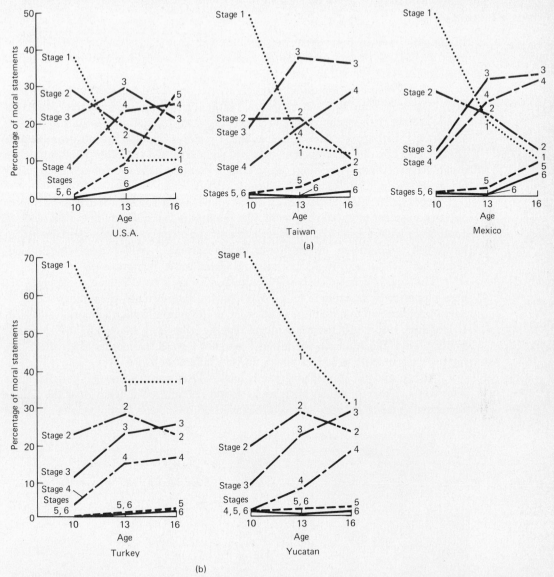

Figure 10.1(a) Cross-cultural age trends in moral judgment among middle-class urban boys in the United States, Taiwan, and Mexico. *Source:* Adapted from Lawrence Kohlberg and Richard Kramer (1969). Continuities and discontinuities in childhood and adult moral development. *Human Development, 12,* 104. Copyright 1969 by S. Karger, AG. Adapted by permission. **(b)** Cross-cultural age trends in moral judgment among boys in isolated villages in Turkey and Yucatan. *Source:* Adapted from Lawrence Kohlberg and Richard Kramer (1969). Continuities and discontinuities in childhood and adult moral development. *Human Development, 12,* 104. Copyright 1969 by S. Karger, AG. Adapted by permission.

SOCIALIZATION AND MORAL DEVELOPMENT IN ADOLESCENCE

Parental Influences

In Chapter 7 we saw that parental acceptance was positively related to moral development and that too strict and punitive control was associated negatively with moral development (Hower & Edwards, 1979).

Also, power assertion disciplinary techniques (physical punishment and deprivation) have been found to foster an external moral orientation (being careful not to get caught) rather than internalized moral standards (M. L. Hoffman, 1970, 1980). Love withdrawal, perhaps because it has a highly punitive quality, has no demonstrable positive effect on the development of moral standards. On the other hand, inductive disciplinary methods (reasoning) do appear to foster internalization of moral standards (M. L. Hoffman, 1980; Hower & Edwards, 1979).

Inconsistency is another aspect of discipline which has been found to be important in adolescent moral development. For example, a classic study found that lack of consistency with regard to parental expectations and consequences of adolescent misbehavior led to confusion, anxiety, poor moral learning, hostility, disobedience, and, sometimes, delinquency in adolescent boys (Bandura & Walters, 1959).

The idea that parents serve as role models for their children and adolescents has been supported by research in moral development. Interestingly, the mother's disciplinary practices seem to have more of an effect on the internalization of moral values (M. L. Hoffman, 1980). Still, there is evidence that the father may affect moral development in other ways. For example, the father's behavior toward the mother often affects the mother's disciplinary practices which, in turn, affect the child.

Also, a study of adults from mainly lower-SES homes who, as children, had been referred to a clinic for antisocial behavior found that antisocial behavior of the fathers correlated significantly with antisocial behavior of the subjects both in adolescence and

Parenting practices play an important role in moral development.

in their mid-40s (Piliavin, Hardyck, & Vadum, 1968). Moreover, the most significant factor in predicting consistent antisocial behavior of the subjects between adolescence and adulthood was the father's antisocial behavior.

A study on the effects of father absence found that seventh-grade boys whose fathers had not been present for at least six months prior to the study scored significantly lower on guilt, internal moral judgment, and confession than did a group of boys whose fathers had been present; this study controlled for IQ and social class differences (M.L. Hoffman, 1971). No such differences were found for girls. A later study of male and female undergraduates found, however, that women's moral judgments were more negatively affected by father absence than were men's judgments and this appeared to be a problem especially when father absence was due to divorce rather than death (Parish, 1980).

Peer Influences

Peers begin to assume more importance for young people in junior high school. When societal, parental, and peer values coincide, the power of the peer group is added to that of the others in reinforcing moral values. Sometimes, however, peer values are different from societal or parental values. In such cases adolescents may experience conflicts in situations that require them to make moral decisions. Peer groups have been found to be important influences in the development of deviant adolescent subcultures such as delinquent gangs and the politically active and alienated youth cultures of the 1960s.

As we have seen, Kohlberg asserts that exposure to more advanced moral reasoning creates a state of cognitive disequilibrium which motivates people with less well-developed moral principles to reexamine their beliefs and impels them toward higher levels of reasoning. Since, in Kohlberg's view, development moves only in a forward direction, youth who are less highly developed are likely to advance when exposed to more developed peers, but the latter should not regress.

Contrary to these predictions, several studies suggest that there is a tendency for children and adolescents to regress to the "lowest common denominator of moral action" when with peers (M. L. Hoffman, 1980, p. 328). One study found such regression to be especially likely among peer-oriented preadolescents (Devereaux, 1970). Those subjects who said that they frequently associated with peers appeared more likely to follow the crowd in committing a deviant act. This was especially true of those preadolescents who preferred gangs to a small number of friends. Furthermore, the peer group experiences of these youth seemed to reduce anxiety and guilt feelings about antisocial behavior which probably originated in the home. It seems that the home loses much of its power to motivate and to control the behavior of gang-oriented children.

The support of a delinquent peer group appears to play an important role in maintaining deviant values among youth. One study found that attraction to such values (for example, "The ability to keep one's mouth shut to the cops" or "The ability to make a fast buck") began early, increased considerably between the ages of 12 and 13, and persisted as a counterattraction to school and work. However, this study also found that without the support of the delinquent peer group, individual delinquent values were likely to shift to the values of the larger society (Lerman, 1968).

A peer group plays an important role in maintaining deviant values among youth.

Media Influences

Television has begun to receive attention as a socializing agent with influence similar to that of parents and teachers. Television-viewing is a significant aspect of American adolescent life. For example, the average teenager watches television almost four hours a day (Liebert, Sprafkin, & Davidson, 1982).

As we saw in Chapter 4, there is evidence that viewers can and do learn attitudes, values, emotional responses, and new behaviors from observing symbolic models on television and in films (Bandura, 1977; National Institute of Mental Health [NIMH], 1982). More specifically, it appears that moral judgments and moral behaviors can be learned by watching these models (Bandura, Grusec, & Menlove, 1966, 1967). While few studies have been done with adolescents, it has been found that children who watch altruistic behavior on television become more helpful and those who watch aggressive behavior perform more aggressive acts than those who don't watch programs with such content (NIMH, 1982).

One author has strongly criticized television because of undue emphasis on sex portrayed as "love," violence, and the idealization of immaturity, materialism, and hedonism (LeMasters, 1974). While this view is unjustifiably harsh as applied to all television programs, it is certainly accurate in many cases.

School Influences

Today, many parents are confused about what to teach their children in the areas of values and behavior. Their confusion has led them to seek the help of the schools in coping with this problem. A 1975 Gallup poll indicated that 79 percent of Americans were willing to have the schools take on some responsibility for moral education (Muson, 1979).

There are three major models of moral education: indoctrination, values clarification, and developmental moral education (Scharf, 1978). The *indoctrination model* seeks to teach conformity to society's code; it attempts to teach socially accepted values by rewarding "good" values and punishing "bad" ones.

Critics of this approach say that it encourages students not to raise questions when making moral decisions, but to conform to what they are told. Secondly, there is considerable evidence that knowing what is "right" doesn't ensure that people will act accordingly.

In response to such feelings as well as to pressures for some attention to moral education in the schools, a second approach arose, that of *values clarification.* Students participate in exercises and peer discussions designed to help them come to terms with moral conflicts. No attempt is made to impose specific value orientations on the student; rather, the goal is to teach the relativity of values and to increase students' awareness of their own values.

Evaluating the effectiveness of this approach has been difficult since it is hard to know what outcomes are viewed as desirable. One review of research concluded that it had no demonstrated effects on students' values (Lockwood, 1978).

Kohlberg's *developmental moral education* approach is a third model of moral education (Kohlberg, 1975). Like the values clarification model, it stresses peer discussion of value dilemmas. The two approaches differ, however, in their goals. The values clarification model seeks to foster awareness of values, whereas the developmental moral education model attempts to stimulate movement to higher stages of moral reasoning.

A review of research on the effects of this approach concluded that direct discussions of moral issues can increase the level of moral functioning by almost half a stage among children and adolescents, but that this doesn't happen in all cases (Lockwood, 1978). Moreover, such discussions appear to be the most effective in advancing reasoning at the lower levels of moral development, from stage 2 to 3 being the most common case.

The most effective discussions appear to be those which induce cognitive disequilibrium among the participants by exposing them to diverse and more cognitively advanced viewpoints and by looking at the inconsistencies of various solutions to moral dilemmas. In order to advance to a higher level of moral development, however, it appears that *active* participation in such discussions is essential (Windmiller, 1980).

Still, it is important to remember that the correlations between moral judgment and moral behavior are not particularly high. Even when individuals function at higher levels of moral judgment, research suggests that the moral behavior of such people is not more "advanced" than that of individuals functioning at lower levels of moral judgment (Wonderly & Kupfersmid, 1980).

More recently, Kohlberg has directed his efforts to promoting a practical educational experiment based on his theory. In this approach, called the Just Community, a group of students and teachers meet for several hours during each class day to set educational and group policies and resolve problems (each person has one vote). The intent of the program is to foster moral development in the areas of "justice and fairness" through open group discussion.

Advocates of the Just Community argue that the way in which American schools are organized and administrated constitutes a "hidden curriculum" which instills obedience to authority rather than an appreciation of democracy. In order to learn the principles of democracy, one needs to practice them, and the Just Community provides that practice.

While the idea of the Just Community is interesting, independent evaluations of several of the programs have not been particularly favorable (Feldman, 1979). Also, it seems that those in traditional positions of power (teachers in schools, guards in prisons) do make unilateral decisions when group decisions are perceived as being intolerable or illegal (Muson, 1979).

In summary, even though there isn't a consensus on whether and/or how the schools should be involved in moral education, the search for approaches to foster moral development will continue.

ROLE OF IDEOLOGICAL COMMITMENT IN IDENTITY FORMATION

A major developmental task of adolescence is the development of a philosophy of life by which to make important decisions or an *ideology,* "a body of attitudes roughly consistent with each other, and more or less organized in reference to a more encompassing, though perhaps tacit set of principles" (Adelson, 1971, p. 121). Erikson saw the development of a philosophy of life (ideological commitment) as perhaps the most significant aspect of identity formation because it provides adolescents with a framework by which to integrate the various aspects of identity: self-concept, sex-role and sexuality, occupational aspirations, and related life-style choices.

The degree to which a personal philosophy can develop is contingent on a combination of factors: increased cognitive capacities, social forces encouraging adolescents to examine previously unquestioned views, and their ability and willingness to explore these issues seriously. As we have said, those who don't struggle to develop a coherent and individualized philosophy of life are classified as foreclosures, those who struggle and succeed are classified as identity achievers, those who are struggling are moratoriums, and those who have given up the quest are diffusions. Studies have shown that identity achievers and moratoriums tend to function at Kohlberg's Stages 5 and 6 and that foreclosures and diffusions are more likely to function at Stages 1 to 4 (Marcia, 1980).

Interestingly, it appears that the importance of developing a philosophy of life is declining in importance among college students. Among 1983 college freshmen, 43 percent of males and 46 percent of females considered this goal to be "very important" or "essential," compared to 79 percent and 86 percent, respectively, in 1969 (Astin, 1980; Astin, Green, Korn & Maier, 1983).

Next, we'll look at two important aspects of ideological commitment: religious values and political and social values.

RELIGIOUS VALUES

In the process of identity achievement, the desired outcome is a personal commitment to spiritual or religious values that can be used as guides for living. Other less desirable outcomes include the unquestioning acceptance of parental religious beliefs or the defensive clinging to rigid beliefs and practices (foreclosure) or spiritual alienation due to a failure to find personally satisfying answers to basic questions about life (diffusion).

Development of Religious Thinking in Adolescence

The cognitive changes which occur during adolescence and exposure to a wider range of viewpoints lead adolescents to view religion in a more abstract and personal way than they did as children (Elkind, 1971; Harris, 1971).

A related issue concerns the development of religious identity. James Fowler (1976) has put forward a six-stage theory of faith development based on the theories of Piaget, Kohlberg, and Erikson, as well as on preliminary research (see Table 10.3). According to Fowler, late adolescence appears to be a significant time for the develop-

Table 10.3 FOWLER'S THEORY OF FAITH DEVELOPMENT

Stage 1. Intuitive-projective faith (minimum age: 4 years)
Children experience the world as magical and unlawful and use fantasy to make sense of things. They seem to realize that death, sickness, and bad luck and their opposites are, to some extent, beyond the power of their parents to control. Hence, they sense that there are powers even stronger than those of their parents.

Stage 2. Mythical-literal faith (minimum age: 6–11)
Children move beyond fantasy as a way of knowing to reliance on the teachings of authorities (parents, religious leaders, teachers, and peers). Religious beliefs are concrete and literal. Children view rules as absolute and believe that God will punish rule-breakers and reward rule-followers.

Stage 3. Synthetic-conventional faith (minimum age: 12–13)
Individuals use faith to bring coherence and meaning to their lives. Faith (and related values) is rooted in the authority of social, legal, and religious conventions, rather than that of significant others. Individuals uncritically accept the tenets of their faith and screen out dissonant information.

Stage 4. Individuating-reflexive faith (minimum age: 18–19)
Individuals move beyond convention as a basis for faith and begin to take personal responsibility for their religious beliefs. People begin to critically evaluate the tenets of their faith, based on their own experiences, values, and judgment.

Stage 5. Paradoxical-consolidative faith (minimum age: 30–32)
Individuals believe that other approaches to spiritual questions are equally valid and that all people belong to the same universal human community. They can find meaning in their vision of faith while recognizing that this vision is limited, partial, and contradicted by the visions of other faiths.

Stage 6. Universalizing faith (minimum age: 38–40)
Individuals experience the "kingdom of God" as a reality—they live in this world, but are not of it. Such people, who are rare, are experienced by others as authentic and deeply accepting.

Source: "Stages in Faith: The Structural-Developmental Approach" by James W. Fowler from *Values and Moral Development* by Thomas C. Hennessy. © 1976 by The Missionary Society of St. Paul the Apostle in the State of New York. Used by permission of Paulist Press.

ment of religious identity. While many adolescents (and adults) function at the level of *synthetic-conventional faith,* some move on to the stage of *individuating-reflexive faith.* This stage, similar to Kohlberg's Stage 5, requires the person to move from a more conventional perspective (foreclosure) to an individualized perspective (identity achievement) on religion. Adolescents who make this transition successfully must come to grips with the need to take full responsibility for their religious beliefs rather than relying on their parents' views.

While Fowler's theory is an interesting one, it requires further testing before we can know how valid it is.

Traditional Religious Beliefs and Practices

A number of studies indicate that 18- to 30-year-olds have the lowest rates of attendance at religious services (Hoge & Roozen, 1979). However, this fact shouldn't be taken to mean that most young people turn away from their childhood religious beliefs, for only a small number do drop out and many religious dropouts return to the church. For example, it has been estimated that the return rate of dropouts during the teenage years is approximately 9 percent; for age 20 to 34, it is about 25 percent (Roozen, 1979, as cited in McAllister, 1981).

Although many adolescents don't attend weekly religious services, they do feel that religion is an important aspect of their lives.

With regard to high school students, a survey of some 24,000 high school juniors and seniors selected for membership in "Who's Who Among American High School Students" found that 80 percent viewed themselves as members of an organized religion and 64 percent attended weekly services ("Nation's teenagers," 1977). Among American college students, surveys have shown that religious commitments and practices have constantly declined since the late 1950s. For example, frequent or occasional attendance at religious services was reported by 89 percent of 1969 college freshmen, but only 85 percent of 1983 freshmen (Astin, Green, Korn, & Maier, 1983; A. Levine, 1980).

Studies of the impact of college attendance on religious beliefs show that there are substantial declines in traditional religious beliefs and behavior during the college years. Exposure to "liberalizing" educational and social experiences appears to produce "a more reasoned, more abstract, less literal interpretation of religion" (Feldman & Newcomb, 1969). A national survey of students at some 600 colleges reported a 20 percent decline from freshmen to senior year in the number of students identifying themselves as Protestant, Catholic, or Jewish. Moreover, the number of students selecting the "no preference" category increased by more than 50 percent (Astin, 1977). Such declines occurred more often among men than women and most often among brighter students.

Some of the religious concerns expressed by a large sample of male and female freshmen and sophomores at a midwestern state university can be seen in Table 10.4.

Alternative Religious Beliefs and Practices

Nonbelievers   A survey of Gallup polls indicated that some 94 percent of American adults have a belief "in God or a universal spirit" (Sigelman, 1977). We would speculate that there would be a larger number of adolescent nonbelievers because they are in the

Table 10.4   RELIGIOUS CONCERNS OF COLLEGE STUDENTS

Item	Percent
Confused in some of my religious beliefs	30
Not going to church often enough	30
Doubting the value of worship and prayer	26
Don't know what to believe about God	26
Wanting to feel close to God	25
Losing my earlier religious faith	24
Dissatisfied with church services	23
Having beliefs that differ from my church	19
Wanting to understand more about the Bible	15
Differing from my family in religious beliefs	9
Affected by racial or religious prejudice	9
Missing spiritual elements in college life	8
Troubled by lack of religion in others	8
Science conflicting with my religion	8
In love with somebody of a difference race or religion	7
Failing to see the relation of religion to life	7
Wanting more chances for religious worship	6

Source: Adapted from Benjamin Beit-Hallahmi. (1974). Self-reported concerns of university underclassmen. *Adolescence, 9,* 333–338. Copyright 1974 by Libra Publishers, Inc. Adapted by permission.

process of formulating their own beliefs. This appeared to be more true in the late 1960s than recently. For example, when asked to indicate their current religious preference (Protestant, Roman Catholic, Jewish, Other, or None), 15 percent of college freshman males and 11 percent of females in 1969 gave "none" as a religious preference. In 1983 only 9 percent of males and 6 percent of females responded similarly (Astin, 1979; Astin et al., 1983). Obviously, then, most youth are not nonbelievers.

The Jesus Movement　Estimates indicate that some 400,000 Americans and some 600,000 individuals worldwide, mainly in their late teens and early twenties, belong to fundamentalist religious groups (Balswick, 1974). This movement consists of a number of diverse groups whose members are known by a variety of names such as "Jesus Freaks," "Street Christians," or "God's Forever Family" (Balswick, 1974). Fundamentalists stress personal salvation and the rejection of sinful activities. Consequently, there are strong prohibitions against drug use, alcohol, gambling, fighting, and sex outside of marriage (Robbins, Anthony, & Curtis, 1975). There is also an emphasis on a literal interpretation of the Bible, a personal relationship with Jesus (Balswick, 1974), and a belief in an imminent apocalypse (Richardson, Harder, & Simmonds, 1972).

Members of the Jesus movement are largely young people from middle- and upper-middle-class backgrounds who have dropped out of school. They come from a variety of religious backgrounds and appear to have been heavily involved with drugs prior to their conversions. Some have been described as dillusioned hippies (Balswick, 1974).

Critics suggest that some adolescents join the Jesus movement to avoid dealing with the challenges of growing up; that is, they are attracted by the black-and-white answers to complex questions because such answers are similar to their childhood views of morality (Simmonds, 1977). The high incidence of drug, alcohol, and tobacco use among Jesus freaks prior to conversion is seen as an indication that the movement represents a form of external support for these youth.

Eastern Religious Groups　During the late 1960s and the early 1970s many counterculture youth joined groups based on Eastern religious orientations. Their interest in Yoga, mysticism, transcendental meditation, Hare Krishna, Zen Buddhism, and similar beliefs, while sincere, also provided a way of rejecting traditional cultural and religious values of American society. Currently, it seems that fewer adolescents are interested in such movements.

Young people join such groups for a variety of reasons: a search for answers to difficult life questions which are different from those offered by other religious groups, needs for friendship, a larger cause with which to identify, escape from adult responsibilities, and more meaningful spiritual experiences.

Religious Cults　The 1970s saw an increase in young people's joining religious cults such as the Divine Light Mission and Sun Myung Moon's Unification Church (the "Moonies"). Potential members of cults are often recruited on college campuses from students who are white and from middle-class and affluent backgrounds (Dean, 1982).

The Moonies have had a lot of negative publicity often focused on the accusation

Some American youth develop interests in Eastern religions.

that they brainwash converts. One study of some 237 Moonies found no evidence of brainwashing or of members' being forced to obey dictates of the group against their will (Galanter, Rabkin, Rabkin, & Deutsch, 1979). Also, this study found that Moonies seemed to have experienced more emotional stress in their lives before joining the group than their age-mates typically report, and the majority of them reported that membership in the group reduced their stress. In some cases, then, it's possible that cults can serve a rehabilitative function for some members by preventing alienation, drug abuse, and suicide (Doress & Porter, 1978). Still, there remain problems related to heavy reliance on outside authorities for direction rather than developing these qualities in oneself. In addition, questions about the membership recruiting practices of some cults haven't yet been answered satisfactorily (at least to this author).

Some parents become so upset by their children's membership in such groups that they forcibly abduct them (even as adults) or obtain a 15-to-30-day conservatorship during which "deprogrammers" attempt to restore previously held values (Hauser, 1981). Leaving aside the issue of possible violation of human rights, such behavior on the part of parents, while understandable, can often lead to the creation of intense hostilities between parents and children.

Interestingly, there is a high turnover rate in the religious cults, apparently because of disillusionment with failed promises and just "growing out of it" as young people mature (Doress & Porter, 1978).

POLITICAL AND SOCIAL VALUES

Developmental Trends in Political and Social Thinking

As would be expected, there are general parallels between the development of political thinking and both Piaget's stages of cognitive development and Kohlberg's stages of moral development.

Joseph Adelson's (1971, 1975) studies of some 1,000 American adolescents between the ages of 11 and 18 revealed some interesting developmental trends in adolescent political thought. Younger adolescents' thinking about political issues is concrete

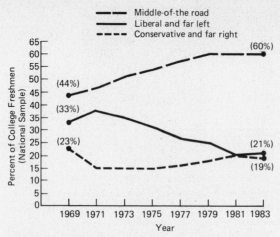

Figure 10.2 Political orientations of college freshmen (males and females) from 1969 to 1983. *Source:* Figure based on data from Alexander Astin, *The American Freshman: National Norms* (for Fall 1969, 1971, 1973, 1975, 1977, 1979, 1981, 1983). Copyright 1969, 1971, 1973, 1975, 1977, 1979, 1981, 1983 by the American Council on Education and the University of California at Los Angeles. Reprinted by permission.

rather than abstract. Consequently, they are likely to propose simplistic solutions to complex political problems. Their thinking is "personalized" in nature such that they tend to equate "laws" with police officers or judges and "governments" with the president or mayor. In addition, younger adolescents are more authoritarian and punitive in their views than are older adolescents.

By 15 to 18 years of age political thinking becomes more abstract and less authoritarian. This change means that older adolescents are able to consider more humanitarian solutions to political and social problems. Research with British and German youth shows similar findings in this area (Gallatin & Adelson, 1971; Gallatin, 1980).

An increase in realism in the political and social values of adolescents has also been reported (Adelson, 1975). For example, when asked what could be done if a city council were not responsive to the problems of the average citizen, 12- and 14-year-olds (and very few 16-year-olds) were inclined to give a simplistic, moralistic answer: "That's not fair" or "Talk to them real nice" (p. 73). Most 18-year-olds gave more pragmatic suggestions such as calling for a new election or appointing people to speak to the council on behalf of the citizens.

In addition, as adolescents mature, they develop the capacity for formulating a reasonably coherent political ideology, that is, "a morally coherent view of how society is and might and should be arranged" (Adelson, 1971, p. 1013). Adelson notes that the development of such a comprehensive political view usually doesn't take place until the end of the high school years. Moreover, he suggests that the extent to which adolescents develop a coherent political ideology is probably overestimated and that relatively few young people really succeed in formulating such a framework.

Contemporary Trends in Political and Social Beliefs and Behaviors

Youth in the late 1970s and early 1980s appear to be more moderate in their political and social views than their counterparts during the late 1960s and early 1970s. Findings from several national surveys of college freshmen report a shift toward middle-of-the-road political orientations (see Figure 10.2, p. 276).

A variety of studies suggest that today's youth are much less concerned about political issues than were their counterparts of the late 1960s and early 1970s. For example, one study found that political interest among adolescents had declined between 1965 and 1975 (although political interest increased with age among 9-, 13-, and 17-year-olds) (R. S. Jones, 1979). Also, in 1983 only 30 percent of college freshman females and 40 percent of freshman males considered "keeping up with political affairs" to be "essential" or "very important" (Astin et al., 1983). In 1969 these percentages were 50 percent and 53 percent, respectively (Astin, 1980).

Despite the fact that 18-year-olds won the right to vote in national elections in 1971, only 36 percent of 18- to 20-year-olds and 43 percent of 21- to 24-year-olds voted in the 1980 national election (U.S. Bureau of the Census, 1981). The number of young people who vote is much lower than the number of people over 25 who vote (the average for age groups over 25 is 64 percent) (U.S. Bureau of the Census, 1981).

Because the number and intensity of student protests has decreased in recent years, there has been a tendency to declare that there is no unrest on campus. Nonetheless, in 1976 it was estimated that one out of five undergraduates had taken part in a demonstration (A. Levine, 1980). It is important to note, however, that the protest issues have changed since the 1960s. Table 10.5 indicates that in 1969 the two most frequent causes for protest were the Vietnam war and minority concerns; in 1978 they

The number and intensity of student protests has decreased in recent years.

were financial aid and campus facilities. Also, the frequency of protests typically varies according to the selectivity, location, size, and programs of a university. For example, protests over the divestment of stock in South African companies occurred in 49 percent of research-oriented universities, but in no two-year colleges (A. Levine, 1980).

Protest tactics in the 1970s have also changed from those in the 1960s: from demonstrations and building takeovers to less visible and more peaceful means such as litigation, lobbying, the use of governance procedures, and education of the public and peers by way of seminars and research reports (A. Levine, 1980).

Current political interests of American college students are directly related to a growing sense of pessimism about the country among the people at large (A. Levine, 1980). When students at 26 colleges were asked which political and historical events had most influenced them, they cited the Vietnam war, Watergate, civil rights protests, and political assassinations. Moreover, three out of four of those surveyed saw the influence of these events as negative. Worse still, these youth have never known things to be different.

It has been suggested that today's students are turning away from larger social and political issues to escape an unfriendly world and are developing a "lifeboat mentality":

> Each student is alone in a boat in a terrible storm, far from the nearest harbor. Each boat is beginning to take on water. There is but one alternative: each student must singlehandedly bail. Conditions are so bad that no one has time to care for others who may also be floundering. (A. Levine, 1980, p. 22)

Among the outgrowths of such a mentality is a reported increase in self-interest groups among college students which typically have a single-issue focus—black, Chicano, gay, or women's issues (A. Levine, 1980).

IDEOLOGICAL COMMITMENT RECONSIDERED

An ideology, like a map, is a way of "making the world look simpler and more consistent than it is" and thereby serves as an "aid to navigation" (Deutsch, 1980, p.

Table 10.5   PERCENT OF INSTITUTIONS EXPERIENCING STUDENT UNREST OVER VARIOUS ISSUES IN 1969 AND 1978

	1969	1978
Vietnam	68	—
Problems of minorities	35	12
Campus rules of student behavior	22	11
Faculty and staff employment	12	18
ROTC and draft	10	—
Student fees and financial aid	2	20
Institutional facilities	3	19
Institutional services	3	12
Administration policies and practices	4	17

Source: Arthur Levine. (1980). *When Dreams and Heroes Died: A Portrait of Today's College Student.* San Francisco: Jossey-Bass, p. 41. Copyright 1980 by Jossey-Bass, Inc., and The Carnegie Foundation for the Advancement of Teaching. Reprinted by permission.

9). It orients us and serves as a useful guide for action. Because human beings seem to need cognitive consistency and because we are constantly exposed to numerous contradictory pieces of information, we use various psychological mechanisms to reduce cognitive dissonance, the discomfort brought about by attending to contradictory messages. Sometimes, we repress or deny such information even when it is essential to our functioning realistically in the world.

According to Karl Deutsch, a political scientist at Harvard University, an "extreme" ideology is one which is closed to useful and important information that doesn't fit an existing cognitive framework. Similarly, he uses the term "reasonable" to describe an ideology which is open to additional useful and "true" information.

We emphasize these points because we believe they have special relevance for adolescent (and adult) development. That is, adolescence and young adulthood are critical periods for the formulation of a personal ideology. This should not be taken to mean, however, that a young adult should have developed an ideology which is impervious to change. Ideally, a philosophy of life evolves in the experience of confrontations with day-to-day events. Because adolescents have not yet experienced a great deal of life, their ideological commitments should be coherent enough to serve as useful guides to action, but also remain open to new and contradictory information.

SUMMARY

A major developmental task of adolescence is developing a coherent philosophy of life, including religious and political ideologies.

The psychoanalytic theory of moral development places heavy emphasis on the development of the superego through the internalization of parental standards and feelings of guilt which result from misbehavior.

Kohlberg's cognitive-developmental theory maintains that moral judgment proceeds according to universal, predictable stages and is closely tied to cognitive development.

Social learning theorists assert that moral judgments and behaviors are learned through observational learning, operant and classical conditioning. Moral judgments and behaviors may be inconsistent, and moral behavior may vary from one situation to another.

Gender, social class, and cross-cultural differences have been noted with regard to moral judgment and behavior.

Parents, peers, and the media all serve as socializing agents in moral development. Several models of moral education in the schools have been used with varying levels of success.

Religious thinking is typically more abstract and personal in adolescence than it is in childhood. Also, dissatisfaction with organized religion is most common during the teenage and early adult years. Since the mid-1950s, religious commitments have constantly declined among college students. Youth who are nonbelievers, members of fundamentalist Christian groups, Eastern religious groups, and cults constitute a small number of adolescents.

Early adolescents' views of political issues tend to be concrete and simplistic. In later adolescence their political thinking becomes more abstract and less authoritarian.

Today's young people appear to be more moderate in the political and social views than were youth in the late 1960s and early 1970s.

GLOSSARY

cognitive disequilibrium   A state that arises when people hear information that contradicts their beliefs; motivates individuals to resolve the contradiction by moving to a higher level of moral reasoning.

conventional level of moral development (Kohlberg)   The second level of moral development, characterized by moral judgments grounded in a concern for being judged as socially acceptable by others.

extreme ideology (Deutsch):   A belief system which is closed to useful and important information that is discrepant with existing ideas.

ideology (Adelson)   A relatively consistent body of attitudes which is organized more or less according to a larger set of principles.

individuating-reflexive faith (Fowler)   A level of faith development, characterized by religious beliefs that have been critically evaluated and have personal meaning to those who hold them.

postconventional level of moral development (Kohlberg)   The highest level of moral development, characterized by moral judgments based on abstract moral principles.

preconventional level of moral development (Kohlberg)   The lowest level of moral development, characterized by moral judgments based on external rewards and punishment.

reasonable ideology (Deutsch)   A belief system which is open to useful and important information even when it is discrepant with existing ideas.

super-ego (Freud):   The moral agent of the personality.

synthetic-conventional faith (Fowler)   A level of faith development in which individuals uncritically accept the tenets of their faith and screen out dissonant information.

GETTING INVOLVED: Exercises and General Questions to Consider

EXERCISE 1: BELIEFS CONCERNING THE NATURE OF GOD

The purpose of this exercise is to help you clarify your ideas about the nature of God. For the exercise, use Worksheet 10.1 below.

Worksheet 10.1 BELIEFS CONCERNING THE NATURE OF GOD

Instructions: Below are listed seven different statements about the nature of God. Read through all the statements and study them carefully before you begin. Your task is to evaluate your feelings about each statement and then rank them in terms of how accurately you feel they describe your beliefs *at the present time*. We realize that this is a difficult task and that you might not feel the same way at some later time. Place a "1" next to the statement you feel is most descriptive of your beliefs, a "2" next to the second-most descriptive statement, etc. Do this for all seven statements.

_____ 1. God is a wise, omnipotent creator.

_____ 2. There is a friendly intelligence working by natural laws.

_____ 3. There is an impersonal spiritual source.

_____ 4. I neither believe nor disbelieve in God.

_____ 5. The only power is natural law.

_____ 6. The universe is merely a machine.

_____ 7. None of these alternatives.

Source: Adapted from Edward W. C. McAllister. (1981). "Religious attitudes among women college students." *Adolescence, 16* (63), 587–604. Copyright 1981 by Libra Publishers, Inc. Adapted by permission.

Note: If you like, you might ask a friend and/or your parents to do their own rankings so you can compare your responses to those of other people. If others are willing to participate, be sure *not* to let them see your rankings. Have them use separate sheets of paper. This procedure will prevent them from being influenced by other individuals' answers.

EXERCISE 2: POLITICAL ORIENTATION

The purpose of this exercise is to assist you in clarifying your political orientation. You will need to use Worksheet 10.2 on page 282.

Note: When you have completed the worksheet, compare your orientation with the responses shown in Figure 10.2 on p. 276.

Worksheet 10.2   POLITICAL ORIENTATIONS

Instructions: Read through the list of political orientations given below. Select the one that best seems to describe you *at the present time.* We realize that these terms have different meanings for different people and that a given orientation might not accurately describe you in all instances. Despite these problems, try to select the orientation you feel best describes your political inclinations as a general rule.

_____   Far left

_____   Liberal

_____   Middle-of-the-road

_____   Conservative

_____   Far right

GENERAL QUESTIONS TO CONSIDER

1. Summarize the major points of the psychoanalytic, social learning, and cognitive-developmental theories of moral development. Note the similarities and differences among the theories.

2. The following words are those of Martin Luther King, Jr., written from a jail in Birmingham, Alabama:

> I do not advocate evading or defying the law. . . . That would lead to anarchy. One who breaks an unjust law must do so openly, lovingly, and with a willingness to accept the penalty. An individual who breaks the law that conscience tells him is unjust, and willingly accepts the penalty of imprisonment in order to arouse the conscience of the community over its injustice is, in reality, expressing the highest respect for the law. (1964, p. 86)

Do you agree with this statement? Why or why not? At which level in Kohlberg's theory do you judge King's remarks to fall? Explain.

3. Reflect on Gilligan's ideas about gender differences in making moral judgments. What are your views about this issue?

4. Do you believe that schools should be involved in moral education? Why or why not?

5. Have your religious beliefs changed as you have matured? Can you describe these changes? Do they seem to follow the pattern suggested by James Fowler? (see pp. 271)?

6. How important are religious beliefs to you in your life? Is membership in a church or other religious institution important to you? Do you attend religious services? Why or why not?

7. Do you feel that your experiences in college have had an impact on your religious and political ideas? If so, what experiences have affected you and how? What other personal experiences have influenced your religious and political views? How?

8. Have you experienced any of the religious problems listed in Table 10.4 on p. 273?

9. Are you aware that your political beliefs have undergone changes as you have matured? Can you describe these changes? Do they seem to follow the pattern described by Joseph Adelson?

10. Do you agree that youth in the 1980s generally have more moderate political views than those in the late 1960s and early 1970s? If so, what are some reasons for this change?

Chapter 11 Outline

chapter *11*

Becoming a Sexual Person

To become a sexual person, the adolescent must integrate sexual thoughts, feelings, and behaviors into the self-concept. In addition, the adolescent must learn how to deal with sexual drives and feelings in ways that are both self-enhancing and socially acceptable. The emotional conflicts and ignorance about sex which permeate American culture make these difficult tasks.

In this chapter we'll focus on a number of questions. What is the process of psychosexual development? What are today's adolescents' attitudes toward sex? Are youth today sexually active earlier than those of previous generations? In addition, we'll discuss sex education, the epidemics of sexually transmitted disease and pregnancy among teenagers, birth control and abortion, and responsible sexual decision-making and behavior. Our coverage of these topics will be limited to adolescents in the United States.

PROCESS OF PSYCHOSEXUAL DEVELOPMENT

Psychosexual development, like other aspects of individual development, is a continuous and dynamic process based on the interaction of two forces (Miller & Simon, 1980). The first force is the individual's unique psychological history, including both sexual and nonsexual aspects. The second force is the particular social context in which the individual acts, including historical, cultural, and interpersonal factors. The adolescent's task is to integrate these internal and external forces. The physical and physiological changes in pubescence and the onset of puberty are significant events in the process of psychosexual development.

Identity, Intimacy, and Sexuality

Erikson's developmental task for young adulthood is to resolve the intimacy versus isolation conflict. Older adolescents and young adults need to learn to be comfortable expressing warmth and affection for others and to accept these feelings from others; at the same time they need to learn to be comfortable and happy by themselves. Negative resolutions of this conflict include social and emotional withdrawal (fearing closeness with others) and fear of being alone.

It's important to distinguish between *emotional intimacy* and *fusion*. For example, it isn't uncommon to see couples (teenagers, especially) who are "madly in love" and who can't bear to be separated. These intense feelings of closeness and of needing to be with each other are often interpreted by a couple as intimacy, but are better described as a state of fusion, according to Erikson (1968). The fact that the partners can't bear to be apart suggests that they are still unsure of "who they are" as individuals and that each is using the other, not necessarily harmfully, to define himself or herself.

True intimacy, according to Erikson, requires at least two things: emotional closeness and separate identities. This condition presents a problem for a female who is reared according to traditional sex-role expectations because she is encouraged not to have a separate identity, but rather to base her identity on being a wife and mother. If a "delayed identity search" is begun after a woman marries, it can cause marital conflict if it causes a woman to challenge or change the couple's original expectations for marriage.

As we saw in Chapter 8, individuals may be classified, according to their responses to interview questions, in terms of the degree of intimacy in their relationships. To review, those who are capable of having friendships with both sexes, which are close and caring and have a high degree of self-disclosure, are classified in the *intimate status*. Their sexual relationships are based on emotional commitment and usually include sexual intercourse. Individuals classified in the *preintimate* status are similar to those in the former group, but prefer sexual relationships without obligations since they seem to have conflicts about making a commitment to another person. Individuals in the *stereotyped* status tend to have superficial relationships with friends of either gender. Dating is often conquest-motivated and relationships usually last no more than several months. While individuals in the *pseudointimate* status give the impression of having close sexual relationships because the relationships are long-lasting, both parties remain mutually isolated on an emotional level and treat each other as conveniences. Those in the *isolate* status have no close friends and rarely date.

In line with Erikson's theory, research provides some confirmation of the importance of identity achievement to emotional and sexual intimacy, at least for males. That is, several studies have found that males who were classified at the more advanced identity statuses (achievement and moratorium) were also likely to be classified in greater numbers in the more advanced intimacy statuses (intimate and preintimate). Foreclosure and diffusion subjects were more likely to be in the stereotyped, pseudointimate, and isolate statuses (Orlofsky, Marcia, & Lesser, 1973; Marcia, 1976a). Studies using male and female subjects have reported similar findings (Fitch & Adams, 1983; Kacerguis & Adams, 1982).

Still, because the nature and process of identity development appear to differ between the sexes, the implications of these findings are not yet clear. That is, interpersonal relationships and religious and sexual issues appear to be key components in identity formation for females and occupational and political issues for males (Fitch & Adams, 1983; Schenkel & Marcia, 1972). Thus, it isn't yet clear whether identity precedes, follows, or in some other way is related to advanced intimacy development in females (Hodgson & Fischer, 1979).

Sex-Role Identity and Sexual Preference

Sex-role identity is the psychological outcome of incorporating culturally valued personality and behavioral sex-role characteristics. Having a particular sex-role identity means that we tend to see ourselves as more or less "masculine," "feminine," or "androgynous." The term *sexual preference,* on the other hand, refers to one's choice of a same-sex, other-sex, or either-sex partner for a mature, sexual-emotional relationship. Such sexual preferences are described, respectively, as homosexual, heterosexual, or bisexual.

Traditional theories of sex-role identification and popular stereotypes hold that sexual preference is directly tied to sex-role identity. However, a critical evaluation of research in this area suggests that such a view isn't warranted (Pleck, 1981a). It is possible for a male with a homosexual preference to have a "masculine" sex-role identity and for a homosexual female to have a "feminine" sex-role identity. Similarly, a person who identifies more strongly with opposite-sex-role characteristics may have a heterosexual sexual preference.

We raise this topic because there is increasing discussion and controversy about

Some adolescents have a homosexual sexual preference.

sex roles and sexual preferences, and societal confusion increases adolescents' difficulties in solidifying sex-role identity and sexual preference. For example, boys who don't like sports or who aren't good at them or girls who do like sports and are good at them may experience *sex-role strain* because they may see themselves as not meeting societal sex-role norms. Because of the tendency to confuse sex-role identity and sex-typed behavior with sexual preference, these adolescents may then worry about being latent homosexuals—still a negative label in our culture, especially for males.

Such fears—or "homosexual panic"—can also arise among older adolescents (especially males, but increasingly females, too) when they perceive that their peers are much more active heterosexually (Coons, 1970). The absence of heterosexual behavior may be interpreted as a sign of homosexuality, despite the fact that there has been no conscious sexual attraction toward same-sex peers. Such fears may be exacerbated if boys have engaged in mutual masturbation or homosexual activities with male peers which, as we shall see, is relatively common during adolescence.

Sex Differences in Sexuality

Sexuality appears to have different meanings for males and females, especially in adolescence. The reasons for these differences are both anatomical and social.

At puberty the increase in male hormones causes uncontrolled frequent erections which serve to focus the boy's attention on his genitals. The greater frequency of masturbation among adolescent males compared to females has been suggested as a key factor in the development of sex differences in sexuality (Gagnon & Simon, 1973).

At the same time powerful societal expectations encourage boys to be aggressive and conquest-oriented with regard to sex. Male adolescent peers play an important role in encouraging sexual experimentation and confirming each other's sexual competency (Gagnon & Simon, 1973; Miller & Simon, 1974). For the most part, therefore, sex becomes a vehicle by which males validate their social status with other males.

Boys are much more likely than girls to talk and brag about sex, to take communal showers, and to try group masturbation. These types of experiences make it less likely that males will experience sex solely, if at all, in the context of love and other tender emotions. Research supports this idea: "Commitment to an emotional relationship with the sexual partner is not a prerequisite to coitus for males and may, in fact, preclude it" (Miller & Simon, 1974).

Rather than learning about sex and orgasms, girls learn about romance and the importance of physical attractiveness and catching a mate (Gagnon & Simon, 1973). Their sexuality has a diffuse sensual focus rather than a genital one. It is not until women actually begin having sexual experiences (masturbation or oral or genital sex) that they begin to see themselves as sexual persons. Hence, for girls, it is the sexual partner and not the peer group who facilitates sexual activity; the female peer group functions to foster positive feelings about romantic love (Miller & Simon, 1974).

The process of sexual socialization appears to take longer in females than in males (J. H. Williams, 1977). Two reasons for this are sexual guilt and negative associations about their genitals and sex which men don't have, such as blood and pain associated with menstruation, fears of penetration, fears of pregnancy, and negative messages about sex and men which have probably come from mothers and awareness of such

occurrences as rape. These negative associations are combined with the positive rewards of dating and emotional intimacy. It is not surprising, therefore, that the sexuality of adolescent (and many adult) females is characterized by ambivalence (Hyde &
Rosenberg, 1980). These feelings can become more negative if sexual partners are
impatient, unskillful, or selfish.

One of the consequences of these sex differences in sexuality is that girls and boys
are likely to enter relationships with different expectations. Boys are interested in
relationships because they provide opportunities for varying degrees of sexual intimacy,
without making binding commitments. Girls, on the other hand, see a relationship as
a means of gaining important social status and as an opportunity for developing an
emotionally intimate relationship which may include sexual intimacy. For example, one
study investigated sex differences in eroticism ("I dream of or desire sexual gratification" or "When I have intercourse, it is most often based on a physical need") and
romanticism ("I think about marriage" or "When I have intercourse, it is most often
based on both physical and emotional needs") (Houston, 1981). Using black and white
college students, it was found that females had significantly higher orientations to
romanticism compared to males and that males had significantly higher orientations
to eroticism compared to females. These sex differences were even greater between
black males and females.

The sexes' different views of sexuality also cause adolescent (and adult) males and
females to be out-of-step with each other, and it takes considerable time before both
move toward a "mature" sexuality in which both have achieved a sense of identity,
accept themselves as sexual persons, and are able to integrate emotional and sexual
intimacy.

SEXUAL ATTITUDES AND STANDARDS OF ADOLESCENTS

In the past 50 years adolescents' sexual attitudes and standards have become more
liberal, especially those of females. Since 1980 college students' attitudes appear to be
shifting in a more conservative direction. Table 11.1 depicts attitudinal trends at a
southern state-supported university and Figure 11.1 depicts trends from a national
survey of college freshmen. The long-term liberal trend has led some to speak of a
"sexual revolution," while others feel the term "evolution" is more descriptive of these
changes. Whichever term we use, there have been significant changes in sexual attitudes
which have had the effect of weakening the long-existing "double standard" for the
sexes.

There have been several attempts to categorize adolescents' standards of premarital sexual behavior (Jurich & Jurich, 1974; Reiss, 1967). For example, one schema
includes the following categories (Jurich & Jurich, 1974):

Traditional: abstinence from sexual intercourse for both sexes prior to
marriage

Double standard: sex before marriage acceptable for males, but not for
females

Table 11.1   PERCENT OF COLLEGE STUDENTS "AGREEING STRONGLY" WITH STATEMENTS ABOUT PREMARITAL SEXUAL RELATIONSHIPS

Statement	Male	Female
I feel that premarital sexual intercourse is immoral.		
1965	33 (N = 129)	70 (N = 115)
1970	14 (N = 137)	34 (N = 158)
1975	20 (N = 133)	21 (N = 295)
1980	17 (N = 167)	25 (N = 237)
A man who has had sexual intercourse with a great many women is immoral.		
1965	35 (N = 127)	56 (N = 114)
1970	15 (N = 137)	22 (N = 157)
1975	20 (N = 138)	30 (N = 296)
1980	27 (N = 166)	39 (N = 234)
A woman who has had sexual intercourse with a great many men is immoral.		
1965	42 (N = 118)	91 (N = 114)
1970	33 (N = 137)	54 (N = 157)
1975	29 (N = 130)	41 (N = 295)
1980	42 (N = 165)	50 (N = 236)

Source: Adapted from Ira E. Robinson and Davor Jedlicka (1982, February). Change in sexual attitudes and behavior of college students from 1965 to 1980: A research note. *Journal of Marriage and the Family,* p. 239. Copyright 1982 by the National Council on Family Relations, 1219 University Avenue Southeast, Minneapolis, Minnesota 55414. Adapted by permission.

Permissiveness with affection: sex before marriage acceptable if the couple is "in love"

Permissiveness without affection: sex before marriage acceptable whether or not two people care for each other

Nonexploitive permissiveness: sex before marriage acceptable provided that there is a mutual understanding and agreement between both partners which may or may not include feelings of love

A study by Anthony and Julie Jurich (1974) of upper-SES male and female students in eight colleges in the Northeast found that females were more likely to favor the traditional standard, whereas males favored either the double standard or the permissiveness without affection standard. Note that abstinence from sexual intercourse doesn't necessarily mean abstinence from sexual activities, that is, some respondents may have interpreted this statement to mean that everything except actual sexual intercourse is acceptable ("heavy" petting, mutual masturbation to orgasm, and oral-genital stimulation). A more recent survey indicated that most adolescents believe that premarital sexual intercourse is acceptable for both sexes as long as affection is present (Dreyer, 1982).

Interestingly, the rates of acceptance are higher than the rates of participation in premarital intercourse among today's adolescents. For example, among 15- to 18-year-old males, 83 percent approved of premarital sex and 56 percent had engaged in it by the age of 18. Among same-aged females, 64 percent approved and 44 percent had engaged in it by the age of 18 (Hass, 1979).

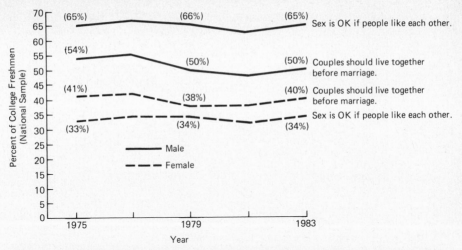

Figure 11.1 Percent of college freshmen (males and females) "agreeing strongly" or "agreeing somewhat" with sex-related statements, from 1975 to 1983. *Source:* Figure based on data from Alexander Astin, *The American Freshman: National Norms* (for Fall 1975, 1977, 1979, 1981, 1983). Copyright 1975, 1977, 1979, 1981, 1983 by the American Council on Education and the University of California at Los Angeles. Reprinted by permission.

SEXUAL BEHAVIOR AMONG ADOLESCENTS

Kissing, Necking, and Petting

A study of middle-class adolescents (13 to 17 years of age) reported that close to 65 percent of them had had some kissing experience by the age of 13 (Vener & Stewart, 1974). Necking (prolonged hugging and kissing) was less common than kissing at all ages and was practiced by 70 percent of 15-year-old males and by 65 percent of 15-year-old females.

With regard to petting, a survey of studies of adolescent sexual behavior reported that about 60 percent have engaged in light petting (fondling above the waist) by the age of 15. By 18 or 19 almost 90 percent of the males and 80 percent of the females reported engaging in light petting (Diepold & Young, 1979).

Adolescents learn to demonstrate emotions and sexual feelings.

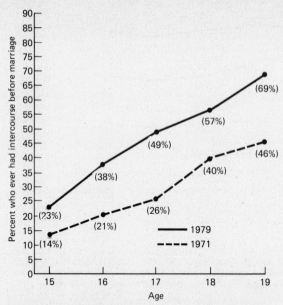

Figure 11.2   Percentage of never-married women aged 15 to 19 who ever had intercourse before marriage in 1971 and 1979. *Source:* Melvin Zelnick and John F. Kantner (1980). Sexual activity, contraceptive use and pregnancy among metropolitan-area teenagers: 1971–1979. *Family Planning Perspectives, 12*(5), 230–237. Copyright 1980 by the Alan Guttmacher Institute. Reprinted by permission.

Research seems to suggest that today's adolescents (both male and female) are engaging in light petting at earlier ages. Nearly 68 percent more males and 83 percent more females report engaging in petting at age 14 than was true in the 1940s (Diepold & Young, 1979).

By age 16 about 30 percent of adolescents have engaged in heavy petting (fondling below the waist) (Diepold & Young, 1979).

Masturbation

Masturbation (the stimulation of one's genitals to produce sexual arousal whether or not orgasm results) is probably the first sexual experience for most individuals.

Probably because of the greater accessibility of male genitalia and also because of different standards of sexual behavior for males and females, masturbation is more common among males than females (W. C. Wilson, 1975). Approximately 80 percent of males sampled have masturbated by the age of 14, 90 to 98 percent by age 18 (Diepold & Young, 1979). These figures have not changed much since Alfred Kinsey's research in the 1930s and 1940s.

For females, data are much more sparse. Kinsey reported that only 20 percent of the females sampled had engaged in masturbation to orgasm by age 15 and only 33 percent by age 19. Data for comparable female age groups some 30 years later indicate that more females now engage in masturbation. For example, a study completed in the early 1970s showed that 23 percent of the sampled 14-year-olds and 37 percent of the 19-year-olds had engaged in masturbation (Diepold & Young, 1979). By 1979 these figures were much higher for 18-year-olds: 40 percent for black heterosexual females, 54 percent for white heterosexual females, 67 percent for white homosexual females, and 83 percent for black homosexual females.

Sexual Intercourse

In the past 50 years, there has been a dramatic increase in the frequency of premarital intercourse among young people, especially among females (see Table 11.2). In addition, there has been a striking decrease in the age at which adolescents first engage in intercourse, again particularly among females. For example, a national survey of black and white females reported that premarital intercourse among 15- to 19-year-olds rose from 30 percent in 1971 to 50 percent in 1979 (Zelnick & Kantner, 1979). From Table 11.3 and Figure 11.2, it can be seen that more adolescent females are engaging in premarital intercourse at earlier ages (14 percent of the 15-year-olds in 1971, compared to 23 percent in 1979). The increases over the same period for 16-, 17-, 18-, and 19-year-old women were even greater.

Estimates of the incidence of premarital intercourse for younger males range from 9 to 38 percent for 13- to 15-year-olds (Miller & Simon, 1974; Vener & Stewart, 1974). Among 16- to 17-year-old males, estimates range from 20 to 34 percent (Miller & Simon, 1980). These estimates are undoubtedly low, because they come from surveys conducted in 1974 and 1975. There is good reason to believe that current estimates, if they were available, would be higher. For example, the most recent survey (1979) of male premarital sexual activity was based on a national sample of black and white males aged 17 to 21. From Table 11.4, it can be seen that 56 percent of 17-year-old and 71 percent of 21-year-old males have engaged in premarital intercourse. As can be seen by comparing Tables 11.3 and 11.4, the percentages of men who have had intercourse before marriage are higher than they are for women at a comparable ages.

Studies on adolescents' sexual behavior have reported the following trends (Diepold & Young, 1979; Zelnick & Kantner, 1980):

Table 11.2 PERCENTAGE OF WHITE HIGH SCHOOL AND COLLEGE STUDENTS REPORTING PREMARITAL INTERCOURSE IN THREE HISTORICAL PERIODS

Period	High school		College	
	Males	Females	Males	Females
1925–1965[a]	25	10	55	25
1966–1973[b]	35	35	85	65
1974–1979[c]	56	44	74	74

[a]Bromley & Britten, 1938; Chilman, 1961; Davis, 1929; Ehrmann, 1959; Kinsey et al., 1953; Peterson, 1938.
[b]Carns, 1973; Christensen & Gregg, 1970; Hunt, 1974; Jessor & Jessor, 1975; Kaats & Davis, 1970; Lake, 1967; Luckey & Nass, 1969; Robinson et al., 1972; Vener & Stewart, 1974; Vener et al., 1972.
[c]Chilman, 1979; Hass, 1979; "What's Really Happening on Campus," 1976.
Source: Philip H. Dreyer. (1982). Sexuality during adolescence. In Benjamin B. Wolman (Ed.), *Handbook of Developmental Psychology.* Englewood Cliffs, N.J.: Prentice-Hall, p. 575. Copyright 1982 by Prentice-Hall, Inc. Reprinted by permission.

Table 11.3   PERCENTAGE OF NEVER-MARRIED WOMEN AGED 15 TO 19 WHO EVER HAD INTERCOURSE BEFORE MARRIAGE, BY RACE, 1979 AND 1971

Age	1979			1971		
	White	Black	Total	White	Black	Total
15	18	41	23	11	31	14
16	35	50	38	17	44	21
17	44	73	49	20	59	26
18	53	76	57	36	60	40
19	65	86	69	41	78	46
Total (15 to 19)	42	65	46	23	52	28

Source: Adapted from Melvin Zelnick and John F. Kantner. (1980). Sexual activity, contraceptive use and pregnancy among metropolitan-area teenagers: 1971–1979. *Family Planning Perspectives, 12*(5), 230–237. Table 1 on p. 231.

Table 11.4   PERCENTAGE OF MEN AGED 17 TO 21 WHO EVER HAD INTERCOURSE BEFORE MARRIAGE, BY RACE, IN 1979

Age	White	Black	Total
17	55	60	56
18	64	80	66
19	77	80	76
20	81	86	81
21	68	89	71
Total (17 to 21)	68	75	69

Source: Adapted from Melvin Zelnick and John F. Kantner. (1980). Sexual activity, contraceptive use and pregnancy among metropolitan-area teenagers: 1971–1979. *Family Planning Perspectives, 12*(5), 230–237. Table 2 on p. 233.

1. Females at all ages (but not males) are engaging more frequently in premarital intercourse than has been true in the past.
2. Lower-SES adolescents are more likely than their higher-SES peers to engage in more frequent premarital intercourse and to begin such activity at an earlier age.
3. Premarital intercourse is more frequent among black males and females than their white counterparts.

What with the commonly held notion about the "dangers" of the back seats of cars, it is surprising to note that adolescents report that their first premarital sexual experience most likely occurred at the home of the partner, usually the male. Perhaps the fact that increased numbers of homes are empty much of the day has made it easier for teenagers to use their own homes for sexual activities (Zelnick & Kantner, 1977).

Homosexual Behavior

Traditional, but inaccurate, views of sexual preference include the following: (1) sexual preference is stable and never changes; (2) you can tell a person's sexual preference by his or her mannerisms; and (3) a homosexual preference is deviant from healthy sexual behavior and reflects serious psychological problems in an individual.

Because of negative societal attitudes, research in this area is sparse (especially concerning lesbians or female homosexuals), and much research has been criticized for having a heterosexual bias (Morin, 1977). In this context we might mention that the American Psychiatric and Psychological Associations no longer consider homosexuality to be a psychological disorder, and what research exists seems to show that there are no meaningful differences between the mental health of homo- and heterosexuals (Freedman, 1975).

Adolescents' attitudes toward homosexual behavior are becoming more accepting, but there is still considerable conflict about this issue. In 1983, 58 percent of college freshman males and 40 percent of females agreed "strongly" or "somewhat" that homosexual relations should be prohibited (Astin, Green, Korn, & Maier, 1983).

Obviously, such attitudes make self-acceptance more difficult for those who see themselves as homosexuals since self-concepts are based on how we believe others see us. In addition, there are few opportunities for young (or older) homosexuals to discuss and discover in positive ways their sexual preference(s). Because adolescents are wrestling with self-acceptance on a number of different "fronts," this process is made even more difficult for those who are struggling with sexual preference issues.

It is important to distinguish between exploratory homosexual experiences and a sexual preference that is predominantly homosexual in orientation. Exploratory homosexual experiences are not uncommon among adolescent males and are usually engaged in out of curiosity or as a response to anxiety about one's sexuality. They should not necessarily be taken as early signs of a long-term homosexual orientation.

Nearly identical rates of heterosexual premarital intercourse have been reported for male heterosexuals (50 percent) and homosexuals (49 percent) and for both female groups (36 percent) (Saghir & Robins, 1973). These findings suggest that adolescence is an important time for working out answers to questions about sexual preference.

Exploratory homosexual behavior becomes less frequent with age and males are more likely to engage in such behavior. Most of these experiences occur between 8 and 13 years of age and are usually exhibitionistic or masturbatory in nature. Recent studies have shown that between 10 to 15 percent of males and 5 to 11 percent of females report having had at least one homosexual encounter during adolescence (Chilman, 1979; Hass, 1979). Among college students in 1976, 12 percent of males and 4 percent of females reported that they had had at least one homosexual experience ("What's really happening," 1976).

Only 3 percent of males and 1.5 percent of females reported participating in an ongoing homosexual relationship (Chilman, 1979).

A Note on Homophobia   Homophobia is the fear of homosexuals. Homophobic individuals usually respond to overt homosexuals or the idea of homosexuality with fear, intolerance, and disgust. Such reactions may be related to the fact that some individuals have difficulty accepting behaviors and values which deviate from traditional norms (Gurwitz & Marcus, 1978). That is, it's not uncommon for people to dislike those whose attitudes are different from their own.

Also, some individuals express hostility toward homosexuals because they feel threatened by their own attraction to members of the same sex or by their homoerotic fantasies (Mosher & O'Grady, 1979). That is, they displace their negative feelings about themselves onto homosexuals. Such homophobic individuals are probably ignorant of the fact that many people who consider themselves exclusively heterosexual have homosexual fantasies from time to time (Masters & Johnson, 1979). If this explanation is accurate, it would seem that one way of reducing homophobia would be to educate people about the actual frequency of homoerotic fantasies so as to allay individuals' negative feelings about them.

Fear of seeming to be gay causes some individuals to exaggerate sex-role characteristics associated with their own sex and to avoid displaying any characteristics associated with the other sex. For example, some adolescent males worry that others will think they are gay if they aren't always "on the make."

Meeting and getting to know overt homosexuals is a useful way of getting rid of such fears and prejudice. Consider, for example, the remarks of a 16-year-old boy who was in a teen rap group with another boy, Ed, who was openly gay:

> When Ed first said he was gay I thought, Let me out of here! But I knew the guy, we were friends already, I knew what he did in his spare time, what kinds of fights he had with his mother, what kind of movies he dug. I mean he's a person. So by now his being gay is just something else I know about him. I never thought I'd be hearing myself saying that. (Bell, 1980, p. 113)

SEX EDUCATION

Inadequate sex education is a serious problem among American adolescents. Moreover, this situation is not uncommon in many cultures (Shipman, 1968). Lack of information causes considerable unnecessary anxiety among young people. It is also a primary cause of the epidemic rates of sexually transmitted disease and unwanted pregnancies among today's American adolescents.

Adolescents' Knowledge About Sex

Adolescents want and need to know more about sex. One study of 13- to 19-year-old adolescents found that over half of the boys and two-thirds of the girls wanted to learn more about sex from their parents, but more than two-thirds reported that their parents didn't talk with them about sex (Sorenson, 1973).

What aspects of sexuality do adolescents want to know more about? The results of one study of the sex-related interests of 15-year-olds are reported in Table 11.5. Based on this study, it appears that adolescents don't see sex as separate from their larger personalities and they do see a connection between love and sex (Thornburg & Thornburg, 1977). Also, males are more interested in learning about intercourse (rank 4), whereas girls rank this last (10). Females, understandably, rank interest in pregnancy and abortion (3 and 4) much higher than do males (7 and 8).

A later study of 13- to 18-year-olds showed high interests in birth control,

Table 11.5   RANK ORDER OF SEXUAL INTERESTS AS REPORTED BY 15-YEAR-OLDS

Males (N = 130)	Rank	Females (N = 130)
Love	1	Self-understanding
Self-understanding	2	Love
Dating	3	Pregnancy
Intercourse	4	Abortion
Venereal disease	5	Child Abuse
Marriage readiness	6	Marriage readiness
Pregnancy	7	Parental roles
Abortion	8	Dating
Premarital sex	9	Venereal disease
Female sex system	10	Intercourse

Source: Adapted from Thornburg, E. E., & Thornburg, H. D. (1977). Personal and family life interests of adolescents. In H. D. Thornburg, *You and Your Adolescent.* Tucson, Ariz.: H.E.L.P. Books, p. 130. Copyright 1977 by H.E.L.P. Books. Adapted by permission.

pregnancy, understanding oneself, and preparing for marriage and parenthood (Shirreffs & Dezelsky, 1979).

Sources of Information About Sex

A series of studies between 1967 and 1979 investigated the initial sources of sex information as reported by high school and college students (Thornburg, 1982). The results of two of these studies are shown in Table 11.6. Apparently, most adolescents rely on their peers for information about sex. Other sources include literature (magazines and books), schools, and mothers.

As might be expected, different sources contribute different kinds of information (Thornburg, 1982). For example, peers contribute information about petting, intercourse, homosexuality, prostitution, and contraception, whereas literature is a source of information about seminal emissions, abortion, ejaculation, and prostitution. We would speculate that young people use literature to obtain information about those issues they feel less comfortable talking about. Over half of the information disseminated by mothers concerns menstruation and conception, although recent studies

Table 11.6   INITIAL SOURCES OF SEX INFORMATION, BY PERCENT

Source	1973 (College students)	1979 (High school students)
Mother	13	17
Father	2	3
Peers	38	37
Literature	21	22
Schools	20	15
Minister	.7	.5
Physician	.6	.3
Street talk or experience	5	5
Don't know	5	10

Source: Adapted from *Development in Adolescence,* 2nd Ed., by H. D. Thornburg. Copyright © 1975, 1982 by Wadsworth, Inc. Reprinted by permission of the publisher, Brooks/Cole Publishing Company, Monterey, California.

suggest that mothers are beginning to discuss abortion as well. Information conveyed by schools seems to focus quite heavily on sexually transmitted disease with some time given to the subject of abortion, seminal emissions, and ejaculation.

These studies didn't investigate television and films as sources of information about sexuality, but we would assume that they play a role. Cable television will no doubt assume increasing importance as a source of information about sex.

Teaching Adolescents About Sex

Why Parents and Adolescents Don't Talk About Sex   Some well-intentioned parents don't talk about sex with their children because they believe that keeping information about sex from adolescents will keep them out of trouble. In fact, just the opposite appears to be true. Adolescents who are well-educated about sex (especially if by their parents) are less likely to engage in premarital intercourse at an early age (Lewis, 1973; Miller & Simon, 1974). Also, well-informed adolescents are more likely to use contraceptives in a responsible way if they do engage in premarital sex.

Parents and children have poor communication about sexual matters for other reasons as well. First, many parents really don't know a lot about sex and may have misconceptions and anxieties about sex. Second, many parents realize that sexual attitudes and behaviors have changed since they were young and they don't want to appear to be "out of it" to their adolescent children. Third, supportive communication between many parents and children on any subject is less common than would be desirable. And, since discussions of sexual issues are quite personal and often anxiety-laden, it is unlikely that parents and children who are uncomfortable talking about personal feelings would find it easy to talk about sexuality. Fourth, adolescents want to appear informed and sophisticated about sex to their parents and peers. This makes it less likely that they will put themselves in the position of asking for information and revealing their ignorance. Also, they may find it difficult to accept themselves (and their parents) as sexual persons, and the idea of discussing sexual concerns with their parents may touch off anxiety. Too, the intimacy of sexual discussions with parents may conflict with adolescents' needs for independence from parents.

Sex Education in the Schools   Sex education poses difficult problems. For all practical purposes, parents don't provide adequate sex education, yet many of them are quite ambivalent about sex education being taught in the schools. For example, one study reported that 82 percent of parents surveyed approved of the idea of sex education in high school, but this figure diminished rapidly as specific topics of the program were identified (Dembo & Lundell, 1979). Ninety percent approval was found for only 4 of 22 topics (VD, contraception, menstruation, and illegitimacy). The authors of this study noted that, ironically, these four topics are the ones most adolescents know about by age 13. Another study of sex education programs in the schools of six states requiring such programs reported that 60 percent were forbidden to discuss birth control (Gordon & Dickman, 1977).

Research indicates that most young people learn significant amounts of information about sex between the ages of 12 and 13 (Thornburg, 1982). This suggests that sex education programs are certainly appropriate during the middle school and junior high school years.

Sex education in the schools can be a controversial issues.

An additional problem with sex education in the schools is that there are serious doubts about whether it has any beneficial effects on adolescents' actual sexual behavior. For example, at least one study found no significant differences between the sexual behavior of students who had taken a sex education course and those who hadn't (Spanier, 1978).

Several writers in this area suggest that the lack of effectiveness of sex education programs is due to the fact that most programs are taught from an academic orientation rather than from the perspective of the adolescents' personal interests and development (Cvetkovich, Grote, Bjorseth, & Sarkissian, 1975; Dembo & Lundell, 1979). That is, most sex education programs avoid those issues that are most important to young people: masturbation, orgasm, and homosexuality, for example. Moreover, they fail to address the personal questions adolescents have, but are usually hesitant to ask.

For effective sex education to take place, parents must become more informed and more comfortable talking about sex with their children, and schools must be encouraged to develop and implement sex education programs that are more useful to adolescents. Unfortunately, both of these options pose immense challenges and make it unlikely that much-needed changes will take place in the near future.

The next two sections will consider two negative consequences of inadequate sex education: sexually transmitted diseases and teenage pregnancy.

SEXUALLY TRANSMITTED DISEASES

Epidemic Rates

Sexually transmitted diseases (STD), formerly called venereal diseases or VD, have grown to epidemic levels in the United States, especially among the young (see Figure

11.3). Over 1,000,000 Americans contracted gonorrhea and syphilis (usually gonor-rhea) in 1981 and more than 50 percent of these cases occurred among people who are less than 25 years of age (U.S. Bureau of the Census, 1983). Moreover, in 1982 it was estimated that some 20,000,000 Americans had genital herpes ("The new scarlet let-ter," 1982). Many cases of STD aren't reported because of fear of social stigma, so these estimates are low. We should mention that the number of reported cases of gonorrhea and syphilis dropped sharply in the first 6 months of 1983—3 percent for gonorrhea and almost 7 percent for syphilis. Experts speculate that these declines are related to reduced sexual activity fueled by fears of herpes and Acquired Immune Deficiency Syndrome (AIDS) ("Reported cases," 1983).

The epidemic rates of STD have been attributed to: (1) an increase in the numbers of young people engaging in sexual intercourse, (2) a decrease in the use of condoms due to an increase in the use of oral contraceptives, and (3) the appearance of penicillin-resistant venereal diseases, some of which were brought back to the United States by Vietnam veterans (Katchadourian, 1977).

Regrettably, large numbers of adolescents appear ignorant about the prevention of STD. For example, a recent survey of adolescent girls reported that 40 percent believed that birth control pills were effective in preventing STD (Silber, 1981). Another study revealed that half of urban, adolescent males who were sexually active by the age of 17 didn't know that condoms could prevent gonorrhea (Finkel & Finkel, 1975).

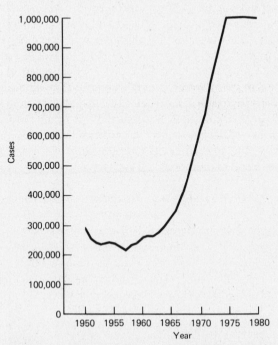

Figure 11.3 Reported cases of gonorrhea in the United States from 1950 to 1979. *Source: STD Fact Sheet, 1979.* Washington, D.C.: U.S. Department of Health and Human Services, 1979.

Gonorrhea

Gonorrhea ("clap") is the most common infectious disease in the country and the most common STD among adolescents (Silber, 1981). Of the 1,000,000 people who develop gonorrhea each year, about 25 percent are teenagers and 38 percent young adults (U.S. Department of Health and Human Services, 1979).

Gonorrhea is almost always transmitted during sexual intercourse, despite the oft-told tales about toilet seats! It is not transmitted by kissing, but may be contracted through oral or anal sex (Katchadourian, 1977).

Symptoms usually appear from several days to a week or so after exposure. Among males they include painful urination and a yellowish, pussy discharge from the penis. Among females, there may be no symptoms or the symptoms may be so subtle as to go unnoticed and, therefore, untreated. Sexually active women may not know that they have gonorrhea and may unwittingly pass it on. Later symptoms include a thin vaginal discharge, painful urination, and stomach cramps, which individuals sometimes mistake for a bladder or urinary tract infection.

Diagnosis of gonorrhea usually requires a relatively simple laboratory examination of the discharge, and treatment is usually straightforward—the administration of antibiotics. Laws such as the "medical rights of minors" have established the right to medical consultation for diagnosis and treatment without parental consent (Silber, 1981). Because many adolescents do not know about this right, they avoid going for diagnosis and treatment for fear of parental reactions.

Having contracted gonorrhea doesn't give lifetime immunity; also, there are no reliable blood tests by which to detect it. Nonetheless, early detection is essential if later complications are to be avoided. The most serious of these include sterility, arthritis, and damage to the heart and brain. Babies born to mothers with gonorrhea may be affected by the disease, which, if untreated, can produce blindness. Dropping silver nitrate in babies' eyes on birth will prevent blindness, and this procedure is mandatory in all American hospitals.

Gonorrhea can be prevented relatively easily: by the use of condoms (but not diaphragms) or by washing the genitals with bactericidal soap after intercourse (Katchadourian, 1977).

Syphilis

Syphilis ("siff" or "pox") is a more serious venereal disease, but less common than gonorrhea; some 73,000 cases were reported in the United States in 1981 (U.S. Bureau of the Census, 1983).

One of the treacherous aspects of syphilis is the fact that the symptoms of the disease change as the disease progresses. However, unlike gonorrhea, it can be detected by a blood test. (The blood test is required before a marriage licence will be issued.) The initial symptom of syphilis is a chancre (a hard, round ulcer with raised edges) which appears on the genitals. The chancre usually appears two to four weeks after the disease has been contracted and usually disappears several weeks after that. Unfortunately, this leads people to believe, wrongly, that they have recovered from whatever infection they thought they had. Treatment of syphilis in the early stages is quite effective with antibiotics, but if the disease is allowed to go untreated, it moves into more dangerous phases.

Syphilis is transmitted whenever the chancre comes in contact with the penis, vagina, rectum, or mouth. Since the sore in males is not always on the penis, condoms do not necessarily protect against syphilis.

One means of reducing the likelihood of contracting syphilis (and other venereal diseases) is to limit the number of one's sexual partners since, statistically, the probabilities of encountering a carrier increase as the number of partners increases.

Herpes Simplex Virus Type II

Herpes viruses are a family of viruses, one form of which, the herpes simplex virus type II, appears to be transmitted through genital and oral-genital contact. Figure 11.4 shows the sharp rise in the rates of genital herpes in the total U.S. population in recent years.

The symptoms of herpes appear from three to seven days after contact. Painful

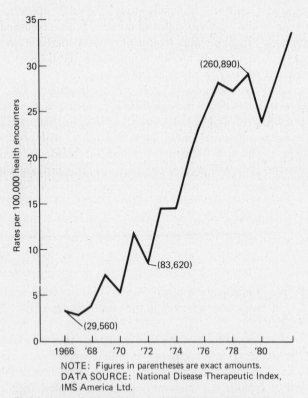

NOTE: Figures in parentheses are exact amounts.
DATA SOURCE: National Disease Therapeutic Index, IMS America Ltd.

Figure 11.4   Estimated rates of patient encounters with private physicians for genital herpes infection, United States, from 1966 to 1979. *Source:* Paul J. Wiesner and William C. Parra (1982). Sexually transmitted diseases: Meeting the 1990 Objectives—a challenge for the 1980s." *Public Health Reports,* September–October, *97*(5), 413.

lesions (resembling cold sores) develop in the genital area; the sores tend to heal within several weeks. While medication may relieve some of the painful symptoms, no cure has been found. The virus remains in the system, and symptoms can recur.

The virus is less likely to be passed on when the disease is in its inactive phase, and the use of a condom during intercourse may help prevent the transmission of herpes.

An association has been found between genital herpes and cervical cancer (Katchadourian, 1977). Also, infants born by vaginal delivery to mothers who have active herpes are likely to be infected with the virus, but delivery by Cesarian section eliminates this danger.

TEENAGE PREGNANCY

Incidence

Research suggests that most teenage pregnancies occur because of ignorance about conception and methods of contraception (Luria & Rose, 1979). This widespread ignorance coupled with the increasing numbers of young people engaging in sexual intercourse have led to near "epidemic" levels of pregnancies among teenagers. Between 1950 and 1980 the illegitmate birth rate for teenagers has more than doubled (U.S. Bureau of the Census, 1983), and in the past decade there has been a 75 percent increase in the birthrate among girls under 18 years of age (McKenry, Walters & Johnson, 1979). In 1980 almost one out of every 100 girls under 15 years of age gave birth to a child (U.S. Bureau of the Census, 1983). Since these figures do not include the numbers of girls who have miscarriages or abortions, they are a conservative estimate. It has been estimated that about 28 percent of sexually active girls aged 15 to 19 become pregnant each year (Zelnick & Kantner, 1978a).

Teenage pregnancy is more frequent among young women from lower-class families (Havighurst, 1980) and among black females (Zelnick & Kantner, 1980). However, teenage birth rates appear to be leveling off or declining among blacks and increasing among whites (Zelnick & Kantner, 1980). Moreover, since blacks comprise only about 15 percent of the national population, the recently reported large increases in teenage pregnancies and births out of wedlock are due to rate increases among white women.

There are many serious medical problems associated with teenage pregnancy. Teenage mothers are more likely to suffer complications such as toxemia, high blood pressure, premature labor, and postdelivery infections (Sugar, 1976). It should be noted, however, that socioeconomic status is a better predictor of pregnancy and delivery complications than is age for females over 14 (Phipps-Yonas, 1980). An important factor here is the strong relationship between inadequate health care and lower socioeconomic status.

Mortality rates for teenage mothers are higher than any other age group except women over 40 years of age. Infant mortality rates are also higher among teenage mothers than among older age groups (Sugar, 1976).

Teenage pregnancy is a serious problem in this country.

Causes

Causes of adolescent pregnancies can be grouped into four major categories: physiological, social, cognitive, and psychological (McKenry et al., 1979).

The *physiological* factors of earlier onset of menarche and better general health of Americans, have increased the potential for pregnancy among young girls. Also, menstrual cycles are often irregular during the teenage years which makes using the rhythm method quite risky.

The *social* factor of poverty is not a cause of pregnancy, but it is related to frequency rates since those who are poor have fewer economic, social, and medical resources for preventing unwanted pregnancy. Also, peers in certain subcultures may reinforce the idea of becoming pregnant at an early age (Havighurst, 1980). Hostile family relationships may put pressure on young girls to get out of the house; for some getting pregnant is the most obvious way to do this.

The *cognitive* factor of ignorance about sexual activity, conception, and contraceptives is a major cause of unwanted teenage pregnancies. For example, one study found that less than 30 percent of teenagers who became pregnant in 1976 intended to do so (Zelnick & Kantner, 1978a). This study also found that only 20 percent of adolescents who didn't want to get pregnant used birth control of some kind.

Many adolescents who don't function at the formal operational level lack the cognitive ability to foresee the consequences of their sexual activity. Also, many youth feel that the use of contraceptive devices makes sex seem planned (Chilman, 1979; Finkel & Finkel, 1975). These irresponsible and irrational beliefs appear to be closely tied to adolescent egocentrism.

Many *psychological* factors may contribute to teenage pregnancy. Research suggests that young women with low ego strength and negative self-concepts may use sexual activity as a means of *acting out* strong impulses. That is, instead of being able to reflect on or talk about powerful impulses or internal conflicts, these girls feel driven to act on them. Also, highly dependent girls with strong needs for affection, those who feel they have little control over what happens to them, and those experiencing social or psychological stress are more likely to become pregnant.

Poor relationships between girls and their mothers or fathers also have been found to be associated with teenage pregnancy. Also, sometimes there may be an unconscious wish to become pregnant (McKenry et al., 1979).

Some pregnancies are designed to manipulate others. For example, one study of pregnant teenagers from poverty-level homes found that among the 27 percent who reported that they had intended to become pregnant, the majority said that they became pregnant either to force a marriage or to get even with a parent (Cobliner, 1974).

It is also important to note that some studies have found no significant differences between unmarried teenage mothers and their nonpregnant peers, except that the latter are luckier than the former (Oskamp & Mindick, 1981)!

We would also add that the process of becoming a sexual person and comfortably acknowledging this fact to oneself and to others is made quite difficult in American society. It wouldn't be unexpected, then, for adolescents to have considerable conflict and ambivalence about their sexual behavior and personal relationships. Such conflict makes it more likely that young people would deny that pregnancy could occur and that they would tend to trust in luck not to get pregnant rather than take responsibility for and control over their activities. Limited access to birth control and the awkwardness and embarrassment of speaking to professionals about one's needs are also issues.

Options for Pregnant Teenagers

Abortion   The issue of abortion is quite controversial in the United States. In 1983, 55 percent of college freshman males and 56 percent of females agreed "strongly" or "somewhat" that abortions should be legal (Astin, Green, Korn, & Maier, 1983).

Regardless of one's views about abortion, it is clear that the 1973 Supreme Court decision making abortions legal during the first three months of a pregnancy has resulted in an increased number of abortions among women, including teenagers. By 1980, 30 percent of all abortions were performed on teenage girls (U.S. Bureau of the Census, 1983). Estimates indicate that abortion is much less frequent among black adolescents than whites. This fact may reflect philosophical differences between the races (K. Thompson, 1980), but no doubt it is also related to the recent court rulings on the public funding of abortions.

There is not a great deal of information on the psychological effects of abortion on adolescents. One summary of research suggests that most youth experience relief and happiness (Dreyer, 1982). The most common negative feelings are mournfulness and guilt, most likely to be reported by those who are Catholic, young, or from lower-SES backgrounds or who feel abortion was forced on them. About 15 percent experience emotional problems which are serious enough to require psychotherapy. In most of these cases, individuals have had a history of psychological problems.

Relinquishing the Child   If a pregnant teenager decides to continue with the pregnancy, she must decide if she will keep or relinquish the child. Statistics show that 94 percent of the babies born to 15- to 19-year olds in this country are kept by the mother (Alan Guttmacher Institute, 1976).

For the teenagers who decide to relinquish the child, two options are available: adoption and foster care. Adoption is the preferred option for the child so that he or she has a permanent home.

Single Parenthood   A third choice for teenage mothers is to keep the child and rear it on their own. As we saw above, this option is chosen by most teenage mothers and particularly by those who are black (Zelnick & Kantner, 1978).

It appears that many teenagers tend to idealize the mother role, suggesting that the personal fable is operating. They are inclined to envision "the 'Carnation Milk' or 'Pampers' baby—clean, smiling, happy, lovable—and the relaxed, rested, glamorous, glowing mother. The night feedings, dirty diapers, squalling infant—all this won't happen with *her* baby" (Juhasz & Sonnenshein-Schneider, 1980, p. 745).

Such idealistic fantasies are far removed from the realities of child care. For example, some researchers have found that adolescent mothers have unrealistically high expectations about their children's rates of development and are more impatient, insensitive, irritable, and inclined to use physical punishment with their children (McKenry et al., 1979). Also, children born to unmarried parents are more likely to be victims of child abuse (Bolton, Laner, & Kane, 1980; Kinard & Klerman, 1980; McKenry et al., 1979).

It is highly unrealistic to expect those who are not yet intellectually, emotionally, or socially mature and who have not yet attained a high school education and financial stability to have the resources to cope successfully with child-rearing. A disturbing statistic is that the suicide rate of teenage mothers is 10 times that of the general population (Cvetkovich et al., 1975).

Parenthood places more than immediate psychological stress on adolescents. Problems related to education and employment have serious long-term implications for the social, economic, and psychological well-being of the mother and the child. At least 50 percent of girls who bear children in high school never complete their education (Furstenberg, 1976; Phipps-Yonas, 1980). In many cases this is because schools expel such students for "moral" reasons. The consequence—increased likelihood of mother and child's dependency on public assistance—has negative effects on both the young family and the larger society. For example, approximately 60 percent of children born out of wedlock require public assistance (Moore & Caldwell, 1977).

In response to the high rates of teenage pregnancy, some high schools have developed alternative programs for pregnant students. These include providing a six-week maternity leave, day care, and special classes relating to child care (Block & Block, 1980).

Relatively little research has been done about adolescent fathers because traditional social norms don't hold men responsible for their sexual behavior or for child-rearing.

Early Marriage and Parenthood   Many teenagers get married because of pregnancy. It has been estimated that a third of teenage girls who marry are pregnant and that in very early marriages 50 to 85 percent of the brides are pregnant (Chilman, 1979; Howard, 1971).

Unfortunately, the divorce rate for teenage marriages is three to four times higher than for later marriages (Howard, 1971). Even among those marriages which "survive," couples married as teenagers report more tension, higher rates of marital dissatisfaction, lower levels of income, and less satisfaction with their standard of living than those who marry later (Lee, 1977).

It should be noted that age at marriage alone probably isn't the determining factor in marital stability. Adolescents who marry are also likely to come from lower-SES backgrounds, to have little education, and to have employment problems—all factors associated with divorce (Chilman, 1979).

Lack of knowledge about child-rearing is as much a problem for couples as it is for the teenage mother who attempts single parenthood. One study of marital adjustment and parenting among teenage couples found that they knew little about child development and underestimated the ages at which children should be expected to sit, walk, talk, etc. (DeLissovoy, 1973). Also, physical punishment was often used, even with very young infants. The author of the study concluded that the young parents generally tended to be "insensitive, impatient, irritable," although he did find "a few notable exceptions" (1973, p. 22).

Because of the increased rate of births to teenagers and the realization that adolescents are unprepared to meet the challenges of child rearing and their own self-development, many states have instituted some form of educational adolescent parenting projects (Magid, Gross, & Shuman, 1979). These projects usually attempt to provide information related to child development, effective parenting techniques, and self-improvement skills for the parents.

TOWARD RESPONSIBLE SEXUAL DECISIONS AND BEHAVIOR

Ideally, adolescents need to learn how to deal with sexual drives and feelings in ways that respect their own, their partners', and the larger society's welfare. The welfare of all concerned depends on information about, access to, and use of contraception. For example, it has been found that the ability of adolescents to discuss birth control with their partners fostered much more effective contraceptive practices (Thompson & Spanier, 1978).

Should Adolescents Have Access to Contraceptives?

In 1977 the U.S. Supreme Court ruled that minors could have access to nonprescription contraceptives and that these birth control devices could be openly displayed and advertised. For prescription devices (pill, diaphragm, IUD), parental consent is required in many states for single females under 18 years of age who have not previously been pregnant. In 1983 the controversial "squeal law" of the Department of Health and Human Services was scheduled to go into effect. This regulation would have required many family planning clinics to notify parents by certified mail within 10 days after their children 17 years or younger had been issued a prescription contraceptive device. However, a permanent injunction was issued against the regulation before it could go into effect.

In spite of the fact that nonprescription contraceptives are openly displayed and advertised, many sexually active adolescents fail to use them.

The issue of whether or not adolescents should have access to contraceptive information and contraceptive devices is obviously a controversial one. Perhaps the most commonly cited reason for restricting information and access to contraceptive services is that their availability will encourage adolescents to engage in sexual intercourse. Considerable research shows that this fear is unfounded. Also, one survey of research reported that the reasons teenagers engage in sexual intercourse have very little to do with the availability of contraceptive services and that almost 75 percent of teenage girls don't come to clinics for contraceptives until they have been sexually active for at least a year (Chilman, 1979).

Ideally, parents and adolescents should talk about sex and contraception. Most, however, do not. Moreover, many adolescents seem to feel that their sexual behavior is their own business. A study of adolescent girls who were patients at a family planning clinic reported that an important barrier to their use of such services was the requirement of parental consent (Urban and Rural Systems Associates, 1976).

Since adolescents do and will continue to engage in sexual intercourse whether or not their parents and others condone it and since the prevention of unwanted pregnancies and sexually transmitted diseases is essential, it seems reasonable that contraceptive information and devices should be made available to adolescents on a confidential basis.

Contraceptive Use Among Adolescents

One survey of research reported that only about 45 percent of sexually active teenagers used any form of birth control at the time of their first intercourse and that only 50 percent of college students and 20 percent of high school students reported using any kind of contraception on a regular basis (Dreyer, 1982). Melvin Zelnick and John Kantner's (1977) comprehensive study of the sexual behavior of 15- to 19-year-old women in 1971 and 1976 reported the following (see also Figure 11.5):

1. Twenty-five percent of white women and 60 percent of black women didn't know the time of greatest risk of conception during the menstrual cycle.
2. Contraceptive use increased with age, for example, 19-year-olds were more likely to use contraception than 15-year-olds.
3. There is about a one-year gap between the time of first intercourse and the first use of contraception. This did not change much between 1971 and 1976.

Between 1976 and 1979, contraceptive use among teenage females increased. For example, in 1976, 29 percent of all sexually active 15- to 19-year-old women reported that they "always used contraceptives and 34 percent reported this in 1979 (Zelnick & Kantner, 1980). However, even though more teenagers (but certainly not the majority) are using contraceptives, pregnancy rates have continued to climb. The most likely cause of this phenomenon appears to be the decline in popularity of the pill (the most effective contraceptive device, but also the one with the most dangerous side-effects) and the substitution of withdrawal (one of the least effective birth control methods). In fact, the use of withdrawal is the most common form of initial birth control (36 percent versus 34 percent for the condom and 19 percent for the pill)(Zelnick & Kantner, 1980). (For information about the various types of contraceptive methods, see Table 11.7.)

One of the few studies of the contraceptive behavior of adolescent males (and their partners) reported that 55 percent did not use a condom nor did their partners use an effective contraceptive (Finkel & Finkel, 1978). The subjects of this study were black, white, and Hispanic high school students in a large, northeastern city. The authors

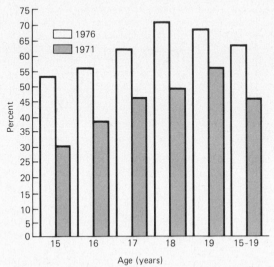

Figure 11.5 Percent of sexually experienced, never-married women aged 15 to 19 who used contraception at last intercourse, by age, in 1976 and 1971. *Source:* Reprinted by permission from Melvin Zelnick and John F. Kantner (1977). Sexual and contraceptive experience of young, unmarried women in the United States, 1976 and 1971. *Family Planning Perspectives, 9*(2), 62.

Table 11.7 SUMMARY OF CONTRACEPTIVE METHODS

Method	User	Effectiveness	Advantages	Disadvantages
Birth control pills	Female	Excellent	Easy and esthetic to use	Continual cost; possible adverse side effects; requires daily attention
IUD or (IUCD) (intrauterine contraceptive device)	Female	Excellent	Requires little attention; no expense after initial insertion	Possible adverse side effects, particularly pain, increased bleeding, expulsion
Diaphragm with cream or jelly	Female	Very good	No side effects; small initial cost of diaphragm and minor continual cost of jelly	Repeated insertion and removal; possible esthetic objections
Cervical cap	Female	Very good	Can be worn 2–3 weeks without removal; no cost except for initial fitting and purchase	Does not fit all women; potential difficulties with insertion
Condom	Male	Very good	Easy to use; helps to prevent venereal disease	Continual expense; interruption of sexual activity and possible impairment of gratification
Vaginal foam, creams, jellies, tablets, and suppositories	Female	Fair to good	Easy to use; no prescription required	Continual expense; unattractive or irritating to some people
Withdrawal	Male	Fair	No cost or preparation	Frustration
Rhythm	Male and female	Poor to fair	No cost; acceptable to Roman Catholic Church	Requires high motivation, cooperation, and intelligence; useless with irregular cycles and during postpartum period
Douche	Female	Poor	Inexpensive	Inconvenient; possibly irritating
Abortion	Female	Excellent	Avoids unwanted pregnancies if other methods fail	Expensive; possible medical complications; psychologically or morally unacceptable to some
Sterilization	Male or female	Excellent	Permanent relief from contraceptive concerns	Possible surgical, medical, psychological complications

Source: Adapted from *Fundamentals of Human Sexuality,* 2nd edition, by Herant A. Katchadourian and Donald T. Lunde. Copyright © 1972, 1975 by Holt, Rinehart & Winston. Reprinted by permission of Holt, Rinehart & Winston, CBS College Publishing.

found that, as with females, the males' contraceptive practices improved with age: only 32 percent of the 15-year-olds were "effective contraceptors" (used condom or partner used contraceptive), compared to 63 percent of the 18- to 19-year-olds.

This same study found that white males were more often effective contraceptors (59 percent) than Hispanics (42 percent) or blacks (40 percent). The reasons males gave for not using contraceptives were that they hadn't brought a condom with them (32 percent), using condoms wasn't important to them (26 percent), their partner was protected (25 percent), and they didn't think that their partner could become pregnant (16 percent). More than half of the noncontraceptors gave the impression that they didn't particularly care whether their partners became pregnant! Clearly, such attitudes are indicative of the need for more responsible sexual decision-making.

Constance Lindemann (1974) has suggested that adolescent contraceptive use progresses through three stages: (1) the natural, (2) the peer prescription, and (3) the expert. The *natural stage* is characterized by doing nothing about contraception. The reasons for not taking responsibility for birth control are related to the infrequency and unpredictability of intercourse and a belief in the spontaneity and naturalness of sex. As the term *peer prescription* suggests, in this stage adolescents rely on friends for information about birth control (misinformation is a major problem) and experiment with various birth control methods. Contraceptive use may be planned or spontaneous and appears to be dependent, in part, on the nature of the couple's relationship.

In the *expert stage* adolescents consult professionals or paraprofessionals in the family-planning field. Movement to this stage typically occurs as a result of an increase in the frequency of *coitus* and a greater commitment to sexual behavior. Interestingly, a regression to earlier stages does occur, usually because of a decrease in the frequency of coitus, typically brought about the termination of a relationship (Lindemann, 1974).

Why Adolescents Don't Use Contraceptives

As we have seen, most adolescent pregnancies are unplanned and unwanted, and most teenagers who become pregnant don't use birth control. Logic dictates that those who engage in sexual intercourse without using contraceptives run a high risk of becoming pregnant. Why, then, don't adolescents use birth control? We've mentioned some reasons before; let's review them.

First, large numbers of teenagers are ignorant about or hold erroneous beliefs about the consequences of sexual activity. Lack of information is a problem which can be corrected by increased efforts in the area of sex education. However, a number of studies show that even when contraceptive information is available to adolescents, it is often distorted or denied. Clearly, then, sex education needs to go beyond the dissemination of information if it is to be effective.

In this context, we mention a second cause of adolescents' failure to use contraception: cognitive immaturity. The effective use of birth control requires the ability to plan for the future and its consequences. Adolescents' failure to use contraceptives can be traced, in part, to lack of formal operational thinking (Cobliner, 1974).

Many adolescents don't like to use contraceptives because it makes sex seem planned. This attitude reflects the operation of guilt and adolescent egocentrism (Cvetkovich et al., 1975). By not using birth control, adolescents can pretend that their sexual behavior isn't intentional and they aren't responsible for it. This helps them to escape disapproval of their actions by the imaginary audience. For younger adolescents, the imaginary audience probably consists of the "idealized images of parents and other adults"; for older adolescents, it consists of "same-age peers . . . and potential sexual partners" (Cvetkovich et al., 1975, p. 262).

The personal fable also appears to play a role in the large number of pregnant teenagers who say, "I just didn't believe that it could happen to me!" (Elkind, 1967a). George Cvetkovich and his colleagues (1975) have extended Elkind's thinking to include two additional personal fables: the *sterility fable* (adolescents believe that they are sterile because intercourse hasn't yet resulted in pregnancy) and the *gamblers' fallacy* (the belief that they can't get pregnant because they've only engaged in sex a few times).

Adolescents also fail to use contraceptives because of difficulties in accepting their sexuality and related feelings of guilt and anxiety. Several studies support the idea that many girls cannot reconcile deliberate planning for sexual activity (implied by the use of contraceptives) with their self-concepts (Dembo & Lundell, 1979).

Another reason for irresponsible sexual behavior stems from the episodic or haphazard nature of adolescents' sexual encounters. In these cases, regular use of contraceptives is difficult to establish (Finkel & Finkel, 1978).

Lastly, we need to point out that human behavior is influenced by situational as well as psychological factors. It has been found that contraceptive knowledge had relatively little impact on sexually active adolescents if they were in sexually stimulating situations. They tended to have intercourse whether or not they were contraceptively protected (Chilman, 1979).

SUMMARY

Adolescents must learn to deal with sexual drives and feelings in self-enhancing and socially acceptable ways. Psychosexual development is based on a continuous and dynamic process of interaction between the individual's unique psychological history and current social setting.

At adolescence males are more likely to have a genitally focused sexuality, whereas the sexuality of females is more diffuse and sensual and often coupled with negative associations. Mature sexuality requires a sense of identity, acceptance of oneself as a sexual person, and a capacity for emotional and sexual intimacy.

Kissing is an early and relatively universal form of sexual behavior among American adolescents. Light petting occurs more often than heavy petting and appears to be starting earlier among today's adolescents. Adolescent males masturbate earlier and more frequently than females.

Greater numbers of adolescents engage in premarital sexual intercourse today. Attitudes of female adolescents, especially, have shown a dramatic decrease in the reporting of negative feelings about engaging in coitus.

Although a predominantly homosexual preference appears to be relatively uncommon, many adolescents (especially males) engage in exploratory homosexual experiences.

The lack of accurate information about sex is a serious problem for adolescents.

Because most parents and adolescents don't discuss sexual matters, adolescents rely heavily on peers, literature, and the schools for this information.

The incidence of both sexually transmitted disease and teenage pregnancy has reached epidemic proportions in recent years. The causes of adolescent pregnancy are quite complex and involve cognitive and emotional dynamics which interfere with rational-decision making.

Only about half of adolescents use any form of birth control at the time of first intercourse. Birth control practices improve as adolescents grow older.

GLOSSARY

coitus sexual intercourse.

expert stage (Lindemann) A stage of contraceptive use in which adolescents consult professionals or paraprofessionals in the family planning field for contraceptive information.

fusion (Erikson) Intense feelings of closeness experienced by partners in a relationship who don't have independent identities.

gamblers' fallacy (Cvetkovich) The personal fable that one can't get pregnant because one has intercourse infrequently.

imaginary audience (Elkind) A consequence of adolescent egocentrism in which young people believe that others are paying more attention to them than is really the case.

intimate (Orlofsky) A more advanced intimacy status characterized by individuals who have close and open relationships with others and who are involved in a committed relationship.

isolate (Orlofsky) A less advanced intimacy status characterized by individuals who are loners and who cannot engage in committed relationships.

natural stage (Lindemann) A stage in contraceptive use in which the adolescent takes no responsibility for birth control.

peer prescription stage (Lindemann) A stage in contraceptive use in which the adolescent relies on friends for information about birth control.

personal fable (Elkind) A consequence of adolescent egocentrism in which young people believe they are special and unique.

petting fondling above the waist (light petting) or below the waist (heavy petting).

preintimate (Orlofsky) A more advanced intimacy status characterized by individuals who have close, open, and reciprocal relationships with others but who have not yet engaged in a committed relationship.

pseudointimate (Orlofsky) A less advanced intimacy status in which individuals are involved in relatively permanent relationships which are characterized by superficiality and manipulation.

sex-role identity A specific aspect of personal identity which refers to an individual's conscious and unconscious identification with the traits, attitudes, and interests that societal norms dictate to be appropriate for a given sex.

sexual preference An individual's preference for a same-, other-, or either-sex partner for an emotional and sexual relationship

sexually transmitted disease (venereal disease) A disease transmitted through genital or oral-genital contact.

stereotyped (Orlofsky) A less advanced intimacy status in which individuals usually see others as objects to be manipulated and cannot make long-lasting commitments.

sterility fable (Cvetkovich) The personal fable that one is sterile because intercourse hasn't yet resulted in pregnancy.

GETTING INVOLVED: Case Studies and General Questions to Consider

CASE STUDY 1: CATHY

Cathy is 16 and a high school junior. On the surface, she appears quiet and reserved, but she opens up when she gets to know someone. She has some friends, but wishes she were more popular. She is mainly worried, though, because she feels that she is unpopular with boys. She has not had many dates and no one has asked her out more than twice in a row.

She knows that she isn't the most attractive girl in her class, but she knows that she isn't exactly "Godzilla" either. She can't understand why boys don't like her any better. She wonders if it's because boys think she's a "prude"—she feels that kissing and necking are all right, but after that she draws the line. Sometimes she finds herself resenting them for not liking her better.

She and her friends (who don't date much either) sometimes speculate that the girls who seem to be popular with guys are "fast." Cathy wonders whether or not her standards are too strict. She feels comfortable with them (for now), but she wonders whether they are harming her social life. She doesn't dwell on these thoughts a lot of the time, but since the junior prom is coming up and she would like to go, it occupies more of her thinking these days.

Questions for Case Study

1. How likely is it that Cathy's lack of popularity with boys is solely related to her sexual standards?
2. Should she try to learn to be more comfortable with boys as a way of increasing her popularity? If so, how might she go about this?
3. Speculate about the possible outcomes of a decision by Cathy to start having sex as a way of becoming more popular with boys. Consider her feelings and perceptions about herself, those of others, the possibilities of STD and pregnancy, the likelihood of having more dates, etc. Also, reflect on the short- and long-term outcomes such a decision might bring about.
4. What could you say to Cathy that might be helpful?

CASE STUDY 2: BOB AND CAROL

Bob and Carol are high school seniors. They have been dating steadily for about nine months. They really enjoy being together, although they have not talked about a "serious" relationship.

Bob genuinely cares for Carol, as she does for him. Eventually, their conversations turn to the topic of sexual intercourse. Bob suggests that this would be a good thing for them, as long as they used contraception. Carol wants the relationship to continue, but she isn't sure that she wants to have sex with Bob at this point because she feels too emotionally vulnerable and fears getting pregnant. She has plans to go to college in the fall. She explains this to Bob, who responds that he feels vulnerable also, but can't really understand her reluctance since they would use birth control. Also, since they love each other, they *should* be having sex, he feels. They end up arguing about it and feeling bad. (For the record, Bob is not a virgin, but he hasn't "slept around" either. Carol's sexual experience has included heavy petting, mainly with Bob, but not oral or genital sex.)

Questions for Case Study

1. What do you think Bob and Carol's options are in this situation?
2. What factors are important in their decision about engaging in sex?
3. What suggestions could you offer them?

GENERAL QUESTIONS TO CONSIDER

1. Need all sexual encounters be based on emotional intimacy? Why or why not? What are your feelings about sexual encounters that are not based on close feelings? Do you feel there might be gender sex differences here?
2. Consider Jurich and Jurich's (1974) standards of premarital sexual behavior (pp. 289–290). Which best describes your values?
3. What kinds of consequences, if any, have you ever heard associated with masturbation? Who told you and did you believe any of them?
4. Do you have any feelings about what age is "too young" for adolescents to engage in sexual intercourse? On what do you base your ideas?
5. Do you have any friends who are openly gay? How did you come to talk about the issue? Was it difficult? What made it so? Has knowing someone who has a homosexual preference had any effect on your ideas about this issue?
6. Where did you first learn about sex—parents, church, school, peers, books, television, films, experience? Were your parents good sex educators? With whom do you discuss your ideas and feelings about sex and sexuality?
7. Who should be responsible for sex education? When should it begin? How should it be taught? Do you plan to talk to your children about sex?
8. If a person has a sexually transmitted disease, does he or she have a responsibility to inform his or her sexual partner about it? Do you think most people would do this? How would you feel if you caught an STD from someone?
9. What would you do if you thought you might have a sexually transmitted disease?
10. What things might a pregnant teenager take into account in her decision whether or not to continue with the pregnancy? Should the beliefs and feelings of the prospective father carry any weight in her decision? Why or why not?
11. To whom would you turn if you discovered you (or your sexual partner) were pregnant?
12. What are some of the reasons adolescents don't practice effective contraception? Focus especially on the cognitive and emotional dynamics. Can you identify with any of these?
13. Should adolescents have free access to both over-the-counter and prescription birth control devices, regardless of age? Why or why not? Should parents ever be informed of their child's request for a prescription contraceptive? Why or why not?

Resources for Adolescents and Parents

BOOKS FOR ADOLESCENTS AND PARENTS

Bell, Ruth. (1980). *Changing Bodies, Changing Lives.* New York: Random House. A good, comprehensive paperback on sex, written by teenagers for teenagers with numerous illustrations.

Gordon, S., Scales, P., & Everly, K. (1979). *The Sexual Adolescent: Communicating with Teenagers About Sex.* Belmont, Calif.: Duxbury Press. A paperback covering many aspects of adolescent sexuality, including a variety of resources for parents, teachers, and professionals.

OTHER INFORMATION

1. The Planned Parenthood Federation of America (listed in the telephone directory) offers excellent resources for numerous sex-related questions: birth control, abortion counseling, workshops to enable parents to talk more comfortably with their children about sexual matters, and so forth.

2. There is a national STD hot line which will provide information about sexually transmitted diseases and make referrals for free or low-cost VD examinations. Callers need not give their names. The hot line is open from 8 A.M. to 8 P.M. Pacific Time, Monday through Friday, and from 10 A.M. to 6 P.M. on Saturdays and Sundays. The number is 1-800-227-8922 (in California: 1-800-982-5883). No charge will be listed on your telephone bill, or if you call from a phone booth, your money will be returned.

Chapter 12 Outline

chapter 12

Choosing and Preparing for an Occupation

Choosing and preparing for an occupation is one of the most important developmental tasks facing adolescents in industrial and postindustrial societies. While this has always been true for most boys, it has become an increasingly salient concern for girls in recent years.

Adolescents in the United States are usually expected to take full financial responsibility for themselves on graduation from high school if they have no further educational plans. And most adolescents who go on to college are expected to pay some or all of their educational and living expenses. Because young people usually understand that their work choices will influence many aspects of their lives, they are concerned about making sound and satisfying vocational decisions. This combination of external and internal forces motivates, and sometimes forces, most adolescents to give high priority to career-choice concerns. Unfortunately, there is considerable evidence that youth know relatively little about careers and the process of choosing an occupation.

In this chapter we'll look at a number of issues related to the task of choosing and preparing for a career: economic, societal, and personality determinants of vocational aspirations and career choice. We'll also consider career opportunities for today's youth. We will focus on youth and occupations in the United States.

CAREER DEVELOPMENT

Career development refers to the process of making occupational choices and preparing for a career. Ideally, this process is based on a matching of personality characteristics and existing social, economic, and occupational realities. Adolescence is a particularly important period for the development of occupational choices.

Difficulties in Career Planning

In the United States the 1930s saw the beginnings of an ever-widening breach between the day-to-day experiences of people and the world of work (Borow, 1976). For various reasons—the need to keep younger people in school longer in order to teach them the necessary skills for functioning in a postindustrial society and the need to protect the jobs of those already working—young people have been increasingly cut off from the work place. Consequently, most adolescents graduate from high school (and college) without the opportunity to explore and test themselves in realistic activities related to this very significant life role. Also, the work role has been increasingly separated from other aspects of adult life, so young people have fewer chances to observe their parents as workers or to get a sense of what it is their parents do for a living. This problem is compounded by the fact that jobs in contemporary America are becoming more and more specialized (and often quickly obsolete) so that learning about adult work roles becomes even more difficult.

In addition, it has been suggested that growing numbers of young people are developing negative attitudes toward work caused, in part, by a decrease in the number of job opportunities and by the boring and repetitive nature of many jobs (Borow, 1976). Such attitudes appear to be more common among youth from upper-middle-class families than among those from blue-collar backgrounds. Today's young people may want interesting and challenging jobs, but we already know that, unfortunately, they can expect to be *underemployed*, that is, overtrained for the jobs they hold or unable to find work in the fields for which they have been trained. This is likely to be a particular problem for college graduates.

Youth from lower-SES and minority families face even greater problems in a time of a tight labor market and boring jobs. As we shall see, unemployment rates among black youth have skyrocketed (close to 50 percent in 1982) and are significantly higher than for their white and middle-class peers (who also face higher unemployment rates today). Also, research shows that the educational and occupational aspirations and the actual attainments of black and ethnic minority youth are lower than among their middle-class and white peers.

Many factors conspire to bring about these disparities in educational and occupational aspirations and attainments. In addition to discrimination in hiring practices, often these young people have had negative life experiences causing them to distrust teachers and school personnel and to be (realistically) cynical about their educational and occupational opportunities.

Since the mid-1960s, compensatory education and work-training programs have been established to help such young people acquire needed education and skills, but the funding for many of these programs has been curtailed in the 1980s.

In summary, then, young people in America today find themselves in a difficult position with respect to career-planning. They need more information and on-the-job experience to enable them to bridge the gap between their personal and educational experiences and the world of work.

Black youth are severely affected by a tight labor market.

Models of Career Development

Trait Measurement and Matching Model   For about the first half of the twentieth century, career choice was seen as being related to an individual's specific personality traits, which were believed to be relatively stable over time. According to this view, psychological testing designed to measure these traits could be used to match individuals to particular jobs.

A more recent version of this same approach has been developed by John Holland (1973). Holland has developed a test, the Self-Directed Search or SDS, which measures six basic personality types based on an individual's responses to a list of occupational titles (See Table 12.1). Holland groups occupations into six different environmental types which correspond to the six modal personality types. Therefore, personality types and occupational environments can be matched so as to provide optimal job satisfaction for an individual. Studies have shown that the SDS has helped students reduce career indecision and select occupations consistent with personality traits (McGowan, 1977; Zener & Schnuelle, 1976).

While this approach is useful, it is based on a static view of how people arrive at occupational choices and fails to take into account the fact that people's interests, skills, motivations, aspirations, and situations change over time. Since about 1950, psychologists have viewed occupational choice as a developmental process rather than a specific event (Crites, 1980). We will look at two such approaches now.

Self-Concept Development Model   Donald Super (1957) views career choice as closely tied to the development of the self-concept. In childhood and adolescence the development of self-concept and career orientation is enhanced by the young person's performance and reality testing in school, play, and work experiences. According to this theory, the process of vocational choice involves five developmental tasks which span the years from 14 years of age through adulthood. Three of these tasks must be dealt with in adolescence. The first, *crystallization of a vocational preference,* requires the image of

Table 12.1   HOLLAND'S PERSONALITY TYPES

1. Realistic
    Values concrete things or tangible personal characteristics (money, status, power); prefers occupations involving the manipulation of objects, tools, machines, and animals; avoids social occupations and situations; perceives self as having mechanical and athletic ability and lacking in social interaction skills
2. Investigative
    Values ideas, problem-solving, and scientific activities; avoids persuasive activities; perceives self as intellectually self-confident, having mathematical and scientific abilities, and lacking in leadership ability
3. Artistic
    Prefers activities and occupations which allow self-expression in language, art, music, drama, and writing; values esthetic qualities; avoids conventional activities and occupations; perceives self as intuitive, original, nonconforming, and disorderly
4. Social
    Prefers being and working with people; avoids activities and occupations requiring manual and technical competence; perceives self as understanding and liking to help others, having teaching ability, and lacking mechanical and scientific abilities
5. Enterprising
    Prefers activities involving the manipulation of others to attain organizational goals or economic success; avoids investigative activities; perceives self as aggressive, popular, sociable, self-confident, possessing leadership and speaking abilities, and lacking scientific ability
6. Conventional
    Prefers a structured environment and explicit, ordered, and systematic manipulation of written and numerical data according to a set plan; likes operating business and data-processing machines; avoids artistic activities and occupations; perceives self as orderly, conforming, and having numerical and clerical ability

Source: John L. Holland, *Making Vocational Choices: A Theory of Careers,* © 1973, pp. 14–18. Adapted by permission of Prentice-Hall, Inc., Englewood Cliffs, N.J.

the self as a worker to be integrated into the self-concept; this usually occurs between 14 and 18 years of age. *Specification of a vocational preference,* the second task, usually occurs between 18 and 21 years and refers to the narrowing of the range of possible career choices and the acquisition of necessary occupational skills and expertise. The third task, *implementation of a vocational preference,* takes place between the ages of 21 and 24. It is during this time that most young people complete their training and education and enter the world of work. *Stabilization,* the fourth task, occurs when an individual settles into a particular job that he or she then evaluates to determine its appropriateness for him or her. This usually occurs around the age of 25. The last task, *consolidation,* usually occurs after age 35. During this period, the individual advances in his or her chosen occupation and, hopefully, attains some degree of success.

Optimizing Satisfactions Model   Eli Ginzberg's theory views career choice as a life-long process of optimizing personal preferences in the context of job requirements (Ginzberg, 1971, 1972). Individuals progress through three major psychological phases in the process of making career decisions. The *fantasy period* is characterized by career choices which are based on personal desires, but which fail to take into account such realistic considerations as ability, training, and job opportunities. Nevertheless, such fantasies are an important aspect of the career development process. Such thinking is characteristic of children up to about age 11.

During the *tentative period,* spanning age 11 to 18, the young person successfully incorporates realistic considerations into his or her thinking: career interests (11 to 12 years); abilities and education (13 to 14 years); personal values and life-style goals (15 to 16 years). Between the ages of 17 and 18 the pressures of having to decide what to do upon high school graduation (go to college, leave home, start work) force a transition to the next phase.

In the *realistic period,* beginning at about age 18, the young person begins to explore specific career options through actual work experiences or continued education and training. Economic and social conditions and actual job opportunities become important factors in making job decisions, along with personal abilities, interests, and motivations.

Career development may extend over an individual's entire working life; note the recent increases in mid-life career changes. According to Ginzberg, vocational decisions made before age 20 are not necessarily crucial, provided the individual is able and willing to make changes which will contribute to career development.

Ginzberg's theory is based on his observations of boys, but he believes that the first two stages are descriptive of girls as well. The reality period, however, is probably different and more complex for most girls because marriage and child-rearing are also important life-style considerations. In addition, he points out that economically disadvantaged and minority youth have fewer occupational choices than the middle-class youth he studied. Accordingly, the process of making specific vocational choices is usually shorter for these young people.

These two developmental theories, while useful, give the impression that career choice proceeds in a straightforward and stepwise fashion and that age is a critical factor in moving from one phase to another. Like most stage theories this approach is somewhat rigid and does not adequately allow for individual differences. Also, while Ginzberg addresses career development in females, Super does not. Nonetheless, the models of Super and Ginzberg do point up the importance of the adolescent period in making career choices.

SOCIALIZATION INFLUENCES ON ADOLESCENT OCCUPATIONAL ASPIRATIONS

Family

Adolescents' career aspirations are significantly related to their parents' motivations for their children's occupational success (Douvan & Adelson, 1966; Marini, 1978). Generally, it has been found that the higher the parents' level of aspiration, the higher the aspirations of the children, even when intelligence and socioeconomic status are held constant.

Mothers and fathers appear to have different effects on their children's work values, depending on the age of the child. One study of the work values of parents and their children in the sixth, ninth, tenth, and twelfth grades found that children's values were more similar to those of the same-sex parent through the tenth grade. Twelfth-grade boys and girls, however, had work values more similar to those of their fathers (Wijting, Arnold, & Conrad, 1978).

Parental influence on children's vocational aspirations is obviously tied to the larger issues of the social roles of adult men and women and to parents' sex-role expectations for their children (Marini, 1978). Any changes in work values would be expected to force changes in marital relationships, especially in the areas of child-rearing and household responsibilities. To the extent that more mothers work, have positive attitudes toward their work and toward themselves as women and workers, they will be able to serve as positive vocational role models for their children. To the extent that fathers are able to adopt positive attitudes toward women (especially their wives) as workers, they will be influential in shaping positive attitudes about working women in both their sons and their daughters.

The socioeconomic status of the family also has a strong influence on parental motivations toward work which, in turn, influences adolescents' aspirations, as we shall see shortly.

Ordinal status within the family (birth order) also has been found to affect vocational aspirations and achievement. Only and first-born children are usually higher achievers than other children, as we saw in Chapter 7.

Obviously, parents can have negative effects on their adolescents' vocational aspirations and adjustment by serving as weak or nonexistent occupational role models or by pressuring their children to select particular careers. Recall here our discussion in Chapter 7 of parental breaches of parent-child contracts to bolster their egos or to satisfy their own needs.

Father's Occupation and Attitudes Toward Work   Most of the research on paternal influence on adolescents' career aspirations has been done with white fathers and sons. Generally, it has been found that middle-class fathers have considerable influence on their son's occupational aspirations, lower-class fathers have less, and the most effective occupational role models are fathers who hold high-status positions and have close relationships with their sons (Mortimer, 1976).

Fathers' attitudes play a large role in the career aspirations of daughters as well. For example, it has been found that daughters of fathers who have positive attitudes toward a career-oriented wife have less conflict about combining a career and marriage. Also, high-achieving daughters have been found to have good relationships with their fathers, characterized by the fathers' encouragement of the daughters' independence and achievement as well as acceptance of them as "female" (L. W. Hoffman, 1974a, 1979).

One study of gifted, middle-class, seventh- and eighth-grade boys and girls found that daughters with high occupational aspirations had personality profiles more similar to their fathers than their mothers (Viernstein & Hogan, 1975).

Mother's Occupation and Attitudes Toward Work   Research findings show that daughters of working mothers tend to be more autonomous and active and to consider their mothers as people they admire and want to be like (L.W. Hoffman, 1974a, 1979). Also, it has been reported that the daughters of working mothers were more likely to value feminine competence, whereas daughters of nonworking mothers tended to devalue feminine competence (Baruch, 1972). The mother's attitudes toward working, whether or not she works, and her ability to successfully combine the roles of worker, wife, and mother are also important influences on her daughter's attitudes toward work, especially with regard to combining career and marriage (Baruch, 1972).

High-achieving women (physicians, attorneys, college professors) typically have high-achieving daughters (L.W. Hoffman, 1974a, 1979). It has been suggested that these mothers encourage independence in their daughters rather than overprotecting them and encouraging dependency, as is the more typical case (L.W. Hoffman, 1972).

The study by Mary Cowan Viernstein and Robert Hogan of gifted seventh-and eighth-graders found that high-achieving boys had mothers who were economically and socially ambitious (as well as fathers who were socially acceptable models and a harmonious and stable family environment). Low-achieving boys were less likely to have achievement-oriented mothers or harmonious home environments.

One study found that mothers in white-collar black and Mexican-American (but not Anglo) intact families play a significant role in the development of occupational aspirations of elementary-school-aged children (Allen, 1978). It was found that the mothers' perceptions of the opportunities for the family's occupational advancement were positively associated with their children's occupational aspirations (the fathers' perceptions weren't measured) (Fields, 1981). Also, another study found that mothers played a more crucial role than fathers in the development of high achievement motivation in black adolescent males from middle- and lower-SES intact families. For high achievement-oriented white male adolescents, fathers played a more central role than mothers (Allen, 1978).

Such findings suggest that working mothers can and do serve as occupational role models for their sons and daughters, as do fathers.

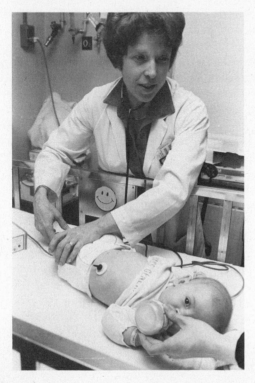

High-achieving women typically have high-achieving daughters.

Peers and Dating Behavior

Adolescent males appear to be positively influenced by the educational and occupational aspirations of their peers (Marini, 1978). There is too little research with female subjects to be able to draw conclusions about girls or sex differences. One study of high school students did note significant sex and race differences in peer influences (Hout & Morgan, 1975). Peers' educational aspirations were found to have a greater effect on white males than on white females, while this pattern was reversed for blacks. In fact, no effect was observed on black males. The influence of peers' occupational expectations was found to be greatest on black females, and greater on white males than on white females.

Dating behavior has been found to have differential effects on boys' and girls' career aspirations. For women, marriage, rather than career, has been the major means to ensure economic well-being and social advancement (Marini, 1978). Accordingly, popularity with the opposite sex has traditionally assumed more importance for females than males, who attain status through their work. What research exists in this area suggests that "frequent and steady dating, particularly at early ages, and the anticipation of early marriage can be seen as deflecting girls away from career preparation" (Marini, 1978, p. 745).

Career Education and Counseling

Career Education   American high school and college curricula are not designed for the purpose of educating young people about careers. Except in vocational or technical schools or in schools with such tracks, the main emphasis has been to educate for literacy. Some critics of the American educational system have suggested that high school and college graduates don't learn marketable skills. Moreover, they say, many students aren't able, by themselves, to see relationships between their academic work and their future careers. For example, a nationally representative study of some 32,000 eighth, ninth, and eleventh graders found that less than 50 percent of the eleventh graders answered correctly more than 75 percent of the items on a test of occupational knowledge (Noeth, Roth, & Prediger, 1975). These inadequacies cause problems for young people in moving from the role of student to that of worker.

Many of these problems can be traced to the increasingly technological nature of our society which causes work to be cut off from other aspects of people's lives and which produces relatively rapid obsolescence of specific job skills. Consequently, what used to be a relatively straightforward process of getting a job has become quite complex.

In response to these problems federal and state governments have allocated millions of dollars for the preparation of testing and curriculum materials for *career education.* This relatively recent innovation has as its purpose informing individuals about current economic and occupational trends, exploring the process of making career decisions, and teaching various occupational skills. Broadly conceived, educational programs expressly for these purposes would be developed and integrated into the existing curricula at all educational levels—kindergarten through college and beyond. It is hoped that students leaving school would be familiar with job availability and requirements suitable to their levels of education and would also have developed marketable skills.

Not everyone approves of career education. The idea of making career preparation and marketability the basis of educational policy is repugnant to many. They feel that the education-for-work ideology limits the functions of educational institutions to those of "reducing expectations, limiting aspirations, and increasing commitments to the existing social structure" (Grubb & Lazerson, 1975). At the same time the more humanistic goals of intellectual and personal development are reduced in importance (Nash & Agne, 1973).

The idea of educating youth merely to be able to fit into an existing job slot—which may shortly be obsolete—seems short-sighted from the point of view of both personal development and social and economic planning. We would argue that the fast-paced changes in occupations and related job skills make it even more imperative that educational goals and curricula be directed to developing literate individuals with meaningful values. Youth who know how to learn—who can read, write, cipher, think logically and critically—and who have developed a "reasonable" ideology (Chapter 10) can learn new ideas and skills as the job market and personal preferences change. Rather than expecting already burdened educational institutions to assume the primary function of occupational preparation, business and industry should be encouraged to assume more responsibility for training and retraining their employees.

As a means of helping students integrate academic and on-the-job learning, some high schools and colleges have adopted work-study programs and courses in experiential education. Depending upon institutional policies, students receive academic credit and sometimes remuneration as well.

Career Counseling   Since the 1970s there have been some attempts to move career education into the classroom and out of the guidance offices, counseling centers, and placement offices. While these changes have occurred in part for the reasons we have just discussed, some of the impetus for change has no doubt come from studies which indicate that guidance counselors are not as effective occupational counselors as they might be. For example, one study showed that 50 percent of eleventh graders surveyed in 33 states reported that they had received no help in career planning from their guidance counselors (Noeth et al., 1975). In addition, many career counselors have stereotypical and sexist attitudes about careers for women and men. For example, girls and women who elect nontraditional careers—engineering, science—often meet considerable resistance from educational and career counselors (Harway & Astin, 1977).

In fairness to guidance counselors, it's important to state that they usually have too many students to see, are required to spend much of their time on administrative tasks, and must spend much of their time with a minority of students with serious problems. First, then, there is a need for increased funding to lighten work loads so that counselors have the time for career counseling and education. In addition, there is a need for educating counselors about nonsexist vocational testing and career counseling, including the availability of computerized systems of occupational decision-making which students can use on their own or in conjunction with counselors (Cassel & Mehail, 1973).

Work Experience

As we have seen, assuming financial responsibility for oneself is usually taken to be an important criterion of adult status. In the United States youth typically make the transition from full-time school to full-time work between the ages of 16 and 24.

More teenagers are working today than at any time since 1940 (Greenberger, Steinberg, & Vaux, 1981). In 1979, the labor force participation rate for 14- and 15-year-olds was 21 percent, for 16- and 17-year-olds, 49 percent, and for 18- and 19-year-olds, 67 percent (Westcott, 1981). In a national sample of high school seniors in 1983, the typical number of hours worked per week was between 16 and 20 (Bachman, Johnston, & O'Malley, in press). Many more would like to have part-time jobs, but cannot find them. Most adolescents want part-time or short-term jobs which mesh with their school schedules. This fact dictates that most will work in service or clerical jobs and will, consequently, receive relatively low wages.

Young people work for a variety of reasons: to earn extra money, to gain some financial autonomy from parents, to experience personal responsibility, to acquire useful job skills, to evaluate skills and interests with regard to long-term career choices, and to broaden their social lives.

Two models have been advanced to describe the effect of early work experience on adolescent occupational socialization (Steinberg, Greenberger, Vaux, & Ruggiero, 1981). The *occupational competence model* maintains that early work experience produces more knowledgeable, competent, and employable workers. The *occupational cynicism model* holds that since adolescents are most likely to work in menial and

Large numbers of adolescents work at part-time jobs.

dehumanizing jobs, working at an early age will lead only to cynicism about work, materialism, and the acceptance of unethical practices in the work place.

Results of several studies generally support the occupational competence model, but provide partial support for the cynicism model as well. For example, working adolescents score higher on certain work-related attitudes (persistence and competence on the job) and on practical knowledge about work (Steinberg et al., 1981). Working appeared to have little impact on long-range occupational reward values (SES and gender are probably more important factors here). On the other hand, workers were more cynical than nonworkers and were more accepting of unethical business practices than were nonworkers. There were no differences between workers and nonworkers on materialistic attitudes (Steinberg et al., 1981). In addition, it has been found that working youth learn to be punctual and responsible, but don't develop more tolerant attitudes toward individual and cultural differences (Steinberg et al., 1981).

Laurence Steinberg and his colleagues (1981) observed some noteworthy sex differences in the development of autonomy. For example, they found that working high school girls showed an increase in self-reliance and a decrease in family closeness, whereas boys showed no increase in self-reliance and an increase in family closeness. Working girls developed more interest than boys in future jobs with opportunities for independent decision-making, and girls developed higher educational expectations, while boys developed lowered expectations. Reasons for these sex differences aren't clear, but the authors speculated that starting to work at an early age may be inconsistent with sex-role expectations for girls, and consistent with those for boys and with male socialization for adulthood. Accordingly, taking a job may be seen and experienced as an independent (yet not rebellious) act for girls and may encourage the development of autonomy. For males working is viewed as an act of conformity and, thus, doesn't necessarily facilitate the development of self-reliance.

The gains of working need to be weighed against the costs. For example, it has been found that early employment leads to less involvement in school, less emotional closeness with friends, and increases in the use of cigarettes and marijuana (Steinberg et al., 1981). The time spent working seemed to be the most important factor predicting these above outcomes. In this context, it has been suggested that 15- and 16-year-olds limit working to 15 to 20 hours per week during the school year in order to optimize the balance between the costs and benefits of working (Steinberg et al., 1981).

In those instances where adolescents have no choice about working or where they appear to have little interest in school, additional problems arise. To combat these difficulties and to increase the connections between school and the work place, the Panel on Youth (a subcommittee of the President's Science Advisory Committee) has recommended that young people be given more opportunities for work experience (Coleman et al., 1974). More specifically, they have suggested that the minimum wage be lowered, more work-study programs be developed, and more flexible school and work schedules be permitted.

Class, Racial, and Ethnic Group Membership

Socioeconomic status has been found to be an important factor related to an adolescent's educational and occupational aspirations, although it appears to have less influence on girls' occupational aspirations because of differential sex-role expectations (Marini, 1978; Marini & Greenberger, 1978a, 1978b).

Socioeconomic status influences males' vocational aspirations for several reasons. First, adolescents usually aspire to educational levels and occupational levels which are familiar. Second, socioeconomic status appears to determine the social acceptability of certain occupations. Middle- and upper-class parents and peers, for example, would be likely to discourage a boy's interest in lower-status jobs. Third, socioeconomic status influences adolescents' perceptions of the occupational opportunities available to them.

A study of Wisconsin high school male seniors found that the lower third of students in terms of SES aspired to high-status occupations significantly less often than would be expected by chance and the upper third aspired to the high-status occupations significantly more often than would be expected by chance (Little, 1967). Thus, it appears that lower-SES adolescents have lower educational and career aspirations than their middle-class peers. However, it is not clear that their lowered aspirations are due to being more familiar with lower-status jobs or to a realistic perception of their chances for higher-status jobs. Lower-SES youths *are* less likely to attain high-status jobs for many reasons: poor academic preparation, fewer opportunities for advanced education because of poor academic preparation and financial constraints, and lack of familiarity and ease with middle-class values and social skills (Borow, 1976). In response to the realistic perception of their deprived circumstances and opportunities for advancement, many lower-SES adolescents reduce their expectations of higher educational and occupational attainment. For example, one study found that between the third and eighth grades, the level of education perceived as necessary to get a good job decreased among a group of low-SES students (from college and beyond to high school and college) and essentially remained the same (college and beyond) among a group of high-SES students (Harvey & Kerin, 1978). This same pattern of findings was observed when low- and high-SES students were asked to indicate the educational level they hoped to attain.

In addition, we should reiterate here that higher SES is associated with higher academic performance which, in turn, is associated with higher educational and vocational aspirations and attainment.

Because racial and ethnic group membership is closely related to socioeconomic status, it is difficult to sort out the independent effects of the two factors. According to several previously cited studies, it seems likely that there are differences among white, black, and Mexican-Americans in the family dynamics related to the development of occupational and educational aspirations (Allen, 1978; Fields, 1981).

PERSONALITY DETERMINANTS OF OCCUPATIONAL ASPIRATIONS

Intelligence, Aptitudes, and Interests

Generally, it has been found that more intelligent adolescents have higher educational and career aspirations than their less intelligent counterparts, although this is less likely to be true for girls (Marini, 1978). Also, brighter adolescents make more realistic career decisions, that is, they are more likely to choose occupations consistent with their actual capabilities, interests, and job opportunities (Hurlock, 1973).

In a summary of research in this area Margaret Mooney Marini (1978) reported that the degree of career commitment among adolescent girls has been found to be positively related to academic ability, especially mathematical ability. Also, it appears that bright females are more likely to maintain or raise their career aspirations over time, compared to their less intelligent peers.

Some occupations require particular aptitudes and talents. For example, manual dexterity may be needed for some jobs, while others may require artistic or musical talents. Typically, various psychological tests are used to measure aptitudes and special abilities as a means of determining the likelihood of a person's success in a particular job.

We would expect particular interest patterns to relate to people's job choices and success. Vocational interest tests measure the degree to which a person's interests parallel the interests of individuals already successfully working in specific jobs. Matching interests suggest career choices.

Since occupational interests and other qualities (such as ability) are not always related, career decisions should take into account more than interests.

Locus of Control

The concept of locus of control (of reinforcement) refers to an individual's beliefs about his or her actions as causes of events (Rotter, 1966). People who believe that what happens to them is a result of their own actions have an *internal locus of control* (the source of reinforcement is internal). People who believe that their successes or failures are due to luck, fate, chance, or the "whims of powerful others" have an *external locus of control* (the source of reinforcement is external).

A relationship has been found between "work personality" (defined as attitudes and behaviors associated with job performance, career choice, and acceptance of responsibility), locus of control, and career maturity (Gardner, Beatty, & Bigelow, 1981). Among other things, the authors of this study suggested that a number of adolescents who have career difficulties—not knowing what they want to do, quitting jobs because they find them boring, irresponsibility on the job—may believe that their career problems are unrelated to their actions (external locus of control). Moreover, they cite evidence in support of a life planning–career development seminar as a means of changing locus of control and career maturity of such high school students. Thus, it appears possible to alter locus of control and, thereby, improve job-related attitudes, performance, and career maturity in some adolescents.

Achievement Motivation

Achievement motivation refers to the need to excel in one's undertakings and to achieve success according to an internalized standard of excellence. Psychologists usually measure the need to succeed by the Thematic Apperception Test. Individuals are asked to tell or write a story about a picture. Those whose stories have themes of working toward a goal or feeling good about accomplishments are scored as having a high need for achievement; people whose stories don't include these themes are considered to be low in this need.

Early research in this area found that achievement motivation scores in men could be increased if the experimenter's pretest instructions stressed the relationship between the subject's story themes and the qualities of intelligence and leadership. For female subjects, these kinds of "arousing" instructions had either no or contradictory effects. Rather than exploring these sex differences, research on achievement motivation began to focus primarily on men. It was not until some years later that interest in women's achievement motivation was renewed through a now well-known study by Matina Horner (1969).

In Horner's study college women were asked to write a story based on a sentence (rather than a picture): "After first-term finals, Anne finds herself at the top of her medical school class." She also asked college men to write a story based on the same sentence, but about "John." The results of her study showed that 90 percent of the men appeared comfortable with John's accomplishment and predicted future successes for him in medicine, but 65 percent of the women wrote stories which contained images or allusions reflecting a motive to avoid success. The most common theme, for example, was that Anne's academic success would lead to social rejection (loss of friends, "datability," and "marriageability"). Other common themes concerned subjects' doubts about their femininity, despair about their success, and guilt.

Since Horner's original study, many researchers have looked at the question of sex differences in achievement motivation with varying and inconsistent results. For example, David Tresemer (1974) found that in 61 studies of female subjects the proportion of women who wrote stories with fear-of-success themes varied from 11 to 88 percent; in 36 studies which used male and female subjects the proportion of (male and female) subjects who wrote stories with fear-of-success themes ranged from 14 to 86 percent. Even though these findings demonstrate that the fear-of-success phenomenon is not limited to women, the nature of the fear appears to be different for men and women. Whereas women associate success with social rejection, men seem to question whether striving for success is really worth the effort (Hoffman, 1974b).

Other interpretations of fear of success have suggested that it is not success that women (or men) fear, but deviation from traditional sex roles (Huston-Stein & Bailey, 1973; Peplau, 1976; Tresemer, 1974). This interpretation appears to have some basis in reality since studies have shown that fear-of-success imagery drops when stories state that half of Anne's medical school classmates are women (Katz, 1973) or that Anne is at the top of her class, but not in medical school (Alper, 1974).

In addition, it has been suggested that women's fear-of-success themes may actually reflect their realistic assessments of social realities rather than deep-seated motives (Condry & Dyer, 1976). Finally, a follow-up study of Horner's subjects showed that the women who had been high in fear of success as undergraduates were more likely to marry, to have children, and to become pregnant for the first time when they and their boyfriends or husbands were on the verge of success (L.W. Hoffman, 1977). Still, the women's fears of success had greatly diminished over the nine years and their actual educational and occupational attainments didn't differ whether they were high or low in fear of success.

It is also interesting to note the differences which have been found in achievement motivation between black and white women and black and white men. For example, Horner (1970) found that while 64 percent of white women and 10 percent of white men demonstrated the motive to avoid success, 29 percent of black women and 67 percent of black men fell into this category. Here, we are probably seeing the effects of a combination of sexism and racism. Black women are typically seen as less threatening than black men by those in power (white males). Therefore, black women are not as discouraged from achievement as either white women or black men. Also, it appears that successful black women are not viewed as threatening to black men as are white women to white men. Because of this, black women's achievement is not so likely to lead to rejection by black men (Weston & Mednick, 1970).

GENDER AND CAREER ASPIRATIONS AND OPPORTUNITIES

Labor Force Participation and Career Orientation

Sex-role expectations have a strong influence on life-style aspirations. Males tend to develop values of power, status, and wealth as criteria of instrumental mastery and masculinity, whereas females develop favorable attitudes toward nurturance, intuition, and childbearing (Vogel, Broverman, Broverman, Clarkson, & Rosenkrantz, 1970). While girls and women are permitted and sometimes encouraged to develop at least some skills associated with the masculine role (work outside the home, for example), males are usually discouraged from developing skills associated with the female role (emotional expressiveness and nurturance, for example). Moreover, males are perceived as choosing "masculine" occupations, whereas females are seen as able to enter either a "masculine" or "feminine" career (White & Ouellette, 1980).

Recently, there is some evidence that a strong career orientation may be declining in importance, at least among college-educated males. At the same time, more men seem to be giving increased importance to family life and leisure-time pursuits (Rogers, 1981; Yankelovich, 1978). Similarly, women appear to be developing increased interests in higher education and careers (Van Dusen & Sheldon, 1976). For example, in 1970 women comprised 41 percent of the college student population, but by 1982 this figure had risen to 52 percent (U.S. Bureau of the Census, 1983).

Between 1950 and 1982 the number of women in the labor force more than doubled, and between 1972 and 1982 it increased by 47 percent from 33 to 48 million (U.S. Bureau of the Census, 1983). Also, the number of women workers is predicted to grow faster than the total labor force through 1990. There are a number of reasons for the increased participation of women: economic necessity, trends toward smaller families, increases in the number of families headed by women due to higher divorce rates, increases in part-time job opportunities and in white-collar jobs in which women are primarily employed, changing attitudes toward careers for women, and legislation prohibiting sex discrimination.

Increasing numbers of women are entering nontraditional or male-dominated jobs, such as the skilled crafts (carpentry, mechanical and electrical trades), the professions (law, medicine, dentistry, engineering), sales, management and administration, and finance (bank officers, financial managers). At the same time men are shifting into female-dominated jobs, such as librarians, elementary school teachers, nurses, and telephone operators (U.S. Bureau of the Census, 1983). These trends have important implications for today's young people.

More women than men are attending college today.

Barriers to Increased Participation and Higher Aspirations of Females

Most women remain in low-status and low-paying jobs. For example, 80 percent of all clerical workers are women, but only 25 percent of managers are women (see Figure 12.1). Moreover, although their numbers are increasing, still relatively few women are employed in such high prestige occupations as medicine (15 percent), law (15 percent), architecture (9 percent), and engineering (6 percent) (U.S. Bureau of the Census, 1983).

Also, while incomes increase with educational attainment for both sexes, there are rather amazing salary differentials between the sexes. For example, a woman with five or more years of university education earns only slightly more than a man with one to three years of high school (Mellor, 1984)! In 1982, among year-round, full-time workers, women's average earnings were only 59 percent of men's—the median annual salary for women was $12,001, compared to $20,260 for men (U.S. Bureau of the Census, 1983). Table 12.2 compares the incomes of men and women in the same job categories, again revealing substantial discrepancies.

Obviously, then, there are still barriers which discourage women from increased participation in the work force, particularly in the more personally and economically rewarding positions. Some of these barriers are external in nature—relative lack of opportunity for challenging, high-status, and high-paying positions, sexual harassment, and sex discrimination. For example, a number of studies have found that males in elementary school and college believe that skillful performance by a female on a "masculine" task is due to luck rather than ability and that female physicians are less competent than male physicians (Deux & Emswiller, 1974; Feldman-Summers &

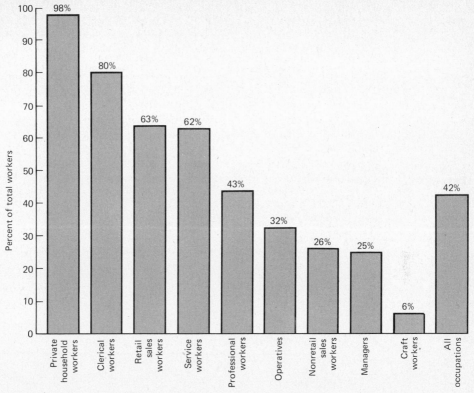

Figure 12.1 Most women are employed in low-status and low-paying jobs. *Source:* Women's Bureau, U.S. Department of Labor (1980, October). "Women are underrepresented as managers and skilled craft workers. Washington, D.C.: U.S. Government Printing Office.

Kiesler, 1974). Moreover, while attitudes about women's roles are becoming more liberal, adolescents (particularly males) still hold stereotypical beliefs in this area (Ditkoff, 1979). For example, a national survey of 1983 college freshmen reported that 32 percent of males but only 17 percent of females agreed "strongly or somewhat" that "The activities of married women are best confined to the home and the family." This same survey also found that 88 percent of males and 97 percent of females agreed "strongly or somewhat" that "Women should receive the same salary and opportunities for advancement as men in comparable positions" (Astin, Green, Korn, & Maier, 1983). See Table 12.3 for related findings.

Also, many high-status and high-salaried jobs require substantial commitments of time and energy (and often travel). Such requirements pose serious problems and role conflicts for women who have strong commitments to household responsibilities and child-rearing and who are either single or whose husbands don't assume an equal share of these responsibilities. Child care can provide some relief in such cases, but it's often difficult to come by and costly.

Other barriers to increased labor force participation and higher aspirations among females are internal in nature, that is, they are a result of learned psychological attitudes and dispositions. For example, females often attribute their own successful

Table 12.2 MEDIAN WEEKLY EARNINGS OF FULL-TIME WORKERS, 1982 ANNUAL AVERAGES

Occupational Group	Weekly earnings (in dollars)		Women's earnings as percent of men's
	Women	Men	
Professional, technical workers	342	484	71
Managers, administrators (except farm)	309	507	61
Sales workers	212	383	55
Clerical workers	236	347	68
Craft workers	247	383	64
Operatives (except transport)	198	311	64
Transport equipment operatives	237	328	72
Laborers (except farm)	205	248	83
Service workers (except private household)	180	246	73
Private household workers	111	(a)	—
Nonfarm laborers	205	248	83
Farm workers	174	192	91

[a]Fewer than 50,000 men.
Source: Adapted from Earl F. Mellor. (1984). Investigating the differences in weekly earnings of women and men. *Monthly Labor Review, 107*(6), 20–23.

Table 12.3 PERCENT OF MALES AND FEMALES AGREEING WITH STEREOTYPICAL STATEMENTS CONCERNING WOMEN'S ROLES

Statement	Males		Females	
	1973[a]	1978[b]	1973[a]	1978[b]
1. The most important work for a woman is that of wife and mother.	87	65	61	36
2. A career should be more important to a man than a woman.	65	63	47	25
3. Affectionate, motherly, housewifey women are more admired by men than career women.	59	46	41	36
4. Women are happier when they work for men rather than for other women.	31	36	64	39
5. Competing with men tends to make a woman less feminine.	67	60	42	34
6. Women should not work outside the home except in cases of financial necessity.	56	38	20	20
7. Men generally like women who are not too intelligent or competitive on the job.	50	33	43	32
8. Men are happier when they work for other men than for women.	70	78	73	71

[a]Tenth, eleventh, and twelfth graders.
[b]Eleventh graders.
Source: Adapted from Gail S. Ditkoff. (1979). Stereotypes of adolescents toward the working woman. *Adolescence, 14*(54), 278. Copyright 1979 by Libra Publishers, Inc. Adapted by permission.

performance and that of other women to luck rather than skill (Deux & Emswiller, 1974), and high school upperclass females tend to downgrade successful females in relation to unsuccessful females, while they upgrade successful males in relation to unsuccessful males (Feather & Simon, 1975).

Female Life-Style Orientations

The societal norms which view the husband/father as the primary economic provider and the wife/mother as the primary helpmate, household worker, and child-care worker cause role conflicts for men and women, but especially for women (Bardwick, 1971; Baruch, 1972). One study examined college women's attempts at reconciling these conflicts through various life-style orientations (Angrist, 1972). Five life-style orientations were identified:

1. *Careerists* aspired to a full-time career along with the roles of wife and mother both at the time of college entrance and graduation. They had educated and working mothers, were interested in working in male-dominated occupations, and believed that others could assist or replace them in household and child-care responsibilities.
2. *Noncareerists* wanted to be full-time wives and mothers, along with some participation in leisure and work activities. In college they were much concerned with selecting a mate and became engaged during their senior year. These women viewed jobs as a means of ensuring financial security if this ever became necessary.
3. *Converts* had no career aspirations as college freshmen, but developed them during their sophomore, junior, or senior years, primarily as a function of their late-emerging competence as students. They were willing to delay marriage and to make flexible work arrangements after marriage.
4. *Defectors* entered college with career aspirations, but shifted to a full-time wife and mother orientation by the time of graduation. They were typically poor students who were not interested in finishing college, but who wanted to marry young and have children.
5. *Shifters* had inconsistent career orientations, experiencing conflict between career and family roles, perhaps because they were top students and also held traditional views of husbands' and wives' responsibilities.

The percent of women in each of these categories at the time of graduation can be seen in Figure 12.2. At the time of graduation and at the time of college entrance, more women had a noncareerist orientation (46 percent) than a careerist orientation (40 percent), and 14 percent were still uncertain of their goals. It seems that the college experience encouraged some women (22 percent) who were previously uncommitted to a career to develop such a commitment. On the other hand, 13 percent of the students moved away from career commitments during the four-year period.

A follow-up study conducted seven years after these women graduated revealed that 50 percent saw themselves as careerists and wanted to work, despite having young children; 28 percent were either currently working or had worked for some time during the seven-year follow-up period, but had no specific career goals. Only 23 percent had

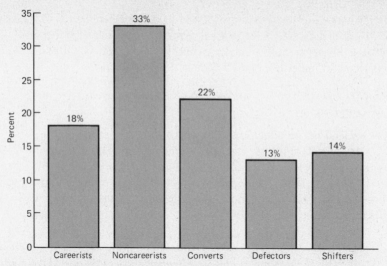

Figure 12.2   Life-style aspirations of female students at the time of graduation (N = 87). *Source:* Adapted from Shirley S. Angrist (1972). Variations in women's adult aspirations during college. *Journal of Marriage and the Family, 34,* 468. Copyrighted 1972 by the National Council on Family Relations, 1219 University Avenue Southeast, Minneapolis, Minnesota 55414. Reprinted by permission.

a noncareerist orientation, engaging in leisure activities and working only occasionally. Thus, many women's career interests increased as they grew older and more realistic about life-style choices and as their child-rearing responsibilities diminished (Almquist, Angrist, & Mickelsen, 1980).

CAREER OPPORTUNITIES FOR TODAY'S ADOLESCENTS

Increasing Adolescents' Awareness of Occupational Information

As we have seen, today's adolescents are uninformed and often unrealistic about career requirements and opportunities. They also typically know very little about their own skills and interests and about the process of occupational decision making (Borow, 1976; Noeth et al., 1975). Moreover, the current economic climate places increased pressures on adolescents to get a job—any job—thus discouraging them from thoughtful career-planning.

In the past young people could rely more on their parents for career information and many simply followed in their parents' "career footsteps" (Mead's model of the postfigurative culture). Because of changes in the economy and the job market, parents are less able to help their children with advice about specific careers.

Consequently, today's adolescents need a variety of resources to aid them in career-planning. One study investigated Alabama high school students' sources of career information: parents, friends, counselors, teachers, books, and the media (Bain & Fottler, 1978). The authors found that students in college preparatory programs, regardless of sex or ethnic group membership, used all six sources significantly more than students in the general high school program. Also, students who had volunteer or part-time jobs used all sources more than those with no work experience, again pointing to the positive role that part-time work experience can play for adolescents. Girls used all six sources more than boys and relied especially on friends, teachers, books, and magazines.

Today's adolescents will have to learn to take more initiative in seeking out career information. This means that high school and college students need to familiarize themselves with career counseling services in guidance offices, counseling centers, and placement offices. Also, they need to know about available printed resources. Important publications which should be on hand in school and public libraries include:

1. *Occupational Outlook Handbook.* This government document, published every two years by the U.S. Bureau of Labor Statistics, is a comprehensive guide to occupations. It includes job descriptions, education and training requirements, advancement possibilities, salaries, and employment outlooks for 250 occupations. In addition, it describes other sources of career education, training, and financial aid information as well as resources for special groups such as youth, the handicapped, veterans, women, and minorities.
2. *Occupational Outlook Quarterly.* This bulletin, published four times a year by the U.S. Bureau of Labor Statistics, is intended to be an up-dated supplement to the *Occupational Outlook Handbook.*
3. *Monthly Labor Review.* This periodical, published by the U.S. Bureau of Labor Statistics, provides current labor statistics and articles describing labor activity in the United States.

Today, adolescents need a variety of resources for career planning.

For local area employment projections, young people should contact the local offices of their state employment service.

The Job Outlook for Today's Youth

Current Trends   The drop in the birthrate during the 1960s has meant that the composition of the current labor force has changed—progressively fewer young people (16 to 24 years) will be in the labor force between 1980 and 1990 (U.S. Bureau of Labor Statistics, 1983). Also, the number of women joining the labor force will continue to increase during the next decade. Of course, employment opportunities are closely tied to the condition of the economy, so long-term predictions are always somewhat risky.

Today's economic climate has had serious effects on youth unemployment nation-wide. Some 2.4 million youth no longer in school but with at least a high school education are looking for work and another 1 million students are looking for jobs (Young, 1981). Black youth have been particularly hard-hit in this area. For example, recent estimates of unemployment rates for black high school dropouts were 44 percent (22 percent for whites); 24 percent for black high school graduates (10 percent for whites); and 23 percent for black college students (8 percent for whites)—see Figure 12.3. Unfortunately, current predictions suggest that high youth unemployment rates will continue throughout the 1980s, particularly for those with less education.

Geographical shifts in population affect the supply of and demand for workers in local job markets. For example, during the decade of the 1980s, the population of the Northeast region of the United States is expected to decrease by 1.7 percent, compared with a 22 percent increase in the West (U.S. Bureau of the Census, 1983).

Occupations are usually divided into the categories of *white-collar* (professional and technical, managerial and administrative, sales, and clerical jobs), *blue-collar* (craft, operative, and transport workers; laborers), *service* (private household workers; food, cleaning, health, personal, and protective service workers), and *farm* workers.

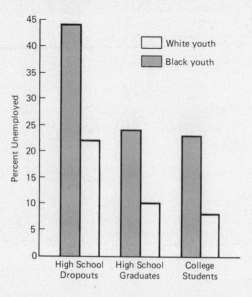

Figure 12.3 Unemployment rates for different age groups and educational levels. *Source:* Anne McDougall Young (1981). Labor force activity among students, graduates, and dropouts in 1980. *Monthly Labor Review, 104*(7), 32.

(For descriptions of these job categories, see Table 12.4.) Since 1960, the number of white-collar and service workers has risen rapidly. In contrast, the blue-collar work force has grown slowly and the number of farm workers has declined.

Currently, job-market "watchers" are predicting that the average rate of growth of all occupations between 1982 and 1995 will be about 25 percent (U.S. Bureau of Labor Statistics, 1984b). As can be seen from Figure 12.4, occupations which are expected to show increases above the 25-percent rate fall primarily in the white-collar occupations and the service worker areas (non-private household workers). All blue-collar jobs are expected to show increases but at rates level with or lower than the 25-percent rate of overall growth. The employment of private household workers and farm workers is expected to decrease substantially (U.S. Bureau of Labor Statistics, 1984a). Many of these trends are, in part, a result of increased mechanization.

Implications for Youth   The current labor predictions mean that young people must give special consideration to education and training in order to match the more specialized nature of today's job market. For example, the educational attainment of the labor force in 1982 was 12.6 years (U.S. Bureau of the Census, 1983). This means that high school dropouts are likely to be at a serious disadvantage when seeking jobs that offer better pay or advancement.

Although the better jobs will continue to go to college graduates, young people should be forewarned that more education will not necessarily guarantee a person a

Table 12.4   OCCUPATIONAL CATEGORIES

White-collar workers

Professional and technical workers	Highly trained workers such as scientists, engineers, medical practitioners, teachers, entertainers, pilots, and accountants
Managers and administrators	Bank officers and managers, buyers, credit managers, and self-employed business operators
Sales workers	Workers in retail stores, manufacturing and wholesale firms, insurance companies, and real estate agencies
Clerical workers	Bank tellers, bookkeepers, accounting clerks, cashiers, secretaries, and typists

Blue-collar workers

Craft workers	Highly skilled workers such as carpenters, tool-and-die makers, instrument makers, all-round machinists, electricians, and automobile mechanics
Operatives (except transport)	Production workers, such as assemblers, painters, and welders
Transport operatives	Workers who drive buses, trucks, taxies, and forklifts, as well as parking attendants and sailors
Laborers	Construction laborers, freight and stock handlers, garbage collectors

Service workers

Private household service workers	Housekeepers, child-care workers, maids, and servants
Other service workers	Firefighters, janitors, cosmetologists, bartenders, etc.
Farm workers	Farmers, farm managers, and farm laborers

Source: Compiled from information in U.S. Bureau of Labor Statistics. *Occupational Outlook Handbook, 1982–1983.* Washington, D.C.: U.S. Government Printing Office, 1982.

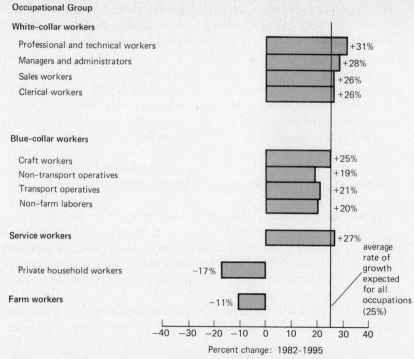

Figure 12.4   Projected change in employment, by major occupational group, 1982–1995. *Source:* Adapted from U.S. Bureau of Labor Statistics, (March 1984). *Employment Projections for 1995.* Washington, D.C.: U.S. Government Printing Office.

higher-paying or higher-status job (Ginzberg, 1980; U.S. Bureau of Labor Statistics, 1982). Not only are there now more college graduates than ever before, but the occupations typically filled by them (professional, technical, and managerial) have not expanded rapidly enough to absorb their growing numbers. Consequently, 20 percent of college graduates who entered the labor market between 1970 and 1982 took jobs not usually requiring a bachelor's degree, and the number of graduates in clerical, lower-level sales, and blue-collar occupations grew (U.S. Bureau of Labor Statistics, 1984b). This trend is likely to continue.

Increased levels of job dissatisfaction among this group are predicted to result in high occupational mobility (rather than unemployment). A proposed solution to job dissatisfaction for some youth is the option of apprenticeships in skilled trades such as carpentry and electrical work. Apprenticeships last from one to six years, during which time the worker is paid a full-time salary while he or she learns a trade by working with a skilled craftsperson (Egan, 1978). Completion of an apprenticeship program can provide a person with a personally satisfying and highly marketable skill that usually leads to a good job with a good salary.

Because of the rapid turnover in jobs and job requirements, many of today's young people will need to reorient their thinking from the traditional view of a highly stable or lifelong career commitment to a more flexible attitude toward occupational choices and long-term career plans. However, a national survey of 1983 male and

Many college-educated youth can expect to be underemployed.

female high school graduates suggests that such an orientation is not widely held among today's youth. For example, 67 percent of the girls and 64 percent of the boys felt that it was important for a job to have a "predictable, secure future" (Bachman, Johnston, & O'Malley, in press).

As might be expected, due primarily to economic conditions, adolescents display attitudes that suggest an increasing concern for their own private welfare, rather than that of the larger society. Such a trend is consistent with Arthur Levine's (1980) "lifeboat mentality" discussed in Chapter 10. For example, the importance ratings for a variety of job characteristics for a national sample of male and female high school seniors in 1976, 1980, and 1983 can be seen in Table 12.5. It is apparent that, in general, males and females say they want the same things from a job. Noteworthy sex differences are evident, however, in that fewer women are concerned about earning a good deal of money (51 percent versus 61 percent of men); more women feel that it's important

Table 12.5 HIGH SCHOOL SENIORS' RATINGS OF IMPORTANT THINGS IN A JOB (PERCENT RATING "VERY IMPORTANT," CLASSES OF 1977, 1980, 1983)

	Males			Females		
	1977	**1980**	**1983**	**1977**	**1980**	**1983**
Interesting to do	84	85	86	92	91	89
Uses skills and abilities	65	68	69	76	76	75
Predictable, secure future	62	64	64	62	65	67
Good chances for advancement	59	65	65	54	61	65
See results of what you can do	55	54	54	61	64	61
Chance to earn a good deal of money	54	58	61	40	50	51
Chance to make friends	47	47	44	61	59	57
Worthwhile to society	39	36	39	50	51	51
A job most people look up to and respect	32	36	36	36	39	41
High status, prestige	22	26	29	18	24	27

Source: Adaption of Table 2 from Chapter by Jerald G. Bachman, Lloyd D. Johnston, and Patrick M. O'Malley. Recent findings from Monitoring the Future: A continuing study of the life styles and values of youth. In Frank M. Andrews (Ed.), *Research on the quality of life* (tentative title; forthcoming in 1985). Ann Arbor, MI: Institute for Social Research of the University of Michigan.

that a job provide a chance to make friends (57 percent versus 44 percent of men); and more women than men feel that it's important that a job be worthwhile to society (51 percent versus 39 percent of men).

SUMMARY

Economic and social factors have produced a breach between the day-to-day experiences of young people and the world of work in industrial and postindustrial societies.

The trait measurement and matching model, Super's self-concept theory, and Ginzberg's theory of vocational development all provide useful views of career development.

Adolescents' career aspirations are related to those of their parents. Both fathers and mothers influence both their sons' and daughters' career aspirations.

Peers usually have less impact than parents on adolescents' vocational aspirations, but quite often parental and peer aspirations are similar so they reinforce one another.

Some schools have instituted career education programs to help adolescents with career-planning and developing immediately marketable skills.

Early work experience has been shown to have both positive and negative effects on adolescents.

Socioeconomic status is related to educational and vocational aspirations, but this is more true for boys than girls. The family dynamics related to the development of achievement motivation appear to differ among white, black, and Mexican-American families.

Intelligence, aptitudes, interests, locus of control, and achievement motivation are related to career aspirations.

Recently, social and economic changes have resulted in many more women choosing to work outside the home. Also, women are seeking higher status, higher paying, nontraditional or male-dominated jobs. Still, most women remain in low-status and low-paying jobs, and even when men and women hold the same job, women are likely to be paid less.

The rapid turnover in jobs and job requirements means that many adolescents will need to develop more flexible attitudes about occupational choices and long-term career plans. Young people will need at least a high school education to obtain better-paying jobs.

GLOSSARY

achievement motivation   The need to excel in one's undertakings and to achieve success according to an internalized standard of excellence.

blue-collar occupations   Craft, operative, transport, and laborer jobs.

career education   Programs in schools designed to inform students about current economic and occupational trends, to train in the process of making career decisions, and to teach them marketable skills.

external locus of control (Rotter)   The belief that what happens in one's life is due to chance, luck, or forces beyond one's control.

internal locus of control (Rotter)   The belief that what happens in one's life can be controlled by one's own actions.

occupational competence model   The idea that early work experience produces more knowledgeable and competent workers.

occupational cynicism model   The idea that early work experience produces negative and materialistic attitudes about work.

optimizing satisfactions model of vocational development (Ginzberg)   The idea that career choice is a lifelong process of optimizing personal preferences in the context of job requirements.

self-concept model of vocational development (Super)   The idea that career choice is a reflection of a person's self-concept.

trait measurement and matching model of vocational development   The idea that particular personality traits are the factors which determine an individual's interest in particular occupations.

underemployed   Term applied to people who are overeducated for the jobs they hold.

white-collar occupations   Professional and technical, managerial and administrative, sales, and clerical jobs.

GETTING INVOLVED: Exercises and General Questions to Consider

EXERCISE 1: WORK VALUES

The purpose of this exercise is to help you clarify your work values. For this exercise, use Worksheet 12.1 below.

Worksheet 12.1. WORK VALUES

Instructions: Read through the six work values listed below and reflect on them. Your task is to indicate how important each value is to you *at the present time.* Use the following categories to evaluate each statement: highly important, moderately important, neither important or unimportant, moderately unimportant, and highly unimportant. Write your ratings to the left of each statement.

_____ Social status of job (social significance of one's job)
_____ Activity (desire to keep busy on the job)
_____ Job involvement (taking active interest in one's work)
_____ Upward striving (seeking high-level jobs and standard of living)
_____ Earnings (financial rewards of working)
_____ Pride in work (satisfaction from doing a job well)

Source: Adapted from Jan P. Wijting, Carole R. Arnold, and Kelly A. Conrad. (1978). Generational differences in work values between parents and children and between boys and girls across grade levels 6, 9, 10, and 12. *Journal of Vocational Behavior, 12,* 249. Copyright 1978 by Academic Press. Adapted by permission.

After you have finished the worksheet, think about the degree to which your current career interests reflect your work values as characterized by this exercise. Are there important inconsistencies between the two? If so, you might consider possible implications for career choice.

EXERCISE 2: ATTITUDES ABOUT WOMEN'S ROLES

The purpose of this exercise is to give you some perspective on your attitudes toward women's roles. For this exercise, use Worksheet 12.2 on the following page.

When you have completed the worksheet, compare your attitudes with the responses shown in Table 12.3 on p. 336.

GENERAL QUESTIONS TO CONSIDER

1. How do you feel about today's unemployment and "underemployment" problems? What are the chances you will be able to find an interesting and challenging career, in your opinion?
2. How do you feel work will fit into your life-style. Do you plan to devote most of your time and energy to your career? To your family? Do you anticipate conflicts between career and family roles?
3. If you have held a job, consider the benefits of your work experience. Have there been any negative consequences?
4. Has your mother or your father (or someone else) been a stronger influence on your career aspirations? Explain in what way.

Worksheet 12.2   ATTITUDES ABOUT WOMEN'S ROLES

Instructions: Below are listed eight statements about the roles of women. Your task is to evaluate your feelings about each statement *at the present time.* So that you may compare your responses with those in Table 12.3, simply indicate whether you agree or disagree with each statement. Write in your response to the left of each statement.

_____ 1. The most important work for a woman is that of wife and mother.

_____ 2. A career should be more important to a man than a woman.

_____ 3. Affectionate, motherly, housewifey women are more admired by men than career women.

_____ 4. Women are happiest when they work for men rather than for other women.

_____ 5. Competing with men tends to make women less feminine.

_____ 6. Women should not work outside the home except in cases of financial necessity.

_____ 7. Men generally like women who are not too intelligent or competitive on the job.

_____ 8. Men are happier when they work for other men than for women.

Source: Adapted from Virginia H. Frye and Siegfried C. Dietz. (1973). Attitudes of high school students toward traditional views of women workers. *Journal of the Student Personnel Association for Teacher Education, 11*(3), 104. Copyright 1973 by the American Personnel and Guidance Association. Adapted by permission.

5. Does your mother work? Does she like working? How does your father seem to feel about your mother's working? How has this situation influenced your attitudes about women working?

6. How are the child-care and household responsibilities in your family handled? Do your mother and father share these tasks equally? What are *your* attitudes? Discuss the implications of this issue for couples' relationships and career choices.

7. What kind of career programs or services, if any, did your high school have? Did you make use of them? Why or why not? How effective did you find them?

8. Based on your own experience, what recommendations would you give to high school guidance counselors to increase their effectiveness in career counseling?

9. Do you have any suggestions for increasing the participation of adolescents in part-time jobs (for example, flexible school and work schedules)?

10. Reflect on some of the reasons that women are employed in low-status and low-paying jobs. Is this state of affairs inevitable as long as women maintain the major responsibility for child care and housework?

11. If you're a woman, in which of Angrist's life-style orientation categories (p. 337) would you place yourself? If you are a man, what orientation best fits your expectations for women and for your (future) wife? Explain.

12. How do you feel college attendance influences women's and men's occupational aspirations?

13. Would you, as a college student or graduate, consider an apprenticeship in a skilled trade? Why or why not?

Chapter 13 Outline

chapter *13*

Hazards in the Adolescent Experience

Because young people are coping with significant personal changes as well as adapting to new roles in the social environment, the adolescent experience can be stressful at times. Nonetheless, most youth progress through this developmental period without serious difficulty.

No doubt because of popular expectations that the adolescent period will be filled with "storm and stress," parents, teachers, and counselors often view the onset of the teenage years with anxiety and dread. Young people, caught up in their own experiences and lacking a broader perspective, may perceive their conflicts and frustrations as being an indication of serious psychological disturbance rather than "normal" responses to adolescent development.

Because the incidence of serious problems—psychological disorders, suicidal behavior, drug and alcohol abuse, and chronic delinquency—is relatively low, attention should be paid to any of these personality or behavior problems that do appear (Weiner, 1970). This is especially true of symptoms other than anxiety or depression. Well-intentioned adults can make serious mistakes by passing off problems as "normal adolescent turmoil" which will be "outgrown" as adolescents mature. Early professional attention in such cases can often prevent more serious problems from developing.

In an attempt to clarify some of this confusion, a number of relevant issues will be discussed in this chapter. Among other topics, we will focus on psychological disturbances and suicide, drug and alcohol use and abuse, chronic juvenile delinquency, and alienation. In addition, we'll review various strategies for working with adolescents with these problems. For the most part, our discussion will be limited to adolescents in the United States.

PSYCHOLOGICAL DISORDERS IN ADOLESCENCE

It is difficult to estimate incidences of specific types of psychological disorders because of professional disagreements about what constitutes "normality," appropriate diagnostic categories, and symptomatology. In addition, record keeping in this area is often inadequate. The incidence of actual psychopathology among adolescents is estimated to be about 20 percent (probably somewhat less). We will discuss some specific types of psychological problems which are particularly important in the adolescent population.

Identity Diffusion

Identity diffusion is the negative pole of Erikson's developmental task of adolescence. He defines this state as "intense feelings of precariousness and disunity of self, doubt about one's ability to cope, and a relentless search for some trustworthy foundation for self-hood" (1968).

When identity diffusion is short-lived and a step on the way to identity achievement, it is seen as a developmental difficulty, not a serious psychological problem. On the other hand, a prolonged period of identity diffusion is usually a serious psychological problem and one which can lead to schizophrenia. Erik Erikson and others have noted that "acute identity diffusion" is similar in many ways to borderline schizophrenia: social isolation and inability to relate intimately with others; loss of time perspective which results in the belief that things can't change; inability to concentrate, work, and compete with others; choice of a negative identity, indicating disdain for (or inability to meet) family and societal standards (Weiner, 1970). Consequently, some adolescents who suffer from chronic identity diffusion may be misdiagnosed as schizophrenics, but for others this diagnosis may be accurate.

Some young people have always been marginally adjusted and find the assumption of adult roles increasingly beyond their capabilities. Other youth may have been able to function quite well in childhood and adolescent roles, but seem unable, for reasons which are unclear, to cope with the adult role demands of autonomy, emotional and sexual intimacy, and work.

Anorexia Nervosa and Bulimia

Anorexia nervosa (literally, "nervous loss of appetite") is characterized by self-starvation and severe loss of weight which can lead to death (usually from cardiac abnormalities induced by the disease or from suicide). Anorexia begins, usually around age 14 or 15, with dieting and can end in avoidance of eating altogether and such extreme weight loss that hospitalization may be required. Interestingly, anorexics deny that they are hungry. A related disorder is *bulimia* in which periods of dieting or fasting alternate with eating binges followed by self-induced vomiting. While these eating disorders appear to occur more often among middle-class, white adolescent females, they have also been diagnosed in males, lower-SES individuals, and blacks.

Anorexics appear to carry to an extreme this culture's preoccupation with the slim female figure. The typical anorexic is intelligent, a good student, helpful and

Anorexia nervosa is characterized by self-starvation and severe loss of weight.

obedient at home. She is somewhat overweight and also overcontrolled, conscientious, and meticulous (Ushakov, 1971).

Anorexics seem to come from families in which there is instability as well as physical illness and psychological problems (Hall, 1978). It has been suggested that the anorexic's rigid control over food intake is an attempt to define who she or he is (identity) and to exert control in her or his life (anorexics often seem to have dominating parents). The need to maintain such a thin body state also suggests that there are difficulties with body image, particularly related to impending sexual maturation and all that this implies.

It has been estimated that bulimia may affect as many as 10 percent of college students. In fact, the National Association of Anorexia Nervosa and Associated Disorders has set up chapters on college campuses in 36 states ("A deadly feast," 1983).

The cause of these disorders is not fully understood. Mental health professionals use a variety of approaches to treat the problems, often focusing on family therapy since the family appears to play an important role in the development of anorexia (Schneider, 1981).

Adjustment and Personality Disorders

Over half of the problems among adolescents are diagnosed as adjustment disorders (also called transient situational disturbances) and personality disorders, making these the most frequently used diagnostic categories for the adolescent population. *Adjustment disorders* are symptoms which appear as a temporary reaction to an overwhelmingly stressful experience in an individual without any apparent underlying serious problems (Spitzer, Williams, & Skodol, 1980). *Personality disorders* are maladaptive behavior patterns which are often antisocial in nature, such as chronic delinquency, promiscuity, and truancy, but are not considered to be neurotic or psychotic. Such young people are sometimes described as *acting out* or expressing in socially unacceptable behavior their internal frustrations and conflicts.

While such traditional diagnoses are sometimes accurate, some psychologists believe that they are often not the most useful means of understanding and treating adolescent psychopathology. This is because a number of serious psychological problems may appear in disguised forms among the adolescent population. As an alternative practice, Weiner (1980) has suggested using a schema of six major categories of adolescent psychological disturbance: (1) schizophrenia, (2) depression, (3) suicidal behavior, (4) problems of school attendance, (5) problems of school achievement, and (6) delinquent behavior. Since we have already discussed school problems in Chapter 9, our focus in this chapter will be on the remaining four categories.

Depression

The incidence of depression among adolescents as diagnosed by mental health professionals is lower than that for the adult population. For example, estimates of depression among young psychiatric patients range from 3 percent among 10- to 14-year olds to 6 percent among 15- to 17-year olds to 10 percent among 18- to 19-year olds; among adult psychiatric patients (25 to 44 years of age), the incidence is about 14 percent (Weiner, 1980).

On the other hand, it has been reported that almost half of adolescent psychiatric patients display depressive symptoms (unhappiness, self-deprecation, crying spells, and suicidal thoughts or attempts). In addition, it has been estimated that between 35 and 40 percent of nonpatient samples of youth report having some feelings typically associated with depression (Albert & Beck, 1975; Weiner, 1980).

Because of cognitive immaturity, younger adolescents are likely to express depression atypically—through overt behavior instead of through the introspective preoccupations which are typically associated with adult depression (Weiner, 1980). According to Weiner, such *masked depression* appears in several forms. For example, fatigue, hypochondriasis, and concentration difficulties are often reported by some youth. While it's true that these symptoms can reflect other causes, such as the "natural" preoccupation with their changing bodies, they may also reflect underlying psychological conflicts which require attention. Other symptoms include increased activity to ward off depression, a need for constant companionship, or an avoidance of people (among those adolescents who fear social rejection).

In addition, depression is sometimes manifested through indirect appeals for help, typically in the form of problem behaviors such as temper tantrums, running away, stealing, truancy, and the like (Weiner, 1980). Here, it is important to distinguish between this type of antisocial behavior and that engaged in by *sociopathic youth*. According to Weiner, there are three distinguishing features of behavior symptomatic of underlying depression: (1) antisocial behaviors are usually atypical of the young person's behavior (whereas this is not so among sociopathic youth who have a history of such acts); (2) the onset of the antisocial behavior can usually be traced to a specific external and depressing experience, such as the divorce of parents, and (3) the behavior is carried out in such a way as to ensure that the young person will be observed or caught, suggesting that such acts are committed for the purpose of getting attention and help.

Depression has been found to occur more frequently among females than males (especially black females), among low- rather than high-income families (Levitt & Lubin, 1975), and among low- and high-SES families characterized by feelings of alienation (Wenz, 1979a, 1979b). Also, it has been estimated that close to 25 percent of the college student population suffers from some symptoms of depression and that about 12 percent will seek professional help for this problem (Beck & Young, 1978).

Suicidal Behavior

Suicidal behavior is closely associated with depression in both adolescents and adults. In both age groups, it has been found that males are three to four times more likely to commit suicide than females (usually by shooting themselves), and that females are three times more likely to make suicide attempts (usually by ingesting a toxic substance) (U.S. Bureau of the Census, 1983). Also, those adolescents and adults who engage in suicidal behavior often have experienced such behavior among their family and friends and therefore have had a "suicidal model" to follow (Weiner, 1980).

Completed suicide is relatively uncommon among young people—those under 18 years of age comprise only 6 percent of known suicides in the United States each year. Suicide ranks as the fourth leading cause of death among 12- to 17-year-olds, after accidents (mainly among white males), homicide, and cancer (Kovar, 1979). On the other hand, adolescents are equally likely as adults to make suicide *attempts;* about 12 percent of known suicide attempts each year are committed by adolescents (Wenz, 1979a, 1979b). This number has at least doubled since 1950 (McAnarney, 1979), and increasing adolescent suicide appears to be a worldwide phenomenon (Greuling & DeBlassie, 1980).

Aside from suicide attempts made by psychotics, most attempts among youth appear to be a desperate "cry for help," whereas among adults they are more likely to reflect a wish to die (Weiner, 1980). Adolescent suicide attempts are sometimes mistakenly thought of as "shallow, histrionic, and impulsive reactions" to relatively minor stressful experiences such as breaking up with a boy- or girlfriend (Weiner, 1980, p. 458). This myth is no doubt perpetuated because these kinds of stresses often *do* precede a suicide attempt. However, these particular events are almost always preceded by a series of serious difficulties and disappointments with which the young person has felt unable to cope.

Adolescents who talk about suicide should be taken seriously. Unfortunately, not all young people will talk openly of suicidal thoughts, so adults must be alert to other indirect signs such as social withdrawal or antisocial behavior. The first suicide attempt usually comes as a complete surprise to both parents and peers of the adolescent, suggesting that they are not paying careful attention. Some professionals report that adults often exhibit a "remarkable blindness" to indirect signals of distress, apparently because they want to avoid dealing with their own problems which would be stirred up by actually looking at the adolescent's problems (Grueling & DeBlassie, 1980). Perhaps, then, it is not surprising to find that suicidal adolescents usually have poor relationships with their families and peers (Wenz, 1979a) and therefore are deprived of important sources of emotional support.

The rising rates of adolescent suicide suggest that young people are experiencing more stress or are less able to cope than previous generations. The loosening of contemporary community and family ties and increased family and social pressures for athletic, academic, and occupational success have all been suggested as important factors contributing to the high rates of stress and increased suicide rates among adolescents (Elkind, 1981; McAnarney, 1979; Wenz, 1979a, 1979b).

Schizophrenia

Schizophrenia is classified as a psychosis, the most serious form of psychological disorder, and is characterized by such symptoms as difficulties in thinking coherently and logically, distorted perceptions of reality including delusions and hallucinations, inappropriate emotional responses, and withdrawal from others (Spitzer et al., 1980).

Schizophrenia often makes its first appearance during or soon after adolescence. The age of highest risk for the onset of schizophrenic symptoms is 17 years of age (Holzman & Grinker, 1974). A substantial number of adolescents who seek professional help are diagnosed as schizophrenic—approximately 25 to 30 percent of adolescents admitted to psychiatric hospitals and from 6 to 8 percent of those seen in psychiatric clinics and private offices (Weiner, 1980).

Schizophrenia is often more difficult to detect in adolescents than in adults; symptoms may be clearly detectable only in 30 to 40 percent of the cases (Weiner,

Schizophrenia is a serious psychological disorder affecting adolescents.

1980). A large number of adolescent schizophrenics show a "mixed picture" in which the schizophrenic symptoms are initially less obvious than other problems or they exhibit behavior which might be symptomatic of other conditions as well. Two such symptoms which are often seen in the early stages of a schizophrenic breakdown are depression and antisocial behaviors such as fighting, stealing, running away, truancy, school failure, and family conflict (Weiner, 1980).

Schizophrenia appears to be caused by both genetic and psychological factors. Children and adolescents who develop schizophrenic symptoms have invariably grown up in disturbed family environments. In addition, one study reported that about three-fourths of adolescent schizophrenics studied had at least one parent who was either psychotic or severely emotionally disturbed (Bender, 1974).

The likelihood of recovering from schizophrenia is not particularly high, and when this disorder begins in adolescence, recovery is even less likely. It has been estimated that only 23 percent of adolescents who have been hospitalized for schizophrenia actually recover; some 25 percent show improvement, but have persistent symptoms or occasional relapses; and 52 percent make little or no progress and remain hospitalized indefinitely (Weiner, 1980). Weiner speculates that recovery rates for adolescent schizophrenics who do not require hospitalization (who can be treated on an outpatient basis) are probably more favorable, but there are no data to support this assertion.

Helping Adolescents with Psychological Problems

Psychotherapists generally acknowledge that working with adolescents is more difficult than treating children or adults. Younger adolescents (unlike most older adolescents and adults) don't come for counseling or psychotherapy on their own initiative. Consequently, they are usually defensive and hostile toward the therapist, at least initially. Also, adolescents who come for therapy often engage in antisocial and self-destructive behavior or threaten to do so; this can be a continuing source of concern and anxiety for the therapist.

A variety of treatment methods have been used with adolescents—individual and group psychotherapy, family psychotherapy, behavior modification, group homes, residential treatment, and "half-way houses" (Weiner, 1970). Typically, treatment aims to establish a warm relationship between the adolescent and the therapist or other group members. It is felt that within such a relationship adolescents can come to understand why they engage in nonfunctional behavior and to recognize and correct distorted perceptions. Since adolescents are in the process of consolidating their personality and building ego strength, attempts to reorganize the personality are considered detrimental rather than therapeutic. Rather, the focus of therapy is on helping adolescents learn effective strategies for coping with their current problems and conflicts. Troubled adolescents seem to prefer a therapist who expresses warmth and concern and who sets firm limits. They emphatically do not want a therapist who is inauthentic or untrustworthy or who tries to act like a peer (Chassin, Young, & Light, 1980).

Not all adolescents who have problems require or will accept professional counseling or therapy. Also, adolescents are more likely to turn to each other than to adults and professionals for help (Ziomkowski, Mulder, & Williams, 1975). Peer assistance has been institutionalized in the form of telephone hot lines, rap centers, and peer group therapies. While not all responses to such innovations are favorable, it appears that some peer-initiated and peer-supported programs can be effective. Teachers, coaches, youth workers, and relatives can also provide much needed support and reassurance for youth who are confused, frustrated, and without necessary role models—*if* young people will seek them out.

USE AND ABUSE OF ALCOHOL AND OTHER DRUGS

The use and abuse of drugs among adolescents is a serious concern of parents, teachers, school administrators, and other adults who work with young people. Whereas many parents and adults could ignore these problems prior to 1965 because they were confined largely to youngsters in the inner cities and slum neighborhoods, this is no longer true. Since the advent of the "hippie movement" in the late 1960s and early 1970s, drug use, especially marijuana and the hallucinogens, has spread throughout the middle and upper classes.

After several years of increases in drug usage, the use of alcohol, cigarettes, marijuana, and hallucinogenic drugs declined between 1979 and 1982 among both the 12- to 17-year-old and 18- to 25-year-old age groups (see Figure 13.1). While these are welcome trends, there is still reason to be concerned about the levels of drug usage among young people, as we shall see in the following discussion.

Alcohol

The most frequently used drug among adolescents is alcohol. For example, a national survey of drug use reported that the incidence of drinking among "current users" (those who reported having used alcohol at least once in the month prior to being surveyed) was 68 percent among 18- to 25-year-olds and 27 percent among 12- to 17-year-olds in 1982. From Figure 13.1, it can be seen that there has been a decline in alcohol use for both groups since 1979.

Small to moderate amounts of alcohol can produce feelings of tranquility and euphoria and may enable socially inhibited or shy persons to be more outgoing. Higher amounts of alcohol lead to drunkenness, characterized by confusion, difficulties in walking and talking, and sleepiness. Some people feel quite relaxed and uninhibited when "drunk," whereas others become depressed or belligerent. Intoxicated individuals often believe that their functioning is enhanced, but many of the more complex intellectual and physical functions appear to be seriously impaired by excessive alcohol intake (Katchadourian, 1977).

Heavy drinking in adolescence is a problem for several reasons. First, some 10,000 young people die each year in car accidents involving drivers who have been drinking. Moreover, research has consistently shown that between 45 and 60 percent of all fatal car crashes with a young driver are alcohol-related (DeLuca, 1981). Second, heavy alcohol consumption can have serious and irreversible adverse effects on the body. Third, alcohol abuse can have negative effects on cognitive, emotional, and social development (such as doing poorly in school and having problems with friends). Fourth, heavy drinking can be a prelude to alcoholism. In fact, it has been estimated

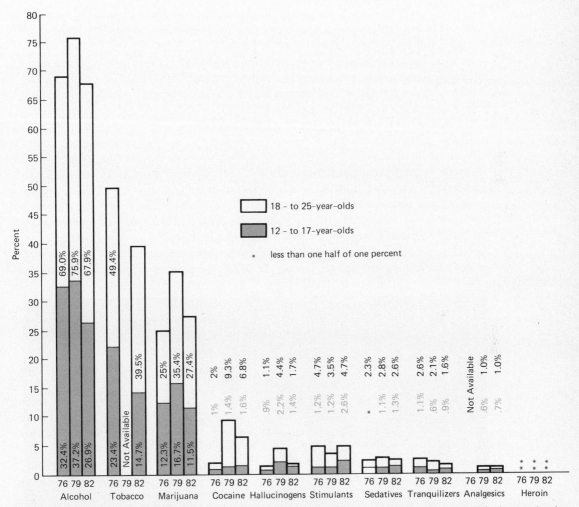

Figure 13.1 Percentage of adolescents and young adults reporting having used drugs at least once in the month prior to being surveyed ("current users") in 1976, 1979, and 1982. *Source:* Judith Droitcour Miller et al. (1983). *National Survey on Drug Abuse: Main Findings 1982.* Rockville, MD: National Institute on Drug Abuse.

that 1 in 10 teenagers is currently or will become an alcoholic; some 450,000 youth under age 21 are currently classifiable as alcoholics (Dykeman, 1979). It has been found that adolescents who drink heavily often come from homes in which the father drinks, where there is little parental control, where there is tension between the father and child, and where the adolescent feels rejected (Prendergast & Schaefer, 1974).

Both parents and peers influence an adolescent's drinking behavior, but it seems likely that parents are the more powerful role models here (Tudor, Peterson, & Elifson, 1980). The peer group appears to serve the function of reinforcing the patterns of drinking learned at home (Barnes, 1977).

Adolescents themselves seem to be getting increasingly concerned about teenage drinking. For example, many have joined Students Against Drunk Driving (SADD), a high school organization that features health education programs for those who plan to get drivers licenses ("Effort launched," 1982).

Tobacco

Tobacco is the second most frequently used drug among adolescents, although the incidence of cigarette smoking among adolescents and young adults has decreased considerably between 1979 and 1982 (see Figure 13.1). "Current use" of cigarettes decreased most dramatically among young people aged 12 to 21 and less so among the 22- to 25-year-old group (Miller et al., 1983). And, although the overall incidence of smoking has declined among the young, there has been a reversal in the proportion of males and females who smoke. During the 1970s, the number of females who smoked

Heavy drinking is a serious problem among today's adolescents.

rose sharply and the number of males declined dramatically so that now, more females smoke than do males.

Adolescents are more likely to smoke if their parents do (Kovar, 1979). They smoke because they are curious about it, in order to gain peer approval, and to express their increasing desire for autonomy (McAlister, Perry, & Maccoby, 1979). One study found that high school smokers had self-images of inadequacy. Males smoked to give the impression of "strength," while females smoked to enhance their attractiveness (Lotecka & Lassleben, 1981).

Most adolescents believe that smoking can harm their health, but they rationalize their behavior by saying that it's OK to smoke as long as they stop before it becomes a habit (Kovar, 1979). Unfortunately, stopping smoking is extremely difficult. This difficulty is reflected by the facts that antismoking education programs have been relatively unsuccessful in affecting adolescents who smoke and that relapses frequently occur among those who attempt to stop (Lotecka & Lassleben, 1981).

Marijuana

Next to alcohol and tobacco, marijuana is the most frequently used drug among adolescents. Twenty-seven percent of 18- to 25-year-olds and 12 percent of 12- to 17-year-olds in 1982 reported that they were "current users" of marijuana. From Figure 13.1, it can be seen that marijuana use among both age groups appears to have peaked in the late seventies. Smoking marijuana is less common among adolescents in elementary school compared to high school, among females, among nonwhite adolescents, and among those living in the South and in small and nonmetropolitan areas (Miller et al., 1983).

Marijuana can produce mild intoxification with pleasurable feelings of well-being, calm, and relaxation, as well as heightened sensory perceptions. Negative effects associated with marijuana do not include physiological dependence (addiction), although psychological dependence is possible. There also appears to be some deterioration in attention span and short-term memory, as well as in coordination when one is "stoned" (Katchadourian, 1977).

Unlike tobacco and alcohol, marijuana is an illegal drug. There is some support for its being legalized or decriminalized (violation would be considered a civil rather than a criminal offense, punishable by a fine).

Other Drugs Used by Adolescents

The number of adolescents using drugs other than tobacco, alcohol, and marijuana is relatively small (see Figure 13.1).

Inhalants Approximately 10 percent of adolescents age 12 to 17 reported ever having used inhalants or solvents such as gasoline, glue, or aerosols in 1979. Usage appears to be more common among the poor and among younger adolescents and elementary-school-aged children. National surveys report no apparent increases in the use of inhalants in recent years (U.S. Bureau of the Census, 1982). Inhalants produce euphoria and giddiness. They don't appear to lead to physical addiction, but high doses can cause irreversible damage to the liver and kidneys and, in some cases, death (Cohen, 1979).

Cocaine and Other Stimulants

The use of cocaine is more common among 18- to 25-year olds than 12- to 17-year-olds. As can be seen from Figure 13.1, the percentage of "current users" among the older group declined between 1979 and 1982; among the younger group, the percentage is much lower and also level over this same period. This age differential is still evident when a more liberal standard of usage is used; 28 percent of the older group and 7 percent of the younger group reported that they had "ever used" cocaine. Since cocaine is expensive, it is more likely to be used by youth who have access to money. Higher usage rates are found among youth who are male, white, and who have attended or graduated from college (Miller et al., 1983). No doubt if the substance were less costly, more adolescents would use it. "Coke" can be chewed, inhaled, brewed in tea, or injected. It produces heightened feelings of euphoria, alertness, and power. It can cause psychological dependence in heavy users, as well as paranoid delusions.

Other stimulants include caffeine and amphetamines ("speed"). These produce a "high" and feelings of increased alertness and activity. Sometimes the high may be followed by a "crash" or period of depression which can be quite severe. Amphetamines are illegal unless they are obtained by medical prescription. Also, they rapidly produce *tolerance,* which means that more pills have to be taken to produce the desired effect. The percentages of 12- to 17-year-olds and 18- to 25-year-olds who reported ever having used stimulants in 1982 were 7 percent and 18 percent, respectively. The percentage of youth who report "current use" is much lower: 3 percent of the younger group and 5 percent of the older group (see Figure 13.1).

Most students who use stimulants do so to study for exams, to increase their athletic performance, or to stay alert while driving. Some use amphetamines in order to reduce hunger and to lose weight. Tolerance and psychological dependence can develop rapidly to amphetamines and long-term use can be extremely dangerous, both physically and psychologically, as can sudden withdrawal.

Hallucinogens   Considerable concern has been expressed about the use among adolescents of PCP (phencyclidine or "angel dust"). The numbers of both younger and older youth who report having "ever used" PCP show a pattern of increase between 1976 and 1979 and a decrease between 1979 and 1982. For 12- to 17-year-olds, the percentages are 3, 4, and 2; for 18- to 25-year-olds, the percentages are 10, 14, and 11 (Miller, 1983). The use of PCP, and other hallucinogens as well, is more common among the 18- to 25-year-old and 26- to 34-year-old age groups than in the 12- to 17-year-old group.

PCP, an illegal drug, has anesthetic and hallucinogenic properties and can induce psychological dependence. In extreme cases PCP can cause bizarre hallucinations and other psychotic symptoms, as well as suicidal and homicidal behavior ("The deadly 'angel dust,'" 1978).

LSD, or lysergic acid diethylamide, is another hallucinogenic drug. In the late 1960s when LSD first became popular among youth, its use increased rapidly. In the early seventies, use among youth reached a plateau, and now appears to be in decline (Abelson et al., 1977; Johnston, Bachman, & O'Malley, 1981).

look at the drug problem from an adolescent's point of view ("In one ear . . .," 1977). Adolescents rate friends and former drug users as more authoritative sources about drugs than health professionals and law enforcement officials (Wong, 1976).

Also, many drug education programs are ineffective because they exaggerate the horrors of drug abuse and fail to address realistically the concerns of most adolescents who might contemplate using a drug in small quantities.

Ironically, American adults' concern about adolescent drug use and abuse reflects a curious blindness to their own role in the problem. In fact, it has often been stated that while drugs are a problem among adolescents, the more important issue is the drug problem in the United States. The use of drugs in this country is quite commonly associated with success in business (the "three-martini lunch"), social sophistication, parties, dating, and other forms of recreation (Carroll & Synigal, 1975). Drugs are considered a socially acceptable and quick means of relaxing from the tensions inherent in our fast-paced society.

Moreover, many parents falsely believe that somehow their own smoking and drinking habits won't have any impact on their children's attitudes and behaviors. At the same time that adolescents are told to stay away from drugs (and grow up), they are bombarded with examples of drug use from their parents, other adults, peers, television programs, and advertising (Carroll & Synigal, 1975). Clearly, then, a truly effective treatment of the teen drug problem requires that serious attention be given to the drug problem in the larger society.

DELINQUENT BEHAVIOR IN ADOLESCENCE

Incidence of Juvenile Delinquency

Legally, a *juvenile delinquent* is someone who has not attained adult status (18 years of age in most states) and who exhibits behavior punishable by law. In 1982, 22 percent of all youth under 18 were arrested. Among all females under 18, 10 percent were arrested; among males, the rate was 34 percent. Adolescents who engaged in delinquent behavior, but who aren't apprehended or don't go to court, are not labeled in crime statistics as "delinquents," even though their behavior would warrant it. Consequently, official estimates of delinquent acts are likely to be lower than the actual incidence of such behavior.

As many as a third of all juvenile offenders are arrested for such behaviors as school truancy, running away from home, incorrigibility (not obeying reasonable demands of parents), and curfew, alcohol, and drug violations. Many states classify these acts as *status offenses,* which means that they are illegal only if juveniles engage in them. Some states report status offenses separately from delinquent behavior, and some consider both together. Such inconsistencies make it difficult to get an accurate picture of the incidence and types of antisocial behavior among adolescents.

The number of juvenile arrests in the United States decreased by 6 percent between 1981 and 1982, and declined 15 percent between 1978 and 1982. Still, it is noteworthy that 6 percent of all people arrested in 1982 were under 15 years of age, 12 percent were between 15 and 17, and 16 percent were between 18 and 21 (Federal Bureau of Investigation, 1983). Taken together, these statistics mean that the arrests of youth under the age of 22 comprised 40 percent of the total arrests made in 1982, and those for people under 25, 53 percent of the total. Figure 13.2 shows the arrest rates for adolescents as a percentage of total arrests made for a number of specific crimes. Of course, these statistics are only arrest rates and, therefore, don't accurately reflect the incidence of delinquent and criminal acts. In fact, one study of self-reported delinquency (whether or not arrests resulted) revealed that more than 80 percent of some 500 adolescents surveyed indicated that they had engaged in delinquent acts, but only 10 percent of them had ever been arrested (Haney & Gold, 1973).

Delinquent behavior is much more common among males. In 1982 for every female under 18 years of age, almost four males were arrested (Federal Bureau of Investigation, 1983). Arrest rates were down for both sexes under 18 years from 1978 at about equal rates of decline (males down 14.9 percent; females, 14.8 percent). However, between 1981 and 1982, there was a much smaller decline showing male arrests falling at a more rapid rate than those of females (6.5 versus 3.9 percent) (Federal Bureau of Investigation, 1983). Sex differences with regard to specific types of crime are shown in Table 13.1.

Research indicates that both the frequency and seriousness of delinquent acts (serious vandalism, theft, assault, shoplifting, and armed robbery) peak at age 15 for

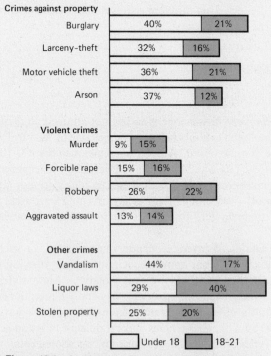

Figure 13.2 Arrests of youth under 18 years of age and between 18 and 21 years of age as a percentage of all arrests in each category, in 1982. *Source:* U.S. Department of Justice (1983). Uniform Crime Reports in the United States. Washington, D.C.: U.S. Government Printing Office.

Table 13.1 ARRESTS OF MALES AND FEMALES UNDER 18 IN 1982

Offense Charged	Males (percent)	Females (percent)
Serious crimes		
Murder and nonnegligent manslaughter	92	8
Forcible rape	98	2
Robbery	93	7
Aggravated assault	84	16
Burglary	93	7
Larceny-theft	74	26
Motor vehicle theft	89	11
Arson	88	12
All other crimes		
Other assaults	79	21
Forgery and counterfeiting	68	32
Fraud	78	22
Embezzlement	73	27
Stolen property; buying, receiving, possessing, etc.	91	9
Vandalism	92	8
Weapons; carrying, possessing, etc.	93	7
Prostitution and commercialized vice	3	97
Sex offenses (except forcible rape and prostitution)	93	7
Drug abuse violations	84	16
Gambling	96	4
Offenses against family and children	63	37
Driving under the influence	89	11
Liquor laws	77	23
Drunkenness	86	14
Disorderly conduct	84	16
Vagrancy	83	17
All other offenses (except traffic)	80	20
Suspicion	81	19
Curfew and loitering law violations	78	22
Runaways	42	58

Source: Compiled from data in U.S. Department of Justice (1982). *Uniform Crime Reports for the United States.* Washington, D.C.: U.S. Government Printing Office.

both boys and girls (see Figure 13.3) (Gold & Petronio, 1980). As we saw in Chapter 8, fears of peer rejection appear to peak about age 15. We would speculate that the increased incidence of reported delinquency at this age may be tied to adolescents' fears of peer rejection.

Class, Gender, and Racial Issues

Official reports of juvenile delinquency show that delinquency is highest among lower-SES youth. Adolescents' self-reports of delinquent behavior, on the other hand, don't show such a relationship (Gold & Petronio, 1980). This discrepancy has led some experts to suggest that more affluent teenagers are less likely to be arrested and to go to court than their lower-class delinquent peers (Erickson, 1973). The reasoning here is that authorities may be more hesitant to antagonize more powerful parents and that

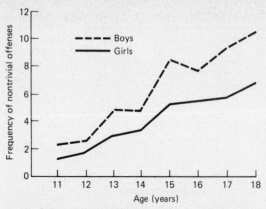

Figure 13.3 Average frequency of nontrivial offenses committed by boys and girls age 11 to 18. *Source:* Martin Gold and Richard J. Petronio (1980). Delinquent behavior in adolescence. In Joseph Adelson, Ed., *Handbook of Adolescent Psychology.* New York: Wiley, p. 504. Copyright 1980 by John Wiley & Sons, Inc. Reprinted by permission.

parents with money and status may find it easier to intervene with authorities on behalf of their children.

     The issue of unequal treatment of male and female delinquents also deserves mention. For example, girls are more likely to be arrested for status offenses involving sexual acting out (Barton, 1976). While we don't want to suggest that promiscuous sexual behavior is desirable, it does seem that a sexist double standard is operating when such activity among males is considered acceptable (and even admirable by some), but is condemned and likely to lead to arrest among females. Also, there is evidence that although girls are less likely than boys to be arrested for criminal behaviors, if they are arrested, girls are treated more harshly. For example, girls are three times more likely than boys to be recommended for incarceration (Barton, 1976).

     With regard to the issue of racial discrimination and arrest rates, one review of the literature on this question could find no compelling evidence that race, per se, was an important factor (Barton, 1976). With regard to the issue of sentencing, however, it appears that probation officers are more likely to recommend black youth for incarceration and white youth for psychiatric examination (Barton, 1976). Other researchers have found that the combination of a prior record and idleness (for example, lack of a job) tends to produce the harshest sentences (Cohen & Kluegal, 1978). Among those black and white youth who have been previously arrested, blacks are likely to be at a disadvantage in sentencing because the unemployment rate is much higher among black youth.

Types of Delinquent Behavior

Juvenile Crime   Crimes against property include burglary, larceny-theft, motor vehicle theft, and arson. Although the incidence of such crimes decreased between 1978 and 1982 by 15 percent among males under 18 and 17 percent among females under 18, they (particularly theft) are the most frequently committed delinquent acts among juveniles (Federal Bureau of Investigation, 1983).

The second most frequent type of crime committed by juveniles is victimless crime. In 1982 the most frequent delinquent acts committed by male juveniles in this area were liquor and drug use, disorderly conduct, curfew violations and loitering, and running away. For females the most frequent acts of victimless crime were liquor use and running away. Overall, there was a decrease in the incidence of this type of crime committed by juveniles between 1978 and 1982.

Violent crimes (murder, rape, robbery, and assault with intent to kill) decreased by almost 4 percent among youth under 18 between 1978 and 1982. Among juvenile males, there was a 4 percent overall decrease, but among females, there was a 2 percent overall increase in violent crime. The specific categories of violent crime which showed the greatest increases between 1978 and 1982 were forcible rape (up 9 percent among males in spite of the decrease in the overall category) and aggravated assault (up 5 percent among females) (Federal Bureau of Investigation, 1983). Robbery is the violent crime for which most youth are arrested.

Gang-Related Delinquency   In the 1960s there seemed to be a decline in the number of large, organized gangs and related delinquent acts and a rise in smaller group and individual crimes (S. Stephens, 1971). Yet in the late 1970s serious juvenile crime increased sufficiently to warrant cover-story status in weekly news magazines ("The Youth Crime Plague," 1977). Street gangs continue to be a problem in the 1980s ("Breaking a deadly," 1983).

Gangs vary in size and are typically composed of same-sex and same-ethnic group members. One study found that black youth gangs were more likely than white gangs to have specific territories (Friedman, Mann, & Adelman, 1976). Although street gangs are predominantly male in composition, there are some female street gangs. It has been estimated that "only" 25 percent of juvenile crimes are committed by urban gangs ("The Youth Crime Plague," 1977), and that the victims of gang violence are more likely to be other gang members (Friedman et al., 1976).

A study of Philadelphia street gangs revealed that the single most powerful predictor of gang membership was a "high proclivity for violence" (Friedman, Mann, & Friedman, 1975). This finding is related to an earlier one which indicated that certain needs of lower-SES youth predispose them to engage in illegal, violent behavior: toughness, excitement, fate, smartness, and autonomy (Miller, 1966).

Street gangs provide a family substitute for some youth, especially lower-SES youth in urban ghettoes. Such youth are expected to join a gang in the neighborhood, and they may be threatened or coerced into doing so (Friedman et al., 1976). There is evidence that such gangs provide important advantages to their members, in spite of their encouragement of illegal behavior. The Philadelphia study found that the second most powerful single predictor of street gang membership was the number of advantages provided by gang membership as reported by members. These advantages included companionship, excitement, heterosexual contacts, and protection. For example, a Chicago youth explained that he joined a gang for "protection, man, protection. I was a skinny little kid, and I was tired of having hassles. You don't last long if you don't belong to a club. You can always count on having someone stand up for you" ("The Youth Crime Plague," 1977).

Defiance of parents emerged as the third most important characteristic of gang members. More specifically, it was found that significantly more incidents of shouting at, cursing at, or striking their parents (primarily fathers) occurred among gang members compared to nongang members (Friedman et al., 1975). Alienation from parents is an initial cause of adolescents' turning toward juvenile delinquency and gang membership. As we have suggested, such youth are forced to rely quite heavily on their peers for emotional and social support and sometimes for physical survival. In the gang, individual members' behavior is often controlled by the threat of physical violence from other gang members (Friedman et al., 1976). Since gangs directly challenge the established authority of social institutions (the family, school, police, community), gang membership usually increases the alienation of members from their families and communities. This fact, in turn, makes it likely that the gang will become an even more powerful influence in the members' lives (Friedman et al., 1976). In this context, the Philadelphia study reported that 44 percent of gang members were forced to fight, 22 percent were forced to stab or injure someone, and 25 percent were forced to shoot at someone (see Table 13.2).

Gang members in the Philadelphia study also seemed to experience significantly less guilt related to delinquent activities compared to nongang members. Similar results

Table 13.2 COERCION OF STREET GANG MEMBERS AND NONMEMBERS TO COMMIT ANTISOCIAL AND ILLEGAL ACTS

Act	Gang (percent)	Nongang (percent)
Stay out all night	17	16
Cause trouble in neighborhood	21	13
Call police names	22	14
Get drunk	32	16
Bother grownups	15	10
Fight	44	21
Get or hide a weapon	29	12
Stab someone or injure someone with a weapon	22	10
Shoot at someone	25	9
Take heroin	7	8
Have sex with a girl	38	14
Have sex with other guys	4	3
Steal	27	13
Fight at school	38	18
Skip homework	25	9
Take hash or marijuana	20	15
Stay away from school	24	13
"Shake down" other guys	24	33
Take speed	7	6
Break up parties	26	9
Destroy public property	20	12
Mark or spray paint on walls	30	15

Source: Adapted from C. Jack Friedman, Fredrica Mann, and Howard Adelman (1976). Juvenile street gangs: The victimization of youth. *Adolescence, 11,* 529. Copyright 1976 by Libra Publishers, Inc. Adapted by permission.

have been obtained in other studies of gang members and juvenile delinquents. Usually, this fact is interpreted to mean that delinquents display sociopathic tendencies. An alternative interpretation is that lack of guilt reflects value differences between gang members and nongang members. If gangs place high value on "interpersonal violence, theft, and open rebellion against the parents" (Friedman et al., 1976, p. 601), it would be expected that members who engage in such behaviors, rather than feeling guilty, would gain in peer status and self-esteem.

Interestingly, the authors of the Philadelphia study found almost no relationship between gang membership and other variables such as lower intelligence, lack of educational preparation, broken homes, criminal histories, and poverty. (Since the youth in this study all came from lower-SES backgrounds, the variable of poverty was studied only within a limited context.)

Running Away   While official estimates put the number of juvenile runaways in 1982 at 115,214, other sources have conservatively estimated that some 600,000 children run away (M. E. Brown, 1979). In the early 1960s there were more male runaways; in 1982 some 58 percent were females (see Table 13.1). Forty-three percent of runaways are under the age of 15.

Most who leave home do so only once and return in a week. These adolescents are alienated from their families but not irreversibly so (Ambrosino, 1971). They tend to be unhappy about their lives at home, often have trouble relating to peers, and have been found to perform poorly in school; they have increasing difficulty as they move through high school.

The "repeaters" or "street runaways" leave home frequently. This group appears

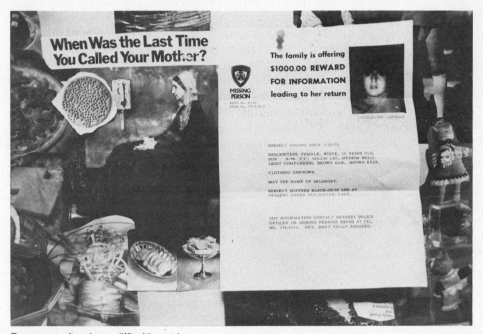

Runaways often have difficulties at home.

to have serious individual or family problems. For them, running away represents an attempt to make a clean break with the past. Tragically, running away usually does nothing to improve their situations and often worsens their plight. It has been estimated that the average runaway has money for three days, and since most cities don't have emergency shelters, they turn to the streets for support almost immediately (Brown, 1979; Wooden, 1976). For many youth (male and female), prostitution is the only means of survival.

Obviously, runaways need shelter, health care, and counseling. Some cities have begun to provide centers which offer a place to eat and sleep and free medical, psychological, and legal services. Since the 1960s, when this phenomenon was first recognized as a serious social problem, approximately 200 runaway shelters have been established, but this number is "pitifully small and inadequate when compared to the number of runaway children" (R. Johnson & Carter, 1980).

Causes of Delinquency

What causes some adolescents to become juvenile delinquents? While biological factors may play some role, most explanations are rooted in sociological and psychological factors.

Socioeconomic Status   Because statistics of law enforcement agencies indicate that more lower-SES youth engage in delinquent behavior, socioeconomic status has frequently been discussed as a major cause of juvenile delinquency. Recently, however, two important facts have come to light which cast doubt on this assumption. First, when researchers use adolescents' self-reports of delinquent activities rather than official statistics of such behavior, social class differences are not apparent. Second, the incidence of delinquency is rising most rapidly in the middle- and upper-middle-class suburbs. Thus, it appears that socioeconomic status alone is not the critical factor that it used to be.

Nonetheless, socioeconomic status is related to other factors, and it seems likely that these factors combine to exert different influences on youth in different social classes. For example, it has been suggested that most lower-class delinquency arises because legitimate avenues for pursuing middle-class opportunities are blocked. However, even though they face limited opportunities, not all lower-class youth become delinquents. Moreover, many middle-class youth do engage in delinquent acts, whether or not they go to court. Obviously, then, other factors must be operating which increase the likelihood that some adolescents will engage in delinquent behavior.

Parent-Adolescent Relationships   Probably, the most significant factor related to juvenile delinquency is inadequate or abusive parenting. Research has consistently shown that parents who do not show affection for their children or who psychologically or physically abuse them are more likely to have delinquent children (Andrew, 1981; Paperny & Deisher, 1983). Increased likelihood of delinquency has been traced to such parenting factors as: (1) early disciplinary techniques that are too lax, too strict, or erratic, (2) discipline that involves more physical punishment than reasoning, (3) parents who are rated by independent observers as hostile, cruel, neglecting, and inclined to ridicule their children, rather than as warm, affectionate, or passive (Loeber & Dishion, 1983; Streit, 1981).

It has been found that delinquent sons have few close ties to their fathers and consider them unacceptable role models. Delinquent children often have absent fathers (R. E. Anderson, 1968). While delinquency has also been associated with "broken homes" (Chilton & Markle, 1972), it is important to note that at least one study has found that the incidence of delinquency is higher in intact homes characterized by considerable emotional strife than in single-parent families characterized by cohesiveness, mutual affection, and support (Ahlstrom & Havighurst, 1971).

Parents who don't encourage positive attitudes toward learning and school and the development of academic skills are more likely to have children who are academic failures or troublesome in the classroom, and difficulty in school has been found to be highly related to delinquency (Andrew, 1981; Gold & Mann, 1972; Loeber & Dishion, 1983). Also, parents who suffer from emotional problems or who have criminal records are more likely to have delinquent children (Andrew, 1981; Loeber & Dishion, 1983).

Peer Relationships   As we have seen, heavy identification with and dependency on peers is an important causal factor in delinquency, regardless of socioeconomic status. Those youth who have been rejected by their parents turn to their peers for support. Such youth probably do poorly in school and look for others like themselves (Andrew, 1981). They need to fit in somewhere and to prove themselves good at something; because they're frustrated and angry, they are likely to engage in antisocial acts and to reinforce one another for doing so. For example, it has been reported that a variable closely associated with delinquent behavior is teenagers' perceptions that their friends are heavily delinquent (Gold, 1969). As we saw in the case of teenage gangs, sometimes young people must join their peers for self-protection as well.

Psychological Factors   Delinquency has been associated with a variety of psychological traits: lower than average intelligence (but not retardation), high levels of inner anger and aggressive behavior, impatience, a need for "thrill-seeking," a lack of empathy with others, and lower levels of moral reasoning (Andrew, 1981). Delinquents have been found to have lower self-esteem than nondelinquents and higher self-esteem than emotionally disturbed adolescents (Offer, Ostrov, & Howard, 1977). Psychologists disagree as to whether psychopathology plays an important role in delinquency. Estimates for the incidence of psychosis and emotional disturbance in the delinquent population have been cited as 25 percent and 32 percent, respectively (Andrew, 1981).

Other factors have also been associated with the increased rates of delinquency: rapid social change and the repeated watching of violent programs on television (National Institute of Mental Health, 1982).

What determines whether delinquents will "grow out of" their antisocial behavior or become adult criminals? Research in this area is sparse, but seems to suggest that only those children and adolescents who engage in a considerable amount of antisocial behavior are likely to become adult criminals (Gold & Petronio, 1980). Many psychologists believe that an early onset of delinquent behavior is indicative of serious, long-term antisocial behavior. It was formerly believed that three symptoms in early childhood —firesetting, bedwetting, and cruelty to animals—were precursors of later sociopathic behavior (Andrew, 1981). A recent review of research suggests, however, that other factors are much more accurate predictors in this regard: fighting, temper tantrums, school problems and truancy, and inability to get along with others (Justice, Justice, & Kraft, 1974).

Treating and Preventing Delinquency

Numerous programs have been designed to reduce delinquency. One article listed the following approaches: "Individual and group psychotherapy, family therapy and family contracting, behavior modification, transactional analysis, recreation, vocational training, alternative schooling, survival camping and wilderness canoeing, incarceration and probation, 'big brothers' and 'big sisters,' community organization, and Bible reading" (Gold & Petronio, 1980, pp. 517-518).

Little research has been done on the results of these programs, but most are probably not effective (Gold & Petronio, 1980). This is partly because many treatment approaches are simply ineffective, but also because the adolescents involved in the programs were those who had already displayed serious problems, and these of course, are the youth least likely to respond to treatment.

Although they are not large in number, some attempts to reduce delinquency have proved successful. Such programs have two essential features: (1) warm and accepting relationships with adults and (2) activities and relationships designed to enhance adolescents' images of themselves as effective and independent individuals both now and in the future (Gold & Petronio, 1980). This finding is consistent with the theories of delinquency that trace its causes to poor parenting and blocked access to middle-class goals. Effective programs incorporating these characteristics have been designed for youth already labeled "juvenile delinquents" and for those labeled "predelinquent."

In the last decade the institutional treatment of delinquent youth has shifted away from the large training school and correctional facility toward community-based programs designed on a family-unit model (Redd, Porterfield, & Andersen, 1979). In one such program, houseparents and up to 10 adolescents live in a group home. During the day residents go to school or work, and in the evening they participate in school-related and recreational activities in the home. Each adolescent has household responsibilities and is asked to participate in decisions on how the house is to "run." The goal of such programs is to give adolescent residents the necessary emotional support and training so that they can acquire the social, academic, and vocational skills necessary for success in society (Redd et al., 1979).

Another type of intervention program that can been effective is behavioral or family contracting. This method originated as a means of dealing with delinquent adolescents and their families whose relationships were so negative that formal agreements had to be drawn up in which parents and adolescents stated in writing what each would do and what rewards would be expected for so behaving.

Family therapy can be helpful in treating delinquency.

An example of behavior contracting within families is illustrated by the case of Candy Bremer (a pseudonym), a 16-year-old delinquent girl who was referred by the court to a federally funded counseling program that used this approach (Stuart, 1971). Candy came from an intact, middle-class family of modest means. At the time she was referred to the program, she had been hospitalized for alleged promiscuity, exhibitionism, drug abuse, and home truancy. Her parents reported that they could not control her behavior and that most of their interactions were hostile and unpleasant. After a series of conferences, a behavioral contract was negotiated (see Table 13.3). Basically, the contract required that Candy abide by her parents' curfew and take responsibility for certain household tasks in exchange for specified privileges and early payment of her allowance. Once the contract was introduced, the parents reported that family interactions improved: the number of arguments decreased considerably and they had learned an effective way (the contract) to resolve some conflicts. According to the therapist, the court's wardship was terminated and no new problems developed.

ALIENATION AMONG TODAY'S ADOLESCENTS

Contemporary American life is characterized by affluence, rapid social and technological change, ascendancy of bureaucracies, and increasing isolation of the nuclear family. These characteristics contribute to a sense of frustration and feelings that we have less and less control over more and more aspects of our lives. In addition, many people feel increasingly isolated from one another. Many people feel lonely. Some feel alienated as well.

Table 13.3 **A BEHAVIORAL CONTRACT USED IN THE FAMILY OF A DELINQUENT GIRL**

Privileges	Responsibilities
General	
In exchange for the privilege of remaining together and preserving some semblance of family integrity, Mr. and Mrs. Bremer and Candy all agree to	concentrate on positively reinforcing each other's behavior while diminishing the present overemphasis upon the faults of the others.
Specific	
In exchange for the privilege of riding the bus directly from school into town after school on school days	Candy agrees to phone her father by 4:00 P.M. to tell him that she is all right and to return home by 5:15 P.M.
In exchange for the privilege of going out at 7:00 P.M. on one weekend evening without having to account for her whereabouts	Candy must maintain a weekly average of "B" in the academic ratings of all her classes and must return home by 11:30 P.M.
In exchange for the privilege of going out a second weekend night	Candy must tell her parents by 6:00 P.M. of her destination and her companion and must return home by 11:30 P.M.
In exchange for the privilege of going out between 11:00 A.M. and 5:15 P.M. Saturdays, Sundays, and holidays	Candy agrees to have completed all household chores before leaving and to telephone her parents once during the time she is out to tell them that she is all right.
In exchange for the privilege of having Candy complete household chores and maintain her curfew	Mr. and Mrs. Bremer agree to pay Candy $1.50 on the morning following days on which the money is earned.
Bonuses and sanctions	
If Candy is 1–10 minutes late	she must come in the same amount of time earlier the following day, but does not forfeit her money for the day.
If Candy is 11–30 minutes late	she must come in 22–60 minutes earlier the following day and does not forfeit her money for the day.
If Candy is 31–60 minutes late	she loses the privilege of going out the following day and does not forfeit her money for the day.
For each half hour of tardiness over 60 minutes,	she loses her privilege for going out and her money for one additional day.
Candy may go out on Sunday evenings from 7:00 to 9:30 P.M. and either Monday or Thursday evening	if she abides by all the terms of this contract from Sunday through Saturday with a total tardiness not exceeding 30 minutes which must have been made up as above.
Candy may add a total of two hours divided among one to three curfews	if she abides by all the terms of this contract for two weeks with a total tardiness not exceeding 30 minutes which must have been made up as above and if she requests permission to use this additional time by 9:00 P.M.
Monitoring	

Mr. and Mrs. Bremer agree to keep written records of the hours of Candy's leaving and coming home and of the completion of her chores.

Candy agrees to furnish her parents with a school monitoring card each Friday at dinner.

Source: Reprinted with permission from *Journal of Behavior Therapy and Experimental Psychiatry, 2,* by Richard B. Stuart, Behavioral contracting within families of delinquents. Copyright © 1971, Pergamon Press, Ltd.

Types of Alienation Specific to Adolescence

Developmental Estrangement   As individuals mature, they move toward new opportunities and relationships, but in this process they also must move beyond the past and leave the comfortable ties and relationships that existed before. In order to learn to become adults, adolescents must abandon childhood ties, roles, and behaviors. According to Kenneth Keniston (1965), *developmental estrangement* in adolescence occurs when the void left by leaving childhood ties and roles is not filled by adult behaviors and roles. The extent of this type of alienation for young people depends on the amount and kind of guidance and support they can derive from family, peers, and larger society. Since rapid cultural and technological changes disrupt the stability of social norms, it isn't always clear to today's parents and adolescents what is appropriate behavior. Consequently, youth feel pressures to "grow up," but often receive too little or inconsistent guidance as to *how* to do this.

Cultural Alienation   Among minorities and the poor, alienation is not a new phenomenon. For individuals who have been discriminated against and deprived by our society —blacks, Hispanics, Orientals, Native Americans, Appalachian whites (and women, in many respects)—feelings of alienation are a natural response to being rejected and left out of the mainstream of our culture. Studies of black high school students have found that large numbers of male and female youth feel alienated from both school and society. For such youth "the American dream becomes a nightmare" (Conger & Petersen, 1984, p. 603).

Identity Diffusion   Identity diffusion is a state of being confused about who one is and can be viewed as being alienated from oneself. In addition, however, some identity diffused adolescents may also be alienated from the larger society, since they appear unable to settle on occupational goals or a meaningful personal ideology. Many adolescents who engage in antisocial behaviors use these actions as a means of avoiding confrontations with their feelings of confusion, frustration, and emptiness. As we have seen, serious and prolonged instances of identity diffusion are more appropriately viewed as psychological rather than psychosocial disturbances.

Today's Alienated Youth

Compared to the youth of the late 1960s and the early 1970s, today's young people appear to be less alienated, at least as measured in terms of social and political activities and withdrawing from mainstream society. The current shift toward middle-of-the-road political orientations and the decline of interest in larger social and political issues reflect a growing sense of pessimism about American society, its institutions, and values. Many students are developing what Arthur Levine has called a "life-boat mentality" and are focusing on their own concerns (1980). As a result, they have been described as the "me generation."

This response, in part, reflects feelings of alienation among today's youth. We would speculate that "me-ism," cynicism, depression, suicide, delinquency, drug use, running away, and religious conversions are all indications that alienation is a problem for many youth in the 1980s.

THE "INVULNERABLES"

In this chapter, we have discussed a number of hazards which can befall adolescents: psychological disorders, drug abuse, delinquency, and alienation. As we have seen, the causes of these problems aren't always well understood, although the family environment and socioeconomic status stand out. Youth with few economic, educational, and social advantages and those whose family environments are not supportive or are abusive are at high risk to succumb to serious problems. Still, not all high-risk youth develop such problems, and some low-risk adolescents do.

By way of ending this chapter (and book) on a positive note, we want to say something about youth who are able to thrive in adversity—the "invulnerables" (Garmezy, 1976). These young people grow up in severely stressful environments, yet they seem to remain relatively invulnerable to and even triumph over them. For example, consider this boy growing up in a dilapidated apartment in the slums of Minneapolis. He lives with "his father, an ex-convict now dying of cancer, his illiterate mother, and seven brothers and sisters, two of whom are mentally retarded. Yet, his teachers describe him as an unusually competent child who does well in his studies and is loved by almost everyone in the school" (Pines, 1979, p. 53).

Until recently, psychologists neglected studying such individuals to focus on those who are maladjusted. Lately, however, there has been an interest in studying those who cope exceptionally well with deprivation and stress in order to learn from their positive examples. There has not been much research to date, but invulnerables seem to possess at least five qualities which enable them to prosper (Pines, 1979):

1. *Strong social skills.* Invulnerables seem exceptionally at ease with both peers and adults. They are invariably popular with fellow students.
2. *Ability to attract and use support of nonparental adults.* These youth are willing and able to reach out to supportive adults (teachers, relatives, babysitters) for the encouragement they don't usually get at home.
3. *Competence and self-confidence.* Invulnerables have an amazingly strong sense of their own abilities to cope and can make something out of very little.
4. *Autonomy.* Invulnerables seem able to carve out a private place for themselves in their environments that gives them both physical and psychological refuge from stressful conditions and individuals.
5. *High achievement needs.* Invulnerables seem to do well at most things they tackle. Also, they tend to develop intense interests in certain subjects at an early age.

In addition, research tentatively points to three other characteristics and conditions shared by invulnerables: (1) a good relationship with at least one adult, especially early in life, (2) the occurrence of challenges in their lives, and (3) an "optimal" number of stresses to manage at any one time—too few stresses aren't challenging enough and too many are overwhelming (Pines, 1979).

Clearly, psychologists are a long way from understanding how invulnerables manage to develop the skills they need to master potentially debilitating environments. Still, the fact that some individuals *are* able to do so well with so little should make us mindful of individual differences and the extraordinary capacities for growth within each person.

SUMMARY

Most adolescents don't experience serious difficulties; therefore, when obvious symptoms of personality or behavior problems appear, they are usually worth noting. Among the psychological disorders of adolescence are acute or chronic identity diffusion, anorexia nervosa, adjustment and personality disorders, depression, suicidal behavior, and schizophrenia.

Among both younger and older adolescents, the use of alcohol, cigarettes, marijuana, and hallucinogenic drugs has declined in recent years. Alcohol remains the most frequently used drug among young people. Compared to usage rates for tobacco, alcohol, and marijuana, the number of adolescents using other drugs is relatively small. The use of cocaine has decreased among older adolescents and the use of PCP has declined among both younger and older adolescents in recent years.

Juvenile delinquency appears to be decreasing in recent years. Most delinquent youth commit crimes against property, but some also commit victimless and violent crimes.

Most intervention programs to reduce delinquency have been unsuccessful. Often this is because only youth with the most serious problems are included in such pro-

Each person has extraordinary capacities for growth.

grams. Group homes and behavioral contracting within families are two of the more effective intervention strategies.

The incidence of "me-ism," cynicism, depression, suicide, drug abuse, running away, and religious conversions are indications that alienation is a problem for many youth in the 1980s.

Some youth seem able to master extremely stressful environments rather than succumb to them.

GLOSSARY

acting out   A maladaptive behavior pattern in which conflicts are directly expressed in antisocial behavior (delinquency, truancy).

adjustment disorder   Temporary maladaptive response to environmental stresses.

alienation   The feeling of being isolated and estranged from society, other individuals, or oneself.

cultural alienation   The experience of being rejected by the larger society because of prejudice.

developmental estrangement (Keniston)   Feeling of alienation that results when adolescents leave childhood roles and ties behind before they are able to take on adult roles.

invulnerables (Garmezy)   Youth who are able to master severely stressful environments.

juvenile delinquent   An individual under the age of 18 (in most states) who engages in illegal behavior.

masked depression   Depression characterized by symptoms which don't typically suggest that depression is present (inability to concentrate, fatigue, or hypochondria).

personality disorder   Enduring and maladaptive pattern of relating to, perceiving, and thinking about oneself and the environment.

schizophrenia   A serious psychological disorder characterized by major cognitive, emotional, and behavioral disturbances.

sociopathic behavior   Antisocial behavior, usually engaged in by an individual without feelings of guilt or remorse.

status offense   An act that is punishable by law only when committed by a juvenile.

GETTING INVOLVED: Case Study and General Questions to Consider

CASE STUDY: MIKE

Mike is a 16-year-old high school junior who has a friend he thinks has a drinking problem. Mike and his friends usually get together after school a couple of times a week and sometimes on the weekends. They usually all drink beer, but recently Jerry has been bringing a pint of whiskey to drink along with the beer. Lately, it seems to Mike, Jerry has been drinking a lot (a six-pack of beer a night when they get together). He also thinks he has smelled liquor on Jerry's breath in morning classes sometimes.

Nobody else seems concerned about Jerry's drinking. In fact, when Mike teasingly made a comment about it in the group one night, everyone, including Jerry, put him down. Then, they proceeded to encourage Jerry to drink even more.

Mike doesn't want to exaggerate the problem—still, it's been going on for about three months and Jerry seems to be getting less and less interested in school. Also, Jerry's father is an alcoholic. (In fact, one of the reasons Jerry likes to go out at night is so that he won't be at home when his dad is there because his dad gets verbally and physically abusive when he drinks.)

Mike and Jerry have grown up together and are good friends. Mike worries about what might happen to Jerry. Could he become an alcoholic like his father? Mike likes to have a good time and a few drinks, but he hates to stand by and watch Jerry go downhill. Still, he doesn't want to "butt in" either. Since Jerry didn't pay any attention before when Mike hinted about his drinking, he wonders whether it would do any good to talk to him anyway. Since the other guys laugh off Jerry's drinking, Mike doesn't feel comfortable talking about it with them either—last time they really put him down.

Questions for Case Study

1. Summarize Mike's situation.
2. Do you think Jerry has a drinking problem? Why or why not?
3. Why do Jerry's peers encourage him to drink, rather than helping him to stop?
4. Should Mike try to help Jerry or should he mind his own business? Why?
5. What could Mike do that might help Jerry? Are there any school or community resources he could call upon?
6. If Mike tries to help Jerry, but nothing comes of it, what could he do to help himself feel better? Are there school or community resources he could use for himself?

GENERAL QUESTIONS TO CONSIDER

1. Why do most young people attempt or commit suicide? Do you know of any adolescent who either attempted or completed suicide?
2. Reflect on the role of inadequate or abusive parenting in the development of psychological disorders in children and adolescents.
3. How regularly do you and your peers drink alcohol? What purposes does "drinking" serve for you and your friends?

4. Did your junior high or high school have a drug education program? Do you feel that it influenced your thinking or attitudes about drugs in any ways? How could it have been more useful?

5. Why does a young person use any drug (tobacco, alcohol, marijuana, etc.) for the first time? Are the reasons for continued use different from those for first-time use, in your experience?

6. What advice would you give to younger adolescent friend or sibling about the use and abuse of specific drugs?

7. Do you feel that adults and the society at large are hypocritical in their concern and condemnation of drug use and abuse in adolescents because most don't practice what they preach? How does this affect your attitudes toward drug experimentation and usage?

8. It is estimated that the highest frequency of delinquent acts occurs at age 15 for both boys and girls. Does this match your impression? Why do you think that more crimes are committed at this age?

9. What do you think accounts for the recent decline in the commission of most categories of crime among adolescents?

10. What role, if any, do you feel alienation plays in the lives of today's adolescents? Elaborate.

11. Do you know of any child or adolescent who could be described as an "invulnerable"? Can you explain how he or she "triumphs over adversity" where most others fail?

Appendix Outline

appendix

Communicating in Small Groups

If you're like most college students, there are aspects of your self that you're still in the process of defining. Hearing other people's opinions and getting their reactions to your beliefs and ideas are good ways of gaining perspective on yourself—something quite helpful, if not essential, in the process of personal growth. Students have convinced me of the usefulness of small group discussions both in relating to the course material and in understanding themselves.

Also, ideas and concepts are not really useful to us *unless* we can make them our own. To do this, we need to be able to associate unfamiliar concepts with related ideas or experiences which are already familiar to us. Small group discussions can be especially useful in this course because they provide you with the opportunity to integrate the subject matter with your personal experiences and those of your classmates.

Accordingly, sharing ideas and experiences is encouraged in this course to help you to relate personally to important concepts in the study of adolescence and to gain perspective on your own developmental status by comparing your experiences with those of others. Because of lack of experience in small group discussions, most students are unsure of what to expect in them. This appendix is included to give you a sense of how these group discussions function and how you can make them work effectively.

HOW SMALL GROUP DISCUSSIONS WORK IN THIS COURSE

Because specific decisions about small groups in your class will be made by your instructor, he or she will be better able to explain how small group discussions will work in your class. For the sake of general clarification, I offer the following information and guidelines:

1. *How often do small groups meet?* The answer to this question will depend on a number of related issues: the number of topics to be discussed, the number of days per week your class meets, and the amount of time your instructor feels can be given to the discussions.
2. *How many people are in each group?* The optimal number is six to eight students in each group.

3. *Do members remain in the same group all semester?* Yes. It takes a while to build up trust and ease in talking together. This doesn't happen unless people get a chance to know each other over a number of meetings.

4. *What is the group attendance policy?* Attendance may be voluntary or required in your class. If it is *voluntary*, you're free to come or not, as you choose. If you do decide to attend, it's a good idea to be consistent in your attendance for the sake of feeling "connected" with the group and for better group functioning. If attendance is *required* of students and you want to attend, there's no problem. However, if you are extremely uncomfortable in small group settings, you might attend one or two groups to see if they're really as awful as you anticipate. If you feel you cannot attend, speak to your instructor to see if other arrangements might be made.

5. *What is discussed in the groups?* Perhaps you can get the best answer to this question by reading through some of the exercises, case studies, and questions at the end of the chapters in Part II of this book. Probably, you and your instructor will decide together which topics the groups in your class will discuss.

6. *How much self-disclosure will be expected?* While it is true that students often use their own experiences in discussing course issues, such self-disclosure is *always* voluntary. You do not have to contribute personal experiences to the discussion; you can make other types of comments that can be just as useful. Trust your feelings in this matter and wait until you feel comfortable with the idea. Also, avoid making your comments too personal, since this makes people uncomfortable and interferes with discussion.

7. *What are the standards of confidentiality?* Most comments people make in the groups could probably be repeated to people outside the group without embarrassment or harm to group members. Nonetheless, just knowing that what you say might be repeated out of context may make you somewhat unwilling to state your ideas freely. While there is no way to guarantee confidentiality, group members will probably feel more comfortable if they all agree to abide by by a minimum standard of confidentiality, that is, in talking to nonmembers about subjects discussed in the group, you agree not to repeat information about a group member *by name*.

8. *Are the group discussions relevant to "older" students?* Since group discussions focus on the concerns and experiences of adolescents, some older students may question whether participation in the groups is appropriate for them. Also, they may have some concerns about how comfortably they can "mix" with younger, late adolescent students. When there is a mixture of ages in the groups, both younger and older students have commented on the usefulness of hearing different perspectives. There may be some initial discomfort because of age differences, but it typically disappears quickly.

SOME BASIC CONCEPTS IN GROUP DYNAMICS

Social psychological research points to two major operations in any group: task accomplishment and group maintenance. As the labels suggest, *task functions* are behaviors and statements which keep the group moving toward the accomplishment of a goal—getting enough votes to pass certain legislation, electing officers, or approving a budget. In addition to these familiar activities, more subtle (and equally important) events take place. These *maintenance functions* include group members' attempts to relieve normal group tension through joking, listening to one another, or encouraging each other to speak.

The purpose of a group will determine the relative importance of these two functions; for example, a student senate would be more concerned with tasks and less concerned with maintenance, whereas an encounter group in a counseling center would place more weight on maintenance and less on tasks.

To clarify the differences between task and maintenance behaviors as they relate to group discussions, some examples are given below based on categories described by William Fawcett Hill (1969).

Task Functions

1. *Initiating discussion:* "Today, I thought we might talk about . . ." or "I recently read Elisabeth Kübler-Ross's *On Death and Dying* and wonder if we could apply her analysis to Mary's feelings about her friend's death [in a hypothetical case study]."
2. *Giving and asking for information:* "Do you have a part-time job?" or "Did you know what you wanted to major in as a freshman?"
3. *Giving and asking for reactions:* "I can really identify with John's problem . . ." or "Do you think Judy's moving out of her parents' house was a good idea?"
4. *Clarifying by restating and giving examples:* "Are you saying that you feel Bob did the right thing?" or "I can still remember studying for my first exam in college. I was so panicked that I studied for days."
5. *Reality-testing for accuracy of statements:* "Well, I guess my experience hasn't been quite the same as yours. I've found that . . ." or "How do the rest of you feel about what Jack has just said?"
6. *Synthesizing and summarizing:* "Well, it sounds like we have all had some similar and some different interactions with our parents on the issue of choosing friends. We seem to be agreeing that . . ." or "In talking about sex education, it appears that most of us learned about sex from our friends. . . . Does anyone have anything to add before we move on?"
7. *Gate-keeping and expediting:* "Bill, we haven't heard from you today. Would you feel comfortable sharing your feelings about the case study?" or "Well, Susan, it sounds like your experience was really frustrating. Has someone else gone through something similar or have your experiences been different?"
8. *Time-keeping:* "We seem to be enjoying this discussion, but we have only 15 minutes left. Do you want to stay on this topic or move to another one?"
9. *Standard-setting:* "How do you feel about how we've handled the discussion so far? Are we hearing from everyone? Are you aware of anything we need to change to help us function better?"
10. *Listening:* Most of us don't listen as effectively as we might, and we miss a lot because of it. Here are some rules of thumb:
    a. It's hard to listen to more than one person talk at a time. If more than one person is talking, request that only one of them speaks.
    b. It's hard to listen to someone else when you're talking! Watch tendencies to interrupt or make comments to the person next to you.
    c. If you didn't hear or understand what someone said, ask the person to repeat or explain.
    d. Don't be a conversation "hog." Give others a chance to talk, too!
    e. Eye contact is important; look at who is talking. And when *you* talk, look around the group. Don't speak only to the group facilitator or one interested person.

Maintenance Functions

1. *Sponsoring:* "Joe, you meant to say something a minute ago. What was it?" or "Beth, you always have good ideas. How do you see this situation?"

2. *Encouraging and supporting:* "Yes, that's a good point, Maria," or "You seem to have given this a lot of thought, Steve." Nods and smiles also fall into this category.
3. *Tension-relieving:* Joking and teasing are ways to take the pressure off a particular person or the edge off an awkward moment. On the other hand, joking can become nonfunctional if it occurs so often and inappropriately that it disrupts the group.
4. *Listening:* Read again the rules of thumb listed above.

Nonfunctional Group Behaviors

In any group, behaviors may arise which interfere with the effective functioning of that group. The following behaviors fall into this category and should not be encouraged:

1. *Interrupting:* stopping another person in mid-conversation, preventing him or her from making a point
2. *Being aggressive:* making insulting statements, being hurtfully sarcastic, using a derogatory tone of voice
3. *Seeking sympathy:* discussing personal circumstances so often or in such a way as to convey an impression that you want others to feel sorry for you
4. *Status-seeking:* talking about things you have accomplished so often or in such a way as to make yourself appear better than others in some respect
5. *Dominating:* taking over the discussion by talking too often or at too great a length at any one time. Pay attention to tell-tale cues from others indicating boredom or frustration.
6. *Inappropriate self-disclosure:* revealing things about yourself which are too personal for the situation. Although participating in discussions involves expressing your feelings and relating your experiences, these groups are *not* encounter or therapy groups. In this class group discussions focus on *topics,* not members' problems. While students are encouraged to relate their own experiences in the group, they are encouraged to do this appropriately. For example, in discussing parent-adolescent conflicts, it would be appropriate for you to describe how your family behaved in a particular situation, but it would be *in*appropriate for you to complain bitterly and at length about how badly your parents have abused you and to state how much you hate them for what they did. (It's not that such feelings aren't valid, only that they aren't appropriate in this type of group.) Statements of this kind in this setting leave everyone feeling awkward.
7. *Withdrawing:* failing to take your share of responsibility for effective communicating and group functioning. While it's true that some people are more shy than others, by not participating in the group discussion, you're missing an opportunity to practice becoming more comfortable talking in small groups. When you don't talk, you may find yourself drifting away from the discussion and not feeling a part of things. Almost everyone feels some degree of discomfort talking to strangers. The "trick" is to realize that the situation is difficult for everyone and to try to do your part.

GROUP FACILITATORS

Role and Responsibilities

While your course may use leaderless group discussions, it's more likely that your group will have a facilitator. The person in this role is a combination of leader and group member. (The title *facilitator* is used to suggest that one person is not solely responsible for what goes on in the group.) The facilitator's function is to promote good discussions by introducing the topic, guiding the members through the various groups exercises, and fostering a warm and accepting atmosphere. The style a facilitator adopts to carry out these functions depends on the facilitator's personality and the needs of the group.

Facilitators will probably be selected by the instructor from volunteers in class. If you're interested, it's a good opportunity to learn about group dynamics and discussion planning.

The facilitator has responsibilities to both the instructor and the members of the group. Specific responsibilities will be determined by the instructor. Listed below is an approach I have used:

1. Responsibilities to professor
   a. Submit brief evaluations of each group discussion
   b. Meet, as a group, with the instructor to evaluate the outcome of the previous discussion and to select the exercises for the next discussion
   c. Write a final evaluation of the groups' and your experience as facilitator
2. Responsibilities to group members
   a. Meet with the group and work toward the best possible discussion of the topic at hand
   b. Foster a warm and accepting atmosphere in the group (directly by your own behavior and indirectly by serving as a role model for other group members)

Characteristics of Effective Facilitators

Students in my classes have reported that good facilitators are:

1. Informed about the topic to be discussed through reading the appropriate chapter in the book
2. Informed about alternative methods for approaching the topic to be discussed
3. Enthusiastic about the group and topic
4. Friendly and outgoing
5. Able to express ideas clearly
6. Open to a variety of viewpoints

As you might guess, students feel that facilitators are *not* as effective when they:

1. Allow discussions to wander off the major topic of concern
2. Dominate discussion by talking at length about their own experiences
3. Block or argue with comments which oppose their own point of view
4. Appear uninformed or uninterested in the topic
5. Fail to direct discussion effectively so that most members participate

GUIDELINES FOR EFFECTIVE GROUP DISCUSSIONS

Because most students have not had much exposure to small groups, I have found it helpful to offer some guidelines by which you can gauge the effectiveness of your group discussions. In this course, the group experience is usually most effective under the following conditions:

1. The purpose of the group is accepted as facilitating personal understanding of academic content.

2. Members attend regularly.

3. Seating is arranged so that all members can see each other clearly and are equidistant from each other. (Circles are a good arrangement.)

4. A warm and nonthreatening atmosphere prevails, that is, members are supportive and encouraging to each other when they speak.

5. Members have given some thought to the topic under discussion.

6. Members LISTEN to each other.

7. Everyone participates by initiating discussion, asking questions, giving examples.

8. Leadership functions are distributed among all group members and not vested only in the group facilitator.

9. The material is adequately and efficiently covered.

10. Evaluation of group effectiveness is accepted as a normal part of group functioning.

A note on evaluation of group effectiveness: some attention to the goals and needs of the group and of group members is necessary to maintain productive discussions. It is often helpful to spend a few minutes at the end of each session talking about how to improve discussion next time. Sometimes, written evaluations (formal or informal) are useful. (If your group decides to use a formal written evaluation, your facilitator can make arrangements with your instructor to have copies made available.)

Students seem to feel that they get more out of group discussions when they make an effort to participate. Don't fall into the trap of assuming that the facilitator is the leader and is totally responsible for group interactions. Remember, effective group discussions depend on contributions from *all* members in the group.

WHAT YOU CAN EXPECT FROM GROUP DISCUSSIONS

Most students report that they are more aware of and are better able to understand issues confronting adolescents as a result of having participated in the group discussions. They also feel that they are better able to understand themselves and fellow students. Listed below are reactions from some of my students:

In my group, one of the most important discussions was on love and sex. I was surprised at the openness and frankness of the conversation, but was glad that people were talking about sex and not running from it.

I learned to interact more fully with people. It's very hard, sometimes, to be honest about your deep personal values, for fear of rejection, but I found in my group that people, while they may not accept your values, usually were willing to listen.

Because I have two teenagers and a preteen, I learned a lot from the discussion on parent-adolescent conflicts. I've learned to listen more and to try to relate in a different manner. It's easier now to identify mistakes at home and to try to correct them.

GETTING STARTED IN SMALL GROUP DISCUSSIONS

Before you meet together in small groups for the first time, your instructor will probably take some time in class to discuss the issues in this appendix. One way to get the groups started is outlined here.

First Group Meeting

1. Your instructor will divide the class into groups of 6 to 8, including your facilitator, trying for a good balance of ages and sexes in each group (10 minutes). To save time, your instructor may announce group assignments prior to the first meeting.

2. The facilitator will initiate introductions (5 minutes). Each member introduces himself or herself by name and tells the group *one* interesting thing about himself or herself (5 minutes).

3. The facilitator will take about 5 minutes to describe the purposes of the small group discussions, his or her goals for group interaction, his or her preferred styles of facilitating and group functioning (refer to "Guidelines for Effective Group Discussions" on pp. 387–388).

4. When members have an idea of how the group will run, you're ready to go on to the task of becoming acquainted with other members. The facilitator then guides you through the "Ice-Breaker" exercise.

5. *Ice-Breaker Exercise*[1] (approximately 30 minutes, depending on group size)

   a. Before the group interview gets under way, the facilitator explains the exercise briefly (as described below), sets the time limits for each interview (2 to 4 minutes per person, depending on the time remaining), stresses each member's right not to answer any question, and emphasizes the importance of not engaging in debate or argument with each other's positions (understanding and acceptance are to be strived for).

   b. A timekeeper is chosen to be sure that the same amount of time is allotted to each group member and that all members are interviewed within the time available.

   c. One by one, the group members (beginning with the facilitator) volunteer to be the "focus person" to be interviewed. The focus person controls the interview by calling on group members as he or she chooses. Focus persons have the option of not answering questions they feel are too personal or inappropriate by saying, "I pass." Each person's interview is over when the timekeeper announces that time is up.

   d. Some questions which might be asked are:

      (1) If you could be any age, which would you choose? Why?

      (2) If you could travel to any part of the world, where would you go?

      (3) Do you believe in God?

      (4) What is one thing you would like to learn before you die?

      (5) What magazines do you read regularly?

      (6) What are your favorite TV shows?

      (7) Do you have a hobby on which you spend a lot of time?

      (8) What is there about you which makes your friends like you?

      (9) Who has been the most important person in your life? Why?

      (10) What do you see yourself doing 5 years from now? 10 years?

      (11) Do you have a favorite food?

      (12) Do you have faith in our political system?

      (13) What is your most prized possession?

      (14) In what ways are you a conformist?

      (15) What book has greatly influenced you?

[1]Adapted by permission of A & W Publishers, Inc. from *Values Clarification: A Handbook of Practical Strategies for Teachers and Students.* New Revised Edition by Sidney B. Simon, Leland W. Howe, and Howard Kirschenbaum. Copyright © 1972; Copyright © 1978. Hart Publishing Company, Inc.

6. After the group interviews are all over, members spend sometime (5 minutes) talking about their reactions to the exercise and how comfortable they feel now compared to how they felt at the start of the exercise.

7. Before ending, the facilitator reminds the group of the topic to be discussed at the next meeting and the relevant reading assignment. He or she reminds them to bring their textbooks to the meeting.

Remaining Group Meetings

The number of group discussions to be held will be determined by your instructor. Your instructor will probably ask you what you think should be discussed and will then assign a topic for each of the discussion sessions.

Each of the discussions will probably be organized into three segments: (1) remarks introducing the topic and the issues to be covered, (2) completing the exercises, case studies, and questions, and (3) wrapping up the discussion and mentioning the topic for the next discussion.

Group facilitators will probably meet on a regular weekly basis with the instructor to decide which exercises, case studies, and questions from the book will be used. Since you will probably use some of the material in the textbook for discussions, you will probably need to bring your book to class on group discussion days.

Glossary

academic subculture (Clark & Trow; Cohen)   High school students oriented toward intellectual and academic achievement; college students oriented toward serious involvement with intellectual ideas.

academic underachievement   Academic performance at levels lower than student's abilities.

achievement and role success pattern (Dellas & Gaier)   One of three identity patterns of contemporary American women which entails achievement in male-valued domains.

achievement motivation   The need to excel in one's undertakings and to achieve success according to an internalized standard of excellence.

achievement test   A test which measures how much has been learned in a specific content area.

acting out   A maladaptive behavior pattern in which conflicts are directly expressed in antisocial behavior.

adjustment disorder   Temporary maladaptive response to environmental stresses.

adolescence   A transitional stage of development between childhood and adulthood, generally beginning around age 13 and ending about age 22.

adolescent growth spurt   A two-year period during which there are sudden increases in height and weight; occurs during pubescence, about age $10\frac{1}{2}$ in girls and $12\frac{1}{2}$ in boys.

adolescent psychology   The study of the physical, cognitive, personality, and social changes which take place in individuals beginning at puberty and continuing until the assumption of adult responsibilities in society.

alienation   The feeling of being isolated and estranged from society, other individuals, or oneself.

androgyny (Bem)   A sex-role identity that combines positive "masculine" and "feminine" traits.

anorexia nervosa   An eating disorder characterized by self-starvation and severe loss of weight.

aptitude test   A test used to determine how well a person might learn new information or skills of a specific nature.

authoritarian parenting style   A parenting style characterized by low parental acceptance of children and rigidly enforced standards.

authoritative parenting style   A parenting style characterized by the setting of firm, but reasonable standards and high parental acceptance of children.

big league shock (McArthur)   Anxieties triggered by the transition from a less to a more competitive school setting (from junior high to senior high school or from high school to college).

bimodal female identity pattern (Dellas & Gaier)   One of three identity patterns of contemporary American women in which there is a commitment to both career and family roles.

blue-collar occupations   Craft, operative, transport, and laborer jobs.

career education   Programs in schools designed to inform students about current economic and occupational trends, to train them in the process of making career decisions, and to teach them marketable skills.

classical conditioning (Pavlov)   The process of repeatedly pairing two stimuli (an unconditioned and a neutral stimulus) with the result that the initially neutral stimulus acquires the capacity to elicit the response elicited by the unconditioned stimulus.

clique (Dunphy)   A type of adolescent peer group primarily characterized by its small size (approximately 6 members).

cofigurative culture (Mead)   Societies characterized by moderate social change in which youth learn from their peers as well as their elders.

cognitive disequilibrium   A state that arises when people hear information that contradicts their beliefs; motivates individuals to resolve the contradiction by moving to a higher level of moral reasoning.

coitus   sexual intercourse.

collegiate subculture (Clark & Trow)   College students oriented toward social and athletic events, with less emphasis on intellectual pursuits.

combined longitudinal and cross-sectional approach   A research approach which combines the features of the longitudinal and cross-sectional designs, with the primary advantage of making it possible to separate age from time-of-birth effects.

competency-based education (CBE)   An educational approach requiring students to demonstrate minimal competence in designated areas in order to pass from one grade to another or to graduate from high school.

conventional level of moral development (Kohlberg)   The second level of moral development, characterized by moral judgments based on a concern for being judged as socially acceptable by others.

cross-sectional approach   A research design in which different age groups are tested at the same time on the same question to ascertain changes and stability in development with age.

crowd (Dunphy)   A type of adolescent peer group composed of about 20 members from different cliques.

cultural alienation   The experience of being rejected by the larger society because of prejudice.

culture-fair tests   Psychological tests that don't favor any particular cultural background.

defense mechanisms (Freud)   The ego's unconscious reactions to threats that deny, distort, or falsify reality—for example, rationalization.

delinquent subculture (Cohen)   A high school subculture whose members actively rebel against the school's academic program and social activities.

developmental estrangement (Keniston)   Feeling of alienation that results when adolescents leave childhood roles and ties behind before they are able to take on adult roles.

developmental tasks (Havighurst)   Attitudes and skills which are best learned at particular stages of development.

discontinuous culture (Benedict)   A culture in which children are taught attitudes and behaviors which they must unlearn to be successful adults.

eclectic   Choosing what appears to be best from a variety of sources.

ego (Freud)   The rational aspect of personality which aids the individual in adapting to the external world.

egocentrism (Piaget)   A cognitive characteristic in which individuals are unable to differentiate their own thoughts and feelings from those of others; diminishes considerably in late adolescence.

empirical   Based on systematic observation or experiment rather than solely on reasoning.

endocrine glands   Ductless glands that secrete hormones directly into the bloodstream (pituitary, adrenals, thyroid, parathyroids, pancreas, and gonads).

expert stage (Lindemann)   A stage of contraceptive use in which adolescents consult professionals or paraprofessionals in the family-planning field for contraceptive information.

extended family   A type of family unit composed of mother, father, immediate children, grandparents, and sometimes other relatives.

external locus of control (Rotter)   The belief that what happens in one's life is due to chance, luck, or forces beyond one's control.

extreme ideology (Deutsch)   A belief system that is closed to useful and important information that is discrepant with existing ideas.

formal operations (Piaget)   The fourth and last stage of cognitive development which begins about age 11 and is characterized by the ability to think logically about abstract ideas.

fun subculture (Cohen)   A high school subculture oriented toward participation and success in extracurricular activities, with less emphasis on academic achievement; similar to the collegiate subculture at the college level.

fusion (Erikson)   Intense feelings of closeness experienced by partners in a relationship who don't have independent identities.

gamblers' fallacy (Cvetkovich)   The personal fable that one can't get pregnant because one has intercourse infrequently.

gang   A type of adolescent peer group characterized by antisocial and illegal activities.

generation gap   The idea that parents and adolescents have different attitudes and values.

genital stage (Freud)   The last stage of psychosexual development, beginning about age 11, when an individual is motivated toward sexual gratification with another person and when the Oedipal or Electra complex is reawakened.

group identity versus alienation (Newman & Newman)   The psychosocial crisis of adolescents from puberty to age 18; the feeling that one "belongs" in a peer group versus feeling isolated.

heterophilic relationship (Sullivan)   A relationship sought because the other person is significantly different from oneself, namely, the opposite gender.

hormones   Substances secreted by endocrine glands into the bloodstream which regulate physiological and sexual development and functioning.

id (Freud)   The structure of personality present at birth, governed by irrational and biological forces, which seeks to gratify basic instinctive needs.

identity (Erikson)   A stable sense of oneself; the developmental task of adolescence.

identity achievement (Marcia)   An identity status characterized by the attainment, after a period of questioning, of a sense of who one is and what one can become.

identity diffusion (Marcia)   An identity status characterized by the failure to develop a stable and integrated sense of oneself.

identity foreclosure (Marcia)   An identity status characterized by the adoption of the beliefs and goals of parents or the status quo without any serious questioning.

ideology (Adelson)   A body of relatively consistent attitudes organized, more or less, according to a larger set of principles.

imaginary audience (Elkind)   A consequence of adolescent egocentrism in which young people believe that others are paying more attention to them than is really the case.

individual identity versus role diffusion (Newman & Newman)   The psychosocial crisis of adolescents age 18 to 21; attaining autonomy from the family and developing a sense of personal identity rather than failing to do so; similar to Erikson's crisis of adolescence.

individuating-reflexive faith (Fowler)   A level of faith development characterized by religious beliefs that have been critically evaluated and have personal meaning to those who hold them.

inductive disciplinary technique (Hoffman)   A disciplinary method that uses reason as a way of inducing the child's compliance to parental standards.

intellectualization   A Freudian defense mechanism in which anxiety-provoking ideas or problems are discussed in an abstract, rational manner in order to avoid focusing on the unpleasant emotional aspects of problems.

intelligence quotient   A means of measuring intelligence calculated by comparing a given test score with other scores in a standardized sample.

internal locus of control (Rotter)   The belief that what happens in one's life can be controlled by one's own actions.

interpersonal theory of psychiatry (Sullivan)   A theory that considers social interactions to be the major factor in personality development.

intimate (Orlofsky)   A more advanced intimacy status characterized by individuals who have close and open relationships with others and who are involved in a committed relationship.

invulnerables (Garmezy)   Youth who are able to master severely stressful environments.

isophilic relationship (Sullivan)   A relationship sought because the other person is very similar to oneself, namely, the same gender.

isolate (Orlofsky)   A less advanced intimacy status characterized by individuals who are loners and who cannot engage in committed relationships.

juvenile delinquent   An individual under the age of 18 (in most states) who engages in illegal behavior.

longitudinal approach   A research design in which the same subjects are tested repeatedly over a long period of time.

love-withdrawal disciplinary technique (Hoffman)   A disciplinary method that uses nonphysical expressions of anger (ignoring, etc.) to induce compliance in a child.

marginal man status (Lewin)   Characterization of adolescents based on the fact that they have no designated social role, being neither children nor adults.

masked depression   Depression characterized by symptoms which don't typically suggest that depression is present (inability to concentrate, fatigue, or hypochondria).

menarche   The first menstrual period.

menstruation   The monthly discharge of blood and uterine material that occurs in sexually mature females.

modern male role (Pleck)   A male sex role in which masculinity is validated by economic achievement, organizational power, emotional control, emotional sensitivity, and self-expression displayed only to women.

moratorium (Marcia)   An identity status characterized by actively struggling to achieve a sense of oneself.

natural stage (Lindemann)   A stage in contraceptive use in which the adolescent takes no responsibility for birth control.

negative identity   The adoption of socially undesirable roles, usually because routes to positive roles are blocked.

neglectful parenting style   A parenting style characterized by low parental acceptance and low parental control.

nonconformist subculture (Clark & Trow)   College students who are deeply involved with intellectual ideas and social issues and who tend to identify with off-campus groups rather than faculty members.

nuclear family A type of family unit composed of mother, father, and immediate children.

observational learning (Bandura) Learning how to do something by watching someone else do it (imitation, modeling).

occupational competence model The idea that early work experience produces more knowledgeable and competent workers.

occupational cynicism model The idea that early work experience produces negative and materialistic attitudes about work.

operant conditioning (Skinner) Strengthening a response by reinforcing it.

optimizing satisfactions model of vocational development (Ginzberg) The idea that career choice is a lifelong process of optimizing personal preferences in the context of job requirements.

ovaries Female sex glands which produce eggs and sex hormones (estrogen and progesterone).

parental exploitation (Elkind) A condition in which parents put their own needs before those of their children or use their children in order to gratify their own needs.

passive-aggressive behavior The passive expression of anger through inactivity.

peer prescription stage (Lindemann) A stage in contraceptive use in which the adolescent relies on friends for information about birth control.

penis The male sex organ.

permissive parenting style A parenting style characterized by high parental acceptance and low parental control.

personal fable (Elkind) A consequence of adolescent egocentrism in which young people believe they are special and unique.

personality disorder Enduring and maladaptive pattern of relating to, perceiving, and thinking about oneself and the environment.

petting Fondling above the waist (light petting) or below the waist (heavy petting).

postconventional level of moral development (Kohlberg) The highest level of moral development characterized by moral judgments based on abstract moral principles.

postfigurative culture (Mead) Societies characterized by relatively little social change in which young people learn from adults.

power-assertive disciplinary technique (Hoffman) A disciplinary method that uses physical punishment or depriving children of possessions or privileges as a means of inducing compliance to parental standards.

preconventional level of moral development (Kohlberg) The lowest level of moral development, characterized by moral judgments based on external rewards and punishment.

prefigurative culture (Mead) Societies characterized by rapid social change in which young people must learn many things on their own (without guidance from adults).

preintimate (Orlofsky) A more advanced intimacy status characterized by individuals who have close, open, and reciprocal relationships with others but who have not yet engaged in a committed relationship.

primary sex characteristics Structures essential for reproduction (testicles, prostate gland, seminal vesicles, and penis in males; ovaries, uterine tubes, uterus, and vagina in females).

pseudointimate (Orlofsky) A less advanced intimacy status in which individuals are involved in relatively permanent relationships which are characterized by superficiality and manipulation.

psychosocial moratorium (Erikson) A time of freedom from adult responsibilities granted by many cultures to adolescents in which young people are expected to "find themselves."

puberty Attainment of sexual maturity; usually about age 13 in females with onset of menstruation; about $14\frac{1}{2}$ in males with ejaculation of sperm.

puberty rites Formal initiation ceremonies that mark the passage from childhood to adult status; characteristic of tribal societies.

pubescence   Two-year period preceding puberty during which rapid physical and physiological changes take place leading to physical and sexual maturity; starts about $10\frac{1}{2}$ in girls and about $12\frac{1}{2}$ in boys.

reasonable ideology (Deutsch)   A belief system that is open to useful and important information even when it is discrepant with existing ideas.

recapitulation theory (Hall)   The view that all individuals repeat the major stages of human evolution as they mature.

reconstituted (blended) family   A family made up of two adults, at least one of whom has been divorced, as well as the children of one or both of them.

role-taking   The ability to take the role of other people so as to understand their thoughts, feelings, and perceptions.

schizophrenia   A serious psychological disorder characterized by major cognitive, emotional, and behavioral disturbances.

school phobia   Refusal to attend school ostensibly because of sickness or complaints about the school situation, but actually because of psychological conflicts.

scrotum   The sac of skin containing the testes.

secondary sex characteristics   Bodily features that distinguish the sexes, but are not essential for reproduction (voice, body hair distribution, breast development, and body shape).

self-concept   An individual's perception of his or her personal qualities, competencies, etc.

self-concept model of vocational development (Super)   The idea that career choice is a reflection of a person's self-concept.

self-disclosure   Revealing one's private thoughts and feelings to another person.

self-esteem   The value placed on oneself; self-worth.

sex-role identification   The process of internalizing societal sex-role expectations.

sex-role identity   A specific aspect of personal identity which refers to an individual's conscious and unconscious identification with the traits, attitudes, and interests that societal norms dictate to be appropriate for a given sex.

sex-role strain (Pleck)   A special type of role strain in which individuals feel they can't adequately meet sex-role expectations which are experienced as rigid and confining.

sexual preference   An individual's preference for a same-, opposite-, or either-sex partner for an emotional and sexual relationship.

sexually transmitted disease (venereal disease)   A disease transmitted through genital or oral-genital contact.

skeletal age   The most reliable criterion for determining the level of maturation, measured by the proportion of bone to cartilage in the hand and wrist.

social cognition   The study of the nature and development of people's thoughts and perceptions about themselves and others.

socialization   The process by which a culture imparts socially accepted standards, values, and behaviors to its members.

sociopathic behavior   Antisocial behavior, usually engaged in by an individual without feelings of guilt or remorse.

status offense   An act that is punishable by law only when committed by a juvenile.

sterility fable (Cvetkovich)   The personal fable that one is sterile because intercourse hasn't yet resulted in pregnancy.

stereotyped (Orlofsky)   A less advanced intimacy status in which individuals usually see others as objects to be manipulated and cannot make long-lasting commitments.

superego (Freud)   The moral agent of the personality, consisting of internalized parental and societal standards, expectations, and values.

synthetic-conventional faith (Fowler)   A level of faith development in which individuals uncritically accept the tenets of their faith and screen out dissonant information.

testes   Male sex glands which produce sperm and sex hormones (androgens).

traditional female role pattern (Dellas & Gaier)   One of three identity patterns of contemporary American women in which there is a commitment to the roles of wife and mother.

traditional male role (Pleck)   A male sex role in which masculinity is validated by physical strength, aggression, and emotional inexpressiveness.

trait measurement and matching model of vocational development   The idea that particular personality traits are the factors which determine an individual's interest in particular occupations.

underemployed   Term applied to people who are overeducated for the jobs they hold.

vocational subculture (Clark & Trow)   College students whose orientations are job-related rather than intellectual or social.

white-collar occupations   Professional and technical, managerial and administrative, sales, and clerical jobs.

youth (Keniston)   A relatively new stage of development composed of older adolescents who haven't yet assumed adult responsibilities; characteristic of postindustrial societies which require postsecondary education of their citizens.

References

Abelson, H. I., Fishburne, P. M., & Cisin, I. (1977). *National survey on drug abuse: 1977. Volume I: Main Findings* (DHEW Publication No. ADM 78–618). Rockville, Md.: National Institute on Drug Abuse.

Adams, J. F. (1964). Adolescent personal problems as a function of age and sex. *Journal of Genetic Psychology, 104,* 207–214.

Adams, J. F. (1981). Earlier menarche, greater height and weight: A stimulation-stress factor hypothesis. *Genetic Psychology Monographs, 104*(1), 3–22.

Addiction: Hows and whys. (1980). *Current Lifestyles, 3*(7), 7–9.

Adelson, J. (1971). The political imagination of the young adolescent. *Daedalus, 100,* 1013–1050.

Adelson, J. (1975). The development of ideology in adolescence. In S. E. Dragastin & G. H. Elder, Jr. (Eds.), *Adolescence in the life cycle: Psychological change and social context* (pp. 63–78). New York: Wiley.

Adelson, J. (1979, February). Adolescence and the generalization gap. *Psychology Today, 12*(9), pp. 33–37.

Advisory Panel. (1977). *On further examination: Report of the advisory panel on the Scholastic Aptitude Test decline.* Princeton, N.J.: College Entrance Examination Board.

Agrawal, P. (1978). A cross-cultural study of self-image: Indian, American, Australian, and Irish adolescents. *Journal of Youth and Adolescence, 7*(1), 107–116.

Ahlstrom, W. M., & Havighurst, R. J. (1971). *400 losers.* San Francisco: Jossey-Bass.

Alan Guttmacher Institute. (1976). *11 million teenagers: What can be done about the epidemic of adolescent pregnancies in the United States?* New York: Planned Parenthood Federation.

Alan Guttmacher Institute. (1979). *Abortions and the poor: Private mentality, public responsibility.* New York: Planned Parenthood Federation.

Albert, N., & Beck, A. T. (1975). Incidence of depression in early adolescence: A preliminary study. *Journal of Youth and Adolescence, 4,* 301–308.

Allen, W. R. (1978). Race, family setting, and adolescent achievement orientation. *Journal of Negro Education, 47*(3), 230–243.

Almquist, E. M., Angrist, S. S., & Mickelsen, R. (1980). Women's career aspirations and achievements: College and seven years after. *Sociology of Work and Occupations, 7*(3), 367–384.

Alper, T. G. (1974). Achievement motivation in college women: A now-you-see-it-now-you-don't phenomenon. *American Psychologist, 29,* 194–203.

Ambrosino, L. (1971). *Runaways.* Boston: Beacon Press.

Amini, F., Salasnek, S., & Burke, E. L. (1976). Adolescent drug use: Etiological and treatment considerations. *Adolescence, 11,* 281–299.

Anderson, R. E. (1968). Where's Dad? Paternal deprivation and delinquency. *Archives of General Psychiatry, 18,* 641–649.

Anderson, T. W. (1965). Swimming and exercise during menstruation. *Journal of Health, Physical Education, and Recreation, 36,* 66–68.

Andrew, J. M. (1981). Delinquency: Correlating variables. *Journal of Clinical Child Psychology, 10*(2), 136–140.

Angrist, S. S. (1969). The study of sex roles. *Journal of Social Issues, 25*(1), 215–232.

Angrist, S. S. (1972). Variations in women's adult aspirations during college. *Journal of Marriage and the Family, 34,* 465–467.

Archer, S. L. (1982). The lower age boundaries of identity development. *Child Development, 53,* 1551–1556.

Arundel, F. D. (1971). Acne vulgaris. *Pediatric Clinics of North America, 18,* 853–874.

Astin, A. W. (1977). *Four critical years.* San Francisco: Jossey-Bass.

Astin, A. W. (1979). *The American freshman: National norms for fall 1979.* American Council on Education and University of California at Los Angeles.

Astin, A. W. (1980). *The American freshman: National norms for fall 1980.* American Council on Education and University of California at Los Angeles.

Astin, A. W., Green, K. C., Korn, W. S., & Maier, M. J. (1983). *The American freshman: National norms for fall 1983.* American Council on Education and University of California at Los Angeles.

Avery, R. K. (1979). Adolescents' use of the mass media. *American Behavioral Scientist, 23,* 53–70.

Bachman, J. G., Johnston, L. D., & O'Malley, P. M. (1980). *Monitoring the future: Questionnaire responses from the nation's high school seniors.* Ann Arbor, MI: Institute for Social Research of the University of Michigan.

Bachman, J. G., Johnston, L. D., & O'Malley, P. M. (in press). Recent findings from Monitoring the Future: A continuing study of the lifestyles and values of youth. In Frank M. Andrews (Ed.), *Research on the quality of life* (tentative title; forthcoming in 1985). Ann Arbor, MI: Institute for Social Research of the University of Michigan.

Bachman, J. G., O'Malley, P. M., & Johnston, J. (1978). *Youth in transition: Vol. VI: Adolescence to adulthood—change and stability in the lives of young men.* Ann Arbor MI: Institute for Social Research of the University of Michigan.

Backman, M. E. (1972). Patterns of mental abilities: Ethnic, socioeconomic, and sex differences. *American Educational Research Journal, 9*(1), 1–12.

Bain, T., & Fottler, M. D. (1978). Sources of occupational information used by Alabama high school seniors. *Monthly Labor Review, 101*(5), 45–46.

Bakan, D. (1971). Adolescence in America: From idea to social fact. *Daedalus, 100,* 979–995.

Balswick, J. O. (1974). The Jesus people movement: A generational interpretation. *Journal of Social Issues. 30,* 23–42.

Balswick, J. O., & Macrides, C. (1975). Parental stimulus for adolescent rebellion. *Adolescence, 10,* 253–266.

Balswick, J. O., & Peek, C. W. (1971). The inexpressive male: A tragedy of American society. *The Family Coordinator, 20,* 363–368.

Bandura, A. (1964). The stormy decade: Fact or fiction? *Psychology in the Schools, 1,* 224–231.

Bandura, A. (1977). *Social learning theory.* Englewood Cliffs, N.J.: Prentice-Hall.

Bandura, A., Grusec, J. E., & Menlove, F. L. (1966). Observational learning as a function of symbolization and incentive set. *Child Development, 37,* 499–506.

Bandura, A., Grusec, J. E., & Menlove, F. L. (1967). Some determinants of self-monitoring reinforcement systems. *Journal of Personality and Social Psychology, 5,* 449–455.

Bandura, A., & Walters, R. H. (1959). *Adolescent aggression.* New York: Ronald Press.

Bandura, A., & Walters, R. H. (1963). *Social learning and personality development.* New York: Holt, Rinehart, & Winston.

Bane, M. J. (1976). Marital disruption and the lives of children. *Journal of Social Issues, 32,* 103–117.

Baranowski, M. D. (1971). Television and the adolescent. *Adolescence, 6,* 369–396.

Bardwick, J. (1971). *The psychology of women: A study of bio-social conflict.* New York: Harper & Row.

Barnes, G. M. (1977). The development of adolescent drinking behavior: An evaluative review of the impact of the socialization process within the family. *Adolescence, 13,* 571–591.

Barratt, B. B. (1977). The development of peer perception systems in childhood and early adolescence. *Social Behavior and Personality, 5*(2), 351–360.

Barton, W. H. (1976). Discretionary decisionmaking in juvenile justice. *Crime and Delinquency, 22,* 470–480.

Baruch, G. (1972). Maternal influences upon college women's attitudes toward women and work. *Developmental Psychology, 6,* 32–37.

Baumrind, D. (1968). Authoritarian vs. authoritative control. *Adolescence, 3,* 255–272.

Baumrind, D. (1971). Current patterns of parental authority. *Developmental Psychology Monographs, 4* (1, Pt. 2).

Baumrind, D. (1974). Coleman II: Utopian fantasy and sound social innovation. *School Review, 83*(1), 69–84.

Baumrind, D. (1975). Early socialization and adolescent competence. In S. E. Dragastin & G. H. Elder (Eds.), *Adolescence in the life cycle: Psychological change and social context.* New York: Wiley.

Baumrind, D. (1978). Parental disciplinary patterns and social competence in children. *Youth and Society, 9*(3), 239–276.

Baumrind, D. (1982). Are androgynous individuals more effective as persons and parents? *Child Development, 53,* 44–75.

Bayh, B. (Chairman). (1975). *Our nation's schools—A report card: "A" in school violence and vandalism. Report of the U.S. Senate Committee on the Judiciary.* Washington, D.C.: U.S. Government Printing Office.

Beck, A. T., & Young, J. E. (1978, September). College blues. *Psychology Today,* pp. 80, 85–86, 89, 91–92.

Bee, H. L. (1978). *The developing child* (2nd ed.). New York: Harper & Row.

Bell, R. (1980). *Changing bodies, changing lives.* New York: Random House. Copyright 1980 by Random House.

Bem, S. L. (1975). Sex role adaptability: One consequence of psychological androgyny. *Journal of Personality and Social Psychology, 31,* 634–643.

Benbow, C. P., & Stanley, J. C. (1980). Sex differences in mathematical ability; Fact or artifact? *Science, 210,* 1262–1264.

Bender, L. (1974). The family patterns of 100 schizophrenic children observed at Bellevue, 1935–1952. *Journal of Autism and Childhood Schizophrenia, 4* (4), 279–292.

Benedict, R. (1938). Continuities and discontinuities in cultural conditioning. *Psychiatry, 1,* 161–167. Copyright 1938 by the William Alanson White Psychiatric Foundation.

Berg, P., & Hyde, J. S. (1976, September). *Gender and race differences in causal attributions.* Paper presented at American Psychological Association Meeting, Washington, D.C.

Berger, B. (1976). The coming age of people work. *Change, 8,* 24–30.

Berndt, T. J. (1979). Developmental changes in conformity to peers and parents. *Developmental Psychology, 15,* 608–616.

Bernstein, R. M. (1980). The development of the self-system during adolescence. *Journal of Genetic Psychology, 136,* 231–245.

Berscheid, E., Dion, K., Walster, E., & Walster, G. (1971). Physical attractiveness and dating choice: A test of the matching hypothesis. *Journal of Personality and Social Psychology, 7,* 173–189.

Biller, H. B. (1974). *Paternal deprivation.* Lexington, MA: Lexington Books.

Biller, H. B., & Davids, A. (1973). Parent-child relations, personality development, and psychopathology. In A. Davids (Ed.), *Issues in abnormal and child psychology* (pp. 48–77). Monterey, Calif.: Brooks/Cole.

Birnbaum, J. A. (1975). Life patterns and self-esteem in gifted family-oriented and career-oriented women. In M. T. S. Mednick, S. S. Tangri, & L. W. Holman (Eds.), *Women and achievement.* New York: Wiley.

Blanchard, R. W., & Biller, H. B. (1971). Father availability and academic performance among third-grade boys. *Developmental Psychology, 4,* 301–305.

Block, J. H. (1973). Conceptions of sex-role: Some cross-cultural and longitudinal perspectives. *American Psychologist, 28,* 512–526.

Block, J. H., Haan, N., & Smith, M. B. (1973). Activism and apathy in contemporary adolescents. In J. F. Adams (Ed.), *Understanding adolescents: Current developments in adolescent psychology.* Boston: Allyn & Bacon.

Block, R. W., & Block, S. A. (1980). Outreach education: A possible preventer of teenage pregnancy. *Adolescence, 15*(59), 657–660.

Blood, L., & D'Angelo, R. (1974). A progress research report on value issues in conflict between runaways and their parents. *Journal of Marriage and the Family, 36,* 486–491.

Bloom, B. (1964). *Stability and change in human characteristics.* New York: Wiley.

Blyth, D. A., Simmons, R. G., & Bush, D. M. (1978). The transition into early adolescence: A longitudinal comparison of youth in two educational contexts. *Sociology of Education, 51,* 149–162.

Blyth, D. A., Thiel, K. S., Bush, D. M., & Simmons, R. G. (1980). Another look at school crime: Student as victim. *Youth and Society, 11*(3), 369–388.

Bolton, F. G., Laner, R. H., & Kane, S. P. (1980). Child maltreatment risk among adolescent mothers: A study of reported cases. *American Journal of Orthopsychiatry, 50*(3), 489–504.

Boocock, S. S. (1974). Youth in three cultures. *School Review, 83*(1), 93–111.

Borow, H. (1976). Career development. In J. F. Adams (Ed.), *Understanding adolescence: Current developments in adolescent psychology* (3rd ed., pp. 489–523). Boston: Allyn & Bacon.

Bowen, H. R. (1977). *Investment in learning: The individual and social value of American higher education.* San Francisco: Jossey-Bass.

Bradway, K., & Thompson, C. (1962). Intelligence at adulthood: A twenty-five-year follow-up. *Journal of Educational Psychology, 53,* 1–14.

Braham, M. (1965). Peer group deterrents to intellectual development during adolescence. *Educational Theory, 15,* 248–258.

Breaking a deadly family tradition: Los Angeles wages war on street crimes. (1983, April 18). *Boston Globe,* p. 3.

Bronfenbrenner, U. (1970). *Two worlds of childhood.* New York: Russell Sage.

Broverman, I. K., Vogel, S. R., Broverman, D. M., Clarkson, F. E., & Rosenkrantz, P. S. (1972). Sex-role stereotypes: A current appraisal. *Journal of Social Issues, 28,* 59–78.

Brown, D. (1957). Masculinity-femininity development in children. *Journal of Consulting Psychology, 21,* 197–202.

Brown, M. E. (1979). Teenage prostitution. *Adolescence. 14*(56), 665–680.

Brownstone, J. R., & Willis, R. H. (1971). Conformity in early and late adolescence. *Developmental Psychology, 4,* 334–337.

Burke, R. J., & Weir, T. (1978). Sex differences in adolescent life stress, social support, and well-being. *Journal of Psychology, 98,* 277–288.

Burke, R. S., & Grinder, R. E. (1966). Personality-oriented themes and listening patterns in teen-age music and their relation to certain academic and peer variables. *School Review, 74,* 196–211.

Burnstein, B., Bank, L. & Jarvik, L. F. (1980). Sex differences in cognitive functioning: Evidence, determinants, implications. *Human Development, 23*(5), 289–313.

Campbell, E. Q. (1969). Adolescent socialization. In D. A. Goslin (Ed.), *Handbook of socialization theory and research.* Chicago: Rand-McNally.

Campbell, M. M., & Cooper, K. (1975). Parent's perception of adolescent behavior problems. *Journal of Youth and Adolescence, 4,* 309–320.

Carroll, C., Miller, D., & Nash, J. C. (1976). *Health: The science of human adaptation.* Dubuque, IA: Brown.

Carroll, J. F. X., & Synigal, M. (1975). Rehabilitating the problem drinker. *Intellect, 104* (2367), 31–35.

Carter, T. P. (1968). Negative self-concepts of Mexican-American students. *School and Society, 96,* 217–219.

Cassel, R. N., & Mehail, T. (1973). The Milwaukee computerized vocational guidance system (VOC-GUID). *Vocational Guidance Quarterly, 21,* 206–213.

Cauble, M. A. (1976). Formal operations, ego identity, and principled morality: Are they related? *Developmental Psychology, 12,* 363–364.

Cavior, N., & Dokecki, P. R. (1973). Physical attractiveness, perceived attitude similarity, and academic achievement as contributors to interpersonal attraction among adolescents. *Developmental Psychology, 9,* 44–54.

Chand, I. P., Crider, D. M., & Willits, F. K. (1975). Parent-youth disagreement as perceived by youth: A longitudinal study. *Youth and Society, 6,* 365–375.

Chassin, L., Young, R. D., & Light, R. (1980). Evaluations of treatment techniques by delinquent and disturbed adolescents. *Journal of Clinical Child Psychology, 9*(3), 220–223.

Chickering, A. W. (1969). *Education and identity.* San Francisco: Jossey-Bass.

Chilman, C. S. (1979). *Adolescent sexuality in a changing American society: Sociological and psychological perspectives.* Washington, D.C.: National Institute of Mental Health.

Chilton, R. J., & Markle, G. E. (1972). Family disruption, delinquent conduct, and the effect of sub-classification. *American Sociological Review, 37,* 93–99.

Clark, B. R., & Trow, M. (1966). The organizational context. In T. M. Newcomb & E. K. Wilson (Eds.), *College peer groups.* Chicago: Aldine.

Clarke, A. E., & Ruble, D. N. (1978). Young adolescents' beliefs concerning menstruation. *Child Development, 49,* 231–234.

Clausen, J. A. (1975). The social meaning of differential physical and sexual maturation. In S. E. Dragastin & G. Elder (Eds.), *Adolescence in the life cycle: Psychological change and social context.* New York: Wiley.

Cobliner, W. G. (1974). Pregnancy in the single adolescent girl: The role of cognitive function. *Journal of Youth and Adolescence, 3,* 17–29.

Cohen, J. (1979). High school structures and the adult world. *Adolescence, 14,* 491–502.

Cohen, L. E., & Kluegal, J. R. (1978). Determinants of juvenile court dispositions: Ascriptive and achieved factors in two metropolitan courts. *American Sociological Review, 43,* 162–176.

Cohen, S. (1979). Inhalants (pp. 213–220). In R. I. Dupont, A. Goldstein, & J. O'Donnell (Eds.), *Handbook on drug abuse.* Washington, D.C.: U.S. Government Printing Office.

Coleman, J. C. (1974). *Relationships in adolescence.* Boston and London: Routledge & Kegan Paul.

Coleman, J. C. (1978). Current contradictions in adolescent theory. *Journal of Youth and Adolescence, 7,* 1–12.

Coleman, J. C. (1980). Friendship and the peer group in adolescence. In J. Adelson (Ed.), *Handbook of adolescent psychology.* New York: Wiley.

Coleman, J. C., George, R., & Holt, G. (1977). Adolescents and their parents: A study of attitudes. *Journal of Genetic Psychology, 130,* 239–245.

Coleman, J. S. (1961). *The adolescent society.* New York: Free Press.

Coleman, J. S., Bremner, R. H., Burton, C. R., Davis, J. B., Eichorn, D. H., Griliches, Z., Kett, J. F., Ryder, N. B., Doering, Z. B., & Mays, J. M. (1974). *Youth: Transition to adulthood.* Chicago: University of Chicago Press.

College Entrance Examination Board. (1982). *National report on college-bound seniors, 1982.* Princeton, N.J.: Educational Testing Service.

College Entrance Examination Board. (1983). *National report on college-bound seniors, 1983.* Princeton, N.J.: Educational Testing Service.

Collins, J. K., & Thomas, N. T. (1972). Age and susceptibility to same sex peer pressure. *British Journal of Educational Psychology, 42,* 83–85.

Comstock, G. A. (1978, Spring). The impact of television on American institutions. *Journal of Communication,* pp. 12–28.

Comstock, G. A., Chaffee, S., Katzman, N., McCombs, M., & Roberts, D. (1978). *Television and human behavior.* New York: Columbia University Press.

Condry, J., & Dyer, S. (1976). Fear of success: Attribution of the cause to the victim. *Journal of Social Issues, 47,* 812–819.

Conger, J. J. (1971). A world they never knew: The family and social change. *Daedalus, 100,* 1105–1138.

Conger, J. J. (1981). Freedom and commitment: Families, youth, and social change. *American Psychologist, 36*(12), 1475–1484.

Conger, J. J., & Petersen, A. C (1984). *Adolescence and youth* (3rd ed.). New York: Harper & Row.

Constantinople, A. (1969). An Eriksonian measure of personality development in college students. *Developmental Psychology, 1,* 357–372.

Coons, F. W. (1970). The resolution of adolescence in college. *Personnel and Guidance Journal, 48*(7), 533–541.

Coopersmith, S. (1967). *The antecedents of self-esteem.* San Francisco: Freeman.

Costanzo, P. R. (1970). Conformity development as a function of self-blame. *Journal of Personality and Social Psychology, 14,* 366–374.

Costanzo, P. R., & Shaw, M. E. (1966). Conformity as a function of age level. *Child Development, 37,* 967–975.

Cox, M., & Cox, R. (1979). Socialization of young children in the divorced family. *Journal of Research and Development in Education, 13,* 58–67.

Crites, J. O. (1980). Career development. In J. F. Adams (Ed.), *Understanding adolescence:*

Current developments in adolescent psychology (4th ed., pp. 396–420). Boston: Allyn & Bacon.

Crites, J. O., & Fitzgerald, L. F. (1978). The competent male. *Counseling Psychologist, 7*(4), 10–14.

Cross, K. P. (1971). *The Undergraduate woman* (Research Report No. 5). Washington, D.C.: American Association for Higher Education.

Crutchfield, S. (1955). Conformity and character. *American Psychologist, 10,* 191–198.

Cureton, T. K. (1964). Improving the physical fitness of youth. *Monographs of the Society for Research in Child Development, 29*(4).

Curran, J. P., & Lippold, S. (1975). The effects of physical attractiveness and attitude similarity on attraction in dating dyads. *Journal of Personality, 43,* 528–539.

Cvetkovich, G., Grote, B., Bjorseth, A., & Sarkissian, J. (1975). On the psychology of adolescent use of contraception. *Journal of Sex Research, 11,* 256–270.

Damico, S. B. (1975). The effects of clique membership upon academic achievement. *Adolescence, 10,* 93–100.

Damon, W. (1979). Why study social-cognitive development? *Human Development, 22,* 206–211.

Dasen, P. R. (1972). Cross-cultural Piagetian research: A summary. *Journal of Cross-cultural Research, 3,* 23–39.

Davidson, B., Balswick, J. O., & Halverson, C. F. (1980). Factor analysis of self-disclosure for adolescents. *Adolescence, 15*(60), 947–957.

The deadly "angel dust." (1978, March 13). *Newsweek,* p. 34.

A deadly feast and famine. (1983, March 7). *Newsweek,* pp. 59–60.

Dean, R. A. (1982). Youth: Moonies' target population. *Adolescence, 17*(67), 567–574.

DeLissovoy, V. (1973, July). Child care by adolescent parents. *Children Today,* pp. 22–25.

Dellas, M., & Gaier, E. L. (1975). The self and adolescent identity in women: Options and implications. *Adolescence, 10,* 399–407.

DeLuca, J. R. (Ed.) (1981). *Alcohol and health: Fourth special report to the U.S. Congress.* Rockville, MD: National Institute on Alcohol and Alcohol Abuse.

Dembo, M. H., & Lundell, B. (1979). Factors affecting adolescent contraception practices: Implications for sex education. *Adolescence, 14*(56), 657–664.

Derbyshire, R. L. (1979). Adolescent identity crisis in Mexican Americans in East Los Angeles. In E. B. Brody (Ed.), *Minority group adolescents in the United States.* Huntington, N.Y.: Robert E. Krieger.

Deutsch, K. W. (1980). *Politics and government: How people decide their fate.* Boston: Houghton Mifflin.

Deux, K., & Emswiller, T. (1974). Explanations of successful performance on sex-linked tasks: What is skill for the male is luck for the female. *Journal of Personality and Social Psychology, 29*(1), 80–85.

Devereaux, E. C. (1970). The role of peer-group experience in moral development. In J. P. Hill (Ed.), *Minnesota symposium on child psychology,* Vol. 4. Minneapolis: University of Minnesota Press.

Devereaux, E. C., Shouval, R., Bronfenbrenner, U., Rodgers, R. R., Kav-Venaki, S., Kiely, E., & Karson, E. (1974). Socialization practices of parents, teachers and peers in Israel: The kibbutz versus the city. *Child Development, 45,* 269–281.

Dickinson, G. E. (1975). Dating behavior of black and white adolescents before and after de-segregation. *Journal of Marriage and the Family, 37,* 602–608.

Diepold, J., & Young, R. D. (1979). Empirical studies of adolescent sexual behavior: A critical review. *Adolescence, 14*(53), 45–64.

Dion, K., Berscheid, E., & Walster, E. (1972). What is beautiful is good. *Journal of Personality and Social Psychology, 24,* 285–290.

Ditkoff, G. S. (1979). Stereotypes of adolescents toward the working woman. *Adolescence, 14*(54), 277–282.

Doress, I., & Porter, J. N. (1978). Kids in cults. *Society, 15,* 69–71.

Douvan, E., & Adelson, J. (1966). *The adolescent experience.* New York: Wiley.

Dreyer, P. H. (1982). Sexuality during adolescence. In B. B. Wolman (Ed.), *Handbook of developmental psychology.* Englewood Cliffs, N.J.: Prentice-Hall.

Duberman, L. (1973). Step-kin relationships. *Journal of Marriage and the Family, 35,* (2), 283–292.

Dulit, E. (1972). Adolescent thinking a la Piaget: The formal stage. *Journal of Youth and Adolescence, 1,* 281–301.

Dunphy, D. C. (1963). The social structure of urban adolescent peer groups. *Sociometry, 26,* 230–246.

Dunphy, D. C. (1972). Peer group socialization. In F. J. Hunt (Ed.), *Socialisation in Australia* (pp. 200–217). Sydney: Angus-Robertson.

Dusek, J. B. (1975). Do teachers bias children's learning? *Review of Educational Research, 45,* 661–684.

Dusek, J. B., & Flaherty, J. F. (1981). The development of the self-concept during the adolescent years. *Monographs of the society for Research in Child Development, 46*(4).

Dusek, J. B., Kermis, M. D., & Monge, R. H. (1979). The hierarchy of adolescent interests: A social-cognitive approach. *Genetic Psychology Monographs, 100*(1), 41–72.

Dykeman, B. F. (1979). Teenage alcoholism—detecting those early warning signals. *Adolescence, 14*(54), 251–254.

Eagly, A. H. (1978). Sex differences in influenceability. *Psychological Bulletin, 85,* 86–116.

Eagly, A. H., & Carli, L. L. (1981). Sex of researchers and sex-typed communications as determinants of sex differences in influenceability: A meta analysis of social influence studies. *Psychological Bulletin, 90*(1), 1–20.

Eagly, A. H., & Whitehead, G. (1972). Effect of choice on receptivity to favorable and unfavorable evaluation of oneself. *Journal of Personality and Social Psychology, 22*(2), 223–230.

Edwards, J. N., & Brauburger, M. B. (1973). Exchange and parent-youth conflict. *Journal of Marriage and the Family, 35,* 101–107.

Effort launched to fight teen drinking. (1982, October 5). *Boston Globe,* p. 3.

Egan, C. (1978). Apprenticeship now. *Occupational Outlook Quarterly, 22*(2), 3–11.

Eisenman, R., & Platt, J. J. (1968). Underachievement and creativity in high school students. *Psychology, 7,* 52–55.

Eitzen, D. S. (1975). Athletics in the status system of male adolescents: A replication of Coleman's *The Adolescent Society. Adolescence, 10,* 267–276.

Elder, G. H. (1962). Structural variations in the child rearing relationship. *Sociometry, 25,* 241–262.

Elkind, D. (1962). Quantity conceptions in college students. *Journal of Social Psychology, 57,* 459–465.

Elkind, D. (1967a). Egocentrism in adolescence. *Child Development, 38,* 1025–1034. Copyright © The Society for Research in Child Development, Inc.

Elkind, D. (1967b). Middle-class delinquency. *Mental Hygiene, 51,* 80–84.

Elkind, D. (1970). Exploitation and the generational conflict. *Mental Hygiene, 54,* 490–497.

Elkind, D. (1971). Measuring young minds. *Horizon, 13*(1), 350.

Elkind, D. (1979, February). Growing up faster. *Psychology Today,* pp. 38–45.

Elkind, D. (1981). *The hurried child.* Reading, MA: Addison-Wesley.

Eme, R., Maisiak, R., & Goodale, W. (1979). Seriousness of adolescent problems. *Adolescence, 14* (53), 93–99.

Emmerich, H. J. (1978). The influence of parents and peers on choices made by adolescents. *Journal of Youth and Adolescence, 7,* 175–180.

Enker, M. S. (1971). The process of identity: Two views. *Mental Hygiene, 55,* 369–374.

Enright, R. D., & Deist, S. H. (1979). Social perspective-taking as a component of identity formation. *Adolescence, 14*(55), 517–522.

Enright, R. D., Lapsley, D. K., & Shukla, D. G. (1979). Adolescent egocentrism in early and late adolescence. *Adolescence, 14*(56), 687–696.

Enright, R. D., Shukla, D. G. & Lapsley, D. K. (1980). Adolescent egocentrism, sociocentrism and self-consciousness. *Journal of Youth and Adolescence, 9*(2), 101–116.

Epstein, S. (1973). The self-concept revisited: Or a theory of a theory. *American Psychologist, 28,* 404–416.

Erickson, M. L. (1973). Group violation, socio-economic status and official delinquency. *Social Forces, 52,* 41–52.

Erikson, E. H. (1950). *Childhood and Society.* New York: Norton.

Erikson, E. H. (1968). *Identity: Youth and crisis.* New York: Norton.

Falbo, T. (1978). Only children and interpersonal behavior: An experimental and survey study. *Journal of Applied Social Psychology, 8*(3), 244–253.

Farris, C. E., & Farris, L. S. (1976). Indian children: The struggle for survival. *Social Work, 21,* 386–389.

Faust, M. S. (1977). Somatic development of adolescent girls. *Monographs of the Society for Research in Child Development, 42*(1, Serial No. 169).

Feather, N. T. (1969). Attribution of responsibility and valence of success and failure in relation to initial confidence and perceived locus of control. *Journal of Personality and Social Psychology, 13,* 129–144.

Feather, N. T., & Simon, J. G. (1975). Reactions to male and female success and failure in sex-linked occupations: Impressions of personality, causal attributions, and perceived likelihood of different consequences. *Journal of Personality and Social Psychology, 31*(1), 20–31.

Federal Bureau of Investigation. (1983). *Uniform crime reports: Crime in the United States.* Washington, D.C.: U.S. Government Printing Office.

Feinberg, M. R., Smith, M., & Schmidt, R. (1958). An analysis of expressions used by adolescents of varying economic levels to describe accepted and rejected peers. *Journal of Genetic Psychology, 93,* 133–148.

Feinstein, S. C., & Ardon, M. S. (1973). Trends in dating patterns and adolescent development. *Journal of Youth and Adolescence, 2,* 157–166.

Feldman, H., & Feldman, M. (1979). The effect of father absence on adolescents. In B. M. Newman & P. R. Newman (Eds.), *An introduction to the psychology of adolescence.* Homewood, IL.: Dorsey Press.

Feldman, K. A., & Newcomb, T. S. (1969). *The impact of college on students.* San Francisco: Jossey-Bass.

Feldman, R. E. (1979). The promotion of moral development in prisons and schools. In R. Wilson & G. Schochet (Eds.), *Moral development and politics.* New York: Praeger.

Feldman-Summers, S., & Kiesler, S. B. (1974). Those who are number two try harder: The effect of attributions on causality. *Journal of Personality and Social Psychology, 30*(6), 846–855.

Fetters, W. B. (1976). *National longitudinal study of the high school class of 1972.* Washington, D.C.: National Center for Educational Statistics, DHEW Pub. No. 76–235.

Fewer score high on Scholastic Aptitude Test. Selective colleges concerned. (1983, January 16). *Chronicle of Higher Education,* p. 7.

Fields, A. B. (1981). Some influences upon the occupational aspirations of three white-collar ethnic groups. *Adolescence, 16*(63), 663–684.

Finkel, M. L., & Finkel, D. J. (1975). Sexual and contraceptive knowledge, attitudes and behavior of male adolescents. *Family Planning Perspectives, 7,* 256–260.

Finkel, M. L., & Finkel, D. J. (1978). Male adolescent contraceptive utilization. *Adolescence, 13*(51), 443–451.

Fischer, J. L. (1981). Transitions in relationship style from adolescence to young adulthood. *Journal of Youth and Adolescence, 10,* 11–24.

Fishkin, J., Keniston, K., & MacKinnon, C. (1973). Moral reasoning and political ideology. *Journal of Personality and Social Psychology, 27*(1), 109–119.

Fitch, S. A., & Adams, G. R. (1983). Ego identity and intimacy status: Replication and extension. *Developmental Psychology, 19*(6), 839–845.

Flavell, J. H. (1977). *Cognitive development.* Englewood Cliffs, N.J.: Prentice-Hall.

Floyd, H. H., & South, D. R. (1972). Dilemma of youth: The choice of parents or peers as a frame of reference for behavior. *Journal of Marriage and the Family, 34,* 627–634.

Follingstad, D. R., Robinson, E. A., & Pugh, M. (1977). Effects of consciousness-raising groups on measures of feminism, self-esteem, and social desirability. *Journal of Counseling Psychology, 24*(3), 223–230.

Forslund, M. A. (1978). Functions of drinking for native American and white youth. *Journal of Youth and Adolescence, 7*(3), 327–332.

Fowler, J. W. (1976). Stages in faith: The structural development approach. In T. Hennessy (Ed.), *Values and moral development.* New York: Paulist Press.

Freedman, M. (1975, March). Homosexuals may be healthier than straights. *Psychology Today,* pp. 28, 30–32.

Freeman, D. (1983). *Margaret Mead and Samoa.* Cambridge, MA: Harvard University Press.

Freud, A. (1937/1966). *The ego and the mechanisms of defense.* New York: International Universities Press.

Freud, S. (1925). Three contributions to the theory of sex. *Nervous and Mental Disease Monograph Series,* No. 7. New York: Nervous & Mental Disease Publishing Company.

Friedenberg, E. Z. (1959). *The vanishing adolescent.* New York: Dell Publishing.

Friedman, C. J., Mann, F., & Adelman, H. (1976). Juvenile street gangs: The victimization of youth. *Adolescence, 11*(44), 527–533.

Friedman, C. J., Mann, F., & Friedman, A. S. (1975). A profile of juvenile street gang members. *Adolescence, 10*(40), 563–607.

Frisch, R. E., & Revelle, R. (1970). Height and weight at menarche and a hypothesis of critical body weights and adolescent events. *Science, 169,* 397–399.

Froming, W. J., & McColgan, E. B. (1979). Comparing the Defining Issues Test and the Moral Dilemma Interview. *Developmental Psychology, 15,* 658–659.

Furstenberg, F. F., Jr. (1976). The social consequences of teen-age parenthood. *Family Planning Perspectives, 8,* 148–164.

Gad, M. T., & Johnson, J. H. (1980, Spring). Correlates of adolescent life stress as related to race, socioeconomic status, and levels of perceived social support. *Journal of Clinical Child Psychology,* 13–16.

Gagnon, J. H., & Simon, W. (1973). *Sexual conduct: The social sources of human sexuality.* Chicago: Aldine.

Galanter, M., Rabkin, R., Rabkin, J., & Deutsch, A. (1979). The "moonies": A psychological study of conversion and membership in a contemporary religious sect. *American Journal of Psychiatry, 5*(3), 327–349.

Gallagher, J. M., & Noppe, I. C. (1976). Cognitive development and learning. In J. F. Adams (Ed.), *Understanding adolescence: Current developments in adolescent psychology* (3rd ed., pp. 199–232). Boston: Allyn & Bacon.

Gallatin, J. (1980). Political thinking in adolescence. In J. Adelson (Ed.), *Handbook of adolescent psychology* (pp. 344–382). New York: Wiley.

Gallatin, J., & Adelson, J. (1971). Legal guarantees of individual freedom. *Journal of Social Issues, 27,* 93–108.

Garbarino, J., & Sherman, D. (1980). High-risk neighborhoods and high-risk families. The ecology of child mistreatment. *Child Development, 51*(1), 188–198.

Gardner, D. C., Beatty, G. J., & Bigelow, E. A. (1981). Locus of control and career maturity: A pilot evaluation of a life-planning and career development program for high school students. *Adolescence, 16*(63), 557–562.

Garmezy, N. (1976). Vulnerable and invulnerable children: Theory, research, and intervention. *Psychological Documents, 6*(4), 1–23. (Ms. No. 1337).

Gaylin, J., (1978, March). What boys look for in girls. *Seventeen,* pp. 107–113.

Gaylin, J. (1979, March). What girls really look for in boys. *Seventeen,* pp. 131–137.

Gecas, V. (1971). Parental behavior and dimensions of adolescent self-evaluation. *Sociometry, 34*(4), 466–482.

Gecas, V., & Nye, F. E. (1974). Sex and class differences in parent-child interaction: A test of Kahn's hypothesis. *Journal of Marriage and the Family, 36,* 742–749.

Gelles, R. J. (1976). Demythologizing child abuse. *The Family Coordinator, 25,* 135–141.

Gergen, K. J. (1971). *The concept of self.* New York: Holt, Rinehart & Winston.

Gesell, A., Ilg, F., & Ames, L. B. (1956). *Youth: The years from ten to sixteen.* New York: Harper & Row.

Gilbert, B., & Williamson, N. (1973, June). Sport is unfair to women. *Sports Illustrated,* pp. 45–58.

Gilbert, L. A. (1981). Toward mental health: The benefits of psychological androgyny. *Professional Psychology, 12*(1), 29–38.

Gilligan, C. (1977). In a different voice: Women's conceptions of self and of morality. *Harvard Educational Review, 47,*(4), 481–517. Copyright © 1977 by President and Fellows of Harvard College.

Gilligan, C. (1979). Woman's place in man's life cycle. *Harvard Educational Review, 49,* 431–446.

Gilligan, C. (1982). *In a different voice: Psychological theory and women's development.* Cambridge, MA: Harvard University Press.

Ginzberg, E. (1971). *Career guidance.* New York: McGraw-Hill.

Ginzberg, E. (1972). Toward a theory of occupational choice: A restatement. *Vocational Guidance Quarterly, 20,* 169–176.

Ginzberg, E. (1980). Education, jobs, and all that. *New York University Education Quarterly, 11*(2), 10–14.

Glick, P. C., & Norton, A. J. (1979). Marrying, divorcing, and living together in the U.S. today. *Population Bulletin, 32*(5), 1–40.

Gold, D., & Andres, D. (1978). Developmental comparisons between adolescent children with employed and non-employed mothers. *Merrill-Palmer Quarterly, 24,* 243–254.

Gold, M. (1969). Juvenile delinquency as a symptom of alienation. *Journal of Social Issues, 25*(2), 121–135.

Gold, M., & Mann, D. (1972). Delinquency as defense. *American Journal of Orthopsychiatry, 42,* 463–479.

Gold, M., & Petronio, R. J. (1980). Delinquent behavior in adolescence. In J. Adelson (Ed.), *Handbook of adolescent psychology* (pp. 495–535). New York: Wiley.

Goldstein, B. (1967). *Low income youth in urban areas.* New York: Holt, Rinehart & Winston.

Goleman, D. (1980, August). Leaving home: Is there a right time to go? *Psychology Today,* pp. 52–53, 55–57, 59–61.

Gordon, S., & Dickman, I. R. (1977). *Sex education: The parent's role* (Public Affairs Pamphlet No. 549). New York: Public Affairs Committee.

Gorth, W., & Perkins, M. R. (1980). *Study of minimum testing programs.* Washington, D.C.: National Institute of Education.

Grabe, M. (1981). School size and the importance of school activities. *Adolescence, 16*(61), 21–32.

Grant, W. V., & Eiden, L. J. (1982). *Digest of education statistics, 1982.* Washington, D.C.: U.S. Government Printing Office.

Graves, A. J. (1972). Attainment of conservation of mass, weight, and volume in minimally educated adults. *Developmental Psychology, 7,* 223.

Greenberger, E., Steinberg, L. D., & Vaux, A. (1981). Adolescents who work: Health and behavioral consequences of job stress. *Developmental Psychology, 17*(6), 691–703.

Grueling, J. W., & DeBlassie, R. R. (1980). Adolescent suicide. *Adolescence, 15*(59), 589–601.

Grinder, R. E. (1966). Relations of social dating attractiveness to academic orientation and peer relations. *Journal of Educational Psychology. 57,* 27–34.

Grinder, R. E., & Strickland, C. E. (1963). G. Stanley Hall and the social significance of adolescence. *Teachers College Record, 64,* 390–399.

Gronlund, N. W., & Anderson, L. (1957). Personality characteristics of socially accepted, socially neglected, and socially rejected junior high school pupils. *Educational Administration and Supervision, 43,* 329–338.

Grossman, A. S. (1982). More than half of all children have working mothers. *Monthly Labor Review, 105*(2), 41–43.

Grotevant, H. D., Thorbecke, W., & Meyer, M. L. (1982). An extension of Marcia's identity status interview into the interpersonal domain. *Journal of Youth and Adolescence, 11,* 33–47.

Grubb, W. N., & Lazerson, M. (1975). Rally 'round the workplace: Continuities and fallacies in career education. *Harvard Educational Review, 45,* 451–474.

Guardo, C. J., & Bohan, J. B. (1971). Development of a sense of self-identity in children. *Child Development, 42,* 1909–1921.

Gurwitz, S. B., & Marcus, M. (1978). Effects of anticipated interaction, sex, and homosexual stereotypes on first impressions. *Journal of Applied Social Psychology, 8,* 47–56.

Guzman, L. P. (1976). *Puerto Rican self-esteem and the importance of social context.* Unpublished doctoral dissertation, State University of New York at Buffalo.

Haan, N. (1963). Proposed model of ego functioning: Coping and defense mechanisms in relationship to IQ change. *Psychological Monographs, 77*(8).

Hall, A. (1978). Family structure and relationships of 50 female anorexia nervosa patients. *Australian and New Zealand Journal of Psychiatry, 12,* 263–268.

Hall, G. S. (1904). *Adolescence* (2 vols.). New York: Appleton.

Hallworth, H. J., Davis, H., & Gamston, C. (1965). Some adolescents' perceptions of adolescent personality. *Journal of Social Psychology, 4,* 81–89.

Hamachek, D. E. (1980). Psychology and development of the adolescent self. In J. F. Adams (Ed.), *Understanding adolescence: Current developments in adolescent psychology* (4th ed.). Boston: Allyn & Bacon.

Hamburg, B. A. (1974). Early adolescence: A specific and stressful stage of the life cycle. In G. V. Coelho, D. A. Hamburg, & J. E. Adams (Eds.), *Coping and adaptation.* New York: Basic Books.

Handleman, C. (1980). Teaching and academic standards today. *Adolescence, 15* (59), 723–730.

Haney, B., & Gold, M. (1973, July). The juvenile delinquent nobody knows. *Psychology Today,* pp. 49–52, 55.

Haney, B., & Kerin, R. A. (1978). The influence of social stratification and age on occupational aspirations of adolescents. *Journal of Educational Research, 71*(5), 262–266.

Hansen, S. L. (1977). Dating choices of high school students. *The Family Coordinator, 26,* 133–138.

Harkness, S., Edwards, C. P., & Super, C. M. (1981). Social roles and moral reasoning: A case study in a rural African community. *Developmental Psychology, 17*(5), 595–603.

Harper, J., & Collins, J. K. (1975). A different survey of the problems of privileged and under-privileged adolescents. *Journal of Youth and Adolescence, 4,* 349–358.

Harris, L. (1971, January 8). Change, yes . . . upheaval, no. *Life,* pp. 22–27.

Hartley, R. L. (1959). Sex-role pressures in the socialization of the male child. *Psychological Reports, 5,* 459–468.

Hartup, W. W. (1970). Peer interaction and social organization. In P. H. Mussen (Ed.), *Carmichael's Manual of Child Psychology, Vol. 2* (3rd ed.), New York: Wiley.

Harvey, M. G., & Kevin, R. A. (1978). The influence of social stratification and age on occupational aspirations of adolescents. *Journal of Educational Research,* 262–266.

Harway, M., & Astin, H. S. (1977). *Sex discrimination in career counseling and education.* New York: Praeger.

Hass, A. (1979). *Teenage sexuality: A survey of teenage sexual behavior.* New York: Macmillan.

Hauser, J. (1981). Adolescents and religion. *Adolescence, 16*(62), 309–320.

Hauser, S. T. (1971). *Black and white identity formation.* New York: Wiley-Interscience.

Havighurst, R. J. (1972). *Developmental tasks and education* (3rd ed.). New York: McKay.

Havighurst, R. J. (1979).' *Developmental tasks and education* (4th ed.). New York: Longman.

Havighurst, R. J. (1980). Subcultures of adolescents in the United States. In J. F. Adams (Ed.), *Understanding adolescence: Current developments in adolescent psychology* (4th ed.). Boston: Allyn & Bacon.

Havighurst, R. J., & Gottlieb, D. (1975). Youth and the meaning of work. In R. J. Havighurst & P. H. Dryer (Eds.), *Youth* (pp. 145–160). Chicago: University of Chicago Press.

Heald, F. P. (1976). Morbidity and mortality. In J. R. Gallagher, F. P. Heald, & D. C. Garell (Eds.), *Medical care of the adolescent.* New York: Appleton-Century.

Healey, G. W., & DeBlassie, R. R. (1974). A comparison of Negro, Anglo, and Spanish-American adolescents' self-concepts. *Adolescence, 9,* 15–24.

Helmreich, R. L., Spence, J. T., & Gibson, R. H. (1982). Sex-role attitudes: 1972–1980. *Personality and Social Psychology Bulletin, 8*(4), 656–663.

Hendry, L. B., & Gillies, P. (1978). Body type, body esteem, school, and leisure: A study of overweight, average, and underweight adolescents. *Journal of Youth and Adolescence, 7*(2), 181–195.

Henggeler, S. W., & Tavormina, J. B. (1980). Social class and race differences in family interaction: Pathological, normative, or confounding methodological factors? *Journal of Genetic Psychology, 137*(2), 211–222.

Herold, E. S. (1979). Variables influencing the dating adjustment of university students. *Journal of Youth and Adolescence, 8,* 73–79.

Herzog, E., & Sudia, C. E. (1973). Children in fatherless families. In B. M. Caldwell & H. N. Ricciuti (Eds.), *Review of child development research, Vol. 3.* Chicago: University of Chicago Press.

Hess, R. D., & Shipman, V. C. (1965). Early experience and the socialization of cognitive modes in children. *Child Development, 36*(4) 869–886.

Hetherington, E. M. (1972). Effects of father-absence on personality development in adolescent daughters. *Developmental Psychology, 7,* 313–326.

Hetherington, E. M. (1979). Divorce: A child's perspective. *American Psychologist, 34*(10), 851–858.

Hetherington, E. M., & Parke, R. D. (1975). *Child psychology: A contemporary viewpoint.* New York: McGraw-Hill.

High schools under fire. (1977, November 14). *Time,* pp. 62–65, 67, 71–72, 75.

Hill, W. F. (1969). *Learning through discussion.* Beverly Hills, CA: Sage.

Hirsch, P., Robinson, J., Taylor, E. K., and Whithey, S. B. (1972). The changing popular songs: An historical overview. *Popular Music and Society, 1,* 83–93.

Hodgson, J. W., & Fischer, J. L. (1979). Sex differences in identity and intimacy development in college youth. *Journal of Youth and Adolescence, 8*(1), 37–50.

Hoffman, L. W. (1972). Early childhood experiences and women's achievement motives. *Journal of Social Issues, 28*(2), 129–155.

Hoffman, L. W. (1974a). Effects of maternal employment on the child: A review of the research. *Developmental Psychology, 10*(2), 204–228.

Hoffman, L. W. (1974b). Fear of success in males and females: 1965 and 1971. *Journal of Consulting and Clinical Psychology, 42,* 335–358.

Hoffman, L. W. (1977). Fear of success in 1965 and 1974: A follow-up study. *Journal of Consulting and Clinical Psychology, 45,* 310–321.

Hoffman, L. W. (1979). Maternal employment: 1979. *American Psychologist, 34*(10), 859–865.

Hoffman, M. L. (1970). Conscience, personality, and socialization techniques. *Human Development, 13,* 90–126.

Hoffman, M. L. (1971). Father-absence and conscience development. *Developmental Psychology, 4,* 400–406.

Hoffman, M. L. (1980). Moral development in adolescence. In J. Adelson (Ed.), *Handbook of adolescent psychology* (pp. 295–343). New York: Wiley.

Hoffman, M. L., & Saltzstein, H. D. (1967). Parent discipline and the child's moral development. *Journal of Personality and Social Psychology, 5,* 45–57.

Hoge, D. R., & Roozen, D. A. (1979). Research on factors influencing church commitment. In D. R. Hoge & D. A. Roozen (Eds.), *Understanding church growth and decline: 1950–1978.* New York: Pilgrim Press.

Holland, J. L. (1973). *Making vocational choices: A theory of careers.* Englewood Cliffs, N.J.: Prentice-Hall.

Holstein, C. B. (1976). Irreversible, step-wise sequence in the development of moral judgment: A longitudinal study of males and females. *Child Development, 47,* 51–61.

Holzman, P. S., & Grinker, R. R. (1974). Schizophrenia in adolescence. *Journal of Youth and Adolescence, 3,* 267–279.

Honzik, M. P. (1973). The development of intelligence. In B. B. Wolman (Ed.), *Handbook of general psychology.* Englewood Cliffs, N.J.: Prentice-Hall.

Horner, M. (1969, November). Fail: Bright woman. *Psychology Today,* pp. 36, 38, 62.

Horner, M. (1970). Femininity and successful achievement: A basic inconsistency. In J. M. Bardwick, E. Douvan, M. Horner, & M. Gutman (Eds.), *Feminine personality and conflict.* Monterey, CA: Brooks/Cole.

House, E. A., Durfee, M. F., & Bryan, C. K. (1979). A survey of psychological and social concerns of rural adolescents. *Adolescence, 14,* 361–376.

Houston, L. N. (1981). Romanticism and eroticism among black and white college students. *Adolescence, 16*(62), 263–272.

Hout, M., & Morgan, W. R. (1975). Race and sex variations in the causes of the expected attainments of high school seniors. *American Journal of Sociology, 81,* 364–394.

Howard, M. (1971). How to look and outreach for the younger father. *American Journal of Orthopsychiatry, 41,* 294–295.

Hower, J. T., & Edwards, K. J. (1979) The relationship between moral character and adolescents' perception of parental behavior. *Journal of Genetic Psychology, 135*(1), 23–32.

Hraba, J., & Grant, G. (1970). Black is beautiful: A reexamination of racial preference and identification. *Journal of Personality and Social Psychology, 16,* 398–402.

Hurlock, E. B. (1973). *Adolescent development* (4th ed.). New York: McGraw-Hill.

Husbands, C. T. (1970). Some social and psychological consequences of the American dating system. *Adolescence, 5,* 451–462.

Huston-Stein, A., & Bailey, M. (1973). The socialization of achievement motivation in females. *Psychological Bulletin, 80*(5), 345–366.

Hyde, J. S., & Rosenberg, B. G. (1980). *Half the human experience: The psychology of women* (2nd ed.). Lexington, MA: Heath.

Inhelder, B., & Piaget, J. (1958). *The growth of logical thinking.* New York: Basic Books.

In one ear . . . (1977). *Human Behavior, 6*(8), 46–47.

Jackson, D. W. (1975). The meaning of dating from the role perspective of non-dating pre-adolescents. *Adolescence, 10,* 123–126.

Jackson, S. (1965). The growth of logical thinking in normal and sub-normal children. *British Journal of Educational Psychology, 35,* 255–258.

Jacquet, C. H., Jr. (Ed.). (1980). *Yearbook of American and Canadian Churches.* New York: Abingdon Press.

Jahoda, M., & Warren, N. (1965). The myths of youth. *Sociology of Education, 38,* 138–149.

Jensen, A. R. (1969). How much can we boost IQ and scholastic achievement? *Harvard Educational Review, 39,* 1–123.

Johnson, A. L., Brehke, M. L., Stronimen, M. P., & Underwagen, R. C. (1974). Age differences and dimensions of religious behavior. *Journal of Social Issues, 30*(3), 43–67.

Johnson, R., & Carter, M. M. (1980). Flight of the young: Why children run away from their homes. *Adolescence, 15*(58), 483–489.

Johnson, S. S. (1975). *Update on education: A digest of the National Assessment of Educational Progress.* Denver: Education Commission of the States.

Johnston, L. D., & Bachman, J. G. (1976). Educational institutions. In J. F. Adams (Ed.), *Understanding adolescence: Current developments in adolescent psychology* (3rd ed.). Boston: Allyn & Bacon.

Johnston, L. D., Bachman, J. G., & O'Malley, P. M. (1976). *The use of marijuana by high school seniors.* Unpublished manuscript, University of Michigan, Institute for Social Research, Ann Arbor.

Johnston, L. D., Bachman, J. G., & O'Malley, P. M. (1981). *Highlights from student drug use in America, 1975–1981.* Rockville, MD: National Institute on Drug Abuse. DHHS Publication No. (ADM) 82 1208.

Jones, R. S. (1979). Changes in the political orientations of American youth: 1969–1975. *Youth and Society, 10*(4), 335–339.

Jones, S. S. (1976). High school social status as a historical process. *Adolescence, 11,* 327–333.

Josselson, R. L., Greenberger, E., & McConochie, D. (1977). Phenomenological aspects of psychosocial maturity in adolescence, Part II: Girls. *Journal of Youth and Adolescence, 6*(2), 145–167.

Juhasz, A. M., & Sonnenshein-Schneider, M. (1980). Adolescent sexual decision-making: Components and skills. *Adolescence, 15*(60), 743–750.

Jurich, A., & Jurich, J. (1974). The effect of cognitive moral development upon the selection of premarital sexual standards. *Journal of Marriage and the Family, 36*(4), 736–741.

Justice, B., Justice, R., & Kraft, I. A. (1974). Early-warning signs of violence: Is a triad enough? *American Journal of Psychiatry, 131,* 457–459.

Kacerguis, M. A., & Adams, G. R. (1980). Erikson stage resolution: The relationship between identity and intimacy. *Journal of Youth and Adolescence, 9,* 117–126.

Kamens, D. H. (1977). Institutional definitions and collective action. The concept of student as source of school authority and student culture. *Youth and Society, 9*(1), 55–78.

Kandel, D. B., & Lesser, G. S. (1969). Parent-adolescent relationships and adolescent independence in the U.S. and Denmark. *Journal of Marriage and the Family, 31*(2), 348–358.

Kandel, D. B., & Lesser, G. S. (1972). *Youth in two worlds.* San Francisco: Jossey-Bass.

Kangas, J., & Bradway, K. (1971). Intelligence at middle age: A thirty-eight-year follow-up. *Developmental Psychology, 5,* 333–337.

Kantor, I. (1974). This thing called rock: An interpretation. *Popular Music and Society, 3,* 203–214.

Katchadourian, H. A. (1977). *The biology of adolescence.* San Francisco: Freeman.

Katchadourian, H. A., & Lunde, D. T. (1975). *Fundamentals of human sexuality.* New York: Holt, Rinehart & Winston.

Katz, M. L. (1973). *Female motive to avoid success: A psychological barrier or a response to deviancy?* Princeton, N.J.: Educational Testing Service.

Keating, D. P., & Clark, L. V. (1980). Development of physical and social reasoning in adolescence. *Developmental Psychology, 16,* 23–30.

Kempe, R. S., & Kempe, C. H. (Eds.). (1978). *Child abuse.* Cambridge, MA: Harvard University Press.

Keniston, K. (1965). *The uncommitted: Alienated youth in American society.* New York: Harcourt Brace Jovanovich.

Keniston, K. (1970a). *Youth and dissent.* New York: Harcourt Brace.

Keniston, K. (1970b). Youth as a stage of life. *American Scholar, 39,* 631–654.

Keniston, K. (1975). Do Americans really like children? *Childhood Education, 52,* 4–12.

Kett, J. (1977). *Rites of passage: Adolescence in America 1790 to the present.* New York: Basic Books.

Kinard, E. M. (1982). Experiencing child abuse: Effects on emotional adjustment. *American Journal of Orthopsychiatry, 52*(1), 82–91.

Kinard, E. M., & Klerman, L. V. (1980). Teenage parenting and child abuse: Are they related? *American Journal of Orthopsychiatry, 50*(3), 481–488.

King, M. L., Jr. (1964). *Why we can't wait.* New York: Harper & Row.

Kinloch, G. C. (1970). Parent-youth conflict at home: An investigation among university freshmen. *American Journal of Orthopsychiatry, 40,* 658–664.

Koch, H. (1956). Some emotional attitudes of the young child in relation to characteristics of his sibling. *Child Development, 27,* 393–426.

Koff, E., Rierdan, J., & Silverstone, E. (1978). Changes in representation of body image as a function of menarcheal status. *Developmental Psychology, 14,* 635–642.

Kohlberg, L. (1958). The development of modes of thinking and choices in years 10 to 16. Ph.D. Dissertation, University of Chicago.

Kohlberg, L. (1966a). A cognitive-developmental analysis of children's sex-role concepts and attitudes. In E. E. Maccoby (Ed.), *The development of sex differences.* Stanford, CA: Stanford University Press.

Kohlberg, L. (1966b). Moral education in the schools: A developmental view. *The School Review, 74*(1), 1–30.

Kohlberg, L. (1969). Stage and sequence: The cognitive-developmental approach to socialization. In D. A. Goslin (Ed.), *Handbook of socialization theory and research.* Chicago: Rand-McNally.

Kohlberg, L. (1975). The cognitive-developmental approach to moral education. *Phi Delta Kappan, 56*(10), 610–677.

Kohlberg, L. (1976). Moral stages and moralization. In T. Likona (Ed.), *Moral development and behavior.* New York: Holt, Rinehart & Winston.

Kohlberg, L., & Kramer, R. (1969). Continuities and discontinuities in childhood and adult moral development. *Human Development, 12,* 93–120.

Kohn, P. M., & Annis, H. M. (1978). Personality and social factors in adolescent marijuana use: A path-analytic study. *Journal of Consulting and Clinical Psychology, 46,* 366–367.

Komarovsky, M. (1973). Cultural contradictions and sex roles: The masculine case. *American Journal of Sociology, 78,* 873–884.

Komarovsky, M. (1976). *Dilemmas of masculinity: A study of college youth.* New York: Norton.

Kovar, M. G. (1979). Some indicators of health-related behavior among adolescents in the United States. *Public Health Reports, 94,* 109–118.

Landis, J. (1970). A comparison of children from divorced and non-divorced unhappy marriages. *Family Life Coordinator, 11,* 61–65.

Landy, F., Rosenberg, B. G., and Sutton-Smith, B. (1969). The effect of limited father-absence on cognitive development. *Child Development, 40,* 941–944.

Larson, L. E. (1974). System and sub-system perception of family roles. *Journal of Marriage and the Family, 36*(1), 123–138.

Lee, G. R. (1977). Age at marriage and marital satisfaction: A multi-variate analysis with implications for marital stability. *Journal of Marriage and the Family, 39,* 493–504.

LeFrancois, G. R. (1981). *Adolescents* (2nd ed.). Belmont, CA: Wadsworth.

Leinhardt, G., Seewald, A. M., & Engel, M. (1979). Learning what's taught: Sex differences in instruction. *Journal of Educational Psychology, 71*(4), 432–439.

LeMasters, E. E. (1974). *Parents in modern America* (rev. ed.). Homewood, IL: Dorsey Press.

Lenney, E. (1977). Women's self-confidence in achievement settings. *Psychological Bulletin, 84,* 1–13.

Leona, M. H. (1978). An examination of adolescent clique language in a suburban secondary school. *Adolescence, 13,* 495–502.

Lerman, P. (1968). Individual values, peer values, and sub-cultural delinquency. *American Sociological Review, 33,* 219–235.

Lerner, R. M., Karson, M., Meisels, M., & Knapp, J. R. (1975). Actual and perceived attitudes of late adolescents and their parents: The phenomenon of the generation gaps. *Journal of Genetic Psychology, 126,* 195–207.

Lesser, G. S., & Kandel, D. B. (1969). Parental and peer influences on educational plans of adolescents. *American Sociological Review, 34,* 213–223.

Levine, A. (1980). *When dreams and heroes died: A portrait of today's college students.* San Francisco: Jossey-Bass.

Levine, E. M., & Kozak, C. (1979). Drug and alcohol use, delinquency, and vandalism among upper-middle-class pre- and post-adolescents. *Journal of Youth and Adolescence, 8,* 91–101.

Levine, J. A. (1978, June). Real kids vs. "the average family." *Psychology Today, 12*(1), pp. 14–15.

Levitt, E. E., & Lubin, B. (1975). *Depression: Concepts, controversies, and some new facts.* New York: Springer.

Lewin, K. (1951). *Field theory and social science.* New York: Harper & Row.

Lewis, R. A. (1973). Parents and peers: Socialization agents in coital behavior of young adults. *Journal of Sex Research, 9,* 156–170.

Liebert, R. M., Sprafkin, J. N., & Davidson, E. S. (1982). *The early window: Effects of television on children and youth* (2nd ed). New York: Pergamon Press.

Life according to TV. (1982, December 6). *Newsweek,* pp. 136–140.

Lindemann, C. (1974). *Birth control and unmarried young women.* New York: Springer.

Little, J. K. (1967). The occupations of non-college youth. *American Educational Research Journal, 4,* 147–153.

Livson, N., & Peskin, H. (1980). Perspectives on adolescence from longitudinal research. In J. Adelson (Ed.), *Handbook of adolescent psychology* (pp. 47–48). New York: Wiley.

Lockwood, A. (1978). Effects of values curricula. *Review of Educational Research, 48*(3), 325–364.

Loeber, R., & Dishion, T. (1983). Early predictors of male delinquency: A review. *Psychological Bulletin, 94*(1), 68–99.

Logan, D. D. (1980). The menarche experience in twenty-three foreign countries. *Adolescence, 15* (58), 247–256.

Lotecka, L., & Lassleben, M. (1981). The high school "smoker": A field study of cigarette-related cognitions and social perceptions. *Adolescence, 16*(63), 513–526.

Lundgren, D. C., & Schwab, M. R. (1979). The impact of college on students: Residential context, relations with parents and peers, and self-esteem. *Youth and Society, 10*(3), 227–236.

Luria, Z., & Rose, M. D. (1979). *Psychology of human sexuality.* New York: Wiley.

Lynn, D. B. (1959). A note on sex differences in the development of masculine and feminine identification. *Psychological Review, 66*(2), 126–135.

Lynn, D. B. (1974). *The father: His role in child development.* Monterey, CA: Brooks/Cole.

MacArthur, R. S. (1973). Some ability patterns: Central Eskimos and Nsenga Africans. *International Journal of Psychology, 8,* 239–247.

Maccoby, E. E., & Jacklin, C. N. (1974). *The psychology of sex differences.* Stanford, CA: Stanford University Press.

Madison, P. (1969). *Personality development in college.* Reading, MA: Addison-Wesley.

Magid, D. T., Gross, B. D., & Shuman, B. J. (1979). Preparing pregnant teen-agers for parenthood. *The Family Coordinator, 28*(3), 359–364.

Malina, R. M. (1974). Adolescent changes in size, build, composition, and performance. *Human Biology, 46,* 117–131.

Marcia, J. E. (1976a). Identity six years after: A follow-up study. *Journal of Youth and Adolescence, 5,* 145–160.

Marcia, J. E. (1976b). *Studies in ego identity.* Unpublished monograph, Simon Fraser University, Burnaby, British Columbia.

Marcia, J. E. (1980). Identity in adolescence. In J. Adelson (Ed.), *Handbook of adolescent psychology* (pp. 159–210). New York: Wiley.

Margolis, G. (1981). Moving away: perspectives on counseling anxious freshmen. *Adolescence, 16*(63), 633–640.

Marini, M. M. (1978). Sex differences in the determination of adolescent aspirations: A review of research. *Sex Roles, 4*(5), 723–753.

Marini, M. M., & Greenberger, E. (1978a). Sex differences in educational aspirations and expectations. *American Educational Research Journal, 15,* 67–79.

Marini, M. M., & Greenberger, E. (1978b). Sex differences in occupational aspirations and expectations. *Sociology of Work and Occupations, 5*(2), 147–178.

Martin, W. H., & Ward, B. J. (1983, February 8). Educational "Winners and losers," The "whos" and possible "whys." *NAEP Bulletin.* Denver: Education Commission of the States.

Masters, W. H., & Johnson, V. E. (1979). *Homosexuality in perspective.* Boston: Little, Brown.

Mayer, G. R., & Butterworth, T. (1983). Preventing school vandalism and improving discipline: A three-year study. *Journal of Applied Behavior Analysis, 16*(4), 355–369.

McAlister, A. L., Perry, C., & Maccoby, N. (1979). Adolescent smoking: Onset and prevention. *Pediatrics, 63*(4), 650–658.

McAllister, E. W. C. (1981). Religious attitudes among women college students. *Adolescence, 16*(63), 582–604.

McAnarney, E. R. (1979). Adolescent and young adult suicide in the United States—A reflection on social unrest. *Adolescence, 14*(56), 766–774.

McArthur, C. C. (1971). Distinguishing patterns of student neuroses. In G. R. Blaine and C. C. McArthur (Eds.), *Emotional problems of the student.* New York: Appleton-Century-Crofts.

McClelland, D. C. (1961). *The achieving society.* Princeton, N.J.: Van Nostrand.

McClelland, D. C. (1973). Testing for competence rather than intelligence. *American Psychologist, 28,* 1–14.

McConaghy, M. (1979). Gender permanence and the genital basis of gender: Stages in the development of constancy of gender identity. *Child Development, 50*(4), 1223–1226.

McGowan, A. S. (1977). Vocational maturity and anxiety among vocationally undecided and indecisive students. *Journal of Vocational Behavior, 10,* 196–204.

McKenry, P., Walters, L., & Johnson, C. (1979). Adolescent pregnancy: A review of the literature. *The Family Coordinator, 28,* 17–29.

Mead, M. (1928). *Coming of age in Samoa.* New York: Mentor.

Mead, M. (1970). *Culture and commitment: A Study of the generation gap.* Garden City, New York: Natural History Press.

Meece, J. L., Parsons, J. E., Kaczala, C. M., Goff, S. B., & Futterman, R. (1982). Sex differences in math achievement: Toward a model of academic choice. *Psychological Bulletin, 91*(2), 324–348.

Meilman, P. W. (1979). Cross-sectional age changes in ego identity status during adolescence. *Developmental Psychology, 15*(2), 230–232.

Meisels, M. M., & Canter, F. M. (1971–2). A note on the generation gap. *Adolescence, 6,* 523–530.

Mellor, E. F. (1984, June). Investigating the differences in weekly earnings of women and men. *Monthly Labor Review,* pp. 17–28.

Milgram, S. (1965). Some conditions of obedience and disobedience to authority. *Human Relations, 18,* 57–76.

Miller, J. D., Cisin, I. H., Gardner-Keaton, H., Harrell, A. V., Wirtz, P. W., Abelson, H. I., & Fishburne, P. M. (1983). *National survey on drug abuse: Main findings 1982.* Rockville, MD: National Institute on Drug Abuse.

Miller, P. Y., & Simon W. (1974). Adolescent sexual behavior: Context and change. *Social Problems, 22,* 58–76.

Miller, P. Y., & Simon, W. (1980). The development of sexuality in adolescence. In J. Adelson (Ed.), *Handbook of adolescent psychology* (pp. 383–407). New York: Wiley.

Miller, W. B. (1966). Violent crimes in city gangs. *Annals of the American Academy of Political and Social Science, 364,* 96–112.

Monge, R. H. (1973). Developmental trends in factors of adolescent self-concept. *Developmental Psychology, 8,* 382–393.

Montemayor, R., & Eisen, M. (1977). The development of self-conceptions from childhood to adolescence. *Developmental Psychology, 13,* 314–319.

Moore, K. A., & Caldwell, S. B. (1977). The effects of government policies on out-of-wedlock sex and pregnancy. *Family Planning Perspectives, 9,* 164–169.

Moos, R. H. (1978). Social environments of university student living groups: Architectural and organizational correlates. *Environment and Behavior, 10*(1), 109–126.

Morgan, B. (1976). Intimacy of disclosure topics and sex differences in self-disclosure. *Sex Roles, 2,* 161–165.

Morgan, E., & Farber, B. A. (1982). Toward a reformulation of the Eriksonian model of identity development. *Adolescence, 17,* 199–211.

Moriarty, A. E., & Toussieng, P. W. (1976). *Adolescent coping.* New York: Grune & Stratton.

Morin, S. F. (1977). Heterosexual bias in psychological research on lesbianism and male homosexuality. *American Psychologist, 32,* 629–638.

Mortimer, J. T. (1976). Social class, work, and the family: Some implications of the father's occupation for familial relationships and sons' career decisions. *Journal of Marriage and the Family, 38,* 241–256.

Mosher, D. L., & O'Grady, K. E. (1979). Homosexual threat, negative attitudes toward masturbation, sex guilt, and males' sexual and affective reactions to explicit films. *Journal of Consulting and Clinical Psychology, 47,* 860–873.

Moshman, D. (1979). Development of formal hypothesis-testing ability. *Developmental Psychology, 15*(2), 104–112.

Mrazek, P. B., & Mrazek, D. A. (1978). The effects of child sexual abuse. In R. S. Kempe & C. H. Kempe (Eds.), *Child abuse* (pp. 223–245). Cambridge, MA: Harvard University Press.

Mullener, N., & Laird, J. D. (1971). Some developmental changes in the organization of self-evaluations. *Developmental Psychology, 5,* 233–236.

Munro, G., & Adams, G. R. (1977). Ego identity formation in college students and working youth. *Developmental Psychology, 13*(57), 523–524.

Musa, H. E., & Roach, M. E. (1973). Adolescent appearance and self-concept. *Adolescence, 8,* 385–394.

Musgrove, F. (1963). Inter-generation attitudes. *British Journal of Social and Clinical Psychology, 2,* 209–223.

Muson, H. (1979, February). Moral thinking: Can it be taught? *Psychology Today,* pp. 48–49, 51, 53–54, 57–58, 67–68, 91–92.

Mussen, P., Conger, J., & Kagan, J. (1979). *Child development and personality* (5th ed.). New York: Harper & Row.

Muuss, R. E. (1982). *Theories of adolescence* (4th ed.). New York: Random House.

Nash, R. J., & Agne, R. M. (1973). Careers: Education and work in the corporate state. *Phi Delta Kappan, 54,* 373–383.

National Assessment of Educational Progress. (1979). *Three assessments of science, 1969–77: Technical summary.* Denver: Education Commission of the States.

National Assessment of Educational Progress. (1980). *Mathematical technical report: Summary volume.* Denver: Education Commission of the States.

National Assessment of Educational Progress. (1981–82). '81 education story: Good news, bad news. *NAEP Newsletter, 14*(4). Denver: Education Commission of the States.

National Commission on Excellence in Education. (1983, April). *A nation at risk: The imperative for educational reform.* Washington, D.C.: U.S. Government Printing Office.

National Institute of Education. (1978, January). *Violent schools—safe schools: The safe school study report to the Congress, Vol. 1.* Washington, D.C.: U.S. Government Printing Office.

National Institute of Mental Health. (1982). *Television and behavior: Ten years of scientific progress and implications for the eighties* (DHHS Publication No. ADM 82-1195). Washington, D.C.: U.S. Government Printing Office.

Nation's teenagers becoming more conservative. (1977, July). *Intellect, 106*(2386), p. 1.

Nawas, M. M. (1971). Change in efficiency of ego functioning and complexity from adolescence to young adulthood. *Developmental Psychology, 4*(3), 412–415.

Neimark, E. A. (1970). A preliminary search for the formal operational structures. *Journal of Genetic Psychology, 116,* 223–232.

Nelson, E. A., & Rosenbaum, E. (1972). Language patterns within the youth subculture: Development of slang vocabularies. *Merrill-Palmer Quarterly, 18*(3), 273–285.

The new scarlet letter. (1982, August 2). *Time,* pp. 62–66.

Newcomb, T. M. (1961). *The acquaintance process.* New York: Holt, Rinehart & Winston.

Newman, B. M. (1979). Coping and adaptation in adolescence. *Human Development, 22*(4), 255–262.

Newman, P. R., & Newman, B. M. (1976). Early adolescence and its conflict: Group identity versus alienation. *Adolescence, 11,* 261–274. Copyright 1976 by Libra Publishers, Inc. Reprinted by permission.

Niles, F. S. (1979). The adolescent girl's perception of parents and peers. *Adolescence, 14*(55), 591–597.

Nixon, H. L., Maresca, P. J., & Silverman, M. A. (1979). Sex differences in college students' acceptance of females in sport. *Adolescence, 14*(56), 755–764.

Noeth, R. J., Roth, J. D., & Prediger, D. J. (1975). Student career development: Where do we stand? *Vocational Guidance Quarterly, 23,* 210–218.

Now it's suburbs where school violence flares. (1979, May 21). *U.S. News and World Report,* pp. 63–66.

Nye, F. I. (1957). Child adjustment in broken and unhappy unbroken homes. *Marriage and Family Living, 19,* 356–361.

O'Donnell, W. J. (1979a). Adolescent self-reported and peer-reported self-esteem. *Adolescence, 14* (55), 465–470.

O'Donnell, W. J. (1979b). Affectional patterns of adolescents. *Adolescence, 14,* 681–686.

Offer, D. (1969). *The psychological world of the teen-ager.* New York: Basic Books.

Offer, D., & Offer, J. B. (1975). *From teen-age to young manhood: A psychological study.* New York: Basic Books.

Offer, D., Ostrov, E., & Howard, K. I. (1977). The self-image of adolescents: A study of four cultures. *Journal of Youth and Adolescence, 6*(3), 265–280.

Okun, M. A., & Sasfy, J. H. (1977). Adolescence, the self-concept, and formal operations. *Adolescence, 12,* 373–381.

Orlofsky, J. L. (1978). The relationship between intimacy status and antecedent personality components. *Adolescence, 13,* 419–441.

Orlofsky, J. L., Marcia, J. E., & Lesser, I. M. (1973). Ego identity status and the intimacy versus isolation crisis of young adulthood. *Journal of Personality and Social Psychology, 27*(2), 211–219.

Oskamp, S., & Mindick, B. (1981). Personality and attitudinal barriers to contraception. In D. Byrne & W. A. Fisher (Eds.), *Adolescents, sex, and contraception.* New York: McGraw-Hill.

Page, E. B., & Grandon, G. M. (1979). Family configuration and mental ability: Two theories contrasted with U.S. data. *American Educational Research Journal, 16,* 257–272.

Paperny, D. M., & Deisher, R. W. (1983). Maltreatment of adolescents: The relationship to a predisposition toward violent behavior and delinquency. *Adolescence, 18*(71), 499–506.

Parish, T. S. (1980). The relationship between factors associated with father loss and individuals' level of moral judgment. *Adolescence, 15*(59), 535–541.

Parish, T. S. (1981). The impact of divorce on the family. *Adolescence, 16*(63), 577–580.

Parish, T. S., & Dostal, J. W. (1980). Evaluation of self and parental figures by children from intact, divorced, and reconstituted families. *Journal of Youth and Adolescence, 9,* 347–351.

Parish, T. S., Dostal, J. W., & Parish, J. G. (1981). Evaluations of self and parents as a function of intactness of family and family happiness. *Adolescence, 16*(60), 203–210.

Parish, T. S., & Kappes, B. (1980). Impact of father loss on the family. *Social Behavior and Personality: An International Journal, 8,* 107–112.

Parish, T. S., & Taylor, J. C. (1979). The impact of divorce and subsequent father absence on children's and adolescents' self-concepts. *Journal of Youth and Adolescence, 8*(4), 427–432.

Parlee, M. B. (1973). The premenstrual syndrome. *Psychological Bulletin, 80,* 454–465.

Paulsen, E. P. (1972). Obesity in children and adolescents. In H. L. Barnett & A. H. Einhorn (Eds.), *Pediatrics* (15th ed.). New York: Appleton-Century-Crofts.

Peck, R. F., & Galliani, C. (1962). Intelligence, ethnicity, and social roles in adolescent society. *Sociometry, 25,* 64–72.

Peevers, B. H., & Secord, P. F. (1973). Developmental changes in attribution of descriptive concepts to persons. *Journal of Personality and Social Psychology, 27,* 120–128.

Peng, S. S., Fetters, W. B., & Kolstad, A. J. (1981). *High school and beyond—A national longitudinal study for the 1980s: A capsule description of high school students.* Washington, D.C.: National Center for Education Statistics.

Peplau, L. (1976). Impact of fear of success and sex-role attitudes on women's competitive achievement. *Journal of Personality and Social Psychology, 34*(4), 561–568.

Peretti, P. O. (1976). Closest friendships of black college students: Social intimacy. *Adolescence, 11,* 395–403.

Peterson, E. T., & Kunz, P. R. (1975). Parental control over adolescents according to family size. *Adolescence, 10,* 419–427.

Phipps-Yonas, S. (1980). Teenage pregnancy and motherhood: A review of the literature. *American Journal of Orthopsychiatry, 50*(3), 403–431.

Piaget, J., & Inhelder, B. (1969). *The psychology of the child* (H. Weaver, trans.). New York: Basic Books.

Pierce, C. M. (1979). Problems of the Negro adolescent in the next decade. In E. B. Brody (Ed.), *Minority group adolescents in the United States.* Huntington, N.Y.: Krieger.

Piliavin, I. M., Hardyck, J. A., & Vadum, A. C. (1968). Constancy effects of personal costs on the transgressions of juveniles. *Journal of Personality and Social Psychology, 10,* 227–231.

Pines, M. (1979, January). Superkids. *Psychology Today,* pp. 53–54, 57–58, 61, 63.

Place, D. M. (1975). The dating experience for adolescent girls. *Adolescence, 10,* 157–174.

Pleck, J. H. (1975). Masculinity-femininity: Current and alternative paradigms. *Sex Roles, 1,* 161–178.

Pleck, J. H. (1976). The male sex role: Definitions, problems, and sources of change. *Journal of Social Issues, 32*(3), 155–164.

Pleck, J. H. (1981a). *The myth of masculinity.* Cambridge, MA: MIT Press.

Pleck, J. H. (1981b). The work-family problem: Overloading the system. In B. Forisha & B. Goldman (Eds.), *Outsiders on the inside: Women in organizations.* Englewood Cliffs, N.J.: Prentice-Hall.

Poffenberger, T. (1964). Three papers on going steady. *Family Life Coordinator, 13,* 7–13.

Potvin, R., Hoge, D., & Nelson, H. (1976). *Religion and American youth.* Washington, D.C.: Catholic University of America, The Boys Town Center for the Study of Youth Development.

Powell, M. (1955). Age and sex differences in degree of conflict within certain areas of psychological adjustment. *Psychological Monographs, 69* (Whole No. 387).

Prendergast, T. J., & Schaefer, E. S. (1974). Correlates of drinking and drunkenness among high school students. *Quarterly Journal of Studies on Alcohol, 35,* 232–242.

Proshansky, H., & Newton, P. (1968). The nature and meaning of Negro self-identity. In M. Deutsch, I. Katz, & A. R. Jensen (Eds.), *Social class, race, and psychological development* (pp. 178–218). New York: Holt, Rinehart & Winston.

Protinsky, H., & Farrier, S. (1980). Self-image changes in pre-adolescents and adolescents. *Adolescence, 15*(60), 887–893.

Protinsky, H., & Hughston, G. (1979). Adolescent conservation. *Journal of Genetic Psychology, 135,* 157–158.

Purnell, R. F. (1970). Socioeconomic status and sex differences in adolescent reference-group orientation. *Journal of Genetic Psychology, 116,* 233–239.

Raphael, D., & Xelowski, H. G. (1980). Identity status in high school students: Critique and revised paradigm. *Journal of Youth and Adolescence, 9*(5), 383–389.

Raschke, H., & Raschke, V. (1979). Family conflict and children's self-concepts: A comparison of intact and single-parent families. *Journal of Marriage and The Family, 41,* 367–374.

Redd, W. H., Porterfield, A. L., & Ande·sen, B. L. (1979). *Behavior modification: Behavioral approaches to human problems.* New York: Random House.

Reiss, I. L. (1967). *The social context of pre-marital sexual permissiveness.* New York: Holt, Rinehart & Winston.

Religion in America, 1979–1980. (1980). Princeton, N.J.: Princeton Religious Research Center.

Reported cases of V. D. decline. (1983, July 1). *Boston Globe,* p. 1.

Rest, J. R., Cooper, D., Coder, R., Mas·ʊ.z, J., & Anderson, D. (1974). Judging the important issues in moral dilemmas. *Developmental Psychology, 10,* 491–501.

Rest, J. R., Davison, M. L., & Robbins, S. (1978). Age trends in judging moral issues: A review of cross-sectional, longitudinal, and sequential studies of the Defining Issues Test. *Child Development, 49,* 263–279.

Rice, F. P. (1978). *The adolescent.* Boston: Allyn & Bacon.

Richardson, J. T., Harder, W. M., & Simmonds, R. B. (1972). Thought reform and the Jesus movement. *Youth and Society, 3,* 185–202.

Rierdan, J., & Koff, E. (1980). The psychological impact of menarche: Integrative versus disruptive changes. *Journal of Youth and Adolescence, 9*(1), 49–58.

Rivenbark, W. H. (1971). Self-disclosure patterns among adolescents. *Psychological Reprints, 28,* 35–42.

Robbins, T., Anthony, D., & Curtis, T. (1975). Youth culture religious movements: Evaluating the integrative hypothesis. *Sociological Quarterly, 16,* 48–64.

Roberts, D. F., & Bachen, C. M. (1981). Mass communication effects. *Annual Review of Psychology, 32,* 307–356.

Roberts, W. R. (1966). *Rhetorica.* In W. D. Ross (Ed.), *The works of Aristotle,* Vol. 11. Oxford: Clarendon Press.

Roche, A. F. (1979). Secular trends in stature, weight, and maturation. *Monographs of the Society for Research on Child Development, 44*(4, Serial No. 179).

Rogers, D. (1981). *Adolescents and youth* (4th ed.). Englewood Cliffs, N.J.: Prentice-Hall.

Roll, S., & Millen, L. (1979). The friend as represented in the dreams of late adolescents: Friendship without rose-colored glasses. *Adolescence, 14*(54), 255–275.

Roper, B. S., & Labeff, E. (1977). Sex roles and feminism revisited: An intergenerational attitude comparison. *Journal of Marriage and the Family, 39,* 113–119.

Rosenberg, M. (1965). *Society and the adolescent self-image.* Princeton, N.J.: Princeton University Press.

Rosenberg, M. (1975). The dissonant context and the adolescent self-concept. In S. E. Dragastin & G. H. Elder, Jr. (Eds.), *Adolescence in the life cycle: Psychological change and social context.* New York: Wiley.

Rosenberg, M. (1979). *Conceiving the self.* New York: Basic Books.

Rosenberg, M., & Simmons, R. G. (1972). *Black and white self-esteem: The urban school child.* Rose Monograph Series. Washington, D.C.: American Sociological Association.

Rosenkrantz, P., Vogel, S., Bee, H., Broverman, I., & Broverman, D. M. (1968). Sex-role stereotypes and self-concepts among college students. *Journal of Consulting and Clinical Psychology, 32,* 287–295.

Rosenthal, D., & Hansen, J. (1980). Comparison of adolescents' perceptions and behaviors in single- and two-parent families. *Journal of Youth and Adolescence, 9*(5), 407–417.

Rosenthal, T. L., & Zimmerman, B. J. (1978). *Social learning and cognition.* New York: Academic Press.

Rotter, J. B. (1966). Generalized expectancies for internal versus external control of reinforcement. *Psychological Monographs, 80*(1, Whole No. 609).

Rubin, I. (1965). Transition in sex values: Implications for the education of adolescents. *Journ~ of Marriage and the Family, 27,* 185–189.

Rubin, Z. (1979, October). Seeking a cure for loneliness. *Psychology Today,* pp. 82–90.

Rubinstein, L., Shaver, P., & Peplau, L. A. (1982). Loneliness. In N. Jackson (Ed.), *Personal growth and behavior.* Guilford, CT.: Dushkin.

Saghir, M. T., & Robins, E. R. (1973). *Male and female homosexuality: A comprehensive investigation.* Baltimore: Williams & Wilkins.

Sampson, E. E. (1962). Birth order, need achievement, and conformity. *Journal of Abnormal and Social Psychology, 64,* 155–159.

Santrock, J. W. (1972). Relation of type and onset of father absence to cognitive development. *Child Development, 43,* 455–469.

Santrock, J. W., & Tracy, R. L. (1978). The effects of children's family structure status on the development of stereotypes by teachers. *Journal of Educational Psychology, 70,* 754–757.

Scarr, S., & Weinberg, R. A. (1976). IQ test performance of black children adopted by white families. *American Psychologist, 31,* 726–730.

Schachter, R. J., Pantel, E. S., Glassman, G. M., & Zweibelson, I. (1971). Acne vulgaris and psychological impact on high school students. *New York State Journal of Medicine, 71,* 2886–2890.

Schachter, S. (1963). Birth order, eminence and higher education. *American Sociological Review, 28,* 757–768.

Schafer, W. E., Olexa, C., & Polk, K. (1970). Programmed for social class: Tracking in high school. *Trans-action, 7*(12), 39–46, 63.

Schaie, K. W., & Strother, C. R. (1968). A cross-sequential study of age changes in cognitive behavior. *Psychological Bulletin, 70,* 671–680.

Scharf, P. (1978). Indoctrination, values clarification, and developmental moral education as educational responses to conflict and change in contemporary society. In P. Scharf (Ed.), *Readings in moral education.* Minneapolis, MN: Winston.

Schenkel, S. (1975). Relationship among ego identity status, field independence, and traditional femininity. *Journal of Youth and Adolescence, 4,* 73–82.

Schenkel, S., & Marcia, J. E. (1972). Attitudes toward premarital intercourse in determining ego identity status in college women. *Journal of Personality, 3,* 472–482.

Scherz, F. (1967). The crisis of adolescence in family life. *Social Casework, 48,* 209–215.

Schneider, S. (1981). Anorexia nervosa: The "subtle" condition. *Family Therapy, 8*(1), 49–58.

Schooler, C. (1972). Birth order effects: Not here, not now! *Psychological Bulletin, 78,* 161–175.

Schratz, M. (1978). A developmental investigation of sex differences in spatial, visual-analytic, and mathematical skills in three ethnic groups. *Developmental Psychology, 14*(3), 263–267.

Schvaneveldt, J. D. (1973). Mormon adolescents' likes and dislikes toward parents and home. *Adolescence, 8,* 171–178.

Sebald, H. (1977). *Adolescence: A social-psychological analysis.* Englewood Cliffs, N.J.: Prentice-Hall.

Sebald, H. (1981). Adolescents' concept of popularity and unpopularity, comparing 1960 with 1976. *Adolescence, 16*(61), 187–193.

Selman, R. (1971). The relation of role-taking to the development of moral judgment in children. *Child Development, 42,* 79–91.

Settlage, C. F. (1972). Cultural values and the superego in late adolescence. *Psychoanalytic Study of the Child, 27,* 57–73.

Sherman, J. (1971). *On the psychology of women: A survey of empirical studies.* Springfield, IL: Charles C. Thomas.

Shipman, G. (1968). The psychodynamics of sex education. *The Family Coordinator, 17,* 3–12.

Shirreffs, J. H., & Dezelsky, T. L. (1979). Adolescent perceptions of sex education needs: 1972–1978. *Journal of School Health, 49*(6), 343–346.

Sigelman, L. (1977). Review of the polls. *Journal for the Scientific Study of Religion, 16,* 289–294.

Silber, T. (1981). Gonorrhea in adolescence: Its impact and consequences. *Adolescence, 16*(63), 537–541.

Simmonds, R. B. (1977). Conversion or addiction: Consequences of joining a Jesus movement group. *American Behavioral Scientist, 20,* 909–924.

Simmons, R. G., Blyth, D. A., Van Cleave, E. F., & Bush, D. M. (1979). Entry into early adolescence: The impact of school structure, puberty, and early dating on self-esteem. *American Sociological Review, 45*(6), 917–931.

Simmons, R. G., Brown, L., Bush, D. M., & Blyth, D. A. (1978). Self-esteem and achievement of black and white adolescents. *Social Problems, 26*(1), 86–99.

Simmons, R. G., Rosenberg, F., & Rosenberg, M. (1973). Disturbance in the self-image at adolescence. *American Sociological Review, 38,* 553–568.

Simon, S. B., Howe, L. W., & Kirschenbaum, H. (1972). *Values clarification.* New York: Hart.

Simpson, E. L. (1974). Moral development research: A case study of scientific cultural bias. *Human Development, 17,* 81–106.

Sistrunk, F., & McDavid, J. W. (1971). Sex variable in conforming behavior. *Journal of Personality and Social Psychology, 17,* 200–207.

Skipper, J. K., & Nass, G. (1966). Dating behavior: A framework for analysis and an illustration. *Journal of Marriage and the Family, 28,* 412–420.

Skorepa, C. A., Horrocks, J. E., & Thompson, G. G. (1963). A study of friendship fluctuations of college students. *Journal of Genetic Psychology, 102,* 151–157.

Slack, W. V., & Porter, D. (1980). The Scholastic Aptitude Test: A critical appraisal. *Harvard Educational Review, 50,* 154–175.

Smith, G. F. (1924). Certain aspects of the sex-life of the adolescent girl. *Journal of Applied Psychology, 8,* 347–349.

Smith, L. M., & Kleine, P. F. (1966). The adolescent and his society. *Review of Educational Research, 36,* 424–436.

Snoek, D., & Rothblum, E. (1979). Self-disclosure among adolescents in relation to parental affection and control patterns. *Adolescence, 14*(54), 333–340.

Snyder, E. E. (1972). High school student perceptions of prestige criteria. *Adolescence, 6*(25), 129–136.

Snyder, E. E., & Kivlin, J. E. (1977). Perceptions of the sex-role among female athletes and non-athletes. *Adolescence, 12*(45), 23–30.

Soares, A. T., & Soares, L. M. (1970). Interpersonal and self-perceptions of disadvantaged and advantaged high-school students. *Proceedings of the Annual Convention of the American Psychological Association, 5*(Part 1), 457–458.

Soares, L. M., & Soares, A. T. (1971). Comparative differences in the self-perceptions of disadvantaged and advantaged students. *Journal of School Psychology, 9,* 424–429.

Sorenson, R. C. (1973). *Adolescent sexuality in contemporary America.* New York: World.

Spanier, G. B. (1978). Sex education and premarital sexual behavior among American college students. *Adolescence, 13*(52), 659–674.

Spanier, G. B., & Fleer, B. (1979). Factors sustaining marriages: Factors in adjusting to divorce. In E. Corfman (Ed.), *Families today.* Washington, D.C.: U.S. Government Printing Office.

Spence, J. T., Helmreich, R., & Stapp, J. (1975). Ratings of self and peers on sex role attributes and their relation to self-esteem and conceptions of masculinity and femininity. *Journal of Personality and Social Psychology, 32,* 29–39.

Spiro, M. E. (1970). *Kibbutz: Venture in Utopia.* New York: Schocken.

Spitzer, R. L., Williams, J. B. W., & Skodol, A. (1980). DSM-III: The major achievements and an overview. *American Journal of Psychiatry, 137*(2), 151–164.

Stanton, M. (1980). Moral judgments among students: A cross-cultural study. *Adolescence, 15*(57), 231–241.

Stark, E. (1984, May). The unspeakable family secret. *Psychology Today,* pp. 41–46.

Stark, P. A., & Traxler, A. J. (1974). Empirical validation of Erikson's theory of identity crisis in late adolescence. *Journal of Psychology, 86,* 25–34.

Steele, B. (1980). Psychodynamic factors in child abuse. In C. H. Kempe & F. E. Helfer (Eds.), *The battered child* (pp. 49–85). Chicago: University of Chicago Press.

Steinberg, L., Greenberger, E., Vaux, A., & Ruggiero, M. (1981). Effects of early work experience on adolescent socialization. *Youth and Society, 12,* 403–422.

Stephens, B., McLaughlin, J. A., Miller, C. K., & Glass, G. V. (1972). Factorial structure of selected psycho-educational measures and Piagetian reasoning assessments. *Developmental Psychology, 6,* 343–348.

Stephens, S. (1971, November 28). The "rat packs" of New York. *The New York Times,* pp. 29 ff.

Stone, L. H., Miranne, A. C., & Ellis, G. J. (1979). Parent-peer influence as a predictor of marijuana use. *Adolescence, 14* (53), 115–122.

Streit, F. (1981). Differences among youthful criminal offenders based on their perceptions of parental behavior. *Adolescence, 16*(62), 409–413.

Stuart, R. B. (1971). Behavioral contracting within families of delinquents. *Journal of Behavior Therapy and Experimental Psychiatry, 2,* 1–11.

Stubbs, M. L. (1982). Period piece. *Adolescence, 17,*(65) 45–55.

Study seeks to dispel acne myths, says some drugs help. (1982, March 23). *Boston Globe,* p. 3.

Sugar, M. (1976). At-risk factors for the adolescent mother and her infant. *Journal of Youth and Adolescence, 5*(3), 251–270.

Sullivan, H. S. (1953). *The interpersonal theory of psychiatry.* New York: Norton.

Sullivan, K., & Sullivan, A. (1980). Adolescent-parent separation. *Developmental Psychology, 16*(2), 93–99.

Super, D. E. (1957). *The psychology of careers.* New York: Harper & Row.

Sussman, M. B. (1978). New family forms and lifestyles. In D. Reiss (Ed.), *The family: Dying or developing?* New York: Plenum Press.

Sutton-Smith, B., Roberts, J. M., & Rosenberg, B. G. (1964). Sibling associations and role involvement. *Merrill-Palmer Quarterly on Behavioral Development, 10,* 25–38.

Swanson, R. B., Massey, R. H., & Payne, I. R. (1972). Ordinal position, family size, and personal adjustment. *Journal of Psychology, 81,* 53–58.

Tangri, S. S. (1972). Determinants of occupational role innovation among college women. *Journal of Social Issues, 28*(2), 177–199.

Tanner, J. M. (1970). Physical growth. In P. H. Mussen (Ed.), *Carmichael's manual of child psychology, Vol. 2* (3rd ed.). New York: Wiley.

Tanner, J. M. (1971). Sequence, tempo, and individual variation in the growth and development of boys and girls aged twelve to sixteen. *Daedalus, 100,* 907–930.

Tavris, C. (1974, September). What does college do for a person? Frankly, very little. *Psychology Today,* pp. 73–78, 80.

Tavris, C. (1976, April). The end of the IQ slump. *Psychology Today,* pp. 69–73.

Tavris, C., & Wade, C. (1984). *The longest war: Sex differences in perspective* (2nd ed.). New York: Harcourt Brace Jovanovich.

Taylor, R. G. (1964). Personality traits and discrepant achievement: A review. *Journal of Counseling Psychology, 11,* 76–82.

Tec, N. (1974). Parent-child drug abuse: Generational continuity or adolescent deviancy. *Adolescence, 9,* 351–364.

Thoday, J. M., & Gibson, J. B. (1970). Environmental and genetical contributions to class difference: A model experiment. *Science, 167,* 990–992.

Thompson, K. (1980). A comparison of black and white adolescents' beliefs about having children. *Journal of Marriage and the Family, 8*(2), 133–139.

Thompson, L., & Spanier, G. B. (1978). Influence of parents, peers, and partners on the contraceptive use of college men and women. *Journal of Marriage and the Family, 40,* 481–492.

Thompson, V. D. (1974). Family size: Implicit policies and assumed psychological outcomes. *Journal of Social Issues, 30*(4), 93–124.

Thornburg, E. E., & Thornburg, H. D. (1977). Personal and family life interests of adolescents. In H. D. Thornburg, *You and Your Adolescent.* Tucson, AZ: H.E.L.P. Books.

Thornburg, H. D. (1982). *Development in adolescence* (2nd ed.). Monterey, CA.: Brooks/Cole.

Thurnher, M., Spence, D., & Lowenthal, M. F. (1974). Value confluence in intergenerational relations. *Journal of Marriage and the Family, 36,* 308–319.

Timmons, F. R. (1977). Incidence of withdrawal from college: An examination of some misconceptions. *Perceptional and Motor Skills, 45,* 651–654.

Tobias, S. (1978). *Overcoming math anxiety.* New York: Norton.

Toder, N., & Marcia, J. E. (1973). Ego identity status and response to conformity pressure in college women. *Journal of Personality and Social Psychology, 26*(2), 287–294.

Tomlinson-Keasey, C. (1972). Formal operations in females from eleven to fifty-four years of age. *Developmental Psychology, 6,* 364.

Trecker, J. L. (1973). Sex stereotyping in the secondary school curriculum. *Phi Delta Kappan, 55,* 110–112.

Tresemer, D. (1974, March). Fear of success: popular, but unproven. *Psychology Today,* pp. 82–85.

Troll, L. E. (1972). Is parent-child conflict what we mean by the generation gap? *The Family Coordinator, 21,* 347–348.

Tudor, C., Peterson, D., & Elifson, K. (1980). An evaluation of the relationship between peer and parental influences in adolescent drug use. *Adolescence, 60,* 783–798.

Turiel, E. (1974). Conflict and transition in adolescent moral development. *Child Development, 45,* 14–29.

Urban and Rural Systems Associates. (1976). *Improving family planning services for teenagers.* Washington, D.C.: U.S. Department of Health, Education, and Welfare.

Ushakov, G. K. (1971). *Anorexia nervosa.* In J. G. Howells (Ed.), *Modern perspectives in adolescent psychiatry.* New York: Bruner/Mazel.

U.S. Bureau of Labor Statistics. (1984a). *Employment projections for 1995.* Washington, D.C.: U.S. Government Printing Office.

U.S. Bureau of Labor Statistics. (1984b). *Occupational outlook handbook: 1984–1985.* Washington, D.C.: U.S. Government Printing Office.

U.S. Bureau of the Census. (1978). *Statistical abstract of the United States, 1978* (99th ed.). Washington, D.C.: U.S. Government Printing Office.

U.S. Bureau of the Census. (1980). *Statistical abstract of the United States, 1980* (101st ed.). Washington, D.C.: U.S. Government Printing Office.

U.S. Bureau of the Census (1981). *Statistical abstract of the United States, 1981* (102nd ed.). Washington, D.C.: U.S. Government Printing Office.

U.S. Bureau of the Census. (1982). *Statistical abstract of the United States: 1982–83* (103rd ed.). Washington, D.C.: U.S. Government Printing Office.

U.S. Bureau of the Census. (1983). *Statistical abstract of the United States, 1984* (104th ed.). Washington, D.C.: U.S. Government Printing Office.

U.S. Department of Health and Human Services. (1979). *STD fact sheet, Edition 35.* (DHHS Publication No. CDC 81–8195). Washington, D.C.: U.S. Government Printing Office.

U.S. Department of Labor. (1982). *20 facts on women workers.* Washington, D.C.: U.S. Government Printing Office.

U.S. National Center for Health Statistics. (1975). Self-reported health behavior and attitudes of youth, 12–17 years, United States. *Vital Health Statistics,* Ser. 11, No. 147.

Van Dusen, R. A., & Sheldon, E. B. (1976). The changing status of American women: A life cycle perspective. *American Psychologist, 31,* 106–116.

Vener, A. M., & Stewart, C. S. (1974). Adolescent sexual behavior in middle America revisited: 1970–1973. *Journal of Marriage and the Family, 36,* 728–735.

Viernstein, M. C., & Hogan, R. (1975). Parental personality factors and achievement motivation in talented adolescents. *Journal of Youth and Adolescence, 4,* 183–190.

Vocational schools get respect. (1983, March 7). *Newsweek,* pp. 79–80.

Vogel, S. R., Broverman, I. K., Broverman, D. M., Clarkson, F., & Rosenkrantz, P. S. (1970). Maternal employment and perception of sex roles among college students. *Developmental Psychology, 3,* 384–391.

Vogt, E. Z. (1983, April 10). The Samoans revisited: Did Mead report myth? *Boston Sunday Globe,* pp. A10–A11.

Wagner, C. A. (1980). Adolescent sexuality. In J. F. Adams (Ed.). *Understanding adolescence: Current developments in adolescent psychology* (4th ed.). Boston: Allyn & Bacon.

Wallerstein, J. S., & Kelly, J. B. (1976). The effects of parental divorce: Experiences of the child in later latency. *American Journal of Orthopsychiatry, 46,* 256–269.

Walster, E., Aronson, E., Abrahams, D., & Rottman, L. (1966). Importance of physical attractiveness in dating behavior. *Journal of Personality and Social Psychology, 4,* 508–516.

Ward, S. H., & Braun, J. (1972). Self-esteem and racial preferences in black children. *American Journal of Orthopsychiatry, 42,* 644–647.

Waterman, A. S., & Waterman, C. K. (1971). A longitudinal study of changes in ego identity status during the freshman year at college. *Developmental Psychology, 5,* 167–173.

Waterman, A. S., & Waterman, C. K. (1972). The relationship between freshman ego identity status and subsequent academic behavior: A test of the predicative value of Marcia's categorization system for identity status. *Developmental Psychology, 6,* 179.

Waterman, C. K., & Nevid, J. S. (1977). Sex differences in the resolution of the identity crisis. *Journal of Youth and Adolescence, 6*(4), 337–342.

Wechsler, D. (1958). *The measurement and appraisal of adult intelligence.* Baltimore: Williams & Wilkins.

Wechsler, H., Rohman, M., & Solomon, L. (1981). Emotional problems and concerns of New England college students. *American Journal of Orthopsychiatry, 51*(4), 719–723.

Weeks, S. G. (1973). Youth and the transition to adult status: Uganda. *Journal of Youth and Adolescence, 2*(3), 259–270.

Weiner, I. B. (1970). *Psychological disturbance in adolescence.* New York: Wiley.

Weiner, I. B. (1980). Psychopathology in adolescence. In J. Adelson (Ed.), *Handbook of adolescent psychology* (pp. 447–471). New York: Wiley.

Weinreich, H. E. (1974). The structure of moral reason. *Journal of Youth and Adolescence, 3,* 135–143.

Weisz, J. R., & Zigler, E. (1979). Cognitive development in retarded and nonretarded persons: Piagetian tests of the similar sequence hypothesis. *Psychological Bulletin, 86,* 831–851.

Wenz, F. V. (1979a). Self-injury behavior, economic status, and the family anomie syndrome among adolescents. *Adolescence, 14*(54), 387–398.

Wenz, F. V., (1979b). Sociological correlates of alienation among adolescent suicide attempts. *Adolescence, 14*(59), 19–30.

Westcott, D. N. (1981, February). The youngest workers: 14 and 15-year-olds. *Monthly Labor Review, 104*(2), 65–69.

Weston, P. J., & Mednick, M. T. (1970). Race, social class, and the motive to avoid success in women. *Journal of Cross-cultural Psychology, 1,* 285–291.

What's really happening on campus. (1976, October 10). *Playboy,* pp. 128–169.

Whisnant, L., Brett, E., & Zegans, L. (1979). Adolescent girls and menstruation. In S. C. Feinstein & P. L. Giovacchini (Eds.), *Adolescent psychiatry, Vol. 7.* Chicago: University of Chicago Press.

White, K. M. (1980). Problems and characteristics of college students. *Adolescence, 15*(57), 23–41.

White, K. M., & Friedman, B. (1977). Conservation of volume in college students: Challenging Elkind. *Journal of Genetic Psychology, 131,* 183–193.

White, K. M., & Ouellette, P. L. (1980). Occupational preferences: Children's projections for self and opposite sex. *Journal of Genetic Psychology, 136*(1), 37–43.

White, K. R. (1982). The relation between socio-economic status and academic achievement. *Psychological Bulletin, 91*(3), 461–481.

Wijting, J. D., Arnold, C. R., & Conrad, K. A. (1978). Generational differences in work values between parents and children and between boys and girls across grade levels 6, 9, 10, and 12. *Journal of Vocational Behavior, 12,* 245–260.

Williams, J. D., & Brekke, B. W. (1979). Relationships among different stages of Piagetian tasks and spatial relations in adolescents. *Journal of Genetic Psychology, 134*(2), 179–184.

Williams, J. H. (1977). *Psychology of women: Behavior in a biosocial context.* New York: Norton.

Wilson, K., Zurcher, L. A., McAdams, D. C., & Curtis, R. (1975). Stepfathers and stepchildren: An exploratory analysis from two national surveys. *Journal of Marriage and the Family, 37*(3), 526–536.

Wilson, W. C. (1975). The distribution of selected sexual attitudes and behaviors among the adult population of the U.S. *Journal of Sex Research, 11,* 46–64.

Windmiller, M. (1980). Moral development and behavior. In J. F. Adams (Ed.), *Understanding adolescence: Current developments in adolescent psychology,* (4th ed.). Boston: Allyn & Bacon.

Wittman, J. S. (1971). Dating patterns of rural and urban Kentucky teen-agers. *The Family Coordinator, 20,* 63–66.

Wolfstetter-Kausch, H., & Gaier, E. L. (1981). Alienation among black adolescents. *Adolescence, 16*(62), 471–485.

Wonderly, D. M., & Kupfersmid, J. H. (1980). Promoting post-conventional morality: The adequacy of Kohlberg's aim. *Adolescence, 15*(59), 609–631.

Wong, M. (1976). Different strokes: Models of drug abuse education. *Contemporary Educational Psychology, 1,* 1–20.

Wooden, K. (1976). *Weeping in the playtime of others: America's incarcerated children.* New York: McGraw-Hill.

Wylie, L. (1965). Youth in France and the United States. In E. H. Erikson (Ed.), *The challenge of youth.* New York: Doubleday.

Wylie, R. C. (1957). Some relationships between defensiveness and self-concept discrepancies. *Journal of Personality, 25,* 600–617.

Yankelovich, D. (1978, May). The new psychological contracts at work. *Psychology Today,* pp. 46–50.

Yarber, W. L., & Packer, K. (1979). School venereal disease education: Perceptions of students, parents, and educators. *Health Values, 3*(5), 206–272.

Yeaworth, R. C., York, J., Hussey, M. A., Ingle, M. E., & Goodwin, T. (1980). The development of an adolescent life change event scale. *Adolescence, 15,* 91–97.

Young, A. McD. (1981, July). Labor force activity among students, graduates, and drop-outs in 1980. *Monthly Labor Review, 104*(7), 31–33.

Young, E., & Parish, T. (1977). Impact of father absence during childhood on the psychological adjustment of college females. *Sex Roles: A Journal of Research, 3,* 217–227.

The youth crime plague. (1977, July 11). *Time,* pp. 18–20, 25–28.

Zacharias, L., Rand, W. M., & Wurtman, R. J., (1976). A prospective study of sexual development and growth in American girls: The statistics of menarche. *Obstetrical and Gynecological Survey, 31,* 325–337.

Zackler, J., Andelman, S. L., & Bauer, F. (1969). The young adolescent as an obstetrical risk. *American Journal of Obstetrics and Gynecology, 103,* 305–312.

Zajonc, R. B., & Markus, G. B. (1975). Birth order and intellectual development. *Psychological Review, 82,* 74–88.

Zellermayer, J. & Marcus, J. (1972). Kibbutz adolescence: Relevance to personality development theory. *Journal of Youth and Adolescence, 1,* 143–153.

Zelnick, M., & Kantner, J. F. (1972). The probability of pre-marital intercourse. *Social Science Research, 1,* 335–341.

Zelnick, M., & Kantner, J. F. (1977). Sexual and contraceptive experiences of young unmarried women in the United States, 1976 and 1971. *Family Planning Perspectives, 9*(2), 55–71.

Zelnick, M., & Kantner, J. F. (1978a). Contraceptive patterns and premarital pregnancy among women 15–19 in 1976. *Family Planning Perspectives, 10*(1), 135–142.

Zelnick, M., & Kantner, J. F. (1978b). First pregnancies to women aged 15–19: 1976 and 1971. *Family Planning Perspectives, 10*(1), 11–20.

Zelnick, M., & Kantner, J. F. (1980). Sexual activity, contraceptive use and pregnancy among metropolitan-area teenagers: 1971–1979. *Family Planning Perspectives, 12,* 230–237.

Zener, T. B., & Schnuelle, L. (1976). Effects of the Self-Directed Search on high school students. *Journal of Counseling Psychology, 23,* 353–359.

Zey-Ferrell, M., Tolone, W. L., & Walsh, R. H. (1978). The intergenerational socialization of sex-role attitudes: A gender or generation gap? *Adolescence, 13,* 95–108.

Ziomkowski, L., Mulder, R., & Williams, D. (1975). Drug use variations between delinquent and non-delinquent youth. *Intellect, 104,* 36–38.

Photo Credits

2, Johnson, Jeroboam;

4, (c)Dietz, 1980, Stock, Boston;

6, (c)Vanoverbeck/Texas Monthly/Picture Group;

7, Pierce, Stock, Boston;

8, Kleun, Taurus;

10, Clark University;

12, Culver;

12, AP/Wide World;

15, Wm Alanson White Psychiatric Foundation, Inc.;

17, (c)Pierce, 1982, Black Star;

20, AP/Wide World;

21, Albert Bandura;

23, Anderson, Monkmeyer;

24, AP/Wide World;

36, (c)Fortin, Stock, Boston;

44, Southwick, Stock, Boston;

54, Franken, Stock, Boston;

55, (c)Kelley/Picture Group;

57, (c)Hedman, Jeroboam;

59, (c)Gatewood, Stock, Boston;

64, (c)Lejeune, Stock, Boston;

67, Siteman, Taurus;

70, Shackman, Monkmeyer;

76, Johnson, Jeroboam;

77, Franken, Stock, Boston;

84, Brown, Stock, Boston;

86, (c)1984 Hazel Hankin;

90, (c)Kroll, Taurus;

93, Zeiberg, Taurus;

95, (c)Muller, Woodfin Camp;

98, (c)Gregory, Southern Light;

104, Leinwand, Monkmeyer;

105, (c)Hazel Hankin;

108, (c)Lejeune, Stock, Boston;

114, (c)Siteman, Taurus;

116, Franken, Stock, Boston;

123, Johnson, Jeroboam;

125, (c)Jensen, Stock, Boston;

128, (c)Siteman, Jeroboam;

129, (c)Adolahe, Southern Light;

130, (c)Spragens, Jr./Picture Group;

138, (c)Herwig, Stock, Boston;

140, Zeiberg, Taurus;

140, (c)Price/Picture Group;

147, (c)Morrow, 1982, Stock, Boston;

150, Hansen, Stock, Boston;

150, (c)Dietz, Stock, Boston;
151, Mercado, Jeroboam;
151, Hayman, Stock, Boston;
158, (c)Reno, 1981, Jeroboam;
160, Holland, Stock, Boston;
162, Menschenfreund, Taurus;
167, Wolinsky, Stock, Boston;
170, (c)Zeiberg, Taurus;
174, (c)Welsch/Picture Group;
177, (c)Gelles, 1980, Stock, Boston;
179, Kagan, Monkmeyer;
194, (c)Siteman, Stock, Boston;
197, Diakopoulos, Stock, Boston;
199, (c)Weisbrot, Stock, Boston;
202, Franken, Stock, Boston;
206, (c)Perlman/Picture Group;
209, Carlson, Stock, Boston;
213, Druskis, Taurus;
218, (c)Abraham, 1976, Stock, Boston;
224, (c)Ackerman/Picture Group;
227, Rawle, Stock, Boston;
232, Gatewood, Stock, Boston;
238, Shackman, Monkmeyer;
242, (c)Diakopoulos/Picture Group;
245, Albertson, Stock, Boston;
248, (c)Diakopoulos, 1974, Stock, Boston;
250, Alphapress, Jeroboam;

256, Lejeune, Stock, Boston;
266, (c)Diakopoulos/Picture Group;
268, Southwick, Stock, Boston;
272, Dietz, Stock, Boston;
275, (c)Lubin, 1972, Jeroboam;
277, Berndt, Stock, Boston;
284, Smolan, Stock, Boston;
287, Skytta, Jeroboam;
291, Franken, Stock, Boston;
299, Herwig, Stock, Boston;
304, Arms, Jeroboam;
308 (c)Anderson, 1981, Woodfin Camp;
318, (c)Alper, Stock, Boston;
321, (c)Hall, 1976, Stock, Boston;
325, (c)Alexanian, Stock, Boston;
328, Simon, Taurus;
334, Rogers, Monkmeyer;
339, Forsyth, Monkmeyer;
343, (c)Howard, Stock, Boston;
348, (c)Druskis, Taurus;
351, (c)Crews, Stock, Boston;
354, Weisbrot, Stock, Boston;
358, (c)Herwig, Stock, Boston;
362, Kroll, Taurus;
369, Simon, Taurus;
373, Vilms, Jeroboam;
377, (c)Saxe/Picture Group.

Name Index

Subject Index